China under Xi Jinping

CHINA UNDER XI JINPING

A New Assessment

Edited by

Qiang Fang and Xiaobing Li

LEIDEN UNIVERSITY PRESS

This book will be made open access within three years of publication thanks to Path to Open, a program developed in partnership between JSTOR, the American Council of Learned Societies (ACLS), University of Michigan Press, and The University of North Carolina Press to bring about equitable access and impact for the entire scholarly community, including authors, researchers, libraries, and university presses around the world. Learn more at https://about.jstor.org/path-to-open/.

Cover design: Andre Klijsen
Cover illustration: *China Dream*, Zhongguo Meng. International Institute of Social History, BG E37/724 / Collection Stefan R. Landsberger.
Lay-out: Crius Group

ISBN 9789087284411
e-ISBN 9789400604810 (e-PDF)
https://doi.org//10.24415/9789087284411
NUR 754

Printed and bound by CPI Group (UK) Ltd, Croydon, CR0 4YY

Table of Contents

Acknowledgements

Since Xi Jinping became the paramount leader of China in late 2012, his ambitious goals and assertive policies such as the Anti-corruption Campaign, Chinese Dream, National Rejuvenation, and the One Belt and One Road diplomacy have captured the attention of politicians and scholars around the world. But the unexpected outbreak of Covid-19 in late 2019 and the disputes over its origin and the ensuing lockdowns have disrupted and compromised both Xi's Chinese Dream and his plan to attain his Common Destiny for Mankind. Against this backdrop, a group of historians and political scientists have decided to examine Xi Jinping's policies before and amid the pandemic through a historical perspective. At the annual conference of the American Historical Association in January 2024, most authors of this book presented their studies in two panels, and they were quite successful and dozens of scholars joined the panels. In the period from 2018 to 2024, the Association of Chinese Historians in the United States (CHUS) organized several scholarly, academic conferences, and on-the-spot social and legal surveys in China and Taiwan. Many authors of this book joined those delegations and spent time, often during the summer, compiling data and sources. In both scope and content, this book is indeed a wealth of splendid scholarly presentations ranging across questions of leadership, policy, law, media, military, and Xi Jinping's foreign policies. For the above-mentioned organization, the heartfelt thanks from the two editors go to each of the authors for their significant contributions to this book and their essential insights into the many important aspects of China under Xi Jinping in the past eleven years. This project received a fund from the James Gao Memorial Fund, which is administered through CHUS.

Qiang Fang wants to express his gratitude to the generous financial support from a number of grants provided by the University of Minnesota Twin Cities and the University of Minnesota Duluth. These grants include but are not limited to the University-wide Grant-in-Aid, Imagine Fund, and special support from the College of Arts, Humanities, and Social Sciences. In addition, Qiang Fang would like to thank Ms. Jing Duan, Harold, and Gerald for their crucial assistance and cooperation throughout the editing of this book.

Xiaobing Li appreciates the University of Central Oklahoma (UCO) for its contribution to this volume. First, Xiaobing Li would like to thank Associate Dean of the College of Liberal Arts Theresa Vaughan and Chairperson of the Department of History and Geography Katrina Lacher. They have been very supportive of the project over the past four years. As the Don Betz Endowed Chair in International

Studies, Li received research funds from the UCO Foundation. Travis Chambers edits some of the chapters.

Finally, the two editors offer thanks to the editor Ms. Saskia Gieling at Leiden University Press for her excellent professionalism and always-timely support during the editorial and production progress of this book. Of course, the two editors are grateful to the two peer-reviewers and copy-editors for their constructive suggestions and first-class editorial expertise, without which this book would not have been presented to the readers on time.

Qiang Fang (University of Minnesota Duluth)
Xiaobing Li (University of Central Oklahoma)

Note on Transliteration

The *Hanyu pinyin* romanization system is applied to Chinese names of persons, places, and terms. A person's name is written in the Chinese way, surname first, such as Mao Zedong. Some popular names have traditional Wade-Giles spellings appearing in parentheses after the first use of the *Hanyu pinyin* in the entry, such as Mao Zedong (Mao Tse-tung), as do popular names of places like the Yangzi (Yangtze) River, Huang (Yellow) River, and Guangzhou (Canton). Exceptions are made for a few figures, whose names are widely known in reverse order like Sun Yat-sen (Sun Zhongshan, or Sun Yixian), and a few places and institutional names, such as Tibet (Xizang) and Peking (Beijing) University.

Abbreviations

ADIZ	Air Defense Identification Zone
AEW	Airborne early warning
ASEAN	Association of Southeast Asian Nations
BRI	Belt-Road Initiative
CCBA	Chinese Consolidated Benevolent Association
CCP	Chinese Communist Party
CASS	China Academy of Social Sciences
CCYL	Chinese Communist Youth League
CECC	Congressional Executive Commission on China (US)
CMC	Central Military Commission (CCP)
CNOOC	China National Offshore Oil Corporation
CPG	Central People's Government
CPPCC	Chinese People's Political Consultative Conference
CPVA	Chinese People's Volunteer Army
DIA	Defense Intelligence Agency (US)
DPRK	Democratic People's Republic of Korea (North Korea)
ECRC	East China Regional Command (PLA)
EEZ	Exclusive Economic Zone
GDP	gross domestic production
GMD	Guomindang (Chinese Nationalist Party, or Kuomintang, KMT)
GNP	gross national product
MFN	most favorable nation
MPS	Ministry of Public Security
MSR	Maritime Silk Road
NATO	North Atlantic Treaty Organization
NGO	nongovernmental organization
NIRA	National Industrial Recovery Act (US)
NKPA	North Korean People's Army
NNSC	Neutral Nations Supervisory Commission
NPC	National People's Congress
PAP	People's Armed Police
PLA	People's Liberation Army
PLAAF	PLA Air Force
PLAN	PLA Navy
POW	prisoners of war

PRC	People's Republic of China
RMB	*Renminbi* (Chinese currency)
ROC	Republic of China
ROK	Republic of Korea (South Korea)
SEATO	Southeast Asia Treaty Organization
SEZ	Special Economic Zone
SLOCs	sea lines of communication
TAR	Tibet Autonomous Region
UN	United Nations
UNC	UN Command
UNCLOS	UN International Convention on the Law of the Sea
UNGA	UN General Assembly
UNHRC	UN Human Rights Commission
UNSC	UN Security Council
USIA	US Information Agency
USN	US Navy
USSR	Union of Soviet Socialist Republics
WASP	Women Air Force Service Pilots (US)
WTO	World Trade Organization
WWI	World War I
WWII	World War II
XPCC	Xinjiang Production and Construction Corps
XUAR	Xinjiang Uyghur Autonomous Region

INTRODUCTION

Xi's Chinese Dream and its Challenges

Qiang Fang and Xiaobing Li

UNIVERSITY OF MINNESOTA DULUTH AND UNIVERSITY OF CENTRAL OKLAHOMA

In late 2012, Xi Jinping, a Communist princeling whose father was a former vice premier in the early People's Republic of China (PRC), came to power when the Chinese Communist Party (CCP) witnessed its third peaceful transition of power since Deng Xiaoping picked Jiang Zemin, then the Party secretary of Shanghai, as the new leader after the 1989 Tiananmen incident. Before Xi Jinping became the paramount leader of the Chinese Communist Party (CCP), he had kept a low profile, which was in stark contrast to Bo Xilai, also a princeling and the Party secretary of the city of Chongqing, who was more flamboyant, aggressive, and ambitious. Because of his underwhelming personality, Xi was deemed by CCP leaders as "weak" and was therefore chosen as the next leader[1] who would, like his recent predecessors such as Jiang Zemin (1989–2004) and Hu Jintao (2002–2012), generally follow the principle of "collective leadership" to share power among members on the Politiburo Standing Committee, which stipulated that it was the premier who would be charged with dealing with the economy and foreign policy. The "collective leadership" was created by Chinese leaders in the aftermath of the disastrous Cultural Revolution due to Mao Zedong's nearly omnipotent and dictatorial power.

The timing of Xi's rise to power is better than that of both Jiang and Hu. While some scholars have argued that the beginning of Xi's era was floundering amid serious official corruption, economic downturn, and domestic disturbances,[2] it is more important to see China's then great economic accomplishments and its significant role in the world that had not been seen since 1949. To cite a few of them, China's GDP surpassed Japan's in 2010 and was second only to that of the United States; in comparison with the U.S. and many Western countries that were still struggling to navigate the Great Recession in 2008, China's economy remained one of the brightest spots and served as a powerful engine to help the West extricate from the recession; China was the "World Factory" and became the largest producer of shoes, clothes, machines, devices including iPhones and computers and so forth. Moreover, unlike

1 Osnos, "Born Red."

2 Fewsmith, "The Challenges of Stability and Legitimacy."

Hu Jintao whose leadership was neutralized by Jiang Zemin's lingering power and influence in the Standing Committee, Xi was on the cusp of becoming the most powerful leader after Mao as he was the president of the state, the Party, and the Central Military Commission with which he could execute both domestic and foreign policies that neither Jiang and Hu could do. Shortly after Xi ascended to the leadership, he, as Xiaojia Hou argues in Chapter Three, revoked the tradition of "collective leadership" and "de-centralization." Xi created two new leading groups in charge of national security and deepening reform that made Xi the paramount leader who would not need to share power with other Party leaders including Premier Li Keqiang.[3] One observer ascribes Xi's swift concentration of power and strongman politics to the backing of other senior Party leaders in the wake of factional struggle, corruption, and above all, the legitimacy crisis of the Party and not to Xi alone.[4]

Capitalizing on China's rising power and might and especially his almost absolute power, a more assertive Xi Jinping was ready to pull off his ambitions and dreams he had secretly harbored for years. As soon as he took power in late 2012, Xi rolled out the notions of "Chinese Dream" and "national rejuvenation," aiming at overtaking the United States as the world leader and restoring China's historical glory as the Central Kingdom. To accomplish his goal, Xi went farther and turned more stringent than his predecessors but less than Mao in snuffing out political contrarians, rights lawyers, and liberal scholars. In 2013, after just a few months in power, Xi issued an order to ban college professors from voicing support for the "Seven Speak-Not (*qibujiang*)" subjects including, inter alia, universal/western values, civil society, judicial independence, freedom of press, and criticism of the CCP.[5] Many professors have since lost their teaching jobs or been fired because of complimenting Western values and "blackening China's name" in classrooms.[6] In 2013, when some rights lawyers called on CCP officials to declare their assets, the police arrested their leader Xu Zhiyong and put him into custody.[7] If the cases of Xu and other rights lawyers were still not enough to attest Xi's new draconian rule and ambition, the kidnapping of several Hong Kong booksellers for selling a gossip book on Xi's private life would be more indicative of the aggressive policies under Xi.[8] The bold and unprecedented infringement of Hong Kong's autonomy by Chinese secret police is unseen even in Mao's era, which foreshadows a more severe and unpopular national security law imposed by the Chinese government in 2020.[9]

[3] Zheng and Gore, *China Entering the Xi Jinping Era:* 6.

[4] Baranvitch, "A Strong Leader for a Time of Crisis."

[5] Lam, "Chinese Government Bans Seven."

[6] Hernandez, "Professors, Beware"; also see Osnos, 2015.

[7] Kaiman, "Trial of Chinese Activist Xu Zhiyong."

[8] Kang, "The Missing Hong Kong Booksellers."

[9] "Hong Kong's National Security Law: 10 Things You Need to Know."

As a well-known concept in international politics correctly says, "Diplomacy is the extension of Domestic Policy,"[10] Xi's assertive diplomacy should be the natural and inevitable spanning and echo of his domestic policies and Chinese Dream. To be sure, prior to Xi's rise to the helm, some top Chinese diplomats and generals emboldened by China's growing power and the Great Recession in the West had already begun to threaten neighbors and to challenge the dominant role of the United States. For instance, in 2009, when Hilary Clinton, America's top diplomat, was meeting with Hu Jintao and some Chinese military leaders in Beijing, one general suddenly stood up and accused the United States of trying to block China's rise. Clinton believed that the general's rare boldness might have been approved by Hu Jintao. Starting from 2009, China has also stepped up its naval buildup and "asserted its claim" to almost all of the South China Sea. In the ASEAN meeting in Hanoi, Vietnam, in 2010, Yang Jiechi, China's then Foreign Minister, reminded Southeast Asian neighbors with an outright threat that China was bigger than any of them, ignoring the presence of Hilary Clinton.[11] After Japan decided to fully administer the disputed Diaoyu Islands (Sankaku Islands for Japan) in September 2012, Chinese leaders permitted nationalists to protest against Japan and some of them attacked Japanese factories and smashed Japanese cars in the streets.[12] In 2016, South Korea deployed the US THAAD anti-missile system to defend its country from northern attack. Fearing that the system could spy on China's military movement and bases, Beijing vented its wrath by urging the boycott of South Korean companies and limited tours to South Korea.[13]

There is no denying that Xi's foreign policies are more chauvinistic than his predecessors'. In addition to sharply raising China's military budget, building a more advanced air force and larger modern warships such as three aircraft-carriers, dozens of destroyers, and nuclear-powered submarines, and expanding China's nuclear arsenals, Xi's government has also sped up the process of building artificial islands in the disputed South China Sea that quickly drew ire from the Philippines and Vietnam. After the Permanent Court of Arbitration in The Hague made a ruling in 2016 outlawing China's claims in the South China Sea, China immediately rebut it and continued its island buildup and militarization.[14]

Although his aggressive and uncompromising domestic and foreign policies have triggered criticisms and protests from both Western states and Asian neighbors, Xi is quite popular in China for his anti-corruption campaign and nationalist

[10] Chu Shulong, *Basic Theories in International Relations*: 3.

[11] Clinton, *Hard Choices*: 76–79.

[12] Gill, *Daring to Struggle*: 18.

[13] Diaz and Zhang, "Angered by U.S. Anti-Missile System."

[14] Periez, "Tribunal Rejects Beijing's Claims"; Ricks, "Could the Chinese Communist Party Survive."

diplomacy. Some Chinese scholars went so far as to assert in 2017 that China had outpaced the United States in three major terms: science, the economy, and comprehensive national strength.[15] In the West, Japan, and Australia, China's vast and lucrative market remains highly magnetic. Western leaders such as German Chancellor Angela Merkel and US former president Donald Trump were eager to woo Chinese investment and markets. Before his visit to China in October 2017, Trump did not conceal his admiration for Xi Jinping. He openly said that he liked Xi and compared him to a "king."[16] Xi strained to cultivate a cordial relationship with Russian president Putin. Since Xi ascended to power in late 2012, he has met Putin in person almost forty times regardless of the tectonic changes in world affairs.[17] Even after Putin decided to annex Crimea and invade Ukraine, Xi has remained one of the staunchest supporters and friends of Putin and continues to purchase large amounts of Russian oil in spite of US sanctions.[18]

Had Covid-19 not broken out in late 2019, Xi Jinping could have inched closer to his Chinese Dream by retaining his relatively harmonious relations with major Western countries while keeping aggressive and stringent policies within and outside China. The scale and scope of the pandemic impact are so enormous that they have caught almost everyone in the world off guard. To Xi Jinping and the CCP, the pandemic and especially the squabbles between China and the West over its origin have upended their relations exponentially. As if the pandemic were not sufficient enough to shatter China's image in the West, Russia's invasion of Ukraine in early 2022 and Xi's ostensibly permissive stance and support for Putin have further compounded China's ties with the West and China's neighbors. When the pandemic started to rage across the world, Western states led by the United States complained about China's initial concealment and the detainment of Doctor Li Wenliang who was among the first to disclose the pandemic on social media. President Trump who had previously admired Xi Jinping was outraged after a Chinese foreign spokesman floated the idea in March 2020 that the US army had brought the coronavirus to China.[19] Trump immediately summoned the Chinese ambassador and lodged a strong protest and soon began naming the virus the "Chinese Virus" that triggered a racist wave of "Asian Hate" in the United States.[20]

The Sino-American relations have quickly spiraled downward to overt hostilities. In June 2020, the Trump Administration barred Chinese students with military

---

[15] Luo, *Semi-Capital: Semi-Capital and China:* 306; also see "Hu Angang Responds to his Allegation."
[16] Philips, "Extraordinary Elevation."
[17] Ramzy, "China's Top Envoy Travels to Europe."
[18] "Russia, China Sign 'Unprecedented' $270 Billion Oil Deal."
[19] Pamuk and Brunnstrom, "U.S. Summons Chinese Envoy over Beijing's Coronavirus Comments."
[20] Kai, "How Trump Fueled Anti-Asian Violence in America."

ties from studying in the United States.[21] On July 23, 2021, Trump demanded that China's Houston Consulate be shut down. A few days later, Secretary of State Mike Pompeo delivered a fiery speech at the Nixon Library in California calling for a new cold war against China.[22] After Russia waged a full-scale war against Ukraine in February 2022, the United States and its allies wasted no time in imposing economic sanctions on Russia and providing Ukraine with military aid. China, contrary to the West, takes a political gambit by not denouncing Russia's aggression and maintaining close trade and economic ties with Russia.[23] Just days before Russia's aggression, Xi Jinping promised Putin that there would be "no limit" on their cooperation and ramped up China's purchase of Russian oil to offset Russia's loss due to Western sanctions, further exacerbating China's tenuous relations with the West.[24]

On October 13, 2022, the Biden administration labeled China and not Russia as America's biggest strategic competitor.[25] The incident of the "spy balloon" in early 2023 intensified the frayed relations between the two superpowers and the intense enmity and distrust between them have not been diminished even after Biden and Xi held their first face-to-face summit in November 2023. Fewer than two weeks after the summit, Commerce Secretary Gina Raimondo called China "the biggest threat" to the U.S. and said that "China is not our friend." She warned US chip makers not to sell advanced chips to China.[26] To avert China from tapping into the Russia-Ukraine war to invade Taiwan, the US has scrambled to form an alliance in Asia entailing Japan, India, and Australia. In August 2023, leaders from Japan and South Korea were invited by Biden to Camp David where they conveyed a stern message to China that they would stand up to any of China's threats to Taiwan, the South China Sea, and Indo-Pacific region.[27] The joint announcement heralds the beginning of a cold-war-like alliance in East Asia. To counter China's growing military might, the US encourages its allies to reinforce their military presence in East Asia and gives a green light to Japan's big stride in military spending and modernization. After China launched military drills around Taiwan in response to House leader Nancy Pelosi's visit to Taiwan, Japanese leaders expressly cautioned China that Japan would oppose China's attack of Taiwan.[28]

[21] Watanabe, "It's the New Chinese Exclusion Act."

[22] For Pompeo's speech see https://www.rev.com/blog/transcripts/mike-pompeo-china-speech-transcript-july-23-at-nixon-library; Accessed March 23, 2022.

[23] Bradsher, "War in Ukraine Has China Cashing In."

[24] Russia-China trade neared $200 billion in 2022. Michael Schuman, "How China is Using Vladimir Putin."

[25] Liptak, "Biden's First Formal National Security Strategy."

[26] Cong, "US Commerce Chief Hypes."

[27] Pierson and Wang, "A Defense Agreement Likely."

[28] Brands, "Why Japan is Gearing Up for Possible War with China."

Seeing growing and coordinated Western criticism, decoupling, and sanctions, the Chinese government under Xi Jinping backed down from its earlier "wolf-warrior (*zhanlang*)" diplomacy with softer rhetoric in dealing with the United States and attempts to improve relations with neighbors such as Australia and Vietnam in the hopes of breaking up the US-led alliance. Xi cautiously refrains from whipping up nationalism against any individual Western or East Asian country which is a far cry from both what Mao did in the Cultural Revolution and what Xi did in 2016 over South Korean deployment of THAAD. At home, however, the Chinese government fights tooth and nail to obliterate Hong Kong protests and imposes a national security law, virtually depriving Hong Kong of civil liberties including its freedom of press and judicial independence promised by Chinese leaders during the retrocession of Hong Kong in the 1980s and 1990s.[29] China's crackdown in Hong Kong, the canary in the coal mine of Asia, leads to sharp backlash in the West and Japan, prodding more Western congressmen to rush anti-Chinese bills. Hong Kong's dire fate has also dimmed the outlook for Taiwan's peaceful reunification with China. During the pandemic, Xi's decision to adopt rigorous lockdowns in the name of reducing the case of infections and saving people's lives was not successful as strict lockdowns and restrictions had markedly disrupted normal economic activities, encroached people's personal freedom, and prevented many patients from obtaining timely treatment in hospital.[30] Despite bungled domestic and foreign policies, Xi insisted on seeking indefinite power at CCP's 20th Party Congress that has reportedly resulted in more discontent.[31] The sudden and mysterious falls of Foreign Minister Qin Gang and Defense Minister Li Shangfu in the summer of 2023 lay bare both the strength and weakness of Xi's power and governance.[32] Moreover, the recent escalations of clashes with the Philippines over disputed reefs and China's increasing military harassments prior to Taiwan's presidential election illustrate Xi's determination not to bow to external pressure.

The drastic changes inside of China and the fraught relations between China and the West in the past ten years have prompted many students across the world to write extensively on Xi Jinping. Yet most of them have centered on the pre-pandemic China when China managed to maintain a cordial relationship with major Western states, Japan, and Russia. In addition, almost all of the researchers are political scientists who have delved into the current policies of Xi Jinping such

[29] Paulson, Jr, *Dealing with China*: 9.

[30] Li, "China's Public Puts on a Show."

[31] Rammeloo, "What Happened to the Man."

[32] The strength is that all the top leaders of CCP are beholden to Xi, which is also the weakness of Xi's power as other leaders may not have the stamina to question Xi's decision. For Qin and Li's cases see Buckley, "China Dismisses Defense Minister Amid Swirl of Speculation."

as foreign, political, or economic policies. Few of them have harked back to Xi's policies such as the Wolf-Warrior diplomacy, his ambitious "national rejuvenation," and the severe crackdown on minorities, dissidents, and people's freedom under previous Communist leaders, much less to the Republican period or the dynasties. For that reason, some scholars' arguments on Xi's China tend to be out of step with the dynamic and everchanging policies of Xi's government after the outbreak of Covid-19 in late 2019. For example, in his latest book, Bates Gill focuses on Xi Jinping's global ambitions through six driving forces: legitimacy, sovereignty, wealth, power, leadership, and idea. He argues that Xi, in spite of facing many challenges, will primarily consider his regime security and would fight hard to overcome the challenges.[33] Michael Dillion's *China in the Age of Xi Jinping* offers a comprehensive study on Xi's China that was published in 2021, which serves better as a textbook for college students of political science who know little about China. Dillion's book also does not cover the dramatic shifts of policies in China in the post-pandemic era.[34]

Some other monographs and edited volumes such as Cheng Li's *Chinese Politics in the Xi Jinping Era*, Ross and Bekkevold's *In the era of Xi Jinping: Domestic and Foreign Policy Challenges*, Zheng Yongnian and Lance L.P. Gore's *China Entering the Xi Jinping Era*, and Willy Wo-Lap Lam's *Chinese Politics in the Era of Xi Jinping: Renaissance, Reform, or Retrogression?* were published in 2015 and 2016 and most chapters in these books use sources in the early 2010s or shortly after Xi came to power.[35] Due to the nature of their preliminary and insufficient sources, some of them have made tangential arguments on Xi Jinping and his policies. To cite one example, Zheng Yongnian and Weng Guifen praise Xi Jinping for his efforts to build a law-based public administration and emphasize the role of the NPC and the CPPCC more than his predecessors. Had Zheng and Weng tracked the staggering law violations in cases of Hong Kong, Xinjiang, and rights lawyers after 2014, they would not have made such premature arguments.[36] In 2016, Steve Tsang and Honghua Men edited a book on Xi's China. Like the other edited volumes, this book studies only the early years of Xi Jinping. In addition, because most of the authors are Chinese scholars and one of the editors works at the Central Party School of the CCP, this book appears more like a propaganda book for the Chinese government than like serious academic research with an unbiased and independent stance.[37] These authors mostly look

[33] Gill, *Daring to Struggle.*

[34] Dillion, *China in the Age of Xi Jinping.*

[35] Li, *Chinese Politics in the Xi Jinping Era*; Zheng and Gore, *China Entering the Xi Jinping Era*; Lam, *Chinese Politics in the Era of Xi Jinping.*

[36] Zheng and Guifeng, "Domestic and Foreign Policy Challenges."

[37] Tsang and Men, *China in the Xi Jinping Era.*

into Xi's policies, organizations, security, and leadership with little ink spilled tracing the historical backdrop, consistency, and practices of Xi's policies.

This book, *China Under Xi Jinping: A New Assessment*, is one of the first scholarly books on Xi's China during the pandemic. Both editors and authors seek to address the following questions: What are the motives behind Xi Jinping's bold and aggressive policies? How does Covid-19 significantly disrupt the relations between Xi's China and the West? What do we learn from CCP history for whether the deterioration of bilateral relations between China and the West will be a long-term or transient one? How does Xi Jinping understand Chinese history, Party media, military power, and the rule of law? Why and how does Xi Jinping remain popular in China despite his bungled shutdowns at home and clumsy diplomacy with the West and its neighbors? To what extent are Xi Jinping's policies similar to or different from those of Mao Zedong or Deng Xiaoping?

This book contains several features that are unmatched by existing scholarship. First, all the authors have studied and taught Chinese and American history or politics in both China and the United States for decades. They are quite familiar with and possess deep understandings of the history, politics, ideology, and society in both countries and therefore their research would be more balanced and nuanced if not more profound than that of many western students. Second, most of the authors are historians. They will examine Xi Jinping's China and China's relationship with the West from historical backdrops and perspectives. Unlike many political scientists who are inclined to pay more attention to Xi's current policies, ideas, and leadership, these historians will explore the historical trajectory, precedents, causes, and problems of Xi's policies and intentions, which will help readers to have a better sense of what Xi and his regime could do in the future. Third, most authors are established and internationally renowned scholars in their respective fields. For example, Xiaobing Li is a prolific scholar on the Cold War and Chinese military; Guolin Yi is a specialist on public media and Sino-US relations; Dean Chen has published expansively on US-China-Taiwan triangle relations. As specialists in their own fields, each author focuses on one specific but important aspect of China under Xi's rule such as, among other topics, law, military, diplomacy, Confucius Institute, public media, and the like that will assist readers from different cultures to gain a panoramic view of Xi's China. The last striking feature of this book is that it will be one of the first studies spanning from Xi Jinping's rise to power in the early 2000s to the pandemic era and beyond. The authors have kept a close eye on the latest developments and sources to analyze and compare Xi's policies as well as his relations with the West before and after the pandemic.

This edited volume is divided into three parts: "Party's Legacy and Continuity," "Global Ambitions and Social Stability," and "Military Outreach and Geopolitical Strategy." Each Part contains three to four chapters. In the first Part, Patrick Fuliang

Shan examines how Xi Jinping utilizes history to cement his power and facilitate his policies before and during the pandemic. Shan argues that the pandemic in late 2019 has resulted in China's isolation, segregation, and lockdowns. To facilitate his political maneuvers, Xi has doubled his use of rich historical resources. Xi has proved to skillfully make full use of China's wealthy resources to initiate new political policies. He launches the revival of the Silk Road by adopting the Road and Belt Initiative in recent years and he has continued to push for its implementation. His repeated calls for the great resurgence of the Chinese nation are intended to restore China's glorious past. His lamentation over the Hundred Year Humiliation is to arouse Chinese nationalism. He has often organized the Politburo members to visit the communist historical sites to reaffirm their oaths purporting to defend their communist faith and to display their determination to solve tough problems. Amazingly, a lot of Xi's new political terminologies are related to history.

Guolin Yi studies the Chinese government's rigorous control of public media since Xi took power in 2012. His chapter centers on two aspects of Xi and CCP's media policies: what the CCP tries to prevent and what it tries to promote. On one hand, the CCP has passed laws and regulations that prohibit private enterprises from newsgathering and broadcasting and adds a new ban on hosting news-related forums. It also tightens the control over online commentaries by shutting down VIP accounts that have stepped out of line. On the other, print media and the main portal websites like Sina, Sohu, and NetEase have been involved in the promotion of Xi Jinping's cult of personality by highlighting his images and quotes. By looking at these measures, Yi's chapter demonstrates the status of the media environment in China under Xi Jinping.

The next chapter is authored by Xiaojia Hou, which looks into the localized centralization of the Party-state system under Xi Jinping. While leaders after Mao have strived to establish collective leadership, decentralize authority, and to balance the power between the party and state, Xi Jinping's rise to power in 2012 and especially his plan to revise the constitution and make his rule indefinite in October 2022, has reversed the trend of de-centralization. Hou investigates how Xi Jinping perceives Party-state relationships and examines the way he reconstructs the decision-making processes to reclaim more power from the state while elevating his own authority within the party. Hou's chapter aims to analyze these changes from a historical lens and explore Xi Jinping's sources of legitimacy and of inspiration from the past. Questions to be addressed include: What lessons did Xi learn from the fall of the Soviet Union? How did he employ Mao's practices of purging and instigating mass movement for political maneuvers? How did he revive Mao's rituals to control official narratives, and use national security to censor public opinion? And how did he overturn a tradition of two-term leadership set by Deng Xiaoping and quickly solidify his grip of power?

Qiang Fang's chapter is the last one in the first part. As a legal historian, Fang spills ink on Xi's understanding of the rule of law with Chinese features, a term Xi coined in early 2021 when the whole world was still struggling with Covid 19. Through the studies of several widely known legal cases such as China's crackdown on rights lawyers, abduction of Hong Kong booksellers, and the strict enforcement of the Hong Kong National Security Law, Fang looks into Xi's definition of the rule of law and compares it with orthodox notions of the rule of law in the West and China. Fang also traces the history of the rule of law in the dynasties, Republic of China, and early periods of the PRC to show the continuity and dynamics of the comprehension and practice of the rule of law in three distinct historical periods. Fang argues that the legal policies and practices of Xi Jinping's "rule of law" with Chinese features should better be referred to as "Rule of the Party Law" as the CCP and Xi would follow a law if it only fits their needs and create a law if existing laws do not serve their policies.

The second Part of the book has a focus on Xi Jinping's economic relations with states in Central Asia, Confucius Institute, and the One Belt and One Road initiative. In her chapter, Yi Sun examines the development of the complex relationship between China and the five Central Asian republics since the early 1990s. Although diplomatic activities initially focused on resolving the border disputes and tackling the uncertainties stemming from the new-found independence of these republics, China's relations with Central Asia have increasingly reflected a desire to protect its economic and security interests in that region since Xi Jinping became Chinese leader. Xi's One Belt One Road Initiative has created a vast infrastructure and network of trade, transportation, and communication, linking China to Central Asia. From 2012–2022, Beijing's economic programs have been accompanied by the practice of cultural diplomacy, evinced in the establishment of many Confucius Institutes and the provision of scholarships to Central Asian students, thus deepening China's economic and cultural influence in the area. Beset by diplomatic woes elsewhere in the world, Sun argues that China under Xi Jinping sees Central Asia as a bright spot in a dramatically changed geopolitical environment.

For years, the Chinese government has been building hundreds of overseas Confucius Institutes in the name of promoting Chinese culture and language. But the growing tensions between China and the United States after the pandemic have prompted some American politicians to ramp up their attacks on Confucius Institutes (CI) for interfering in academic freedom and to call for their closure. According to a former director of a Confucius Institute, the number of Confucius Institutes in the US dwindled from around 120 before 2017 to fewer than ten in 2023.[38] In her chapter, Shuhua Fan studies Confucius Institutes in the Xi Jinping

[38] Editor's talk with former directors of Confucius Institute at Troy University and University of Utah in 2022 and 2023.

era with a focus on their expansion and decline in the United States. In 2004, China established its first CI to export Chinese language and culture overseas. After Xi rose to power, the Confucius Institutes expanded significantly across the world, with about 118 in the US. However, when China became more aggressive in both domestic and foreign policies and when US-China relations sharply deteriorated, US leaders urged the closure of Confucius Institutes. By early 2023, there were only about a dozen left in the US. Fan wants to address questions such as Why did China establish the Confucius Institutes worldwide? Why were they popular in the early stages? Why did we see increasing resistance to those institutes in the West? Why have there been CI mass closures in the US recently? In addition, Fan also argues that the Confucius Institute is part of China's cultural diplomacy to promote China's international image and expand its cultural/educational influence overseas. China's outright campaigns to export soft power and the US' increasing resistance are both driven by national interests.

The last chapter in this part starts with Ting Jiang's research on Xi's One Belt and One Road initiative, which is called the modern Silk Road. During his first term (2013–2018), Xi Jinping proposed the Belt and Road Initiative as China's grant strategy. From 2012 to 2022, the Chinese government made great efforts to transition Xi's strategy from policy to reality. However, many regions and countries on the New Silk Road seemed unready for China's historical program. Jiang explores the spirit and legacies of the Silk Road over a 1600-year period to addresses the following questions: What is the spirit and legacies of the Maritime Silk Road? How does it contribute to the ideological framework of Xi's Belt and Road Initiative? Jiang demonstrates how temporal dimensions of social life of the past could leave profound marks on the current conditions of life, for example, in conceptualizing the Belt and Road Initiative in the 2020s.

Four papers are included in the third part of the book entitled "Global Strategy and China-US-Taiwan Relations." Dean Chen studies the so-called 1992 Consensus between the GMD (aka. KMT) and the CCP when the GMD was still the dominant party and power in Taiwan. The Consensus agreed that there was only one China. However, in the ensuing decades, the Consensus has increasingly lost its legitimacy as the GMD no longer holds a political majority and the independent-leaning Democratic Progressive Party (DPP) refuses to accept the Consensus. After the GMD lost the 2016 and 2020 presidential elections, the GMD has not been able to settle on a strategically sound position to cope with the PRC's offensives, instead opting to grapple with a near-moribund formula known as the "1992 consensus" to maintain ties with the CCP. The GMD's huge electoral win in the 2022 mayoral races boosted the party's confidence somewhat, but municipal elections are less about national security/cross-strait issues than domestic affairs hence the GMD's prospect to recover Taiwan's presidency in 2024 is far from ensured. Yet, if the

GMD returns to power in 2024, its inability to effectively address Taiwan's public anxieties/identity preferences for a free and democratic Taiwan and the deepening U.S.-PRC struggles may become a strategic liability for Washington, the island's strongest security backer. Since 2016, though the GMD has strived to redefine its framing of the "1992 consensus," it has failed to escape its "one-China" precept that has become so sensitive given China's President Xi Jinping had equated, in 2019, the political formulation with the PRC (as well as the "one country, two systems"). Chen's chapter sets out to analyze the changing GMD and CCP stances on the "1992 consensus," as conceived by both Xi and successive GMD leaders since 2013 and attempts to illustrate how a domestic security imaginary (to use Jutta Weldes' concept from 1999) that is deeply rooted in history, culture, and identity has prevented them from adopting a pragmatic arrangement, hence exacerbating the overarching cross-strait relationship as well the U.S.-PRC ties.

After Xi Jinping became the paramount ruler in China, he immediately commenced an ambitious plan to accelerate the pace of military modernization especially the navy and geared up for a potential military showdown with the United States and its allies over Taiwan and the South China Sea. Xiaobing Li's chapter centers on Xi Jinping's military buildup. For example, as Asia's largest air force, the Chinese Air Force (PLAAF) has over 2,250 combat aircraft, including 1,800 fighters, strategic bombers, tactical bombers, multi-mission tactical and attack aircraft. The Air Force continues to promote the "leap-over" approach for aviation technological improvement. By 2020, the Chinese Navy (PLAN) had 240,000 naval officers and sailors with an overall battle force of 350 surface ships and submarines—the USN had 293 warships at that time. The Chinese Navy also had 15,000 marines and 26,000 naval aviation personnel with 690 aircraft. Its tonnage totaled 1.82 million in 2019 as the second largest navy in the world, only after the US Navy. It continued its expansion into the 2020s, commissioning new warships and constructing more naval facilities. Li argues that the rapid development of the PLA's air, naval, and strategic forces enabled Beijing to reposition China as the Asia-Pacific regional epicenter, despite experiencing unprecedented demands, facing new challenges, and creating new problems.

Like Xiaobing li, Lei Duan's chapter also examines Xi's military reform and expansion with a focus on militia reconstruction. Since Xi Jinping came to power in late 2012, China's armed forces have undergone unprecedented reforms in their scale and scope of organizational and strategic changes. Hoping to modernize and strengthen the Chinese military, Xi has adopted the most sweeping and radical reforms on military efficiency, technological innovation, and joint operations in the 2020s. Seeing the formation of a powerful military as an integral part of the China Dream, Xi has shifted the national security strategy to a defensive-offensive one. China has also consolidated its Mao-era militia organization and training works.

In particular, China's maritime militia has undergone significant building and modernization. Many sources suggest that China's armed fishing militia has dual-use capabilities for both military and civilian purposes. As an official component of China's armed forces, the maritime militia has been integrated closely with the regular navy and has played an increasing role in supporting China's territorial claims in the South China Sea in the past ten years. Duan's chapter aims to take a fresh look at the Chinese military reform by focusing on the cooperation and coordination of the People's Liberation Army and the militia force from 2012 to 2022. He argues that the government has integrated both regular military and paramilitary forces in pursuit of China's ambition.

Soon after Donald Trump won the presidential election in late 2016, his new administration blamed China for the lopsided trade between the two countries. Trump launched a trade war with China by imposing high tariffs on imported Chinese goods that triggered intense Chinese anger. Chinese media including the nationalistic tabloid Global Times and Weibo, Chinese Twitter, waged massive criticism against what they claimed "an epic trade war in human history." Lin Mao's chapter presents an argument that, although Xi Jinping's government tries to maintain a tight control over public opinion, it cannot always shape the narrative of the trade war based on official policies. Lin examines how popular nationalism evolved over the early pandemic period and shaped China's response to the trade war, focusing on the influential *Global Times* and how it used the social media platform, Weibo, to frame the trade war. During the early months of the trade war, China's response was largely defensive. Chinese public opinion claimed China was an innocent victim of the trade war, initiated by a reckless Trump administration. Many, especially those in social media, were also optimistic, believing that the trade war would be over soon once the U.S. government came to it senses. After Washington imposed sanctions on Huawei, a popular Chinese high-tech company, the public opinion shifted to an offensive mode. Many now argued that America was not looking for fair trade policies but trying to block China's rise as a global power. Furthermore, the Chinese popular nationalism started to argue that China's model of development was superior to America's liberal democracy. Other issues on Xi Jinping's policy toward Taiwan, Hong Kong, Tibet, Xinjiang, and the South China Sea from 2018–2022 further confounded the bilateral relationship and led to the rise of popular nationalism.

The chapters in this volume cover a wide variety of key areas in the Xi Jinping era. Most of the authors seek to explore Xi's policies, whether they are successful, effective, or counterproductive, through their historical roots and changes over the course of CCP's century-long history. It is the wish of both the editors and the authors that this volume will shed new light on the nature, motives, dynamism, and continuity of not only Xi Jinping's Chinese Dream, domestic policies, and his visions toward media, military, law, rights lawyers, and Taiwan but also his diplomacies toward the West and China's neighbors. The studies seek to illustrate the continuities and differences between Xi and earlier Communist leaders, especially Mao Zedong and Deng Xiaoping. As the enlightened emperor Tang Taizong said in the seventh century, history was a mirror.[39] We hope the scholarly findings in this book will be a mirror that can provide readers with a picture of what China's national and international trajectories could be in Xi's third or even fourth term as CCP's president.

Bibliography

Baranvitch, Nimrod. "A Strong Leader for a Time of Crisis: Xi Jinping's Strongman Politics as a Collective Response to Regime Weakness" in *Journal of Contemporary China*, 2021, Vol. 30, No. 128, pp. 249 265.

Bradsher, Keith. "War in Ukraine Has China Cashing In" in *The New York Times*, December 21, 2023.

Brands, Hal. "Why Japan is Gearing Up for Possible War with China" in *Bloomberg News*, November 6, 2022. https://www.bloomberg.com/opinion/features/2022-11-06/why-japan-is-gearing-up-for-possible-war-with-china-over-taiwan; Accessed January 28, 2023.

Buckley, Chris. "China Dismisses Defense Minister Amid Swirl of Speculation" in *The New York Times*, October 25, 2023. https://cn.nytimes.com/china/20231025/china-defense-minister-ousted/dual/. Accessed December 1, 2023.

"China Responsible for 'Serious Human Rights Violations' in Xinjiang Province" in *UN Human Rights Report*, August 31, 2022; https://news.un.org/en/story/2022/08/1125932; Accessed January 26, 2023.

Chu, Shulong, *Basic Theories in International Relations* (*Guoji guanxi jiben lilun*). Beijing: Qinghua daxue chubanshe, 2003.

Clinton, Hilary. *Hard Choices*. New York: Simon & Schuster, 2014.

Diaz, Adriana and Zhang, Shuai. "Angered by U.S. Anti-Missile System, China Takes Economic Revenge" in CBS News, April 7, 2017. https://www.cbsnews.com/news/china-retaliates-south-korea-us-thaad-missile-defense-lotte-and-k-pop/; Accessed January 27, 2023.

Dillion, Michael. *China in the Age of Xi Jinping*. U.K.: Routledge, 2021.

Editor's talk with former directors of Confucius Institute at Troy University and University of Utah in 2022 and 2023.

Fewsmith, Joseph. "The Challenges of Stability and Legitimacy" in Robert S. Ross and Jo Inge Bekkevold, eds., *China in the Era of Xin Jinping*. Washington: Georgetown University Press, 2015.

Gill, Bates. *Daring to Struggle: China's Global Ambitions under Xi Jinping*. Oxford: Oxford University Press.

Hernandez, Javier C. "Professors, Beware. In China, Students Spies Might Be Watching" in *The New York Times*, November 1, 2019.

"Hong Kong's National Security Law: 10 Things You need to Know" in Amnesty International, July 17, 2020; https://www.amnesty.org/en/latest/news/2020/07/hong-kong-national-security-law-10-things-you-need-to-know/; Accessed January 26, 2023.

[39] Sima, *The Comprehensive Mirror*: 61–84.

"Hu Angang Responds to his Allegation 'China Has Sweepingly Surpassed the United States'" in Guanchazhe Net, April 1, 2018. https://www.guancha.cn/economy/2018_04_01_452304.shtml; Accessed January 27, 2023.

Kaiman, Jonathan. "Trial of Chinese Activist Xu Zhiyong May Be Imminent, Says His Lawyer" in *The Guardian*, January 14, 2014. https://www.theguardian.com/world/2014/jan/14/trial-chinese-activist-xu-zhiyong-immenent-lawyer, Accessed January 26, 2023.

Kai, Jin. "How Trump Fueled Anti-Asian Violence in America" in *The Diplomat*, June 8, 2021. https://thediplomat.com/2021/06/how-trump-fueled-anti-asian-violence-in-america/. Accessed January 27, 2023.

Kang, John. "The Missing Hong Kong Booksellers Saga Explained" in *Forbes*, June 17, 2016. https://www.forbes.com/sites/johnkang/2016/06/17/missing-hong-kong-booksellers-saga-explained/?sh=3ab46e314d80; Accessed January 26, 2023.

Lam, Oiwan. "Chinese Government Bans Seven 'Speak-Not' Subjects" in *Global Voices*, May 16, 2013. https://globalvoices.org/2013/05/16/chinese-government-bans-seven-speak-not-school-subjects/ Accessed January 26, 2023.

Lam, Willy Wo-Lap. *Chinese Politics in the Era of Xi Jinping: Renaissance, Reform, or Retrogression?*. U.K.: Routledge, 2015.

Li, Cheng. *Chinese Politics in the Xi Jinping Era: Reassessing Collective Leadership.* Washington D.C.: Brookings Institution Press, 2016.

Liptak, Kevin. "Biden's First Formal National Security Strategy Identifies China as 'America's Most Consequential Geopolitical Challenge'" in CNN News, October 12, 2022. https://www.cnn.com/2022/10/12/politics/national-security-strategy-joe-biden/index.html; Accessed January 28, 2023.

Luo, William. *Semi-Capital: Semi-Capital and China.* New York: Shijie huayu chubanshe, 2018.

Osnos, Evan. "Born Red: How Xi Jinping, an Unremarkable Provincial Administrator, Became China's Most Authoritarian Leader Since Mao" in *New Yorker*, March 30, 2015. https://www.newyorker.com/magazine/2015/04/06/born-red; Accessed January 2023.

Pamuk, Humeyra and David Brunnstrom. "U.S. Summons Chinese Envoy over Beijing's Coronavirus Comments" in *The Reuters News*, March 13, 2020. https://www.reuters.com/article/us-health-coronavirus-china-diplomacy/u-s-summons-chinese-envoy-over-beijings-coronavirus-comments-idUSKBN2102XW; Accessed January 27, 2023.

Paulson, Henry M. Jr. *Dealing with China: An Insider Unmasks the New Economic Superpower.* New York, Grand Central Publishing, 2015.

Periez, Jane. "Tribunal Rejects Beijing's Claims in South China Sea" in *The New York Times*, July 12, 2016.

Philips, Tom. "'Extraordinary Elevation': Trump Kowtows to Kingpin Xi" in *The Guardian*, October 25, 2017. https://www.theguardian.com/us-news/2017/oct/26/extraordinary-elevation-trumps-kowtow-unlikely-to-win-favours-from-xi-jinping; Accessed January 26, 2023.

Pierson, David and Wang, Olivia. "A Defense Agreement Likely to Deepen Chinese Rancor" in *The New York Times*, August 21, 2023.

Pompeo, Mike. "Mike Pompeo China Speech Transcript July 23 at Nixon Library" https://www.rev.com/blog/transcripts/mike-pompeo-china-speech-transcript-july-23-at-nixon-library; Accessed March 23, 2022.

Rammeloo, Eva. "What Happened to the Man who Led the Chants against Xi Jinping?" in The Economist, November 29, 2022. https://www.economist.com/1843/2022/11/29/what-happened-to-the-man-who-led-the-chants-against-xi-jinping; Accessed January 30, 2023.

Ramzy, Austin. "China's Top Envoy Travels to Europe" in *The Wall Street Journal*, February 16, 2023.

Ricks, Thomas E. "Could the Chinese Communist Party Survive Dropping South China Sea Claims?" in *Foreign Policy*, June 29, 2017.

"Russia, China Sign 'Unprecedented' $270 Billion Oil Deal" in *Fox* News, December 3, 2015; https://www.foxnews.com/world/russia-china-sign-unprecedented-270-bn-oil-deal; Accessed January 26, 2023.

Schuman, Michael. "How China is Using Vladimir Putin" in The Atlantic, December 29, 2022. https://www.theatlantic.com/international/archive/2022/12/china-russia-xi-jinping-vladimir-putin-friends/672586/; Accessed January 28, 2023.

Sima, Guang. *The Comprehensive Mirror in Assisting Governance* (*zizhi tongjian*). Beijing: Zhonghua shuju, 2010.

Tsang, Steve and Men, Honghua. *China in the Xi Jinping Era: The Nottingham China Policy Institute Series*. Palgrave Macmillan, 2016.

Wang, Cong. "US Commerce Chief Hypes 'China Threat' Illusion, Assaulting Chip Firms 'Counterproductive'" in *Global Times*, December 3, 2023.

Watanabe, Teresa. "It's the New Chinese Exclusion Act: How a Trump Order Could Hurt California Universities" in Los Angeles Times, June 7, 2020. https://www.latimes.com/california/story/2020-06-07/trump-move-to-bar-entry-of-some-chinese-graduate-students-stirs-campus-anxiety-anger; Accessed January 27, 2023.

Yuan, Li. "China's Public Puts on a Show of Zero Covid for an Audience of One" in *The New York Times*, September 13, 2022.

Zheng, Yongnian and Weng, Guifeng. "Domestic and Foreign Policy Challenges" in Ross and Bekkevold, 2016.

Zheng, Yongnian and Gore, Lance L.P. *China Entering the Xi Jinping Era*. U.K:. Routledge, 2016.

PART ONE

Party's Legacy and Continuity

CHAPTER ONE

What did the CCP Learn from the Past? An Analysis of Xi Jinping's Dexterous Utilization of History

Patrick Fuliang Shan

GRAND VALLEY STATE UNIVERSITY

Abstract: *China is one of the oldest civilizations and its rich historical resource has been utilized by Chinese rulers for governance in the past millennia. Ever since Xi Jinping came to power, he has used this wealthy resource to initiate new policies, persuade citizens to follow him, and endeavor to consolidate his power. He launched the revival of the Silk Road through the Road and Belt Initiative. He called for the resurgence of the Chinese nation, purporting to bring back China's ancient glory. He often leads the Politburo members to visit the communist historical sites to reaffirm their oaths, reassert their faith, and repledge their dedication to their party. His political terminologies are, more or less, related to history. This article investigates Xi's approaches of using Chinese history to legitimize his rule, attract support to his regime, and woo the people to join his campaign of national revival.*

Keywords: Xi Jinping; History; Politics; Nationalism; Civilization

Introduction

Xi Jinping has been China's paramount leader for over ten years after he started his third five-year term recently, which is unprecedented since Deng Xiaoping's reform. Without a doubt, Xi has brought about significant changes, caused heated debates and diverse perspectives. Consequently, voluminous publications have explored his political moves, assessed his administrative style, and examined his ideological viewpoints. Yet, Xi's use of history has been much neglected, in particular, outside China. Through a careful reading of Xi's speeches, writings, and publications, a reader becomes bombarded with all manner of citations of bygone stories, ancient anecdotes, and ageless axioms. More often than not, Xi's employment of history provides him a solid ground to ponder the relationship between the past and the present, offers him an opportunity to persuade the Chinese to stick to his way, and convinces his compatriots to support his government. In a sense, he has elevated the use of history to a high limit, which is an extraordinary case among the current world leaders and which necessitates scholarly exploration, requires public attention, and demands intellectual inquiry.

Xi Jinping is neither a historian nor a history-related professional. However, he becomes so captivated with the past that he never shies away from serviceable historical precedents with which he spreads his ideas that are bound to be shared with his fellow compatriots. To him, history encompasses the study of the bygone days but more importantly it renders a convenient tool of political governance. Cognizant of the efficacy of history, Xi emphasizes that history is "the best teacher" (*zuihaode laoshi*) who imparts knowledge and who guides students.[1] He argues that history is "the best textbook" (*zuihaode jiaokeshu*) from which a learner can acquire valuable information.[2] He vividly compares history to "a mirror" from which one can see what lies behind.[3] To Xi, history is a source of wisdom, as it records departed events, serves as an informative encyclopedia, and offers stern lessons.[4]

From the broad historical perspective, Xi Jinping regards contemporary China under his administration as the New Era (*xinshidai*), which is the organic continuity of the long Chinese civilization.[5] As for post-1949 China, its history is partitioned into three distinctive eras: Mao Zedong enabled China to stand up, Deng Xiaoping turned China into a relatively prosperous nation, and Xi grants China a status of strong power. For Xi, his model for modernization is deeply rooted in China's past and becomes inseparable from China's long civilization.[6] He asks the Chinese to acquire "historical self-confidence" (*lishi zixin*) and doubles down this rhetoric during the three-year pandemic.[7] His ten-year rule testifies his skillful use of history from which he develops his political notions which are transformed into famed terminologies, such as "the Belt and Road Initiative" to revive the Silk Road, and "the Two Centennials" to utilize the dates of the founding of the CCP [Chinese Communist Party] and the PRC [People's Republic of China] to encourage the Chinese to reach two noble targets: the goal of "moderate prosperity" for the Chinese people in 2021, and the target of turning China into a moderately developed country in 2049.

In order to recapture the gist of Xi Jinping's utilization of history, this article makes full use of his own publications which have been released into public circulation in the past decade. The four volumes of his *The Governance of China*

1 Xi Jinping, *Lun Zhongguo gongchandang lishi* [On the History of the Chinese Communist Party], Beijing: Zhongyangwenxian, 2021, 11. This book is abbreviated LZGGCDLS.

2 Xi Jinping, *Lun Zhongguo gongchandang lishi*, 7.

3 Xi Jinping, *Lun Zhongguo gongchandang lishi*, 9.

4 Yu, "Yong kexuejingshen yu lishi duihua." 43– 44.

5 Jin and Zhou Liangshu, "Xi Jinping dalishiguan dui lishiweiwuzhuyi." 7.

6 Zhou, and Shu Yibiao, "Xi Jinping guanyu lishiwenti zhongyaolunshu de lilunyiyun." 24.

7 Lu, "Shenke linghui Xi Jinping guanyu jianding lishizixin de zhongyao lunshu." 19.

(*tanzhiguo lizheng*) were published in 2014, 2017, 2020, and 2022 which include his speeches, addresses, talks, instructions, orders, and others. Pamphlets ascribing him as the author were also issued, although they might be similar to the pieces inside *The Governance of China*, but thematically assembled together, such as clean government, national resurgence, continual reform, and so forth. An anthology titled *On the History of the Chinese Communist Party* (*lun zhongguo gongchangdang lishi*) was published in 2021 to relay Xi's speeches, quotes, and sayings concerning CCP history. The above-mentioned materials are available online and they all should be seen as primary sources. Altogether, those publications reveal that history plays a far more powerful role in Xi's political life than one can simply imagine. It is fair to claim that one cannot comprehend Xi's way of running China without an understanding of his ties with the past.

Ancient History as an Inspirational Source

Many ancient civilizations once dominated diverse geographical regions in the world, but China appears to be the only one that enjoys a continual development without interruption throughout the past millennia, which becomes a source of Xi Jinping's national pride.[8] He designates China as "a splendid civilization" with a history of five thousand years,[9] during which China has produced great thinkers, published fascinating literature, invented marvelous wonders, and built gigantic projects, which prove that China is "a great and creative nation."[10] In particular, he is proud of the Four Great Inventions including paper-making, gunpower, printing, and the compass and their significant impacts upon the world.[11] He argues that "the Chinese nation is the greatest nation which has a long civilized past and which has offered its indelible contributions to the progress of human civilization."[12] Xi's understanding of China's destiny in the context of this unbroken link with the past results in his historical confidence for his culture, his people, and his nation.[13]

It is this sense of national pride along with the subsequent historical confidence that prompts Xi Jinping to explicitly advocate the idea of China's national

[8] Xi Jinping, *Guanyu shixian zhonghuaminzuweidafuxing de zhongguomeng lunshu zhaibian* [Quotes from Xi Jinping on realizing the Chinese Dream for the Great Rejuvenation of the Chinese Nation], Beijing: Zhongyangwenxian, 2013, 3.

[9] Xi Jinping, *The Governance of China (II)*, 13. (This book is abbreviated TGOC).

[10] Xi Jinping, *Zhiguolizheng* [The Governance of China], 3:141. (This series of books is abbreviated TZGLZ).

[11] TZGLZ, 1:261.

[12] TZGLZ, 4:17.

[13] TZGLZ, 1:39.

resurgence, purporting to restore the ancient glory. He envisions China's bright future with his proposition of "the Chinese Dream" (*zhongguomeng*) immediately after he became the national leader in late 2012.[14] However, he warns the Chinese by citing ancient statesman Guanzi to counsel them to work hard, as he reasons that "the great dream is not to be waited or to be taken with hands down. It must be realized through diligence and productivity."[15] He utilizes *The Book of Change* to promote the self-strengthening spirit and advises the Chinese to be valiant in their strife for national prosperity.[16] In his political rhetoric, history and reality are deeply intertwined, for which he asks two reflective questions: "If there was not Chinese civilization for five thousand years, where did we get Chinese characteristics? Without Chinese characteristics, where do we get today's successful Chinese socialism with Chinese characteristics?"[17]

As China's economy has grown rapidly in recent decades, the country is no longer lying at the edge of the global community; rather, it plays an increasingly important role in it, which creates a fear among some who have watched over China warily. To alleviate this fear, Xi Jinping assures the international community that China's development will be a peaceful rise for which he makes the use of history for his verification. He proclaims that "the Chinese people since the ancient times have been a peaceful people."[18] He reiterates a Confucian saying, "If you do not want to have it yourself, you should not impose it upon others," to express China's peaceful intent.[19] In 2017, Xi quoted Chen Shou, a third century scholar, to plead with the whole world to support his plan to establish "the community of shared future for mankind," because Chen Shou once said that "delicious soup is made by combining different ingredients."[20] Xi mentions a popular saying of the Ming Dynasty to validate the peaceful co-existence of diverse peoples in the world: "One flower does not signify the spring, and hundred flowers in blossom mean the true arrival of springtime."[21] When he visited the United States, Xi promised to his American hosts that the Chinese two thousand years ago were aware of the truth that "the great yet belligerent state is doomed to fail," for which China must assume a defensive military policy.[22] During his visit to Germany, Xi tells the Germans that

14 Xi Jinping, *Xi Jinping zongshuji xilie zhongyao jianghua duben* [Important thematic quotes from General Secretary Xi Jinping], Beijing: Renminchubanshe, 2014, 25.

15 TZGLZ, 3:197.

16 TZGLZ, 4:126.

17 TZGLZ, 4:315.

18 Xi Jinping, *Guanyu shixian zhonghuaminzuweidafuxing de zhongguomeng lunshu zhaibian*, ibid, 65.

19 TZGLZ, 4:428.

20 TGOC, 2:588.

21 TZGLZ, 1:258.

22 Wang, Wang and Wang, "Xi Jinping lishisixiang shulun," 7.

"China did not keep a record of colonialism and aggression" and that China is a peace-loving nation.[23] In 2021, he declared that the Chinese always endorse peace and "there is no gene in the Chinese blood for hegemony and aggression."[24]

While rejecting the wholesale import of the Western political system in the name of its inapplicability, Xi Jinping favors the traditional notion of "Grand Unity" (*dayitong*), intending to lure support for his party-state system. He utilizes the ancient saying: "To the south of the Huai River grow orange, while to the north grow bitter orange."[25] Indeed, the same orange tree, if planted in the north of the Huai River, will not produce orange anymore. Thus, the Western political system does not fit well into China's circumstance. On the contrary, the notion of Grand Unity suits China's needs. Xi claims that Confucius brought forth this very idea which has become the dominant Chinese political value since the Qin Dynasty and the Han Dynasty.[26] In this way, as Louis Bernard Schmidt claims, Xi intends "to awaken a consciousness of the unity of the past with present."[27] At an ethnic conference held in 2019, Xi cited *The History of Han Dynasty* to support this idea of Grand Unity which guarantees peace and which ensures ethnic harmony in the PRC.[28]

In order to build a modern state worthy of respect of the Chinese people, Xi Jinping brings forth the notion of "the people-centered development philosophy" to safeguard "the fundamental interests of the overwhelming majority of the people,"[29] for which he has parroted diverse classics and historical precedents. Once he quoted a Tang Dynasty saying, that "the same water that keeps a ship afloat can also sink it."[30] Xi also uses Emperor Taizong's proclamation that "the people are what we should concern in the immense heaven and on the extensive earth."[31] He brings forward Confucian classics to warn officials to be alert to the people's interest: "Heaven sees as the people see; Heaven hears as the people hear."[32] The work of the Han Dynasty writer Wang Fu's emphasis of the people's power is also chosen as an allegory: "The big bird's flying power does not rely on a single feather and the galloping power of a horse does not come from just one hoof."[33] Here, Xi tries

[23] TZGLZ, 1:266.
[24] TZGLZ, 4:25.
[25] TGOC, 2:312.
[26] Yu, "Yong kexuejingshen yu lishi duihua," 44.
[27] Schmidt, "The utility of history." 255.
[28] TZGLZ, 3:269.
[29] TGOC, 2:235.
[30] TGOC, 2:55.
[31] TZGLZ, 4:182–184.
[32] TGOC, 2:324.
[33] TZGLZ, 3:281.

to convince Chinese officials to forge a close tie with the people and avoid being trapped in or bound by the bureaucratic shackle.

Perhaps, no other move is more explicit in using history than Xi Jinping's launching of the Belt and Road Initiative in 2013, purporting to revive the Silk Road and intending to strengthen China's tie with the countries along the ancient trading route. For doing so, the Chinese government has signed memorandums, agreements, and contracts with Asian, European, and African countries for China's investment, commercial transaction, infrastructural establishment, and so forth. Xi himself is delighted, because his hometown in Shaanxi Province was the starting point of the Silk Road, for which he romantically states that "while I stand over there reflecting upon history, it seems to me that I can hear the resonant sound of the jingling bells from the camels in the nearby mountains and that I can see the floating smoke across the desert."[34] Whenever he visits any of the countries on the Silk Road, he mentions China's historical relationship with them. When he met an Italian speaker on March 22, 2019, Xi told him that "the ancient Silk Road has long connected our two countries."[35] Naturally, it is hard to estimate the outcome of the Belt and Road Initiative, which might have wasted China's economic resource as some complain about, and which has already drawn Western criticism. Indeed, Westerners become skeptical of Xi's intention and are suspicious of his move. Ingrid d'Hooghe and Frank N. Pieke criticize it for Xi's "state-driven globalization" to "better align" it with "China's needs and interests."[36] Whatever consequences it may cause, Xi's overhaul of history for this initiative is quite apparent.

It is interesting to note that Xi Jinping has literarily and figuratively applied ancient legal approaches to promote the rule of law. According to Xi's understanding, "China first systematically compiled code of written laws" during the Zhou Dynasty and established "a fully developed set of written laws during the Han Dynasty and the Tang Dynasty." Henceforth, China's legal professionals should pay attention to the traditional legal practice and "selectively integrate these elements into our present initiatives."[37] Xi capitalizes on Lord Shang's legal ideas to warn the Chinese to abide by the law.[38] Yet, preventative measures are equally indispensable, as Xi mentions Sun Simiao, a medical doctor of the Tang Dynasty, who suggested eliminating a minor problem before it becomes a major trouble and to treat an ailment before it turns to be a serious illness.[39] Xi draws on Song Dynasty politician

[34] TZGLZ, 1:287.

[35] TZGLZ, 3:146.

[36] Pieke and Iwabuchi, *Global East Asia into the Twenty-first Century*, 294.

[37] TGOC, 2:125.

[38] TZGLZ, 4:251–252.

[39] TZGLZ, 4:293.

Wang Anshi's saying to push for the idea of "establishing good laws" for peace, order, and stability.[40]

Xi Jinping's rhetoric on official management can be spotted throughout his publications. He has set up rules, offered warnings, and admonished officials to be moral, prudent, and efficient administrators. As the number of Chinese officials is huge, the control of this gigantic bureaucracy becomes one of his major concerns. He asks officials to practice Confucian self-examination three times daily to become self-disciplined, self-controlled, and self-renovated administrators.[41] Seeing some officials' footloose behaviors, Xi employs Confucius' advice to children who must inform their parents their whereabouts in case of traveling afar. Xi warns that "some officials become unstrained like a heavenly horse flying in the sky, which sooner or later will lead them to making big mistakes."[42] He admonishes officials to obligate their duties, as if they are to take an examination (gaokao), like ancient scholars trying to succeed in the Civil Service Examination System in the national capital.[43] In case they make minor mistakes, officials should correct themselves, for which Xi refers to Tang scholar Han Yu's self-admonition that "it is not courageous for a person who knows his error but refuses to correct it."[44]

Nevertheless, Xi Jinping does not show his mercy to corrupt officials against whom he started the anti-corruption campaign soon after he became the national leader. To him, corruption poses a serious challenge to his regime as it wreaks harm upon the legitimacy of his rule. Thus, he ordered to arrest corrupt officials and meted out punishments according to the degree of violation. Here, particular attention should be paid to his adoption of ancient preventive approaches. He demands officials be cautious to prevent corruption and to avoid making even minor mistakes, for which he refers to Han Fei's allegory: "The embankment of a thousand miles can be broken by a colony of ants."[45] Xi brings forth Mencius' statement that "survival in worries and death in indulgence" to admonish officials not to lead a luxuriously debauched life. He alarms them that "our party is the largest political organization in the world. No external force can defeat us. Those who could cause our collapse must be the ones among us."[46] He draws the wisdom

40 TZGLZ, 4:299.

41 Xi Jinping, *Guanyu dangfenglianzhengjianshe he fanfubeidouzheng lunshuzhaibian* [Quotes from Xi Jinping on the clean government following the party's policies and on the struggle against corruption], Beijing: Zhongyangwenxianchubanshe, 2015, 145.

42 Ibid, 39.

43 Xi Jinping, *Xi Jinping zongshuji xilie zhongyao jianghua duben* [Important thematic quotes from General Secretary Xi Jinping], Beijing: Renminchubanshe, 2014, 158.

44 TZGLZ, 3:79.

45 Xi Jinping, *Guanyu dangfenglianzhengjianshe he fanfubeidouzheng lunshuzhaibian*, 83.

46 TZGLZ, 3:415–416.

of Tang officials, in particular their concept of "purifying officials," to ensure incorruptibility.[47] Xi avails himself of Ming Dynasty scholar Lu Kun's thoughtfulness for acquiring a mindset of fear, as he tells officials that "without a frightened heart, a corrupt official can do the worst thing."[48] Very often, Xi dispatches inspectors to provinces and hopes that they will function as an intimidating force, just like the ancient imperial commissioners (*qinchai dachen*), to forestall corruption.[49]

To reach the goal of building a modernized country, Xi Jinping underscores the importance of training talented individuals (*rencai*), who are well-educated citizens, creative scientists, dexterous technicians, erudite intellectuals, and experienced administrators. According to Xi, "it is China's long tradition to treasure talented individuals."[50] He attributes the rise of the Zhou Dynasty to King Wen whose policy of alluring talents assisted him and his descendants to build a great dynasty. Xi quotes Han Fei's statement that "prime ministers must have served as local officials and great generals must have risen from the ranks" to emphasize the importance of officials' personal experience at the grassroots level.[51] In Xi's eyes, China has lagged behind in science and technology, which started during the late Ming and early Qing era. Yet, some rulers were truly interested in science, including Emperor Kang Xi who studied science enthusiastically. The lack of talented individuals did not turn the then science into practical use, because science was but a restricted knowledge inside the imperial palace.[52] To entice talented scientists to come to China, Xi ambitiously projects to turn China into a scientific base in the world, for which he extracts a poem from *The Classic of Odes*, which advises planting a big sycamore tree in order to entice "golden phoenixes."[53]

Needless to say, Xi Jinping sees it his utmost duty to develop the Chinese economy for which he has taken measures for industry, mining, transportation, international trade, and others. Yet, he pays particular attention to food security, and views food as "the life of the people and a precious treasure of the state," which is a watchword of ancient merchant Fan Li. In this way, he elevates food security to be vital to national survival. To guarantee food production, Xi requires retaining sufficient arable land, for which he refers to Guanzi's statement about its importance.[54] Like ancient monarchs who saw the taming of the Yellow River as a responsibility, he calls on officials to learn from Great Yu, Emperor Wudi,

47 TZGLZ, 4:59.

48 TZGLZ, 4:515.

49 Xi Jinping, *Guanyu dangfeng lianzhengjianshe he fanfubai douzheng lunshuzhaibian*, 109.

50 TZGLZ, 1:127.

51 TGOC, 2:152.

52 TZGLZ, 1:124–125.

53 TZGLZ, 4:207.

54 TZGLZ, 4:383.

Emperor Kangxi, and other ancient rulers to fix China's "mother river."[55] Although the Chinese economy has thrived in recent decades, Xi advises the Chinese to be frugal, for which he brings up the Tang Dynasty writer Li Shangyin's poem: "Success comes from frugality and failure results from extravagance."[56] Purporting to maintain sustainable growth for his country, he spearheads a drive for environmental protection for which he enumerates the warnings of Confucius, Xunzi, and Lu Buwei who insinuated retaining natural resources rather than exhausting the existing reserves, as Confucius himself "fished with a line but not with a net."[57]

The rapid growth of the Chinese economy has caused a myriad of issues and one of them is economic disparity as some linger in poverty. The reasons for this unfortunate situation are multiple. Whatever the factors might be, poverty itself is an urgent issue to handle, because it may trigger social instability. Xi Jinping calls attention to Lu Buwei's statement: "To govern the country, the priority is to realize equality with which the stability will follow."[58] In particular, Xi focuses on those severely impoverished areas. He uses Sunzi's advice of "strength is weakened once divided" to caution the serious consequence of poverty.[59] In Xi's view, his anti-poverty campaign is to allow all citizens "to share the fruits of reform and development" and to realize "social equality and justice."[60] On many occasions, he has told the ethnic minorities that not a single ethnic group will be left out from China's prosperity. It is hard to assess the long-term effectiveness of his anti-poverty campaign, although he declares victory against it and often speaks proudly of it.

It is worth noting that Xi Jinping demands that the Chinese identify themselves with Chinese culture by following the traditional values. As China is increasingly becoming an aged society, he resorts to the Confucian classics to underline that "filial piety is the root of morality" to coach the Chinese to be dutiful to their old parents and aged grandparents.[61] Xi quotes the Han Dynasty thinker Xun Yue's saying, "family is essential under Heaven," to foster a harmonious family tie.[62] The other way around, the parents should follow ancient models to educate their children well, such as Mencius' widowed mother who relocated her home three times, purporting to find the best residence for her son's education. Xi selects Yue Fei's mother's teaching to her son to press Chinese parents to offer patriotic education

[55] TZGLZ, 3:328.

[56] Xi Jinping, *Guanyu dangfenglianzhengjianshe he fanfubaidouzheng lunshuzhaibian*, 70.

[57] TGOC, 2:230.

[58] TGOC, 2:220.

[59] TGOC, 2:93.

[60] TGOC, 2:220.

[61] TZGLZ, 3:307.

[62] TGOC, 2:382.

at home.[63] Xi quotes *The Analects* to highlight the value of rituals, etiquettes, and ceremonies, which should be the occasions of indoctrinating the people to be polite, nurturing their sense of belonging, and enhancing their patriotic awareness.[64]

The Lessons from Modern History

The ancient civilization bequeaths Xi Jinping with national pride with which he tries to foster patriotism, brings forth a lofty target of national resurgence, and utilizes the millennium-old wisdom for problem-solving. Yet, the ancient glory came to an end in 1840, according to Xi, because the imperialist powers started to invade China, cede Chinese territories, and impose unbearable demands upon the Chinese people. For about a century between 1840 and 1949, China bled profusely and became "the sick man of East Asia." Thus, the feeling of national pride is replaced by frustration, antipathy, and fury. Ever since 1840, the Chinese have suffered from a trauma syndrome, developed an inferiority complex, and espoused a passion for national salvation. Xi's publications are full of those sensitive touches concerning the modern era, which pose a striking contrast to his gratified view of ancient history. Nevertheless, he does not fall into a persistent, pessimistic, and passive depression; rather, he utilizes modern history as "a nationalistic legitimizer," as Frank Stricker elaborates.[65] Modern history, though not that glorious, becomes a tool to Xi to foster Chinese nationalism.

In fact, Xi Jinping never eludes an outward expression of China's sufferings in the hands of the imperialist powers. Time again, he implores the Chinese to remember what had happened after the Opium War. As soon as he comes to power, he states that "ever since the beginning of the modern era, our nation was inflicted upon with sufferings and the Chinese nation truly encountered the most dangerous moment."[66] The imperialist powers forced China to pay reparations, give up land, and surrender national interests, all of which collectively turn to be "the hundred-year humiliation" (*bainian chiru*). Xi laments over this shameful century, as he states: "After the Opium War (1840–1842), China's self-sufficient economy began to disintegrate, and the country failed to seize the opportunity of the Industrial Revolution ... China was as a whole an impoverished, backward, and war-torn

[63] TGOC, 2:384.

[64] Xi Jinping, *Guanyu quanmianshenhua gaige lunshuzhaibian* [Quotes from Xi Jinping on the Overall Deepening Reforms], Beijing: Zhongyangwenxianchubanshe, 2014, 89.

[65] Stricker, "Why History? Thinking about the uses of the past," 300.

[66] TZGLZ, 1:3.

country, falling way behind. This remained the situation for more than 100 years."[67] Henceforth, he plays the victim card, not fabricating or exaggerating what occurred but utilizing modern history to inflame nationalism in order to motivate the people to transform China into a powerful country. Only in that way can China avoid a similar repetition of what took place after the Opium War.

One of the most serious lessons Xi Jinping has learned, by using his own words, from modern history is: "Lagging behind will bring us defeats, but development will enable us to reach the goal of self-strengthening."[68] In order to reach the goal of modernization, the Chinese must develop a thriving economy, train a strong army, advance in science and technology, and retain sustainable growth. Thus, the rationale for being a strong country is a survival strategy, a way of avoiding feebleness, and an approach of fending off potential invasions. Modern history is to enhance nationalistic awareness, encourage the hardworking spirit, and avert possible humiliation. In particular, China's military modernization is an overriding urgency, as Xi reasons that "once military backwardness occurs, its impact is fatal to national security. I often read historical materials concerning modern Chinese history. I feel bitterly heartbroken, whenever I see the miserable scenes in which China lagged behind and was beaten time again."[69]

To Xi Jinping's delight, patriotic individuals during the century of humiliation fought bravely for national revival. National salvation was their faith and national resurgence their ideal.[70] Xi selects examples to promote his goal of national resurgence. In particular, he chooses Sun Yat-sen as an extraordinary individual. He praises Sun as the first man to propose the notion of "Chinese revival," for which Sun adopted a state-building strategy which was the first blueprint for China's modernization.[71] Xi hails Sun as a great patriot while complimenting Sun's statement that "the most important duty for the Chinese to know is how to love their country."[72] What Xi wants to do here is to foster Chinese nationalism; at the same time, though, he perhaps intends to hit two birds with one stone. By praising Sun Yat-sen, Xi could establish a tie with Taiwanese politicians who still respect Sun as the Father of the Nation.

Xi Jinping always expresses his gratitude to those foreigners who supported China. While the Chinese agonized over the imperialist invasions, peace-loving individuals from all over the world came to China's aid. When the Chinese

[67] TGOC, 2:269.

[68] TZGLZ, 1:36.

[69] Xi Jinping, *Guanyu quanmianshenhua gaige lunshuzhaibian*, 118.

[70] Xi Jinping, *Guanyu shixian zhonghuaminzuweidafuxing de zhongguomeng lunshu zhaibian*, 33.

[71] TZGLZ, 4:163.

[72] LZGGCDLS, 243–244.

celebrated the victory over the fascist regimes on September 3, 2020, Xi enumerated famous foreigners who came to China during World War Two (WWII), including the Flying Tigers led by Claire Lee Chennault who commanded American pilots to assist China's war against Japan.[73] Xi portrays China's resistance to Japan as a just war for national liberation, for which foreign friends contributed to it, including Norman Bethune from Canada, Dwarkanath Kotnis from India, and many others.[74] By acknowledging their sacrifice to China's national liberation, Xi expects to improve China's relationship with their home countries. Whenever Xi visits those countries, he would mention those individuals as shared heroes. For example, when he is in Moscow, Xi voices his thanks to Soviet pilots who fought against the Japanese invasion in the 1930s, while many of them sacrificed their lives in China.[75]

In the century of foreign invasions, the Chinese people had suffered while the invaders wreaked havoc upon lives and property. Unfortunately, it was the Chinese who paid reparations. After WWII, however, the Chinese did not seek reparation, although they were left with horrendous damage by the Japanese army. Sadly enough, the right-wing politicians in Japan in the recent decades have denied Japan's wartime crimes and even further glorified Japan's war, which infuriates the Chinese and other Asians. Encountering this new phenomenon, Xi Jinping condemns the Japanese invaders, as he sternly affirms that "Japanese militarists' inhumanly aggressive actions, outrageously murderous crimes, beastly plunders, and ruinous destructions had brought horrific calamities to the Chinese and other Asian peoples."[76] According to Xi, thirty-five million Chinese died at the hands of the Japanese troops during WWII.[77] Henceforth, the Japanese invasion in the 1930s and 1940s was "the darkest page of Chinese history."[78] When Xi met the former Japanese prime minister, Sinzo Abe, at an international conference in Indonesia on April 22, 2015, Xi warned that "the historical issue" is so grave that the Japanese government must face it squarely and should send out "positive messages" about it.[79]

Nevertheless, the Chinese would not seek retaliation; instead, as Xi Jinping announced, China will follow the path of a peaceful rise to achieve a win-win situation with all nations. Because China had suffered in the modern era, China will not become an aggressor to invade other countries, for which Xi assures the international community of China's nonbelligerent intent. Xi quotes Sun Yat-sen's advice of following the global trend and Xi himself identifies peace as a necessity

[73] LZGGCDLS, 278–279.

[74] LZGGCDLS, 279.

[75] TZGLZ, 1:277.

[76] LZGGCDLS, 280.

[77] TZGLZ, 1:267.

[78] LZGGCDLS, 275.

[79] Wang, Wang and Wang, "Xi Jinping lishisixiang shulun," 2.

for today's world. Xi continues: "history tells us that a country that wants to thrive must follow the peaceful global trend. Otherwise, it will be abandoned by history."[80] Xi uses the writer Cao Yu's maxim of relying on reason rather than force to showcase China's desire to stick to a peaceful rise and China's determination to reject hegemony, overbearing, and bullying.[81]

However, China will not isolate itself from the international community and will continue to learn from others, although the Chinese will not wholly transplant the Western political system into their country. In particular, Xi Jinping repudiates the idea of wholesale implementation of Western democracy. He draws a conclusion from modern history that "a simple copy of various models of the Western political system could not enable the Chinese nation to accomplish their goals of national salvation, political stability, and social security."[82] Xi takes what happened after the fall of the Qing Dynasty as a historical lesson, as he states: "China had experimented with constitutional monarchy, imperial restoration, parliamentary politics, multi-partisan arrangement, presidential system, and others. All diverse political forces came unto the historical stage but none of them had successfully offered 'a correct answer' to the question of national salvation."[83] He argues that all those previous endeavors prove that the Western political system does not fit well into China's national circumstance. Therefore, according to Xi, the only path for China to take is socialism with Chinese characteristics, which will enable China to enjoy national resurgence.

Quite often, Xi Jinping exploits historical events to enhance patriotic awareness, boost nationalistic sentiment, and sway public opinion. On the 100th anniversary of the May Fourth Movement in 2019, Xi delivered a long speech in which he praised it as a patriotic movement for saving the country out of a national crisis, defending China's national dignity from an international emergency, and uniting the people to challenge the imperialist powers at a critical moment. He hails Chinese patriotism as "a powerful spiritual and motivating force" with which the Chinese are able to change their country, transform their nation, and modernize their state. Because most of the participants of the May Fourth Movement were young people, Xi extols the youth as a reliable force for national resurgence. He calls on the Chinese to take care of the youth, assist their careers, and guide them to be talented citizens.[84]

Perhaps, no other historical leftover problem is more taxing than the Taiwan issue, which was caused by foreign invasion, Japan's colonization, and the Chinese

[80] TZGLZ, 1:267.

[81] TZGLZ, 4:423.

[82] Wang, Wang and Wang, "Xi Jinping lishisixiang shulun," 6.

[83] LZGGCDLS, 92.

[84] ZGGCDLS, 240.

Civil War, according to Xi Jinping's narrative. When Xi met the Nationalist leader Ma Ying-jeou in Singapore in 2015, he stated that the Japanese colonization of Taiwan has thrown "the whole nation into anguish."[85] He told Lien Chan, another Nationalist leader, that "history has left a trauma to our Taiwanese compatriots, but it is also a pain for all Chinese as we all feel it constantly."[86] Yet, Xi emphasizes that the sovereignty of Taiwan was fully restored after the island was handed back to China in 1945, which ended "half a century of humiliation" in the history of Taiwan.[87] More importantly, the Chinese across the Taiwan Straits belong to the same nation and share a blood bond.[88] Henceforth, Mainland China and Taiwan are of "one family."[89] Xi pays tributes to Sun Yat-sen's statement that "unification enables all Chinese to enjoy happiness but division will make all suffer" to underscore the Chinese pursuit of national unification.[90] Xi won't tolerate the move towards the independence of Taiwan, even if he promises that "the Chinese will not fight against the Chinese."[91]

In a similar vein, Xi Jinping interprets the history of Hong Kong and Macao from the nationalistic perspective. When he visited Hong Kong on July 1, 2017 to celebrate the 20th anniversary of its handover to China, Xi declared that the Chinese nation was bogged down in agony as modern history reveals national weakness, humiliations, and sufferings. It was during this historical period that Hong Kong was ceded by Britain as a colony.[92] Xi divides the history of Hong Kong into several distinctive periods and deliberately draws Hong Kong into the Chinese orbit. Before 1949, Hong Kong grieved under Britain's colonial rule. Yet, the three decades between 1949 and 1978 witnessed the shared fate between Mainland Chinese and Hong Kongers. After 1978, Hong Kongers actively participated in and contributed to the motherland's economic growth. As for Macao, Xi is glad to see it "as a historical city where Chinese and Western cultures meet" and he himself appreciates Macao's "unique charm that belongs to a culture typical of South China yet with a distinctive European touch."[93] Though he promises to continue to carry on the One Country Two System Policy in both Hong Kong and Macao, the recent demonstrations in Hong Kong have posed a serious issue for him to handle.

85 TGOC, 2:469.

86 TZGLZ, 1:237.

87 TGOC, 2:469.

88 Xi Jinping, *Guanyu shixian zhonghuaminzuweidafuxing de zhongguomeng lunshu zhaibian*, 57.

89 TZGLZ, 1:232.

90 TZGLZ, 4:402.

91 TZGLZ. 3:343.

92 Chang, "Xi Jinping zongshuji lun gang'ao lishi jiqi zhongyaoyiyi," 2.

93 TGOC, 2:460.

Although the Korean War occurred just beyond the timeline of the modern era, it is a significant event to Xi Jinping's historical interpretation. To be straightforward, it is the Korean War that ended the century of China's national humiliation. To commemorate the 70th anniversary of the Chinese entrance into this war on October 23, 2020, Xi delivered a long speech in which he praised Chinese soldiers for their heroism, patriotism, and lofty spirit. Their bravery, sacrifice, and triumph enabled China to "stand firmly." More importantly, "the Chinese people through this war completely swept away the humiliation of the past hundred years during which China was trampled upon and the Chinese people had to live at others' mercy." The Korean War was vital to Chinese history, as Xi argues that it is this war that serves as the finale of China's struggle for being an independent nation. China thus has "removed its cap as 'the sick man of East Asia,' for which the Chinese people could truly hold their heads high."[94]

Xi Jinping's publications reveal that he has quoted from ancient classics numerous times. In a striking comparison, his citations of modern instances are not a match. Nevertheless, he has started to use more aphorisms from the modern era. For the purpose of training talented citizens, Xi selects Wei Yuan's advice: "producing talents will be followed by more talents; yet, neglecting talents will lead to a shortage of talents."[95] Xi picks up Tan Sitong's idea that "Heaven regards new as a normal phenomenon and the people respect new as the rebirth of life" to promote renovation, reform, and request for national prosperity.[96] In late 2021, at an anti-poverty conference, Xi highlighted Sun Yat-sen's ideal society in which "all people lead a happy life and not a single man will be deprived of his necessity," purporting to deliver his own message for poverty alleviation.[97] When he meets faculty and students of Beijing Normal University, Xi values Lu Xun's allegory that "a genius comes out of diligence" to exhort Chinese intellectuals to labor for academic accomplishments, work for Chinese economic growth, and strive for national resurgence.[98] To celebrate the 40th anniversary of Chinese reform in 2018, Xi cited Lu Xun's famous axiom that "the road is a path paved out of the wilderness" to appeal the Chinese to march on the road of socialism with Chinese characteristics.[99]

[94] ZGGCDLS, 295.

[95] TZGLZ, 3:206.

[96] TZGLZ, 4:48.

[97] TZGLZ, 4:140.

[98] TZGLZ, 1:172.

[99] ZGGCDLS, 228.

Seeking Confidence in CCP History

Although CCP history overlaps modern history for nearly three decades, it is treated as a separate resource by Xi Jinping to legitimize the rule of the party, enhance the people's confidence in the socialist path, and assure the Chinese people that the CCP has labored continuously, persistently, and wholeheartedly for the nation. In the century since its founding in 1921, the CCP has made sacrifices to the people, according to Xi. Thus, monuments are erected, museums established, books published, and places designated for tourism. Exemplary communists are selected to parade their heroic deeds, inspire the people to emulate them, and motivate the Chinese to inherit "the red gene."[100] Xi vividly regards CCP history as "the best nutrient," which means that it functions like protein, vitamins, minerals, carbohydrates, fat, and water. Thus, CCP history assists the normal function of the Chinese nation, provides "positive energy" (*zhengnengliang*) to the people, and directs the Chinese to the right path. It also boosts the immune system, prevents deviation, and maintains strength.[101] Henceforth, Xi demands that the whole nation regard CCP history as a compulsory course to take seriously and to pass successfully.[102]

Pointing at the year 1921 when the CCP was founded, Xi Jinping reminds the Chinese communists of this date and requests that they remember the CCP's original intent, sacred calling, and divine mission. According to him, Beijing University was the first place for the Chinese to study communism, which served as a midwife for the birth of the party.[103] The early communists established the CCP for just one purpose which was national salvation, for which Xi advises the Chinese communists: "Never forget the original intent and stick firmly to the mission." According to Xi, Shanghai was the birthplace of the party.[104] In 2017, Xi brought with him Politburo members to visit the historical building in Shanghai where the First CCP National Congress was convened and to tour the Red Boat in Jiaxing, Zhejiang Province where the last day of the congress was held.[105] He labels those two places as "the spiritual homes" of the communists and admonishes them to reflect over history, enhance their sense of responsibility, and boost their confidence in the party's mission.[106]

Purporting to perpetuate the legacy of CCP history, Xi also considers 1949 as another milestone as the Chinese communists defeated Chiang Kai-shek, won the Chinese Revolution, and established a national regime in that year. At the 70th

100 ZGGCDLS, 107.
101 ZGGCDLS, 24.
102 Xi Jinping, *Xi Jinping zongshuji xilie zhongyao jianghua duben*, 179.
103 ZGGCDLS, 10.
104 ZGGCDLS, 159.
105 Yan, "Buwang hongchuan chuxin, laoji lishi shiming," 5.
106 ZGGCDLS, 184.

anniversary to commemorate the establishment of the PRC, Xi remarked that 1949 completely changed the previously miserable national situation. From then on, the Chinese people have embarked on a national revival.[107] On one occasion, Xi spoke of two miracles after 1949: the rapid economic growth and the long-term social stability.[108] On another occasion, he uncovers three miracles of CCP history: the party led a victorious revolution, established a new political system, and conducted a successful economic reform.[109] Xi is so passionate about 1921 and 1949 that he uses the two dates to yardstick his lofty "Two Centennials" to turn China into a moderately prosperous country in 2021 and to make China a middlingly developed nation by 2049.[110]

A serious lesson Xi Jinping learns from CCP history is his party's long tradition of controlling the army. In other words, the military belongs to the party. Xi is familiar with Mao Zedong's adage that political power comes out of the gun barrel, with which Xi emphasizes the CCP commandership over China's military forces. At the 90th anniversary of the Nanchang Uprising of 1927 which marks the birth of the communist army, Xi remarks that the uprising is "an epochal event" because "the people's army" ever since has begot the strong leadership of the party.[111] On October 31, 2014 when Xi visited Fujian to commemorate the Gutian Conference of 1929, he spoke highly of it, because this conference brought forth the CCP principle that the party must lay a firm control over the army.[112] Henceforth, Xi makes it clear that it is a long convention for the Chinese soldiers to be loyal to the party, defend the party, and fight for the party.

Xi Jinping wastes no time in giving prominence to special historical events to accentuate the hardship the communists have endured, draw attention to the path the party takes, and encourage the people to follow his leadership. The Long March is one such example. When he spoke to commemorate the 80th anniversary of the Long March in 2016, he praised the Red Army for its heroism, extoled the Long March as an epochal expedition, and lionized it as a remarkable accomplishment for strategic relocation, which helped preserve the communist forces and allowed the communists to start anew. He always reminds the Chinese that China is now on a new Long March for national resurgence and the people should emulate the Red Army to overcome potential difficulties and retain their confidence in the party.[113] In May 2019, Xi went to Yudu in Jiangxi Province to visit the starting point of the Long March where he remarked that "we should always remember the origin of

[107] ZGGCDLS, 268.
[108] TZGLZ, 3:105.
[109] ZGGCDLS, 15.
[110] TZGLZ, 1:100.
[111] ZGGCDLS, 169.
[112] ZGGCDLS, 96.
[113] LZGGCDLS, 149, 157.

the red regime, keep in mind the way how New China was established, never forget history, and not ever neglect our original intent."[114]

Drawing on the revolutionary stories, Xi Jinping intends to prove the close tie between the CCP and the Chinese people, purporting to woo their support to his blueprint of state-building. On several occasions, he narrates a story about three female communist soldiers during the Long March on which they stayed at the home of Xu Jiexiu. Upon departure, the three female soldiers cut their quilt, which was the only possession they had, into two halves, and gave half to Xu's family. By recounting this story a number of times, Xi reiterates that the CCP would like to give to the people whatever it has and would always put the people's interests first.[115] Xi dedicates the victory of the Chinese Revolution to the support of the Chinese people. During his visit to Anhui Province in August 2020, he remarked that the Huaihai Campaign in late 1948 and early 1949 in Central China was a decisive military battle for the communists to win the Civil War. Yet, "the victory of the Huaihai Campaign was achieved through the support of the people who had pushed the small carts to offer assistance." Thus, the CCP should never forget the people to whom all communists should always serve as dedicated servants.[116]

On a number of occasions, Xi Jinping expresses his gratitude to the Chinese people for their contributions to the victory of the Chinese Revolution, with whom he expects to strengthen the existing tie. During his visit to Henan Province in late 2019, he spoke highly of the people's sacrifice to the CCP. He is proud of the O-Yu-Wan Base for producing more than 340 generals. In particular, he labels Xinxian County in Henan Province as "a cradle of generals" and Zhugou "the Little Yan'an." He does not forget the people in the O-Yu-Wan Base who sacrificed two hundred thousand lives to the Chinese Revolution. In Xinxian County alone, half of its population died for it. Xi comments that "Henan is the place of heroes, while the revolutionary martyrs Yang Jingyu, Peng Xuefeng, and Ji Hongchang all came from Henan."[117] He advises the communists that "we should not forget the diggers of the well from which we are drinking water. We should not forget those revolutionary martyrs and the people of those 'Old Areas' (*laoqu*)" which refer to the communist bases during the revolutionary years.[118]

In order to learn more about CCP history, inherit "the red gene," and carry on the revolutionary cause, Xi Jinping encourages the Chinese to visit the CCP-related historical sites. Through personal visits, as he argues, one can experience history,

114 LZGGCDLS, 12.

115 LZGGCDLS, 151.

116 LZGGCDLS, 13.

117 LZGGCDLS, 262.

118 LZGGCDLS, 47.

understand the difficulties the party went through, and support the party's rule. He declares that he visited diverse places inside China more than seventy times between 2012 and 2022. Each time, he examines revolutionary relics, spends time at museums, and tours historical sites on which he restudies CCP history, reflects on the party's past, and receives rebaptism. He recommends that the Chinese should visit those places to acquire "historical confidence" in the socialist cause.[119] During his visit to Xiangshan in Beijing's suburb, he himself rediscovered historical confidence, as Xiangshan served as the CCP headquarters for half a year in early 1949 during which the CCP successfully accomplished its strategic transition from rural revolution to urban management.[120]

During the pandemic when the world suffered from excruciating pain, Xi Jinping in 2021 called on the Chinese to study CCP history, purporting to strengthen faith (*xinyang*), enhance belief (*xinnian*), and boost confidence (*xinxin*).[121] According to Xi, the resolute and unchanged trust in the communist leadership should be seen as "the Learning of Heart" (*xinxue*) with which the communist martyrs had intrepidly sacrificed their lives.[122] Xi reminds the Chinese to stick to the correct direction under the CCP guidance.[123] His lofty call for firm faith in the socialist cause can be viewed as a type of religious fervor. Yet, a close examination shows that Xi is to demand the Chinese follow his rule, obey his policies, and materialize his plans. He entreats the communists to review the oath they pledged when they joined the party, reread the party program, and self-examine themselves frequently.[124] The "faith" here is more about strict disciplines which can be retrieved again from CCP history.

From CCP history, Xi Jinping often selects communist heroes for the Chinese people to imitate. Those heroes have become nationally recognized icons with whom the people should identify themselves. Xi labels legendary places with a magnificent title of "spirit" (*jingshen*), narrates heroes' feats there, and inspires the people to emulate "the Jinggangshan Spirit," "the Yan'an Spirit," "the Yimeng Spirit," and "the Daqing Spirit." Individual heroes are selected as well, such as "the Lei Feng Spirit," "the Wang Jie Spirit," and "the Iron-man Spirit."[125] The common feature of those communist heroes, whether groups or individuals, is that they pledged their allegiance to the party, devoted themselves to the party, and even sacrificed themselves to the party. When Xi visited Lankao County in Henan Province in 2014, he emotionally recalled his own familiarity with Jiao Yulu's story when he

119 TZGLZ, 4:62.

120 ZGGCDLS, 259.

121 TZGLZ, 501.

122 TZGLZ, 4:504.

123 TZGLZ, 3:89.

124 ZGGCDLS, 272.

125 LZGGCDLS, 35–36.

was young. Xi still remembers that he cried over Jiao's heroism during his middle school years and affirms that he respects Jiao as his own model.[126] To support his call for self-reliance, Xi selects Gong Quanzhen as an exemplary, because Gong accompanied her husband, a Red Army general, to live in his home village during the difficult years while she contributed to rural education as a teacher.[127] To encourage the Chinese to be pioneers for their new jobs assigned by the party, Xi highlights the career of Xiao Jinguang, who was a Red Army man, but later became the commander-in-chief of the Chinese navy.[128]

One of the serious lessons Xi Jinping draws from CCP history is that the party cannot thrive without the young people. As Xi elaborates, the party's achievement is the crystallization of the young people's "enthusiasm and dedication."[129] For national resurgence, as Xi confidently states, the youth are the vanguards.[130] Henceforth, Chinese communists must pay attention to the youth, assist them, listen to their concerns, befriend them, guide them to the socialist cause, absorb them into the noble undertaking, and recruit them as CCP members. Xi cites Li Dazhao's article on the youth to stress the importance of the young people who are destined to be the successors of the great enterprise of national resurgence.[131]

As for CCP history, two gigantic figures cannot be avoided: one is Mao Zedong who co-founded the CCP, established the PRC, and ruled over the country for nearly three decades; and another is Deng Xiaoping who was a veteran revolutionary, served as the paramount leader after Mao, and implemented his reforms soon after Mao's death. To commemorate Mao's 120th birthday in late 2013, Xi Jinping praised Mao as a great leader who contributed to China as a nation and the CCP as a political organization. According to Xi, Mao creatively worked out practical solutions to solve a number of tough issues for the Chinese Revolution. Yet, as Xi comments, Mao committed "serious mistakes" during his last years.[132] As for Deng Xiaoping, Xi's assessment is positive, because Deng was the major leader of the party, initiated the economic reform, and contributed to China's recent prosperity. Thus, Deng "not only changed the historical fate of the Chinese people, but he also transformed the historical progress of the world."[133] By endorsing Mao and Deng, Xi aims at using their fame to legitimize his status as a rightful successor of the socialist cause, a lawful leader of the party, and a justifiable head of state.

126 LZGGCDLS, 29.
127 LZGGCDLS, 28.
128 TZGLZ, 4:517.
129 ZGGCDLS, 137.
130 ZGGCDLS, 242.
131 ZGGCDLS, 137.
132 ZGGCDLS, 56.
133 ZGGCDLS, 78.

Seldom does Xi Jinping publicly eulogize his father, Xi Zhongxun (1913–2002), who played a role in establishing the Northwest Base to welcome the Long Marchers including Mao Zedong in the mid-1930s. During the Deng Xiaoping era, Xi Zhongxun was a high-ranking leader. The scanty mention demonstrates Xi Jinping's purposeful restraint to avoid an impression that the CCP has established a family rule, avoid being viewed as an inheritor of his father, and validate his own accomplishment via his own ability. Occasionally, he mentions his father. Once during his visit to Gansu Province, he put his father's name after Liu Zhidan and Xie Zichang in referring to the building of the Northwest Base.[134] In 2021, when he brought up his father's name, he revealed his father's altruism, emphasized his father's honesty, and underlined his father's loyalty to the party. According to Xi Jinping, his father, who was a local leader of the communist base in North Shaanxi in 1943, tried to protect the alleged victims during an aggrandized purge, fight against forced confession, and correct the leftists' wrongdoings. In his eyes, his father was faithful to the party, speaking the truth, risking his life to protect others, and safeguarding the local communist organization.[135]

Conclusion

William H. McNeil once remarked that "history knowledge," for many, is to construct "collective memory," share ideas, and reorganize "human groups."[136] Indeed, Xi Jinping's dexterous utilization of history has created a special version of collective memory, alerted the Chinese to remember their glorious civilization, draw grim lessons from modern history, carry on the great enterprise out of CCP history, and unite the Chinese people to share a common fate. Being grounded in brilliant civilization, as Xi elaborates, Chinese history has progressed in a linear approach but was unfortunately paused by the Opium War which started the modern era during which the Chinese people grieved over the sorrow at the hands of the imperialist powers. Although the hundred-year humiliation inflicted on China an eternal trauma, China has stood up and quickly become a developing country. Now, China is marching towards the lofty target of modernization, as Xi confidently expounds. The cumulative result of Chinese history, ushers the country into "the New Era" logically, naturally, and inevitably, while the Chinese people are "standing at a new starting point in history."[137] By utilizing the past, Xi parades his

[134] ZGGCDLS, 256.

[135] TZGLZ, 4:509.

[136] Gagnon (ed.), *Historical Literacy*, 103-06.

[137] TGOC, 2:105.

intention of building a modernized country by blazing a new trail, emboldening the people to overcome potential difficulties, and ultimately restoring the ancient glory. All in all, Xi's China is the corollary of the long Chinese civilization.

Xi Jinping is not a professional historian; on the contrary, he is an adroit politician. Yet, he knows the importance of history to politics. From the historical kaleidoscope, he draws lessons, absorbs nutrients, shares bygone insights, and admonishes the people to learn more. In a particular sense, history becomes essential to politics, and politics is inseparable from history. Henceforth, he holds constant dialogue with the past and uses history for his political moves. A close examination demonstrates that he utilizes ancient history to boost cultural confidence, employs modern history to arouse nationalistic fervor, and resorts to CCP history to bring forth confidence in the existing political system. History is so vital to China that Xi mentions Gong Zizhen's statement recurrently: "To destroy a country, the first thing to do is to eradicate its history."[138] In other words, the people must study national history, find roots in it, avoid cultural amnesia, and vouchsafe assurance in Xi's leadership during the New Era.

Without a doubt, we are living in a future-oriented society and relying increasingly on new scientific inventions to sustain our daily life; however, the past still lingers with us. Differing from Westerners who tend to be forward-looking, the Chinese people are truly passionate over their past. Sometimes, this backward-looking mentality makes the boundary between history and reality permeable, transferrable, and interchangeable, which inevitably assists the ruler to utilize history. Nevertheless, it is hard to assess the effectiveness of Xi Jinping's utilization of it, although the Chinese media is full of praise. The only criticism can be found in the media of overseas Chinese dissidents. Li Yuanhua, a former professor at Beijing's Capital Normal University, argues that Xi's use of history demonstrates that he lacks self-confidence and that his power remains unstable. According to Li, Xi's utilization of history is to inject "a shot in the arm" as a cardiac booster.[139] Lai Jianping told *Sound of Hope* on December 27, 2023 that Xi's high-profile celebration of Mao Zedong's 130th birthday one day before is to "maintain the rule of the CCP." In Lai's eyes, Mao was but "a devil."[140] This kind of voice cannot be heard in China at this moment, but such a tone may be louder in the future, which could mean that it might be a pitfall for Xi to continue to use history as a political tool.

In any case, Xi Jinping's use of the past exhibits the power of history, which at the same time raises a serious question regarding the proportion of the communist ingredient in his political thought. Indeed, a reader can easily find that Xi uses

[138] Xi Jinping, *Xi Jinping zongshuji xilie zhongyao jianghua duben*, 19.

[139] Ning and Luo Ya, "Zhonggong de 'lishizixin' xinmo."

[140] Wang Xiao, "Mao Zedong 130 zhounianmindan Xi Jinping jianghua shiweixian xinhao."

more Chinese history than he does the communist doctrine. The innermost core to his thought tends to be the traditional element, although communist ingredients are present. Xi's publications reveal that he has persistently utilized history.[141] As he always links the present with the past, addresses issues through the lens of historical precedents, and retrieves solutions from the bygone history, one may argue that his move seems to validate Samuel P. Huntington's hypothesis that nations would return to their original civilizations for which "the clash of civilizations" would be inevitable.[142] Whether China is returning to its traditional civilization is open to debate. What Xi has done with history clearly displays the profound naturalization, deep indigenization, and gigantic homegrown process of Chinese style communism, which is termed the third Sinification of Marxism, after Mao Zedong's modification of the communist revolutionary approach from city to countryside, and Deng Xiaoping's implementation of the market economy instead of sticking to a planned economy.[143] Xi's way, which differs from the previous two, is to reach the goal of national resurgence by resorting to traditional values, utilizing long-gone precedents, and applying the deep-seated wisdom to solve the new problem.

Dr. **Patrick Fuliang Shan** is a professor at Grand Valley State University where he teaches Chinese history, East Asian history, and world history. He has published several monographs including *Taming China's Wilderness: Immigration, Settlement, and the Shaping of the Heilongjiang Frontier, 1900–1931* (Ashgate, 2014) and Yuan Shikai: A Reappraisal (Vancouver: UBC Press, 2018). He has also authored many journal articles, critical essays, and others. He served as president of the Chinese Historians in the United States (2009–2011). Email: shanp@gvsu.edu.

Bibliography

Chang, Le. "Xi Jinping zongshuji lun gang'ao lishi jiqi zhongyaoyiyi" [General Secretary Xi Jinping's perspective on the history of Hong Kong and Macao and its significance]. *Shenzhenxinxizhiye-jishuxueyuanxuebao* 17, no. 4, (August 2019): 1–7.

Li, Chien-pin. "An Analysis of the US Indo-Pacific Strategy in US-China Competition." *American Journal of Chinese Studies* 30, no. 1 (April 2023): 43–59.

Gagnon, Paul (ed.). *Historical Literacy: The Case for History in American Education.* Boston: Houghton Mifflin Company, 1989.

141 For Xi Jinping's use of history during the time when he was the leader of Zhejiang Province, see Xi Jinping, *Zhijiang xinyu* [The New Remarks from Zhejiang], Hangzhou: Zhejiangrenmin, 2014.

142 Huntington, "The clash of civilizations?" 25.

143 Wu, "Xi Jinping zongshuji guanyu lishi zixin zhongyao lunshu de sanchong luoji." 24.

Huntington, Samuel P. "The Clash of Civilizations?" *Foreign Affairs* 72, no. 3 (1993): 22–49.

Jin, Meng, and Zhou Liangshu. "Xi Jinping dalishiguan dui lishiweiwuzhuyi de chuangxinxing fazhan" [Xi Jinping's grand historical perspective and its creative contribution to historical materialism]. *Lilunshiye* no. 6 (2020): 5–11.

Lu, Kuan. "Shenke linghui Xi Jinping guanyu jianding lishizixin de zhongyao lunshu" [Fully understanding Xi Jinping's important remarks on enhancing our historical self-confidence]. *Dangdewenxian* no. 2 (2022): 18–26.

Ning, Haizhong, and Luo Ya. "Zhonggong de 'lishizixin' xinmo" [The cardiac demon of the CCP's 'historical confidence']. *Dajiyuan* January 18, 2022. https://www.epochtimes.com.

Pieke, Frank N., and Koichi Iwabuchi. *Global East Asia into the Twenty-first Century*. Oakland, CA: University of California Press, 2021.

Schmidt, Louis Bernard. "The Utility of History." *Social Science* 6, no. 3 (July 1931): 255–258.

Stricker, Frank. "Why History? Thinking About the Uses of the Past." *The History Teacher* 25, no. 3 (May 1992): 293–312.

Wang, Sihuai, Wang Zongyun, and Wang Zhen. "Xi Jinping lishisixiang shulun" [An analysis of Xi Jinping's historical thought]. *Shangluoxueyuanxuebao* 34, no. 1 (February 2020): 1–10.

Wang, Xiao. "Mao Zedong 130 zhounianmindan Xi Jinping jianghua shiweixian xinhao" [Xi Jinping's speech at the 130th anniversary of Mao Zedong's birth releases a dangerous signal]. *Xiwangzhisheng* [Sound of Hope], December 27, 2023. https://www.soundofhope.org.

Wu, Xiaotao. "Xi Jinping zongshuji guanyu lishi zixin zhongyao lunshu de sanchong luoji" [The triplicity of logic concerning Xi Jinping's important discourse over historical confidence]. *Makesizhuyizhexue* no. 6 (2022): 20–26.

Xi, Jinping. *Guanyu shixian zhonghuaminzuweidafuxing de zhongguomeng lunshu zhaibian* [Quotes from Xi Jinping on realizing the Chinese Dream for the Great Rejuvenation of the Chinese Nation]. Beijing: Zhongyangwenxian, 2013.

Xi, Jinping. *Guanyu quanmianshenhua gaige lunshuzhaibian* [Quotes from Xi Jinping on the Overall Deepening of Reforms]. Beijing: Zhongyangwenxianchubanshe, 2014.

Xi, Jinping. *Xi Jinping zongshuji xilie zhongyao jianghua duben* [Important thematic quotes from General Secretary Xi Jinping]. Beijing: Renminchubanshe, 2014.

Xi, Jinping. *Zhijiang xinyu* [The New Remarks from Zhejiang]. Hangzhou: Zhejiangrenmin, 2014.

Xi, Jinping. *Tanzhiguolizheng* [The Governance of China]. Beijing: Waiwenchubanshe, Vol. 1, 2014. (This series of books is abbreviated TZGLZ).

Xi, Jinping. *Tanzhiguolizheng* [The Governance of China]. Beijing: Waiwenchubanshe, Vol. 2, 2017. (The English edition is used as shown below).

Xi, Jinping. *Tanzhiguolizheng* [The Governance of China]. Beijing: Waiwenchubanshe, Vol. 3, 2020. (https://marx.guat.edu.cn/info/1037/2236.htm – accessed on May 20, 2023)

Xi, Jinping. *Tanzhiguolizheng* [The Governance of China]. Beijing: Waiwenchubanshe, Vol. 4, 2022. http://www.sxddy.com/e/wap/show.php?classid=8&id=2493&style=0&bclassid=0&cid=8&cpage=1, accessed on May 21, 2023.

Xi, Jinping. *Guanyu dangfenglianzhengjianshe he fanfubaidouzheng lunshuzhaibian* [Quotes from Xi Jinping on the party style for clean government and the struggle against corruption]. Beijing: Zhongyangwenxian, 2015.

Xi, Jinping. *The Governance of China (II)*. Beijing: Foreign Language Press, 2017. (This book is published in English and is abbreviated as TGOC).

Xi, Jinping. *Lun Zhongguo gongchandang lishi* [On the History of the Chinese Communist Party]. Beijing: Zhongyangwenxian, 2021. (This book is abbreviated as LZGGCDLS).

Yan, Lan. "Buwang hongchuan chuxin, laoji lishi shiming" [Never forget the original intent developed at the Red Boat and stick to the historical mission]. *Zhongxuezhengzhijiaoxuecankao* no. 5 (2019): 5–9.

Yu, Huamin. "Yong kexuejingshen yu lishi duihua – Xi Jinping tongzhi guanyu lishikexue de zhongyao lunshu" [To hold dialogue with history in the spirit of science – Studying the important discourse on historical science by Comrade Xi Jinping]. *Shixuelilunyanjiu* no. 1 (2021): 43–50.

Zhou, Ting, and Shu Yibiao. "Xi Jinping guanyu lishiwenti zhongyaolunshu de lilunyiyun" [Theoretical implication of Xi Jinping's important exposition on historical issues based on the perspective of Marxist historical view]. *Zhonggongyilizhouweidangxiaoxuebao* no. 1 (2021): 21–25.

CHAPTER TWO

From "Seven Speak-Nots" to "Media Surnamed Party": Media in China from 2012 to 2022

Guolin Yi

PROVIDENCE COLLEGE

Abstract: *Between 2012 and 2022, the media ecosystem in China witnessed a trend characterized by the decline of critical journalism and the expansion of the party media, which has increasingly "taken over the microphone." Through judicial rules and mostly bureaucratic regulations, the Chinese government has tightened its control over the traditional party media, the commercial outlets, and the Internet. At times, journalists and netizens have used creative means to push the space for expression. However, they mostly cause the government to resort to more repressive means of control to "plug the loophole." Government rules and regulations have become more and more repetitive, expansive, and elaborative in restrictions. With Xi becoming the most powerful leader since Mao, the Chinese media has been used to promote his cult of personality.*

Keywords: Xi Jinping; Chinese media; Media management; Cult of personality

Between 2012 and 2022, the Chinese government used a series of measures to tighten its control of the media. The control expanded from the party media to commercialized outlets and the Internet. During these years, official rules, policies, and regulations about the media became more extensive and elaborate in its restrictions. As a result, the space of freedom for Chinese journalists to operate has shrunk dramatically. Using chronological and thematic methods, this chapter documents the development of the media ecosystem in China in the decade under Xi Jinping's rule.

Different from liberal democracies where freedom of the press has been regarded as essential to watch for government abuses, authoritarian regimes tend to view the media as tools for political control. Mao Zedong has laid the theoretical foundation for the media control in China since the establishment of the People's Republic of China (PRC) in 1949. He had drawn from the Leninist propaganda model to construct a media system that served as the "mouthpiece of the Party" and of himself personally.[1] In his talk at the Yan'an Forum on Literature and Art during the Yan'an Ratification Campaign in 1942, Mao argued that newspapers and arts are not neutral and should only "serve politics." For him, Western ideas of humanism such as individualism and dissenting views in arts and literature should be stopped because they don't serve the solidarity of the revolutionary cause. He was clear that reporting the dark side of the revolution should be forbidden.[2] As the Chinese Communist Party (CCP) equalizes itself with the government, the people, and the country, it would describe any negative reporting of the party or the government as harmful to the country and the people and thus not acceptable. A good example to show the importance of Mao's Yan'an Talk can be seen in May 2012, when 100 Chinese writers and artists participated in the hand-copying of the document to celebrate its 70th anniversary. Among them was Mo Yan, who won the Nobel Prize for Literature later that year for using "hallucinatory realism" in social criticism in his novels. When asked about the hand-copying of Mao's Yan'an Talk after winning the Nobel Prize, Mo had to say that he had no regret having been part of the celebration.[3]

Golden Age of Critical Journalism

Even though traditional media in China is controlled by the state, Chinese journalists including those who work for the state-owned media organizations, just like their Western colleagues, at one time were able to push for social progress through critical journalism. The golden age of critical journalism in China existed in the late 1990s and early 2000s. With the intensification of market reforms, the government started to allow some subsidiaries of party-owned newspapers to find ways to support themselves financially. While party newspapers are funded by the state and mainly distributed in the offices of the government and state-owned enterprises, commercialized newspapers (or "market-oriented newspapers"), even though still owned by the state, must rely on revenue from advertising and retail from newsstands. They were given more autonomy and freedom in terms of content—and they had to produce non-propaganda content in order to attract readers and advertisers. This structural change laid the foundation for the emergence of better-quality journalism in China as journalists and editors become more professionalized and sought to distinguish their work, for commercial reasons as much as idealistic ones.[4]

[1] Bandurski and Kecheng, "The Rise and Fall of *Southern Weekly*"; Introduction to Guan Jun, *Silencing Chinese Media.*" xi.

[2] Mao Zedong, "Talk at the Yan'an Forum."

[3] Hu Tao, "Mo Yan"

[4] Bandurski and Fang, "The Rise and Fall of Southern Weekly" xi–xii.

In this context, many news outlets began to run less propagandistic stories and more about social problems and official corruption, which led to the flourishing of investigative reporting. Even at the state level, Chinese Central Television (CCTV), China's main national television network, had a program Focus Report (*jiaodian fangtan*) that ran expose stories. It became so popular that during a visit to the station in 1998, Premier Zhu Rongji, a tough reformer known for his unpretentious style, broke his own taboo and decided to write a few words praising it as a tool of *yulun jiandu* or media supervision. Many ministerial officials at the time said that they had to watch the program before meeting with Zhu just in case they might be questioned by the premier about the problems exposed in the program.[5] It can be seen that the Chinese government at one time was willing to accept the media as something like a "watchdog," a role similar to that in Western democracies.

Besides the national media outlet, newspapers of the Nanfang Media Group stationed in the southern city of Guangzhou (or Canton) demonstrated how critical and investigative journalism could impact the life of the people as well as policies of the state. In 2003, *Southern Metropolis Daily* (*SMD*)'s coverage of two incidents will be remembered in the history of Chinese media. The first was the revelation of the SARS epidemic in the spring when the Chinese government was still trying to cover up the crisis. The story in *SMD* forced the government to acknowledge the seriousness of the situation and became more transparent, which helped the handling of the health emergency. The other was the coverage of the death of Sun Zhigang, a college student who was beaten to death by the police in a repatriation center in Guangzhou. The intensive coverage of Sun's death led to nation-wide discussions on the unpopular Custody & Repatriation Law, which allowed police to use "extreme" force to detain and imprison a person who cannot provide proof of a legal residence permit in China. Having involved lawyers and legal scholars who questioned the constitutionality of the law, the debates produced tremendous pressure on the government, who ultimately abolished the law.[6]

The extraordinary performance of the *SMD* in these events earned the anger of the provincial party boss Zhang Dejiang, who received his college education in North Korea. Zhang ordered the punishment of the journalists of this newspaper. Cheng Yizhong, the editor of *SMD* and two of his colleagues were charged with "leaking state secrets" and thrown in jail. Due to the protests of journalists and pressure from retired party officials, he was finally cleared of all charges and walked free five months later.[7] Chen was later named by The United Nations

5 Chu, "Rise of Fall of Investigative Reporting."

6 Pan, *Out of Mao's China*", 256–257.

7 Pan, *Out of Mao's China*, 237, 257, 267.

Educational, Scientific and Cultural Organization (UNESCO) as the laureate of the 2005 Guillermo Cano World Press Freedom Prize.[8]

Newspapers in the Nanfang media group had earned so much international approval that during his state visit to China in 2009, President Barack Obama turned down an interview request from CCTV and chose to sit with journalists from Southern Weekly (*nanfang zhoumo*), a sister newspaper of *SMD* also known for a "push-the-envelope approach to the government's ever-present censorship."[9] The impacts caused by the quality journalism of liberal newspapers, particularly those under the Nanfang Media Group, and the releasing of Cheng Yizhong, show that at one time the media in China could play an important role in promoting social justice. That was indeed the golden age of critical journalism in China.

"Seven Speak-nots"

Xi Jinping became the general secretary of the CCP in 2012, one year after the Arab Spring, when the power of the Internet in mobilizing social movements was shown. At the same time, his government faced the problem of a discontented society due to the widening income gap, rampant corruption, and high unemployment to list just a few. On one hand, Xi started a high-profiled anti-graft campaign to win public support and to purge his political enemies. During the campaign, Chinese netizens, particularly bloggers with many followers, also joined the efforts to expose the corrupted behavior of public officials. The participation of the popular force was out of the control of the CCP, who were worried about the subversive power of the Internet. On the other, the state-led anti-corruption campaign ironically paralleled its silencing and jailing of anti-corruption activists, who had demanded that high-level officials declare their assets to the public. Central officials, therefore, were demanded to "manage the campaign from the top," granting little space for bottom-up activists to take part in exercising oversight.[10]

In contrast to his predecessors as Patrick Shan discusses in Chapter One, who have referred to the media in more general terms, Xi has specifically pointed to the official, commercial and new media being unified by the objective of 'correct guidance' of public opinion. Some analysts and observers note the 'all-dimensional nature' of Xi's control over the media, encompassing all layers of the media ecosystem, from flagship party media, to commercialized outlets, to the vibrant social media space.[11]

8 Congressional Executive Committee on China, "Chinese Journalist Cheng Yizhong Awarded."

9 LaFraniere and Ansfield, "In Obama Interview, Signs of China's Heavy Hand."

10 Repnikova, *Media Politics in China*, 211

11 Ibid: 210.

In early 2013, word began to spread on the Chinese web space about a government directive called "seven speak-nots," which included seven topics that should not be discussed: "universal values, press freedom, civil society, human rights, historical mistakes of the CCP, crony capitalism, and legal independence." The core of these "Western" values is human freedom which, as the foundation of modern liberal democracies, is supposed to protect the citizens FROM the abuses of the government. Obviously, they ran contrary to the Leninist state that expects its people to follow the ruling party without raising any questions.

One of the first citizens to expose the directive to the public was Zhang Xuezhong, a law professor from East China University of Political Science and Law in Shanghai known for making bold statements advocating for press freedom and the independence of the legal system. On May 10, 2013, Zhang stated on his Sina Weibo account, the equivalent of Twitter in China, that he had received a directive from his university administrators that professors should not talk about those seven topics in class. Zhang also demanded the authorities to step up and make clarifications if it was simply a "rumor." Instead, the government chose to silence him by shutting down his Weibo account. Nevertheless, there were other professors who testified that they had received similar directives from their own universities' administrators.[12] Zhang's problem with the authorities did not end there. At the end of the year, he was fired by his university due to his open support for press freedom. Two months earlier, Xia Yeliang, a professor of economics from Beijing University who openly supported democratic values, had been fired by his university as well.[13]

Since it was the first year of Xi Jinping's office, people were still not sure whether the "seven speak-nots" reflected his idea. The directive naturally caught the attention of international media, which tried to verify its existence. On May 13 and 14, 2013, the BBC and *The New York Times* ran stories that the General Office of the CCP had issued a memo "Concerning the Situation in the Ideological Sphere." They discovered the websites of local governments that mentioned "seven major areas" with ideological problems to be addressed even though they did not provide specifics. For example, the *Times* used a website of the Commission of Urban-Rural Development of Chongqing, a municipality in southwest China, which stated "the central leadership has made a thorough analysis of and shown a staunch stance toward seven serious problems in the ideological sphere that merit attention, giving a clearer understanding of the acuteness and complexity of struggle in the ideological sphere." The BBC also pointed out the same wordings from the websites

12 Lin, "The Revelation of the Seven Speak-nots."

13 Jacobs, "Chinese Professor Who Advocated Free Speech Is Fired."

of other local governments and cited speculations that the document might be the official version of the "seven speak-nots."[14]

By summer 2013 the picture had become much clearer. On August 20, the *Times* ran an article that gave further evidence to the existence of the party memo, which was also known as Document No. 9 when it was mentioned publicly by local governments back in May. Claiming that the memo had been released by the central party office and had been verified by four sources close to senior officials, including an editor with a party newspaper, the *Times* article described the document as bearing the "unmistakable imprint of Xi Jinping."[15] Almost at the same time, *Mirror Weekly*, a news magazine in Hong Kong, claimed that it had obtained an official copy of the memo, which it claimed was issued on April 22, 2013 and had been marked with the direction that "the document has been approved by the CCP central leadership and it was to be circulated to the level of city, metropolitan and [army] division level."[16]

The revelation of Document No. 9 by the *Times* and the news magazine in Hong Kong seemed to have angered the CCP leadership. Less than a year later, on May 8, 2014, CCP's official news website announced that Gao Yu, a prominent independent journalist, had been arrested for leaking "state secrets" to foreign agencies. It alleged that Gao had obtained a classified document in June 2013, which it did not specify, and passed it to an "overseas website," which then published it in full and got reposted by many websites. In an article covering the court trial by the *Times* two years later, the court document claimed that Gao Yu had passed on the document to *Mirror Weekly*.[17]

Since Gao had been a vocal critic of the Chinese government and a Guillermo Cano prize winner, international media followed her case closely. In their coverage, both the BBC and the *New York Times* ran stories about a woman with a blurred face on CCTV who had confessed "her crimes." They pointed out that it was the third time Gao had been arrested and the second time she had been charged with "leaking state secrets." Since the announcement of her arrest happened a few weeks before the 25th anniversary of the Tiananmen movement in 1989, they viewed it as a possible official step to deter dissenting voices in the society.[18]

The ideas in "seven speak-nots" provide a clear blueprint of media policies of the new administration. They show exactly what China is lacking as a modern state, but the CCP's only concern was how to stay in power at any cost. To some

[14] "CCP Issued a Document of Ideological Control"; Buckley, "China Warns Against 'Dangerous' Western Values,"

[15] Buckley, "China's New Leadership Takes Hard Line in Secret Memo."

[16] ChinaAid, "Gao Yu Leaking State Secrets—Document No. 9."

[17] Lina and Chang, "Gao Yu Arrested by Beijing Police"; Buckley, "Journalist Gao Yu who had been Charged."

[18] Buckley, "Dissident Journalist Held Ahead of Tiananmen Anniversary"; "China journalist Gao Yu Detained in Tiananmen Lead-up."

extent, it also became a foundation for Xi Jinping's policy of ideological work. Even though an article in *Qiushi*, the CCP's ideological magazine, disclaimed the "seven speak-nots" in early 2014,[19] the firing of college professors for speaking out and the jailing of journalists in the early years of Xi's office shed light on how far the new administration was willing to go to deal with ideological challenges.

When China passed the National Security Law in 2015, it had a separate clause about "cultural security." The 23rd article reads, "The state shall adhere to developing an advanced socialist culture, inherit and carry forward the fine traditional culture of the Chinese nation, cultivate and practice the core values of socialism, prevent and resist the impact of harmful culture, maintain its ideological domination, and enhance the overall cultural strength and competitiveness."[20] Here the wording "to prevent and resist the impact of harmful culture" can be interpreted as echoing the "seven speak-nots" that might threaten the CCP's hold on power. It gives the government the power to crack down on the spread of Western values in the name of "national security." More importantly, when the maintenance of ideological domination was viewed as an issue of national security, it gave the state expansive power to justify the crackdown on the media when needed.

"500 Reposts"

From the time he entered office, Xi demonstrated special interest in the control of the Internet. On August 19, 2013, he made his first major speech on the propaganda work since taking office as the Chinese president. The published version was filled with bureaucratic clichés such as the "leading role of Marxism in the propaganda work," the "principle of positive coverage," and the responsibility of those in charge of propaganda to "hold the ground" etc.[21] In an unpublished version, however, Xi's messages were clearer and even menacing. In November 2013 *DW* and *Radio France Internationale* (RFI) gave the readers a more genuine taste of his position by quoting an article from a Hong Kong newspaper. According to the article, Xi described the Internet as something that can "cause the demise of the Party and the state" and a "battleground of public opinion" that concerns the security of ideology and the state. He demanded CCP officials to "show the sword" to the enemies in order to "grab the positions."[22]

[19] Zhu, Zheng, and Wang, "Hot Topics."

[20] "National Security Law of the People's Republic of China."

[21] Xi Jinping, "Keep the Big Picture in Mind."

[22] Wu, "Xi Jinping's 8.19 Talk Widely Spread."; Zheng, "Xi Jinping's 8.19 Talk in the Internally Circulated Version."

Xi's talk coincided with a campaign against "big Vs," meaning VIP bloggers or influencers with millions of followers. Between June and December 2013, the Ministry of Public Security in China started a campaign against cybercrimes.[23] In the official narrative, the targets included fraud, hacking, and invasion of personal information. In reality, it was a crackdown on social media activists or commentators who had exposed corruption or stirred up interest in social issues.

The campaign became particularly intense in late August, right after Xi's 8/19 talk. One of the most prominent targets in 2013 was Charles Xue, better known as Xue Manzi on social media, a Chinese American investor and commentator with twelve million followers. On August 26, 2013, the Beijing police announced that they had arrested Xue on charges of soliciting prostitution. In the next few days, the party media outlets gave intensive coverage of Xue's arrest and highlighted his identity as a "big V" in their news stories and opinion pieces. Eight months later, Xue again became the headline when he went on CCTV to "confess his crimes" and expressed his "wholehearted support" for the government crackdown on social media. At the same time, his confession letter was published on the website of *People's Daily* the party organ. On the blog space, there was speculation that Xue had been set up and that his arrest might be an attempt to stifle online commentary.[24] The government essentially made Xue an example in the campaign. When the party mobilized its propaganda machines against an individual, it sent a chilling message to other VIP bloggers to be careful in their online commentaries.

A few days after the high-profiled arrest of Charles Xue, on September 9, 2013, the Supreme People's Court and the Supreme People's Procuratorate of China issued a joint judicial interpretation about how to handle criminal cases such as libeling on the Internet. According to this rule, anybody whose online post has been either viewed more than 5,000 times or reposted 500 times would be charged with the crime of libeling for violating the first clause of Criminal Law Article 246. The rule also stipulates that all those who intimidate others and those who issue or spread false information would be charged with "picking quarrels and provoking trouble," a charge frequently used for street protestors. Tong Zhiwei, a law professor also from East China University of Political Science and Law, argued that it was a progress for the government to draw boundaries for libeling on the Internet through judicial interpretations, but his concern was that the interpretations would further limit the space of expression on the Internet and that it would greatly expand the scope of actions that might be criminalized.[25]

[23] Zhou and Shi, "Ministry of Public Security."

[24] Barboza, "Chinese American Commentator and Investor Is Arrested in Beijing"; Buckley, "Xue Manzi Warns VIP Bloggers."

[25] *New York Times* Beijing Office, "Judicial Interpretations Might Cause Further Restrictions."

Tong also said the threshold of "5000 views" is much easier to cross than the threshold of "500 reposts." *DW* quoted an online commentator who said that it would be very easy to set up someone for criminal charges if the troll army was mobilized to go after certain individuals. In an editorial, *Global Times*, the nationalist tabloid under the auspices of *People's Daily*, argued that September 9 would become a "significant day in the history of China's Internet" because the judicial interpretations would limit the spread of "illegal information" on the Internet and that it symbolizes the end of the era of "big-character posters" on the Internet.[26]

Liu Xiaoyuan, a prominent lawyer and human rights advocate, however, expressed his disagreement with the "big-character poster" characterization by *Global Times* by pointing out that many of his own posts that had nothing to do with libel had been deleted by the authorities without any explanation. He argued that they are drummed up due to the government's fear of the Internet particularly in the middle of Xi's anti-graft campaign when netizens openly called out corrupted officials for scrutiny. One commentator even joked that the new interpretation was "good news and a safety net for corrupted officials." Liu also questioned the legality of the judicial interpretations by the Supreme People's Court and the Supreme People's Procuratorate because he argued that the authority should come from the National People's Congress (NPC), China's highest legislative body, to whom he then submitted a petition for a judicial review for interpretations.[27]

Two weeks after the announcement of the judicial interpretations, Yang Hui, a 16-year-old middle school student from the northwest province of Gansu, was taken from school by the police and became the youngest detainee according to the new rule. What had happened was that an employee at a local Karaoke parlor died on September 12 abruptly, but his family and friends expressed doubt over how the police had conducted the investigation. Yang then wrote three blog posts claiming that there might be hidden stories behind it. The police claimed that Yang was arrested because his Weibo entries had been reposted 500 times, but the public questioned whether it was really the case because his original posts had been deleted, which did not even give people the opportunity to verify. Moreover, many advocacy lawyers offered to work for Yang's defense.[28] Under public pressure, local police revoked the decision of criminal arrest of Yang and changed it to administrative detention and released him later. That was not the end of the story, however. On November 10, Yang revealed through his Weibo account that he had

[26] Zhang, "Evidence of Speech Crime: Reposted 500 Times."

[27] *New York Times* Beijing Office, "Judicial Interpretations Might Cause Further Restrictions."

[28] Zheng, "Middle Schooler Became the Youngest Detainee."

been physically assaulted by the police while in custody in September. After that, his post was deleted, and he was dismissed from his middle school.[29]

Cyberspace Administration of China (CAC)

Besides using judicial means to crack down on online activism, Xi also used executive means to make rules and regulations for the Internet. The most important government agency in charge of the Internet was the Cyberspace Administration of China (CAC), which had been established in 2011 under the jurisdiction of the State Council. After taking office, Xi greatly expanded its power and elevated its position in the bureaucracy. On February 27, 2014, he established the Central Cyberspace Security and Information Leading Group and made himself its head, adding another title for himself among the heads of other leading groups, a form of concentrating power to himself.[30] No longer under the State Council, the CAC now became a party apparatus under the direct control of Xi himself. When "security" was added to "information" as part of CAC's missions, it received much more priority than the latter. In March during the "two sessions" of the NPC and the Chinese People's Political Consultative Conference (CPPCC), an advisory body for the CCP, "Cyber Security" was written into the government report to be approved by the national legislature for the first time and elevated as an issue of national strategy.[31]

In May 2014, Lu Wei, who became the head of the CAC a year earlier, was promoted to become the deputy minister of CCP's Publicity Department (formerly Propaganda Department),[32] further raising the position of the CAC in the party bureaucracy. After assuming the leadership of the CAC, one of the most high-profiled activities Lu Wei conducted was to summon prominent "Big Vs" to the new building of CCTV on August 10, 2013 and lectured to them on how to assume more "social responsibilities" and to "spread more positive energy."[33] Interestingly, one of those summoned was Charles Xue, who would be arrested two weeks after the meeting. Neither Xue's meeting with Lu Wei nor his arrest looked like accidents.

After the establishment of the CAC, it issued a series of regulations about the Internet, the most important ones are known as "WeChat Ten Rules," "Account Ten

[29] An, "Yang Hui of Gansu Province."

[30] Shang, "Xi Jinping is in Direct Control of China's Cyberspace Security"; the Leading Group would be renamed Central Cyberspace Affairs Commission in 2018.

[31] Gao and Han, "Written into the Government Report for the First Time."

[32] Li, "Central Commission for Discipline Inspection of the CCP."

[33] Li, "CAC Commissioner Lu Wei Talks."

Rules,” and “Regulatory Talks Ten Rules.”[34] Even though regulations issued by the CAC are not considered law, they played an important role in controlling China’s cyber space. According to a meta-analysis of Chinese Internet policies between 1994 and 2017 conducted by Miao Weishan, Jiang Min, and Pang Yuxia, nearly 90 percent of the 358 Internet policies were issued as “departmental rules” or “regulatory documents,” whereas only four are “laws” passed by the National People’s Congress. These regulations or directives lack systematic, overarching legal frameworks and often impose arbitrary rules. Regulatory rules issued by the CAC can circumvent the more arduous process through the NPC and allows China’s top leadership to exert considerable power over policy directions in a fast-changing economic, political, and international environment. As they stated, Chinese Internet policies did not follow the principle of “rule of law,” but “rule by directives.”[35] Rule by directives is in line with the Chinese policy tradition of “rule by law,” where the government makes rules for the people but not for itself.

“Media Surnamed Party”

As Xi’s grip on power became more solid, his position on the media became even more hardened. On February 19, 2016, he made a rare and high-profiled tour of the three most important state-run media outlets: *People’s Daily*, Xinhua News Agency, and CCTV. When he arrived at CCTV, officials displayed a huge banner carrying three slogans: “CCTV’s Surname is The Party. Absolutely Loyal. Ready for Your Inspection.” Later in the day, Xi convened a forum on the media and propaganda in which he said “The media run by the party and the government are the forefronts of propaganda and must have the party as their surname. All the work by the party’s media must reflect the party’s will, safeguard the party’s authority, and safeguard the party’s unity. They must love the party, protect the party, and closely align themselves with the party leadership in thought, politics, and action.” According to Willy Lam, an expert on elite Chinese politics at the Chinese University of Hong Kong, Xi was raising standards for state media by requiring them to obey the will of the Communist party’s core leadership, which is increasingly defined by Xi himself in another sign of how he had accrued more personal authority than either of his two predecessors. He called it “a very heavy-handed ideological campaign” to drive home the point of total loyalty to the party core.” As Lam wrote, “on one hand, Xi’s influence and power are now unchallenged, but on the other hand, there is

[34] State Council Information Office of the PRC, “What Do the Three ‘Ten Rules’ about Internet Management Mean?”

[35] Weishan, Min and Pang, “Historicizing Internet Regulation in China.”

a palpable degree of insecurity."[36] Even "*Mao's Talks at* the *Yan'an Forum on Arts and Literature* in 1942 was not as authoritarian as Xi in demanding the absolute submission of the media.

Xi's talk about "media surnamed party" caused resistance in the society. The next day, the Shenzhen edition of the liberal *Southern Metropolis Daily* featured two headlines on the front page. One is "The party- and government-run media are a propaganda front and must be surnamed 'party.' Just below it was a large photo of people sorrowfully tipping the ashes of Yuan Geng, a prominent southern businessman, into the sea accompanied by a headline: "Soul Returns to Sea." If the last two characters of each line are read together, it would mean "The media has the Party as its surname. Its soul returns to the sea." That would be seen as a possible lament for the fate of Chinese journalists under the party's tightening restrictions. This was widely interpreted as a "hidden poem," a form of expressing political dissent in imperial China. Obviously "protest" of this kind is not tolerated. A few days later, the party committee of the paper's owner Nanfang Media Group had to post a statement acknowledging a "serious mistake" and denying it as an intentional action. According to the statement, three journalists had been punished. Ren Tianyang, the editor in chief, had made an "in-depth apology"; his deputy, Wang Haijun, had received demerits; and Liu Yuxia, the front-page editor responsible, had been fired.[37]

The other prominent challenger of the policy was Ren Zhiqiang, a property tycoon known for his outspokenness on financial and political issues with more than thirty million followers on social media. On the night Xi made the speech about "media surnamed party," he wrote on his Weibo account "When did the people's government turn into the party's government?" in one post. In another he wrote, "Don't use taxpayers' money to do stuff that doesn't provide services to the taxpayers" and "The people have been tossed into a forgotten corner."[38]

Ren's open defiance of Xi's media comments did not go unpunished. Starting from February 22, state-run media outlets began to run articles condemning him. It started with an article on Qianlong, a website run by the Beijing municipal government, which claimed that netizens should "give Ren a class on party principles."[39] On February 28, the CAC announced that all social media accounts of Ren were shut down due to his "illegal statements."[40] The next day, the CCP branch of Beijing's Xicheng District where Ren lived issued a notification denouncing him and promised

36 "Xi Jinping Asks for "Absolute Loyalty' from Chinese State Media."

37 Tatlow, "Hidden Message."

38 Buckley, "Chinese Tycoon Criticizes Leader."

39 Li, "Why Should Netizens Give Ren Zhiqiang a Lesson of the Party."

40 CAC, "Spokesperson of the Cyberspace Administration of China."

to punish him severely. On this day, state-run media outlets such as *Xinhua*, *People's Daily*, and *China Daily* engaged in coordinated attacks on Ren as well.[41]

The attacks on Ren caused several liberal scholars and party intellectuals to defend him. One of them was Cai Xia, a professor from the Central Party School of the CCP. She used the charter of the CCP to defend Ren's rights to speak out as a party member. She argued that the difference of opinion was normal, but that using the language of the Cultural Revolution to turn it into something about principle and an ideological line was "abnormal" and constituted a form of political persecution. Her defense of Ren caused fury in the state-run media as well and became their target of public denunciation.[42]

The other defender of Ren is Jiang Hong, a professor from Shanghai University of Finance and Economics and a member of the CPPCC. During that year's "two sessions" in spring, Jiang openly expressed his concern for freedom of speech. On March 2, when interviewed by the influential and respected news organization Caixin Media, Jiang said that "certain events," which would be interpreted as what had happened to Ren Zhiqiang, had cast a shadow over the meetings, leaving attendees "a bit dazed" and not wanting "to talk too much." The article with the interview was then removed from its English website. After that, Caixin published another interview with Jiang on March 5, who said that the censorship of his interview was "terrible and bewildering," and that he could not understand what laws and regulations he had violated that warranted the article's removal. The Caixin article was removed again.[43] Caixin then published another article "Story about Advisor's Free Speech Comments Removed from Caixin Website" on March 7. The article was removed as well.[44]

The support for freedom of speech around Ren's case caused the Party to further crack down on him. On May 2, the CCP branch in Xicheng District announced that Ren would be put on a one-year probation, a punishment reserved for CCP members, for writing online comments that went against the policies and guidelines of the party. People knew that his real mistake was criticizing Xi Jinping's propaganda policies. As *The New York Times* pointed out, the government chose to make the announcement of Ren's punishment on May 2, during the one-week holiday of May Day, probably not wanting to attract too much attention due to the popularity of Ren.[45] In addition, Ren's case was included in the disciplinary actions

[41] Buckley, "Chinese Tycoon Criticizes Leader, and Wins Surprising Support."
[42] Kou, "Professor Cai Xia of Central Party School."
[43] Forsythe, "Chinese Publication, Censored by Government."
[44] An, "Advisor Expressed Viewpoints."
[45] Buckley, "China Puts a Tycoon, Ren Zhiqiang, on Probation."

against three other corrupted officials.[46] It can also be interpreted as a government effort to keep Ren's case low profile.

Decline of Investigative Journalism

Under the rule of Xi Jinping, investigative journalism declined dramatically and those engaged in it were either arrested or forced to switch to other professions. Xi's party-state does not see investigative journalism as an aid to "remedying social ills and improving governance," but a threat to social stability or to the party control. In January 2018, Zhang Zhi'an, Dean of the School of Communication and Design (now School of Journalism and Communication) at Sun Yat-sen University in Guangzhou, published an *Annual Report of Chinese Journalism in 2017*. The report called attention to the trend in which the mainstreamed party media are "retaking the control of the microphone." For example, the number of journalists in China increased around 30 percent from the previous year, but they mostly happened in web portals run by the party-controlled media outlets. In contrast, the number of investigative journalists was quickly declining. As the report stated, there were only 175 investigative journalists in China in that year, a decrease of 57.5 percent from six years earlier. As a result, journalists' sense of identity with their own profession decreased dramatically, the space of freedom shrank, and the job loyalty was filled with more uncertainty.[47] This trend would continue in the following years.

In 2019, *The New York Times* published a few articles tracking the status of Chinese investigative journalists and explained why the profession was declining. One case is about the quitting of Liu Wanyong, who had earned the nickname "Tibetan Mastiff," a dog known for aggressiveness and stubbornness, because of his reports that had caused the jailing of corrupted officials and because of his perseverance at the *China Youth Daily*, a paper run by the CCP but with a reputation for "bending the rules" sometimes. According to him, as the government tightened its control, at least 100 "juicy" articles with the *Youth Daily* had been "killed" over the past two years. Gradually he became tired of the response "just wait," which to him meant "Don't even dream of tackling the topic" when discussing story ideas with editors. He left his beloved job and joined an asset management firm. In response, a social media account run by Chinese reporters declared that the departure of "a pillar of the profession" meant investigative journalism would never be the same."[48]

[46] Beijing Xicheng District, "Xicheng District Announced the Disciplinary Actions."

[47] "Breaking News! Annual Report of Chinese Journalism in 2017."

[48] Perlez, "For China's Leading Investigative Reporter, Enough Is Enough."

Another story is about Mrs. Zhang Wenmin, once viewed as one of China's "most feared journalists," who had roamed the country uncovering stories about police brutality, wrongful convictions, and environmental disasters. According to the story, she had to deal with police intimidating her sources and authorities shutting down her social media accounts. Unable to find news outlets that would publish her work, she lost her source of income and had to live largely off her savings. As Zhang said, "the space for free speech has become so limited that it's now dangerous to say you are an independent journalist." According to the *Times* article, besides political restrictions, economic considerations had also contributed to the disappearance of in-depth reporting. Many news outlets in China, like those elsewhere in the world, are struggling with big losses in print advertising revenue and have eliminated investigative reporting teams, which typically require more time and resources and produce fewer stories.[49]

The control of the media reached new heights in 2019 when the CCP required all journalists to take tests before getting their license renewed. On October 19, a notice issued by China's National Press and Publication Administration stipulated that all the people involved in news gathering would be tested on the contents including Xi Jinping's thoughts on socialism, the Marxist theories of the press, along with news ethics and laws. The notice required all news agencies to organize the training sessions to prepare for the tests. Even though it recommended a combination of self-study and group study, it requires the latter to "be no less than 24 hours," during which the participants could possibly watch each other. It also recommended the use of a mobile App called Xuexi Qiangguo in preparing for the test.[50]

Xuexi Qiangguo (or Studying to Strengthen the Nation) has been developed by Alibaba, China's largest e-commerce platform, for CCP's Publicity Department. It is widely viewed as a platform to propagate Xi's ideas on government. "Xuexi" is a pun which can mean both "learning" or "learning from Xi" in Chinese. At first only the CCP members were required to download it and spend a certain amount of time reading the contents. Before long, the requirement was expanded to government functionaries, employees of the state-owned enterprises, teachers at public schools, and even non-CCP members.

Featuring a cartoon showing journalists kowtowing to a portrait of Xi, a BBC article said that one of its journalists had downloaded the app and tried a mock test. It found that only one-third of the questions are about fundamentals and legal questions of journalism while the majority were about the party's policies and Xi's quotations about propaganda. For one study question "What is the responsibility and mission of the party's work on the media and public opinion?" the system will

[49] Hernández, "We're Almost Extinct."

[50] Shi, "Training of News Gatherers."

mark it wrong if people pick "adhering to the truth" whereas the correct answer is "adhering to the promotion of positive news."[51] The Xuexi Qiangguo app can be compared to Mao's Little Red Book using the 21st century technology that has more surveillance capabilities.

Restriction of Non-public Capital in the Media

Before Xi took office, private investment could still be involved in the news industry. It can be seen in some government documents. For example, in one released by the State Council in 2005, private investors were allowed to hold shares in certain news industries such as publishing, advertisement, the production of music, science, sports and entertainment on radio and TV stations on the condition that the public sector accounts for more than 51 percent of the ownership. At the same time, private capital was not allowed to establish or manage wire services, publishing, TV, or radio stations. Since the Internet was relatively new and online news was still rare at the time, the regulation did not touch upon this topic.[52] The involvement of private investment partly explains the success of liberal newspapers like *Southern Metropolitan Daily* and *Southern Weekly* in the late 1990s and early 2000s.

In another one issued by the General Administration of Press and Publication in 2010, the government still encouraged the "guidance and regulation of nonpublic capital entering the news and publishing industries in an orderly way" in order to "liberate the productive forces of new cultural industries." The document also encouraged "nonpublic cultural entities" to expand into the overseas news and publishing markets.[53] The 2010 document was released after the 2008 Summer Olympics Games in Beijing during which Western media covered the protests in Tibet and human rights problems in China. In response to the negative stories in the Western media, the Chinese government increased its investments in the media to magnify its own voice all over the world, an initiative known as Great External Propaganda. In this context, the involvement of private news organizations would blunt the image of sharp power caused by state-owned media outlets to foreign audiences.[54]

Since Xi Jinping came to power in 2012, the government has gradually tightened the control of private funds entering the news industry. In this year, the General Administration of Press and Publication issued a rule that non-public capital was

51 Wang, "China Requires Tens of Thousands."

52 State Council of the PRC, "Decisions of the State Council on the Entrance."

53 State Council of the PRC, "General Administration of Press."

54 He, "The Localization Strategy"; Zhen, "Chinese Government Reiterates the Ban."

not allowed during the transition and merging of newspaper companies.[55] With the rise of the Internet, traditional print media gradually lost ground. In time a new generation of media channels hosted by large internet portal websites such as Tencent, Sina, Sohu, and Jinri Toutiao gradually became important channels people would turn to for news information. They are private or publicly traded companies. Although they are not technically allowed to hire journalists to do original reporting, many of these channels still managed to push the envelope—"hitting line balls" is the Chinese phrase often used—and produce original content under the guise of "special column," or through seemingly harmless genres such as "nonfiction writing."[56]

But the most competitive feature of these portals is not the content, but the fact that they own the major platforms. The news apps of Jinri Toutiao (meaning "today's headline"), Tencent, Sina, Sohu, and iFeng are ranked the top ones in app stores, and Sina and Tencent have Weibo and WeChat in their hands. As more and more Chinese read news on their smartphones, editors and algorithms of the commercial digital media overwhelmingly determine what Chinese people read every day. Not surprisingly, the state enforces strict censorship on them and punishes them when something sensitive is published.[57]

With the new development, the CCP also modified its policy and expanded its control from print media to the Internet and mobile apps. In 2017, the Cyberspace Administration of China (CAC) issued a rule stipulating that nonpublic capital should not be allowed to be involved in Internet news gathering. In 2018, the government introduced the system of a negative list which designated areas where private funds were not allowed. The list reiterated the ban of newsgathering by Internet companies.[58]

As time went by, the rules in the negative list became much more elaborate. In September 2021, the National Development and Reform Commission, the country's central economic planning agency, released a draft regulation that promised to expand restrictions on the involvement of nonpublic capital in swaths of the news industry. It was an update to the restrictions on private investment in the media. In contrast to the 2020 edition which only had one sentence that forbade non-public capital from getting involved in Internet news gathering and any organization from establishing jointly owned or managed or foreign investments from running Internet news service, the 2021 edition has six specific clauses. Among the most important, it banned private capital firms from running news organizations' webpages, radio frequency, channels, columns, and social media accounts. It

55 Guo, "General Administration of Press."

56 Bandurski and Fang, "The Rise and Fall of Southern Weekly."

57 Kuo, "China's Media Market Competition."

58 "China Strictly Forbids Private Investment in News Gathering".

also banned private investment in platforms that provide live-streaming content related to the economy, sports, education, and other topics "related to political affairs, public opinion and value orientations." Moreover, the draft regulation added a new ban on hosting news-related forums or award ceremonies. Another major difference is that the general phrase "not allowed to get involved" that had been used in the past is now "not allowed to undertake, "not allowed to invest in or to set up," "not allowed to operate," and "not allowed to import."[59]

Xi's Cult of Personality

While the media in traditional forms and online platforms has been tightly controlled, it has been increasingly used to promote the cult of personality for Xi. On December 4, 2015, for example, the party organ *People's Daily* ran eleven headlines and one sub-headline mentioning Xi on its front page. The prominence did not stop at the front page. On the second page, there was a "nine-photo spread of Xi meeting with African leaders, while half of page three was taken up by the text of an op-ed piece on China-Africa relations written by Xi and published in the Johannesburg-based Star newspaper." State media's overwhelming focus on Xi certainly had set him apart from his immediate predecessors and made China watchers all over the world wonder whether China was going back to the path of another personality cult similar to the one that surrounded Mao Zedong in the 1960s and '70s.[60]

According to the *Wall Street Journal*, the University of Hong Kong's China Media Project in a study released in July 2015 found that Xi's name had appeared on the pages of the *People's Daily* more than any other Chinese leader since Mao. As it indicated, in the first 18 months since he rose to power, Xi was mentioned by name in the paper 4,725 times, compared with 2,405 and 2,001 times for his predecessors Hu Jintao and Jiang Zemin during a similar period. The cult of personality happened on television as well. In one newscast in 2015, state broadcaster China Central Television (CCTV) devoted nearly all of its evening newscast to Xi during his recent travels abroad. And state media has sought to promote his speeches both domestically and abroad through online quizzes, cartoons and the ubiquitous "Governance of China," a 515-page book compiling his greatest hits.[61]

In fall 2017, after Xi was awarded a second five-year term as the highest leader of the CCP and of China, the *Times* also found that Xi was trying to "put himself

[59] "China Strictly Forbids Private Investment in News Gathering"; Lin, "China Targets News Media."

[60] Sonmez, "China's *People's Daily* Runs 11 Xi Jinping Headlines."

[61] Ibid.

on a pedestal." It discovered a striking difference from the past in the layout of the *People's Daily*'s front page. As it pointed out, for decades, the newspaper had embodied "collective leadership" when none of the party leaders was overly highlighted. It used the front pages of the party organ in 1982, 1987, 1992, 1997, 2002, 2007, and 2012 that documented the transition of power. On those front pages, even though the CCP general secretary was placed above other leaders in the Standing Committee of the Political Bureau, the most powerful body of China, at least their faces were demonstrated with separate headshots. However, on the front page of October 26, 2017, when Xi's second term was officially announced, his beaming face was above a small group photo of all the members of the standing committee of the CCP political bureau with six members' faces barely visible. The *Times* also noticed that the government-printed Xi writings often featured in lavish displays with stars and ribbons, which are different from the more restrained exhibits of many of his predecessors.[62]

As mentioned earlier, when Chinese people increasingly turned to mobile devices to get their news, the CCP would use them for propaganda and Xi's cult of personality as well. For popular news apps such as Jinri Toutiao, Tencent, Sina, Sohu, and iFeng, the state imposes "a super algorithm," meaning that the stories at the very top of every news website and news app have to be about Xi Jinping.[63] The cult of personality for Xi could become bizarre at times. In November 2017, for example, *South China Morning Post*, an influential newspaper stationed in Hong Kong, reported that Christians in a poverty-stricken village in China's Jiangxi Province, were urged to replace the posters of Jesus with portraits of Xi as part of a local government poverty-relief program that seeks to "transform believers in religion into believers in the party."[64]

Another example to show Xi's cult of personality in the Chinese media can be found in July 2021 when the heaviest rainfall on record occurred in Zhengzhou, the capital of the mid-China province of Henan. The situation became so severe that local authorities opened the floodgate of a reservoir to discharge the flood without prior notification to the residents who might be affected. As a result, the flashflood caused great destruction to property and human lives. The worst happened when subway lines and underground tunnels were submerged with passengers trapped inside.[65]

While people were suffering and waiting for help, *Henan Daily*, the mouthpiece of the CCP in Henan and *People's Daily* did not mention anything about the flooding

[62] Hernandez and Carlsen, "Why Xi Jinping's (Airbrushed) Face."

[63] Kuo, "China's Media Market Competition."

[64] Gan, "Want to Escape Poverty?"

[65] Myers, "'Please Save Us!"; Ye, "7.20 Flooding Catastrophe in Zhengzhou?"

on their front pages on July 20 or 21, the first two days of the disaster. Instead, the official organs were running stories about Xi's talk at the celebration of the 100th anniversary of the CCP. Similarly, instead of covering the disaster in China, *Global Times* and CCTV were showing the miseries in other countries by reporting the flooding in Europe with details about death toll and mismanagement by officials. During the flooding, Xi Jinping, different from his predecessor who had visited the disaster-stricken area, chose to take a high-profile inspection tour of Tibet. For the flooding in Henan, he simply sent a "key instruction" about the importance of people's lives. The most striking scene occurred on July 24 when *Henan Daily* and *People's Daily* placed Xi's instructions about how to promote the "toilet revolution in the countryside" at the upper right corner of the front page, a practice reminiscent of the Cultural Revolution when Mao's quotations were placed there. Stories about the flooding were still absent from the front pages of the two newspapers even though it was already four days into the disaster.

Conclusion

Between 2012 and 2022, the media ecosystem in China witnessed a trend characterized by the decline of critical journalism and independent voices and the expansion of the party media, which has increasingly "taken over the microphone." Through judicial means such as criminalizing posts that have been viewed 5000 times or reposted 500 times as well as bureaucratic means such as expanding the power of the CAC and the exclusion of private investment in the news industry, the CCP have tightened its control of the traditional party media, the commercial outlets, and the Internet. At times, journalists and netizens used creative means to push the space for expression. However, they would mostly cause the government to resort to more repressive means of control to "plug the loophole." Government rules and regulations have become more and more repetitive, expansive, and elaborative. As Xi became the most powerful leader since Mao, the Chinese media have been used to promote his cult of personality. His prominence in the flagship media as well as commercial web portals can be compared to the practice during the Cultural Revolution.

Under Xi's rule, critical journalism went into a sharp decline as journalists were harassed, arrested, or forced out of the profession. During these years, the number of journalists thrown in jails increased. According to Reporters without Borders, by 2022, China had become the world's largest jailer of journalists with more than 100 behind the bars.[66] The crackdown on critical journalists has gone hand-in-hand

[66] "Press group: China Biggest Global Jailer of Journalists."

with the crackdown on advocacy lawyers. Liu Xiaoyuan, who submitted the petition to challenge the "500 posts" in 2013 and who had been involved in defending human rights cases, was stripped of his license to practice law in June 2019.[67]

When this chapter was written in 2023, China was facing more serious problems. Besides those mentioned at the beginning of this chapter, the biggest change since 2012 was the deterioration of China's relations with the world particularly with the United States. When Xi abandoned Deng Xiaoping's policy of "keeping a low-profile and biding one's time" and pursued a more aggressive foreign policy, the United States gave up the hope that China would become more open or free as it grows richer and turned to identify it as a major strategic threat. As a result, Washington introduced many measures to deprive China of the capability to threaten the US. One of the most important was to deny its access to advanced semiconductor chips, which is a vital element for China's technological advancement.

Moreover, the "wolf warrior diplomacy" since Xi's takeover angered many foreign governments and caused the further isolation of China from the world community. Many world companies have transferred their supply chains to India and Southeast Asia or are in the process due to worries about geopolitical conflicts between the United States and China and about the uncertainty in Chinese policies as seen in the drastic measures during the COVID-19 epidemic. The deteriorating foreign relations would ultimately hurt an already slowing Chinese economy which relies heavily on international trade. The worsening domestic and international environments facing China would make the CCP feel more insecure about its grip on power. As a result, Xi will govern China in a "crisis mode," which means the media ecosystem in China will not see much improvement in the near future.

Dr. **Guolin Yi** is a Visiting Assistant Professor at Providence College and an Associate in Research at the Fairbank Center for Chinese Studies at Harvard University. His research interests cut across the fields of history and communication with a focus on the cultural history of modern China, especially the media in the larger context of its interactions with the West. He has published a book *The Media and Sino-American Rapprochement: 1963–1972: A Comparative Study* (Louisiana State University Press, 2020) and written for the *Journal of American-East Asian Relations, American Journalism, Chinese Historical Review, World History Bulletin*, and H-Net among others.

[67] Feng and Ao, "Beijing Rights Attorney Liu Xiaoyuan."

Bibliography

Newspapers and News Portals

Associated Press
BBC
ChinaAid
Diplomat
DW News
Guardian
New York Times
People's Daily
Phoenix New Media
Qianlong
Radio France Internationale
Radio Free Asia
Reuters
Shanghai Observer
Sina
South China Morning Post
Voice of America
Wall Street Journal
Xinhua News Agency

Government Documents

Beijing Xicheng District. "Xicheng District Announced the Disciplinary Actions Against Four Cadres." http://www.bjxch.gov.cn/XICxwdt/XICxcdt/XICxcdtxxxq.ycs?GUID=582905 Accessed May 24, 2023.

CAC. "Spokesperson of the Cyberspace Administration of China Made a Statement about the Shutting Down of Ren Zhiqiang's Weibo Accounts." February 22, 2016. http://www.cac.gov.cn/2016-02/28/c_1118181170.htm?TB_iframe=true&width=921.6&height=921.6 Accessed May 23, 2023.

Congressional Executive Committee on China. "Chinese Journalist Cheng Yizhong Awarded UNESCO /Guillermo Cano World Press Freedom Prize," April 13, 2005.https://www.cecc.gov/publications/commission-analysis/chinese-journalist-cheng-yizhong-awarded-unescoguillermo-cano-world#:~:text=Chinese%20Journalist%20Cheng%20Yizhong%20Awarded%20UNESCO%2FGuillermo%20Cano%20World%20Press%20Freedom%20Prize,-April%2013%2C%202005&text=As%20editor%20of%20Nanfang%20Dushi,new%20ground%20in%20Chinese%20journalism. Accessed May 16, 2023.

"General Administration of Press and Publication Issued a Document Guiding the Institutional Reforms in Newspaper Editing Offices," August 10, 2012. https://www.gov.cn/gzdt/2012-08/03/content_2197787.htm Accessed May 31, 2023.

"Hot Topics in the Ideological and Theoretical Spheres in 2013," *People's Daily Online*, January 13, 2014. https://web.archive.org/web/20180915111310/http://theory.people.com.cn/n/2014/0113/c143843-24096298.html Accessed June 8, 2023.

"Ministry of Public Security to Start a Special Operation Focusing on Cybercrimes," Central People's Government of the People's Republic of China, June 18, 2013. https://www.gov.cn/jrzg/2013-06/18/content_2428774.htm Accessed June 9, 2023.

"National Security Law of the People's Republic of China," Peking University (2015), http://lawinfochina.com/display.aspx?id=19663&lib=law Accessed May 22, 2023.

State Council Information Office of the PRC. "What do the Three 'Ten Rules' about Internet Management Mean?" May 4, 2015. http://www.scio.gov.cn/zhzc/8/5/Document/1433040/1433040.htm Accessed May 24, 2023.

State Council of the PRC. "Decisions of the State Council on the Entrance of Non-Public Capital in Cultural Industries,", issued April 13, 2005.https://www.gov.cn/gongbao/content/2005/content_64188.htm Accessed May 31, 2023.

State Council of the PRC. "General Administration of Press and Publication's Guiding Principle on How to Push Further the Development of News and Publishing Industries," issued January 1st, 2010. https://www.gov.cn/gongbao/content/2010/content_1671253.htm Accessed May 31, 2023.

Books and Articles

"Breaking News! Annual Report of Chinese Journalism in 2017 Has Been Released. Click Here for the Full Text," Shanghai Observer, January 9, 2018. https://www.shobserver.com/staticsg/home Accessed May 29, 2023.

"CCP Issued a Document of Ideological Control, but the Announcement has Disappeared Mysteriously," BBC. May 13, 2013.https://www.bbc.com/zhongwen/simp/china/2013/05/130513_china_politics_ideology Accessed May 19, 2023.

"China journalist Gao Yu Detained in Tiananmen Lead-up," BBC, May 8, 2014, https://www.bbc.com/news/world-asia-china-27321241 Accessed May 19, 2023.

"China Strictly Forbids Private Investment in News Gathering. Would the New Ban Cause a Shock to the Industry?" BBC, October 13, 2021. https://www.bbc.com/zhongwen/simp/chinese-news-58883616 Accessed May 31, 2023.

"National Security Law of the People's Republic of China," Peking University (2015), http://lawinfochina.com/display.aspx?id=19663&lib=law Accessed May 22, 2023.

"Press group: China Biggest Global Jailer of Journalists," Associated Press, May 5, 2023. https://apnews.com/article/china-press-censorship-hong-lai-2caeedd86717ef4667ada868abf67eba. Accessed May 18, 2023

"Xi Jinping Asks for "Absolute Loyalty' from Chinese State Media," Guardian, February 19, 2016. https://www.theguardian.com/world/2016/feb/19/xi-jinping-tours-chinas-top-state-media-outlets-to-boost-loyalty Accessed May 22, 2023.

An Jing, "Advisor Expressed Viewpoints. Caixin Encountered the Removal (of its articles)" DW News. March 8, 2016. https://www.dw.com/zh/%E6%94%BF%E5%8D%8F%E5%A7%94%E5%91%98%E8%A1%A8%E8%A7%82%E7%82%B9-%E8%B4%A2%E6%96%B0%E9%81%AD%E9%81%87%E4%B8%89%E8%BF%9E%E5%88%A0/a-19102819 Accessed May 24, 2023.

An Pei, "Yang Hui of Gansu Province, the first Detainee Violating the 'Law of Reposted 500 Times,' Has Been Dismissed from School," RFI, November 18, 2013 https://www.rfa.org/mandarin/yataibaodao/meiti/aw-11182013145421.html Accessed May 25, 2023.

Bandurski, D and Fang Kecheng. "The Rise and Fall of Southern Weekly and the Changing Landscape of Journalism in China: A Pivotal Moment," Introduction to Guan Jun, *Silencing Chinese Media: The*

"Southern Weekly" Protests and the Fate of Civil Society in Xi Jinping's China.* Translated by Kevin Carrico (Lanham: Roman & Littlefield, 2020), xi.

Barboza, David. "Chinese American Commentator and Investor Is Arrested in Beijing," NYT, August 26, 2013 https://cn.nytimes.com/china/20130826/c26xue/dual/ Accessed June 9, 2023.

Beijing Xicheng District, "Xicheng District Announced the Disciplinary Actions Against Four Cadres."http://www.bjxch.gov.cn/XICxwdt/XICxcdt/XICxcdtxxxq.ycs?GUID=582905 Accessed May 24, 2023.

Buckley, Chris. "China Puts a Tycoon, Ren Zhiqiang, on Probation for Criticizing Policies," NYT, May 3, 2016. https://cn.nytimes.com/china/20160503/c03chinaren/dual/ Accessed May 23, 2023.

Buckley, Chris. "China's New Leadership Takes Hard Line in Secret Memo," NYT, August 20, 2013. https://cn.nytimes.com/china/20130820/c20document/dual/ Accessed May 19, 2023.

Buckley, Chris. "Chinese Tycoon Criticizes Leader, and Wins Surprising Support," NYT, March 18, 2016. https://www.nytimes.com/2016/03/19/world/asia/china-ren-zhiqiang-weibo.html Accessed June 15, 2023.

Buckley, Chris. "Chinese Tycoon Criticizes Leader, and Wins Surprising Support," NYT, March 21, 2023. https://cn.nytimes.com/china/20160321/c21chinaren/dual/ Accessed May 23, 2023.

Buckley, Chris. "Dissident Journalist Held Ahead of Tiananmen Anniversary," NYT, May 8, 2014, https://cn.nytimes.com/china/20140508/c08journalist/dual/ Accessed May 19, 2023.

Buckley, Chris. "Journalist Gao Yu who had been Charged with Leaking State Secrets Received Two Year Sentence Reduction and to Serve the Term out of Jail," NYT, November 26, 2015. https://cn.nytimes.com/china/20151126/c26gaoyu/ Accessed June 8, 2023.

Buckley, Chris. "Xue Manzi Warns VIP Bloggers by Using Himself as an Example," NYT April 18, 2014 https://cn.nytimes.com/china/20140418/c18xue/ Accessed June 9, 2023.

ChinaAid, "Gao Yu Leaking State Secrets—Document No. 9," April 17, 2015.https://www.chinaaid.net/2015/04/blog-post_19.html Accessed June 7, 2023.

Chu Tuanzhang. "Rise of Fall of Investigative Reporting: Where are the Investigative Journalists?" Sina, July 23, 2018. https://tech.sina.com.cn/csj/2018-07-23/doc-ihftenhz2197657.shtml. Accessed May 12, 2023.

Feng Gao and Jia Ao, "Beijing Rights Attorney Liu Xiaoyuan Stripped of License After Online Photo," RFA, June 19, 2019. https://www.rfa.org/english/news/china/license-06192019121640.html Accessed June 12, 2023.

Forsythe, Michael. "Chinese Publication, Censored by Government, Exposes Article's Removal," NYT, March 8, 2016. https://www.nytimes.com/2016/03/09/world/asia/china-censorship-caixin-media.html Accessed May 24, 2023.

Gan, Nectar. "Want to Escape Poverty? Replace Pictures of Jesus with Xi Jinping, Christian Villagers Urged," South China Morning Post, November 14, 2017. https://www.scmp.com/news/china/policies-politics/article/2119699/praise-xi-jinping-not-jesus-escape-poverty-christian Accessed June 5, 2023.

Gao Jie and Han Jie, "Written into the Government Report for the First Time, "Maintaining Cyber Security" Has Been Raised to an Issue of National Strategy," People's Daily Online, March 8, 2014. http://media.people.com.cn/n/2014/0308/c40733-24573359.html Accessed June 27, 2023.

Guan, Jun. *Silencing Chinese Media: The "Southern Weekly" Protests and the Fate of Civil Society in Xi Jinping's China.* Translated by Kevin Carrico. Lanham: Roman & Littlefield, 2020.

Guo Yongguo. "General Administration of Press and Publication Issued a Document Guiding the Institutional Reforms in Newspaper Editing Offices," August 10, 2012. https://www.gov.cn/gzdt/2012-08/03/content_2197787.htm Accessed May 31, 2023.

He Qinglian. "The Localization Strategy of China's Great External Propaganda," Human Rights in China (HRIC), October 19, 2010; https://hqlenglish.blogspot.com/2011/06/localization-strategy-of-chinas-great.html Accessed March 22, 2024.

Hernandez, Javier C. "'We're Almost Extinct': China's Investigative Journalists Are Silenced Under Xi," NYT, July 15, 2019. https://cn.nytimes.com/china/20190715/china-journalists-crackdown/dual/ Accessed May 29, 2023.

Hernandez, Javier C., and Audrey Carlsen, "Why Xi Jinping's (Airbrushed) Face Is Plastered All Over China," NYT, November 9, 2017. https://www.nytimes.com/interactive/2017/11/09/world/asia/xi-propaganda.html Accessed June 5, 2023.

Hu Tao. "Mo Yan: No Regret Having Hand-copied the Yan'an Talk. It Has Reasonable Elements," Phoenix New Media, October 12, 2012.https://culture.ifeng.com/huodong/special/2012nuobeierwenxuejiang/content-3/detail_2012_10/12/18218915_0.shtml Accessed June 5, 2023.

Investment in News and Media Service," Voice of America (VOA), October 18, 2021. https://www.voachinese.com/a/china-outlaws-privately-funded-news-outlets-20211018/6274911.html Accessed May 31, 2023.

Jacobs, Andrew. "Chinese Professor Who Advocated Free Speech Is Fired," NYT, December 11, 2013, https://cn.nytimes.com/china/20131211/c11professor/dual/ Accessed May 19, 2023.

Kou, Tianli, "Professor Cai Xia of Central Party School of the CCP Got Denounced after Defending Ren Zhiqiang," RFA, February 28, 2016. https://www.rfa.org/mandarin/Xinwen/12-02282016155135.html Accessed May 23, 2023.

Kuo, Mercy A. "China's Media Market Competition: Insights from Kecheng Fang," The Diplomat, December 7, 2017. https://thediplomat.com/2017/12/chinas-media-market-competition/ Accessed June 5, 2023.

LaFraniere, Sharon and Jonathan Ansfield. "In Obama Interview, Signs of China's Heavy Hand," The New York Times (NYT), Nov. 19, 2009. https://www.nytimes.com/2009/11/20/world/asia/20china.html Accessed May 17, 2023.

Li Jiming, "Why Should Netizens Give Ren Zhiqiang a Lesson of the Party," Qianlong, February 22, 2016. https://china.qianlong.com/2016/0222/380735.shtml Accessed May 23, 2023.

Li Wenke, "Central Commission for Discipline Inspection of the CCP: Lu Wei, former Deputy Minister of the Central Publicity Department, Suspected of Serious Violation of Discipline, is under Party Investigation," Reuters, November 21, 2017. https://www.reuters.com/article/china-ccdi-luwei-investigation-1122-idCNKBS1DM04J Accessed May 24, 2023.

Li Yandan, "CAC Commissioner Lu Wei Talks about Social Responsibilities with "Big V"s on the Internet," August 12, 2013.https://web.archive.org/web/20131228225022/http://news.xinhuanet.com/2013-08/12/c_132621768.htm Accessed June 9, 2023.

Lin, Liza. "China Targets News Media in Xi Jinping's Campaign to Expand Communist Party Control," Wall Street Journal (WSJ), October 12, 2021.

Lin, Xin. "The Revelation of the Seven Speak-nots at Universities Has Caused Controversies," Radio Free Asia (RFA), May 10, 2013, https://www.rfa.org/mandarin/yataibaodao/kejiaowen/gx-05102013112922.html Accessed May 20, 2023.

Lina Yang and Xuemei Chang, "Gao Yu Arrested by Beijing Police, Accused of Leaking State Secrets to Foreign Agencies," People's Daily Online. May 8, 2013. http://cpc.people.com.cn/n/2014/0508/c87228-24992668.html Accessed June 8, 2023.

Mao Zedong. "Talk at the Yan'an Forum on Literature and Art, May 1942," Marxists.https://www.marxists.org/reference/archive/mao/selected-works/volume-3/mswv3_08.htm Accessed June 3, 2023.

Miao, Weishan, Min Jiang, and Yunxia Pang. "Historicizing Internet Regulation in China: A Meta-Analysis of Chinese Internet Policies (1994–2017)," *International Journal of Communication* 15 (2021), 2022, 2003.

Myers, Steven Lee. "'Please Save Us!' Grim Scenes in China as Flood Inundates a Subway," NYT, July 21, 2021. https://cn.nytimes.com/china/20210721/china-flooding-zhengzhou-subway/dual/ Accessed June 6, 2023.

New York Times Beijing Office, "Judicial Interpretations Might Cause Further Restrictions on the Freedom of Speech," NYT, September 13, 2013. https://cn.nytimes.com/china/20130911/cc11libel/ Accessed May 25, 2023.

Pan, Philip. *Out of Mao's China: The Struggle for Soul of a New China.* New York: Simon & Schuster, 2008. 256–257.

Perlez, Jane. "For China's Leading Investigative Reporter, Enough Is Enough," NYT, June 11, 2019. https://cn.nytimes.com/china/20190611/china-journalist-liu-wanyong/ Accessed May 29, 2023.

Repnikova, Maria. *Media Politics in China: Improvising Power under Authoritarianism* (New York: Cambridge University Press, 2017), 211.

Shang Qing, "Xi Jinping is in Direct Control of China's Cyberspace Security," BBC News, February 27, 2014. https://www.bbc.com/zhongwen/simp/china/2014/02/140227_china_xi_web_security Accessed May 24, 2023. The Leading Group would be renamed Central Cyberspace Affairs Commission in 2018.

Shi Jingnan. "Training of News Gatherers under way to Prepare for Their License Tests for 2019," Xinhua News Agency, October 11, 2019. http://www.xinhuanet.com/politics/2019-10/11/c_1125092734.htm Accessed May 24, 2023.

Sonmez, Felicia. "China's People's Daily Runs 11 Xi Jinping Headlines on its Front Page," WSJ, December 14, 2015. https://www.wsj.com/articles/BL-CJB-28272 Accessed June 5, 2023.

Tatlow, Didi, Kirsten "Hidden Message Suspected on Chinese Front Page, and Speculation Swirls," NYT, March 3, 2016. https://cn.nytimes.com/china/20160303/c03chinapaper/dual/ Accessed May 24, 2023.

Wang Jianing. "China Requires Tens of Thousands of Journalists to Take Online Tests on Xi Thoughts," BBC, October 14, 2019. https://www.bbc.com/zhongwen/simp/chinese-news-50039867 Accessed May 24, 2023.

Wu Yu. "Xi Jinping's 8.19 Talk Widely Spread: Show the Sword to Grab Positions," DW News, November 7, 2013. https://www.dw.com/zh/%E4%B9%A0%E8%BF%91%E5%B9%B3819%E8%AE%B2%E8%AF%9D%E7%83%AD%E4%BC%A0%E4%BA%AE%E5%89%91%E6%8A%A2%E9%98%B5%E5%9C%B0/a-17212550 Accessed June 8, 2023.

Xi Jinping. "Keep the Big Picture in Mind, Grasp Big Trends, and Focus on Big Events. Strive to Do a Better Job in the Propaganda Work," People's Daily Online, August 21, 2013. http://jhsjk.people.cn/article/22636876 Accessed June 8, 2023.

Ye Bing. "7.20 Flooding Catastrophe in Zhengzhou: How much Natural Cause? How much Human Error?" VOA, August 8, 2021. https://www.voachinese.com/a/china-zhengzhou-floods-investigation-causes-effects-politics-20210808/5994418.html Accessed June 6, 2023.

Zhang Ping. "Evidence of Speech Crime: Reposted 500 Times," DW News, September 10, 2013.https://www.dw.com/zh/%E8%A8%80%E8%AE%BA%E7%BD%AA%E8%AF%81%E8%BD%AC%E5%8F%91500%E6%AC%A1/a-17080719 Accessed May 25, 2023.

Zhen, Jiang. "Chinese Government Reiterates the Ban on Private Investment in News and Media Service," *Voice of America (VOA)*, October 18, 2021. https://www.voachinese.com/a/china-outlaws-privately-funded-news-outlets-20211018/6274911.html Accessed May 31, 2023.

Zheng Hanliang. “Xi Jinping’s 8.19 Talk in the Internally Circulated Version: Internet to Cause the Demise of the Party and the State,” Radio France Internationale (RFI), November 6, 2013. https://www.rfi.fr/cn/%E4%B8%AD%E5%9B%BD/20131106-%E4%B9%A0%E8%BF%91%E5%B9%B3819%E8%AE%B2%E8%AF%9D%E4%BC%A0%E8%BE%BE%E7%89%88%EF%B-C%9A%E4%BA%92%E8%81%94%E7%BD%91%E4%BA%A1%E5%85%9A%E4%BA%A1%E5%9B%BD Accessed June 8, 2023.

Zheng Hanling. “Middle Schooler Became the Youngest Detainee Violating the Law of Internet Rumor Reposted 500 Times,” RFI, September 23, 2013. https://www.rfi.fr/cn/%E4%B8%AD%E5%9B%BD/20130923-%E5%88%9D%E4%B8%AD%E7%94%9F%E2%80%9C%E7%BD%91%E8%B0%A3%E2%80%9D%E8%A2%AB%E8%BD%AC%E5%8F%91500%E6%AC%A1%E6%88%90%E4%B8%BA%E2%80%9C%E4%B8%A4%E9%AB%98%E7%BD%91%E7%BB%9C%E2%80%9D%E6%9C%80%E5%B9%B4%E8%BD%BB%E5%88%91%E6%8B%98%E7%8A%AF Accessed May 25, 2023.

Zhou Wei and Shi Jingnan. “Ministry of Public Security to Start a Special Operation Focusing on Cyber-crimes,” Central People’s Government of the People’s Republic of China, June 18, 2013. https://www.gov.cn/jrzg/2013-06/18/content_2428774.htm Accessed June 9, 2023.

Zhu Nianfeng, Liping Zheng, and Xueling Wang. “Hot Topics in the Ideological and Theoretical Spheres in 2013,” People’s Daily Online, January 13, 2014. https://web.archive.org/web/20180915111310/http://theory.people.com.cn/n/2014/0113/c143843-24096298.html Accessed June 8, 2023.

CHAPTER THREE

China's Shift to Personalistic Rule: Xi Jinping's Centralization of Political Power

Xiaojia Hou

San Jose State University

Abstract: *There have been three generations of Chinese leadership since Mao Zedong pursued the establishment of collective leadership and a balanced power structure between the Party and the state. However, since Xi Jinping's ascent to power in 2012, he has deviated from this trajectory. This chapter aims to examine the consequential shifts initiated by Xi in the decision-making processes, along with the elevation of his own authority within the Party. Specifically, it explores how Xi Jinping assimilated lessons from the disintegration of the Soviet Union to redefine party leadership, drew inspiration from Mao to enforce ideological rule, implemented Maoist-style campaigns to consolidate personal hegemony, restructured the roles of the Party and the state, and exercised control over historical narratives to bolster his legitimacy.*

Keywords: Xi Jinping; Xi administration; Party-state; Chinese politics; Personalistic rule

Three generations of Chinese leaders after Mao Zedong had strived to establish collective leadership, decentralize authority, and strike a power balance between the Party and the state. In November 2012, Xi Jinping was elected by the 18th Party Congress as the General Secretary of the Central Committee of the Communist Party of China (CC CCP) and took the post of Chairman of the Central Military Commission (CMC). In the following March he assumed the President of the People's Republic of China (PRC) at the 12th National People's Congress (NPC). Although he inherited the three most prominent positions and was officially the leader of China, it was then generally believed that the "collective leadership" principle would continue and Xi "was a relatively weak, conciliatory figure surrounded by the cautious protégés of Jiang [Zemin] and Hu [Jintao]."[1] Contrary to this view, however, at the 19th Party Congress Xi filled the top positions of the Politburo Standing Committee (PSC) with

1 Fewsmith, "The 19th Party Congress."

mostly his supporters.[2] In the 20th Party Congress, all the members of PSC and the Politburo were considered Xi's adherents.[3] Not only did Xi secure his third term as the Party leader, he also avoided naming a successor. In ten years, Xi Jinping dramatically centralized authority under his personal leadership. This may lead us to wonder—how did he achieve it?

Chinese scholars have published a great deal of studies on Xi's accomplishments, but few could criticize Xi.[4] Foreign government agencies and think tanks followed Xi's policies promptly and provided a variety of reports.[5] A number of political analysts closely watched Chinese politics and shared their views.[6] Scholars published manuscripts on Xi's China, particularly on Xi's anti-corruption campaigns, regarding which several theories about Xi's objective have emerged.[7] However, most of these studies focus on current issues, and are weak at contextualizing Xi's strategies in a historical perspective. A few reporters and scholars noticed similarities between Xi Jinping and Mao Zedong, but did not provide analysis in detail.[8] By adopting a historical lens, this chapter sheds light on Xi's pursuit of personalistic rule. In particular, it examines how Xi assimilated lessons from the disintegration of the Soviet Union to redefine party leadership, drew inspiration from Mao to enforce ideological rule, implemented Maoist-style campaigns to consolidate personal hegemony, restructured the roles of the Party and the state, and exercised control over historical narratives and linguistic constructs to bolster his legitimacy.

For Xi Jinping, it was vital that CCP should not repeat the fate of the Communist Party of the Soviet Union (CPSU). Right after Xi's ascent to power, he asked in an internal meeting, "Why did the Soviet Union disintegrate? Why did the Communist Party of the Soviet Union collapse?" He found that because of persistent intense

[2] Economy calculates four of the seven members of the PSC and 15 out of 18 Politburo members were allies of Xi. Economy, *The Third Revolution*, p18.

[3] Wu, "Killing."

[4] One main source for Chinese scholars is a four-volume collection of speeches and writings by Xi Jinping, *The Governance of China*.

[5] For example, the internet assessable ones include Economic and Security Review Commission, *2022 Report*; European Council on Foreign Relations, China's "New Era".

[6] To name a few, Nathan Andrew, Wu Guoguang, and Susan L. Shirk.

[7] The most popular one is that Xi primarily used the campaign to purge the rivals and consolidate power. Pei, *China's Crony Capitalism*. Li Cheng contends that the campaign aims to address public disillusionment and enhance the Party's legitimacy. Li, *Chinese Politics*. Yuen Yuen Ang examines the economic dimensions of the anti-corruption campaign and discusses how the campaign aligns with Xi's economic reform agenda and the pursuit of market efficiency. Ang. *China's Gilded Age*. Bell discusses the importance of moral values in Chinese governance and suggests that Xi Jinping's anti-corruption campaign aims to strengthen moral standards and promote a more virtuous political culture. Bell, *The China Model*.

[8] Zhao, "Xi Jinping's."

ideological struggles, the CPSU negated its own history, negated the legacies of Lenin and Stalin, and thus lost the control of party organizations at all levels. He reasoned, "the disintegration of a regime often starts from the ideological area," and once "ideological defenses are breached, other defenses become very difficult to hold." The CCP must learn from it.[9] In the same year, all the CCP members were required to watch a documentary film on the fall of the CPSU titled "20 years' Reflection on Soviet Communist Party's Decline" (*sulian wangdang wangguo ershinian ji*).[10] The film made it clear that, even as the Soviet people continued to overwhelmingly support the CPSU, corruption and ideological confusion drove Soviet leaders like Mikhail Gorbachev and Boris Yeltsin to weaken the Party and destroy it from above and within.[11] In the 1950s, the Soviet Union was China's guide, but in 2013, it became a dire warning that yesterday's USSR may become China's tomorrow.[12] To prevent a similar failure, three actions were critically needed: to revive the faith in ideology, to reinvigorate political campaigns, particularly against corruption, and to strengthen the authority of the CCP.

Section 1 The Return of Ideological Rule

In a 2004 television interview, Xi, who was then a provincial leader, said, "I truly see myself as a Yan'an native," "even now, many of the fundamental ideas and basic features that I've developed were formed in Yan'an."[13] At the time few people saw this as more than just rhetoric, but in hindsight, it was a prophecy. Xi was firm that "the selection of path is a life-or-death issue for the future of the CCP," and he told the new leadership in early 2013 that "we should unswervingly uphold socialism with Chinese characteristics."[14] Then, in May, 2013, the "directive on the current state of the ideological field" was quickly circulated. This document identified seven perceived threats to the Party's power: constitutional democracy in the West, universal values, civil society, neoliberalism, Western media views such as freedom of the press, promotion of historical nihilism, and doubts about Chinese economic reforms. Xi's administration called to prevent the proliferation of the above-mentioned materials into China via the Internet or other media.[15] What was more important was to restore faith in socialism. Recognizing that Marxist

[9] Xi, "2013 nian" (Speech on January 5, 2013).

[10] *World Socialism Research Center, Sulianwangdang (20 years' reflection).*

[11] Shirk, "China in Xi."

[12] Borokh, "From Rethinking."

[13] Buckley, "An Interview."

[14] Xinhua, "Xi Jinping: Pursuing."

[15] Kojiam, "Politics under Xi."

ideals had become little more than empty slogans, Xi searched for a new ideological package to legitimize the rule of the CCP. What he discovered was the so-called "Chinese Dream." In the following decade, he and the state-controlled media would fill this term with historical, cultural, ideological and personal essence.

The Creation of the "Chinese Dream"

Two weeks after his November election in 2012, Xi announced that he "firmly believe[d] that the great dream of the renewal of the Chinese nation will come true." This would be called the "Chinese Dream." The term holds significant meaning, as it bridges the gap between the dialectical and the rhetorical in addition to the argumentative and the storytelling.[16] Under Mao, the Party did not dare encourage people to dream because of material shortages. Conversely, under Xi the government invited people to dream, having recognized China's remarkable economic and geopolitical success in the past decades. "To dream" was not just encouraged, but also an obligation. The crucial aspect of the plan was to foster a shared dream, allowing individuals to find common ground in their aspirations.[17] When Xi first deployed the term in 2013, he spoke that "everyone has an ideal, ambition and dream," but "in my opinion, achieving the rejuvenation of the Chinese nation has been the greatest dream of the Chinese people since the advent of modern times." Xi claimed this was not just shared by people at a particular time: "this dream embodies the long-cherished hope of several generations of the Chinese people, gives expression to the overall interests of the Chinese nation and the Chinese people, and represents the shared aspirations of all the sons and daughters of the Chinese nation."[18] The "Chinese Dream" not only recognized the significant process of individualization that took place within Chinese society during this period; more significantly, it evoked emotions like pride, confidence, hope, and excitement that eventually served Xi's nationalist political mission.[19]

The Chinese dream has multi-layered components. Fundamentally, it is the fulfillment of Marxism-based socialism, but the dream also embraces the revival of Chinese culture and nationalism. For example, in November 2013, Xi Jinping visited the hometown of Confucius and paid homage to the sage. Xi said, "the development and prosperity of Chinese culture is one of the preconditions for China's great rejuvenation. The moral standards passed on by forefathers should be inherited, adapting ancient forms for present-day use and weeding through the old

[16] Brown, "Knowing and Feeling."

[17] Ibid.

[18] State Council Information Office, *The Governance of China.*

[19] Brown, "Knowing and Feeling."

to bring out the new."[20] In 2014, Xi claimed three times that he "gets intimate with 'Confucian teaching.'"[21] Xi considered the Party a faithful successor and promoter of China's excellent traditional culture.[22] As Chapter One investigates, Xi constantly seeks to find a traditionalist basis of legitimacy for his regime.

Nationalism is another crucial cornerstone of the dream, as will be discussed in Chapter Ten. Going along with the Chinese Dream is the concept of "a new era." As Xi stated on July 26, 2017, from 1949 onwards, China had gone through a "historic rise from standing up (1949–1976), growing rich (1978–2012) to getting strong (2012 onwards)," and it was time to enact a new era of socialist modernization.[23] This speech may have contributed to the final term "Xi Jinping Thought on Socialism with Chinese Characteristics for a New Era (*Xi Jinping xinshidai zhongguo tese shehuizhuyi sixiang*)."[24] The term "new era" provided a common starting point in terminology, and this new era centers on Xi.

Crusade against Historical Nihilism

Since the CPSU had negated its own history, Xi determined not to make the same mistake. In the beginning of 2013, Xi cautioned the new CCP leadership of the old Chinese saying, "to destroy a country, one must first erase its history." Xi warned, "hostile forces at home and abroad often use China's revolutionary history and the history of New China to attack, discredit and defame them."[25] Therefore, the interpretation of CCP and PRC history became a crucial political issue where Xi waged war against historical nihilism.

The government promoted the preservation of historical sites, the commemoration of revolutionary heroes, and the promotion of patriotic education to instill a sense of national pride and unity.[26] For example, in 2015, Xi made a highly symbolic visit to Yan'an, a key site during the revolution years. During his visit, Xi emphasized the importance of studying and promoting the history of the Party's revolutionary activities in Yan'an. He called for a renewed focus on the principles of Marxism-Leninism, Mao Zedong Thought, and the Party's revolutionary traditions. After the visit, Yan'an became a hotspot for tourism. The city saw more than 40.25 million tourist visits in 2016, which rose to 73.08 million in 2019. Red tourism flourished hence after. Official data show that from 2014 to 2019, the number of such trips rose

[20] Xinhua, "Chinese President Xi."
[21] Cui, "yinian nei" (Getting intimate).
[22] Tatlow, "China's Cosmological Communism."
[23] Ren, *Xuexi guanche* (Studying), p 1–9.
[24] European Council on Foreign Relations, "China's 'New Era.'"
[25] Xi, "2013 nian."
[26] For a detailed analysis on Xi's utilization of history, see Chapter One.

from 140 million to 1.41 billion.[27] Meanwhile, historical locations related to Xi also became red tourist sites. For example, Liangjiahe, the village where Xi lived for 7 years during the Cultural Revolution, now is an open-air shrine dedicated to him.

To the CCP, it was pivotal to command the historical narrative. The Xi administration intensified censorship over dissenting voices and alternative narratives that deviated from the official Party line. The government tightened control over the media, internet, and education system to ensure that historical narratives align with the Party's ideology. For example, Xi was personally concerned with how Mao Zedong was presented. "Imagine if Comrade Mao Zedong had been totally repudiated. Would our party be able to withstand that?" he asked in early 2013, "would our country's socialist system be able to withstand it?" Xi answered, "they wouldn't, and when they wouldn't, it would be great turmoil under the heavens."[28] Xi emphasized not putting the reform period in opposition to Mao's era. He asserted that without the foundations established by Mao, "reforms and openness would have had a very difficult time moving forward successfully."[29] Disastrous events like the Great Famine and the Cultural Revolution were downplayed and criticism of Mao's years were nearly eliminated from media. In other words, the several decades that China spent developing within the framework of the Soviet model were regarded a constructive stage, and denying the historical importance of this stage was unacceptable.[30]

In 2017, on the centenary of the Russian Revolution of 1917, Liu Qibao, Politburo member and head of CC CCP Propaganda Department, assessed that the Russian Revolution "opened an unprecedented new model of modernization in world history," which allowed the USSR to quickly transform a "state of small peasants" into a world industrial power. He admonished the audience that "the epoch-making historical achievements of the October Revolution and the enormous successes of the Soviet socialist system achieved in the past are by no means canceled out by the dissolution of the USSR."[31] Xi and his circle undoubtedly acknowledged the shortcomings of the Soviet model. Nevertheless, the task of examining the Soviet experience as a "mirror" was much broader than just criticizing the USSR, but rather objectively evaluating Soviet modernization practices.[32] From this perspective, the Soviet experience served as a starting point for the CCP, which then

[27] Red tourism refers to Chinese people visiting locations with historical significance to Chinese communism. *China Daily*, "Red tourism."

[28] Buckley, "Chinese President Returns."

[29] Xi, "guanyujianchi" (Several Questions).

[30] Borokh, "From Rethinking."

[31] Liu, "在 'shiyue'" (Speech at).

[32] Zhou, "bunengdui" (There should be).

developed its own path of socialist construction.[33] This new assessment indicated that Xi could reinstate practices and policies of Mao Zedong's and Soviet origins.

Re-certification of Historical Narratives

Efforts to stream the official history reached its peak in the release of the "Resolution of the Central Committee of the Communist Party of China on the Major Achievements and Historical Experience of the Party over the Past Century," (hereafter as the Resolution) in July 2021.[34] Historically, the CCP has only released three resolutions on the Party history. Mao released the resolution on "Certain Questions in the History of Our Party" in 1945, through which he inserted an official narrative of the CCP history and confirmed his leadership of the Party. In 1981, Deng Xiaoping promoted the approval of the "Resolution on Certain Questions in the History of Our Party since the Founding of the People's Republic of China" which criticized Mao's major mistakes, thus facilitated Deng's reform. This one, offered Xi's view of the Party's past and how he would want to be remembered in history.

The Resolution was divided into four sections. The first one was about the great victory of the Communist Revolution. It began with China as a splendid civilization weakened by the aggression of Western Powers. The CCP, headed by an infallible Mao and armed with Marxism, saved China. The second part was on socialist construction under Mao who aimed to "integrate the basic tenets of Marxism-Leninism with China's realities." Mao Zedong Thought was "a summation of theories, principles, and experience on China's revolution and construction that has been proven correct through practice, and put forward a series of important theories for socialist construction." It quickly glazed over mistakes like the Great Leap Forward. The Resolution maintained Deng's evaluation that the Cultural Revolution was catastrophic, but blamed it mainly on the Gang of Four instead of Mao. The next section was about the Reform Era. According to the Resolution, Deng Xiaoping, Jiang Zemin and Hu Jintao all focused on questions of "what socialism is and how to build it" and "what kind of party to build and how to build it" in order to explore the best path to building socialism in China. The last section was about the New Era of Socialism with Chinese Characteristics. It appraised 13 sectors in which Xi has inherited problems from his predecessors that he has resolved or is solving. Xi's success was dazzling, as the words in this section exceeded the first three combined.[35]

The Resolution adopted Marxist dialectic materialism. As the history advances through the three stages of thesis, antithesis and synthesis, the Resolution presented

33 Borokh, "From Rethinking."

34 Xinhua, "Resolution."

35 Ibid.

"Mao as the thesis, Deng Xiaoping as the antithesis who reacted against certain excesses of Mao, and Xi Jinping as the synthesis who incorporated the best of Mao and Deng."[36] All the CCP leaders sought to answer the question of "what socialism is," and in the end, "Xi Jinping Thought on Socialism with Chinese Characteristics for a New Era" provided the answer to this question, "on the basis of adapting the basic tenets of Marxism to China's specific realities and its fine traditional culture."[37] The Resolution substantivized the "four upholds" through recounting history. The first was "uphold Marxism," the second "uphold the Chinese Communist Party," the third "uphold the Central Committee" and the fourth, "uphold Comrade Xi Jinping's core position on the Party Central Committee and in the Party as a whole."[38]

The official narrative presented a historical perspective that emphasized the importance and inevitability of past events while maintaining a consistent notion of progress that ultimately reached its pinnacle in the Xi Jinping era. The Resolution demonstrated Xi's exceptional accomplishments in Marxist theory, implying that he was philosophically more "correct" than Mao Zedong or Deng Xiaoping, which paved the way for Xi's ascendancy to theoretical leader within the Party.[39]

Elevation of Xi as the Theoretical Leader

The constitution of the CCP can be amended only once in five years, during the National Party Congress. The Party constitutions have persistently held Marxist-Leninism and Mao Zedong Thought as the official ideology. Before Xi, no current leaders' name was listed in the constitutions. In 1997, after Deng's death, "Deng Xiaoping theory" was announced as a new addition to Marxist-Leninism and Mao Zedong Thought. In 2002, Jiang Zemin's name was included in the constitution, and his "Theory of Three Represents" (*sange daibiao*) was pronounced as the most recent development in the ideology, but this did not bear Jiang's name in the 2002 constitution. The same rule applied to Hu Jintao in the 2012 version of the Party constitution. However, Xi Jinping departed from this tradition. In 2017, the 19th Party Congress enshrined Xi Jinping's theory into the new Party constitution, known as "Xi Jinping Thought on Socialism with Chinese Characteristics for a New Era." This was the first time since Mao's era that a current Chinese leader's political ideas have been named and included in the Party constitution. Furthermore, the phrase "leadership core" was applied to Xi in an unprecedented way. In the following year, the 13th NPC revised the PRC constitution and mentioned Xi Jinping Thought

36 Introvigne, "Resolution on CCP History."
37 Xinhua, "Resolution."
38 Ibid.
39 Introvigne, "Resolution on CCP History."

in the preamble.[40] In the same year, the Party Discipline Punishment Ordinance was revised to incorporate the doctrine of the "two safeguards" (*liangge weihu*). It bound party members to "safeguard the 'core' status of General Secretary Xi Jinping within the CCP" and "to safeguard the centralized authority of the Party."

The aforementioned documents laid the textual foundation for Xi Jinping's position as the core and served as a theoretical confirmation of his role as China's paramount leader. Meanwhile, Xi launched a series of mass campaigns to broadcast these ideals and eliminate dissenting voices.

Section 2 Regime of Campaigns

Taking valuable insights from Mao's approaches, Xi swiftly initiated a range of campaigns from the very outset of his leadership to fortify his authority, beginning with a seemingly popular anticorruption campaign.

Ever-expanding Anticorruption Campaign

After diagnosing corruption as a major cause of CPSU's fall and recognizing the fact that corruption was a plague to the CCP during the Reform Era, Xi Jinping described corruption as a "matter of life and death" upon assuming office. In his keynote speech in the 18th Party Congress, Xi highlighted corruption as one of the greatest challenges for the Party and pledged to address it through comprehensive and systematic measures. In November 2012, Xi designated the Central Commission for Discipline Inspection (CCDI) as the highest internal-control institution within the Party, for investigating corruption cases, monitoring Party discipline, and enforcing anti-corruption measures.

The anti-corruption campaign was carried out with incredible force. The CCDI conducted rigorous inspections, audits, and disciplinary measures to uncover corrupt practices and illegal activities. The campaign gained momentum with the investigation and prosecution of several high-profile figures. The most notable case was Zhou Yongkang, former security chief and member of the PSC. Aside from Zhou, other prominent convicted officials included: Sun Zhengcai, the youngest member of the 18th Politburo; Ling Jihua, right-hand of former party chief Hu Jintao; Guo Boxiong and Xu Caihou, both members of the 17th Politburo and vice chairmen of the 17th CMC; Bo Xilai, former Chongqing Party Secretary; Su Rong, former Jiangxi Party Secretary. The campaign was certainly a purge with military and security agencies as the primary targets.

[40] Grzywacz, "How Xi."

In Xi's first term, the national disciplinary and supervisory agencies handled 2.674 million leads on problems and disciplined 1.537 million individuals. Among them, more than 8,900 officials were at the ministerial and bureau levels, over 63,000 officials at the county and division levels, and 278,000 grassroots party members. There were 440 cases involving party members and other central cadres at the provincial level, including 43 members of the 18th Central Committee and alternate members of CCP, as well as nine members of the CCDI.[41] Li Ning estimates that these accounts for 10.4 percent of central cadres (*zhongguan ganbu*), while only 1.7 percent of lower or non-ranked were disciplined.[42] Undoubtedly, the ratio of conviction was significantly higher among high-ranking officials.

The anti-corruption campaign became Xi's signal operation. In his second term, the campaign maintained its momentum and convicted over two million cadres.[43] Moreover, Xi Jinping expanded the campaign's reach by strengthening disciplinary measures and regulatory frameworks. The Party initiated stricter internal supervision, auditing, and inspection processes to uncover corrupt practices. During the long duration of this campaign, old institutions were rejuvenated (like CCDI), new institutions were created (such as the National Supervisory Commission, hereafter as NSC), and old ones were sometimes merged with newer ones. Using this process, Xi systematically drew more power into the center and for himself, as will be discussed in the next section.

The campaign also shouldered a broader function of governance. First, it advanced other government policies and programs.[44] For example, the anti-corruption campaign could be easily synchronized with the education movements of the time. It served to validate the campaign for ideology as well through immediate enforcement measures. Furthermore, the anti-corruption campaign officially established a connection between the investigation of political offenses and anticorruption efforts. Prior to the campaign, the relationship between politics and anticorruption remained ambiguous and subject to speculation. By formally linking these two offenses, any uncertainty regarding the "political" aspect of the Party's anticorruption endeavors was eliminated, thereby preserving Xi's ability to enforce political loyalty.[45]

The campaign's scope continued to expand. Investigations targeted not only corruption within the Party but in other sectors, including the military, state-owned enterprises, and the financial industry in order to support a variety of policies

[41] Xinhua, "dangdeshijiu" (The 19th Party Congress).

[42] Li, "Politics of Anticorruption."

[43] Wu, "Killing."

[44] Carothers, "Xi's Anti-Corruption."

[45] Li, "Politics of Anticorruption."

and directives.[46] For example, in January 2018, the Party launched a nationwide anti-crime campaign and instructed the NSC and CCDI to treat anti-crime work as a component of anti-corruption work. Another example was that in 2020, when the NSC and CCDI joined a campaign to root out disloyalty and indiscipline among "political-legal personnel." In 2019 and 2020, the NSC and CCDI investigated corruption within the Belt and Road Initiative. In 2020, after the breakout of Covid-19, the CCDI launched new initiatives against medical corruption.[47]

Revival of Political Campaigns

Rectification campaigns were most famous during Mao's Era. The best-known campaign was the 1942 Yan'an Rectification Campaign through which Mao purged his rivals and established paramount authority. Mao frequently used rectification campaigns as a mechanism to discipline the Party or enforce his policies. In the 1990s, rectification campaigns were rebranded as the Party's Education Programs on Selected Themes (*dangde zhuanti jiaoyu huodong*, hereafter PEP), but occurred with much less frequency. For example, Jiang Zemin organized one PEP during his last term in 1997–2002; Hi Jintao led two PEPs between 2002 and 2012. However, Xi resumed Mao's style and launched three in a single term.[48]

In 2013, Xi initiated his first PEP, called Educational Activities, regarding the Party's Mass-Line Policy (Mass-Line Program). It targeted leading party cadres in order to rectify four types of harmful behaviors, the so-called "four party styles" formula (*sifeng*).[49] This demanded the cadres in the program to conduct self-examination and self-criticism in front of their subordinates and solicit criticism from the latter. In 2014, the Mass-Line Program campaign was replaced by a campaign focusing on self-discipline and honest conduct known as "three-strict and three honest (*sanyansanshi*)."[50] The targets remained high-ranking cadres. In 2016, the Party launched a new campaign called "two-studies and one-become (*liangxue yizuo*)," and this was mandatory for all party members. Two new concepts were introduced during these programs: political discipline (*zhengzhi jilu*) and political protocol (*zhengzhi guiju*). In 2014, Zhou Yongkang was openly denounced for violating political discipline; Su Rong was denounced for violating both political discipline

[46] Carothers, "Xi's Anti-Corruption."

[47] Ibid.

[48] Li, "Politics of Anticorruption."

[49] The Four party-styles are: formalism, bureaucratism, hedonism and prodigality.

[50] The "three honests" are: Be honest in making decisions; Be honest in forging a career; Be honest in personal behavior (zuorenyaoshi). The "three stricts" are: Be strict in moral conduct; Be strict in exercising power; Be strict in disciplining oneself. Available at: https://en.wikipedia.org/wiki/Three_Stricts_and_Three_Honests

and political protocol. These two concepts were vague and fully subjected to the Party leader's interpretation. For instance, they included offenses like "voicing dissenting opinions of central Party policies with the purpose to defy the authority of the Party Centre (*wangyi zhongyang*), "manifesting deceptive obsequiousness regarding important decisions of the Party Centre (*dui zhongyang fangzhen zhengce he zhongda juece bushu yangfeng yinwei*)," "being untruthful and disloyal to the Party (*dui dang buzhongcheng bu laoshi*)" and "resisting investigation of the Party organization (*duikang zuzhi diaocha*)."[51] These offenses resembled the charges given to counter-revolutionaries in Mao's era, which were used arbitrarily.

In Mao's era, Mao was the center of the Party and the country, and so is Xi in his. Lately, Xi Jinping has been preoccupied with shoring up loyalty to himself and the Party. In 2014, the collection of Xi's speeches and works called *Xi Jinping: The Governance of China* was released, which was followed by a nationwide campaign to promote the study of Xi Jinping's lectures and thoughts. In January 2018, Xi called on all officials to remain loyal to the Party "at any time, and under any circumstance."[52] He also revived Mao's practice of requiring all Party officials, including major provincial leaders and the Politburo, to engage in criticism and self-criticism in addition to pledging loyalty to the Party's central apparatus as well as to Xi's position as the core.[53] In 2016, CCP CC issued "Guidelines on Intra-Party Life in the New Situation," demanding the CCP committees at each level regularly organize these meetings, overseen by the Party's disciplinary apparatus. At the central level, Politburo members were required to attend such meetings at least once a year. During these sessions, officials were encouraged to openly acknowledge and repent for their own misconduct while also highlighting the shortcomings of their colleagues.[54] In 2019, the Publicity Department of the CCP distributed software called "Learning and Strengthening the Nation (*xuexi qiangguo*)," specifically designed for teaching Xi's lectures and thoughts.[55]

These rituals serve not only to flatter Xi, but also to impede other politicians from organizing collectively against his rule. Party members are told to shun any "improper discussion" that questions central policies, and the recruitment of new members now requires stricter loyalty standards, as will be discussed in the next section.[56]

[51] Li, "Politics of Anticorruption."

[52] Xinhua. "Xi Asks."

[53] Xinhua. "Xi Stresses."

[54] Doyon. "Clientelism by Design."

[55] Kojiam, "Politics under."

[56] Shirk, *China in Xi's "New Era."*

Section 3 Institutional Concentration of Power

Xi Jinping pronounced proudly in January 2016, "Party, state, military, civilian life, and education. North, south, east, west, and at the center, the Party leads everything (*dang zheng jun min xue, dong nan xi bei zhong,dang shi lingdao yiqie de*)."[57] This section focuses on how Xi constructed a system that strengthened his authority while bolstering the Party's control over the country at the same time. Xi has revived many of Mao's governance strategies, but unlike how Mao disregarded bureaucracy, Xi opted to preserve the bureaucracy as long as it adhered to his prescribed framework and functioned under his close oversight.

Centralizing Decision-making

In the Reform Era, the central government allowed local governments to implement institutional innovation in specific fields, which gave the latter a high level of autonomy when executing policies from above and let them adjust policies to local circumstances. Over the decades, enormous problems accumulated like wasteful over-investment in economic sectors, risky local government debt accumulation and rampant corruption. Xi Jinping was determined to overcome these. Once in power, he immediately reversed the trend toward governmental decentralization and reasserted top-down political steering.[58]

First, in the central party organization Xi added several new "Leading Small Groups (*lingdao xiaozu*, hereafter as LSG)" covering a wide range of areas such as the economy, national security, foreign affairs, and greatly elevated their authority.[59] Each LSG functioned as a high-level decision-making body responsible for policy formulation, coordination, and implementation within its respective domain. The most notable LSG was the "Central Leading Group for Comprehensively Deepening Reforms (*zhongyang quanmian shenhua gaige lingdao xiaozu*)," which oversaw and coordinated major reform initiatives across multiple sectors. Xi was the head of this group, as well as of seven other LSGs.[60] Gradually Xi converted many LSGs into permanent commissions. Many of the LSGs' functions overlapped with ministers of the State Council, and thus de facto took decision-making power away from

[57] Xinhua. "Xijinpingzhuchi" (Xi Jinping Chairs Meeting).

[58] Schubert, "Studying."

[59] The CCP had established LSGs in the 1950s, some groups had important decision making power under Mao. But during the Reform Era, leading small groups usually were tasked oriented, short-term groups.

[60] Carothers, "Xi's Anti-Corruption."

the State Council. Many of their offices were even physically located within the corresponding State Council ministries.[61]

One key component of Deng's reform was to rebuild the Party-state relationship by leaning towards the separation of the Party and the state. Starting from the 1990s, the Party and the state had their own respective responsibilities, with each having separate management of cadres. Xi's administration publicly challenged the notion of party-state separation. In March of 2018, the "Plan to Deepen Reform of Party and State Institutions" (hereafter, Plan to Deepen Reform) was released and adopted at the third Plenary Session of the 19th CCP CC. The Plan to Deepen Reform laid out a comprehensive plan for the transformation of both Party and state structures. It called for the "strengthening of the Party's centralized and unified leadership over the civil servant ranks." Six Party commissions were established that intended to move key functions from the State Councils to party leadership.[62] Of these, the NSC was the most important. It centralized and strengthened anti-corruption efforts by merging various corruption-fighting agencies and expanded the scope of anti-corruption work beyond the Party to cover all public officials—including those in government, judiciary, and state-owned enterprises. The NSC and the CCDI shared offices, organizational structures, and personnel. This arrangement allowed for the seamless integration and coordination of their efforts in combating corruption and enforcing disciplinary measures over the whole public sector.

Other new commissions included the Central Financial and Economic Affairs Commission that consolidated economic policymaking and coordination at the central level; the Central Cyberspace Affairs Commission that oversaw cybersecurity, internet governance, and information management; and the State Administration for Market Regulation which merged several regulatory bodies. These institutions were primarily under the control of the Party, thus ensuring party dominance in key decision-making processes and policy implementation at the expense of state autonomy. Meanwhile, these centralized bodies further concentrated decision-making power in the hands of a few top leaders, and Xi served as head in most of the aforementioned commissions.[63]

[61] He, "Top-Level Design."

[62] Economic and Security Review Commission, *2022 Report*.

[63] As of May 2019, Xi Jinping served as Chairman and Chief of the National Security Commission of the CCP Central Committee, the Central Committee for Finance and Economics, the Central Committee for Foreign Affairs, the Central Committee for Overall Reform, and the Central Cyberspace Affairs Commission.

Monitoring Execution from Above

A top-down government structure enhanced central power, but it also raised concerns about execution from lower levels. One method Xi used to mitigate this was the institutionalization of central inspection teams (*zhongyang xunshizu*, CITs).

The CCP has a longstanding tradition of deploying inspection teams to oversee party and state affairs throughout the country, but it was never a prominent supervisory mechanism. By the late 2000s, the inspection systems had become stagnant and faced various challenges because the teams were often captured by local interests or overwhelmed by their workload. Under Xi, CITs went through a number of reforms. The number of CITs was increased from ten to fifteen in 2016. The appointments of inspection team leaders were no longer permanent. Instead, leaders were replaced after the completion of each task to reduce vulnerability towards local capture and prevent collusion between the inspectors and the inspected. CITs were given more specific, problem-oriented instructions. In 2014, the CCP CC authorized CITs to inspect all institutions under the supervision of the Party Centre, including key Party functionaries and powerful factional strongholds. These included the Department of Propaganda and the Central Secretariat, none of which the CITs previously had access to. State institutions, which had been previously exempted from inspection due to their autonomous status guaranteed in the PRC Constitution (like the National People's Congress and the Supreme People's Courts), were also placed under inspection from CITs.[64]

The comprehensive inspecting power of the CITs enabled them to uncover and collect a great volume of information concerning disciplinary infractions committed by the Party leaders under inspection. At the end of 2017, the CITs had inspected 277 Party committees and Party groups that were directly monitored by the Party Centre; and provincial-level inspection teams inspected more than 8,362 Party committees and Party-groups. The scope of inspection was unparalleled in Party history. In 2017, the Party revised the Inspection Directive to authorize the staffing of Party inspection offices at all administrative levels, which turned the inspection teams into a regular institutional setup with full-time staff.[65]

Some inspections targeted political rivals to aid Xi in solidifying power, but the inspections in general were too broad and complex to only carry out political attacks. They served as a multi-purpose governance tool for information gathering and feedback collection.[66] CITs focused on corruption control in the early years,

[64] Li, "Politics of Anticorruption."

[65] Ibid.

[66] Carothers and Zhang argue that the Xi administration has utilized inspection processes to pursue distinct governance objectives, encompassing the following areas: 1) enhancing the management

but priorities gradually shifted to improve organizational management over time. Scholars find that inspection reports began making fewer references to corruption policies and more to Xi's instructions. After 2016, more extensive measures were enacted to ensure loyalty to the Party leadership compared to anti-corruption.[67]

The Personalization of Power

The increased concentration of power in the hands of Xi Jinping aligned with the simultaneous reinforcement of Party leaders' positions at all levels. While Xi Jinping exerted pressure on senior officials through the Party's disciplinary apparatus, he also granted them greater autonomy regarding personnel recruitment and advancement.[68]

Prior to Xi Jinping's leadership, the CCP had established well-defined mechanisms for recruitment and promotion, and state organs had done the same. For example, the Ministry of Personnel was established in 1988 to take charge of the management of cadres in government organizations, service units, and public enterprises, institutionally independent from the CCP. However, the Plan to Deepen Reform in 2018 absorbed the State Administration for Public Service, which oversaw civil servants—now 10 million in number, into the Party's Central Organization Department. The Organization Department was also to exert direct control over the State Commission Office for the Public Sector, which was in charge of allocating personnel and organizational resources. These institutional changes put the Party in direct control of all personnel management and human resource allocations for both the party and the government.[69]

Meanwhile, in 2014 and 2019, the Xi administration revised the Work Regulations on Party and government cadres twice. Before Xi, statistical assessments of performance, particularly the gross domestic product growth of a locality, were a crucial part of the evaluation. The 2014 version added more factors like the level of employment, public income, technological innovation, education, healthcare, and social security in the assessment. The 2019 revision set forth changes insisting on cadres' moral and political correctness. It introduced a "political standard" as the most important criterion for evaluation. These vague

and organization of targeted institutions; 2) combating corruption; 3) supporting the implementation of overarching policies; 4) reinforcing the role of the Party in governing both governmental and non-governmental institutions; and 5) ensuring allegiance to the Party and its leadership, which includes the promotion of ideology. Carothers, "From Corruption Control."

[67] Ibid.

[68] Doyon, "Clientelism by Design."

[69] Ibid.

terms left much leeway for local party leaders to decide what to focus on when evaluating their subordinates.

The Xi administration also modified the process of promotion evaluation. In the early 2000s, intra-Party democracy procedures were introduced to enhance transparency in the promotion. One significant step was the implementation of "democratic recommendation," which was considered essential in selecting cadres for advancement. Prior to 2019, appointments of leading officials were required to ("had to") go through this process, but the 2019 regulation merely recommended ("should") democratic recommendation. In the selection of central party leadership during the 19th Party Congress, these new practices were already implemented. Instead of relying on internal elections, the selection process for the central party-state leadership was carried out through face-to-face consultations. Instead of a formal voting process, discussions and consultations took place among party members to reach a consensus on appointments. Xi Jinping personally engaged in meetings with 59 senior and retired party-state leaders to solicit their input and advice regarding final personnel decisions.[70]

The increased flexibility given to local Party leaders in recruitment and evaluation procedures tended to reinforce the clientelist aspects of the Party-state cadre management system. A recent survey conducted among Chinese officials revealed that recognition from superiors was considered the most crucial criterion for promotion, surpassing competence or achievements. By granting local Party leaders greater authority and discretion over recruitment and promotion decisions, the subjectivity of the Party secretary becomes increasingly central, just like in Mao's era.[71]

Another maneuver Xi made was in the retirement age. The 1982 PRC Constitution imposed a two-term limit on the state presidency. For party and state officials, Deng Xiaoping had instituted age limits for promotion and a fixed retirement age. Those formulas were widely acknowledged and followed, such as two-term limits for top party posts; and Politburo members being ineligible for reelection after the age of 67.[72] Xi boldly broke the two-term limit rule for the state presidency by revising the PRC constitution in 2018. Although the role of state president was largely symbolic, Xi sent out a clear message that he and his crew would not be bound by the tacit norm. One after another, tacit rules were broken. As Xi breached norms, his personal rule deepened.

70 Ibid.

71 Ibid.

72 Nathan, "China: Back to the Future."

Epilogue

Xi's aforementioned actions corresponded to and reinforced each other, bringing his concentration of authority to a new height. In the 20th Party Congress, held in 2022, Xi Jinping solidified his dominant authority over the highest ranks of the CCP. The Politburo consisted of 24 members and not 25 like previous ones. The average age was 63.4, with quite a few members exceeding the normal retirement age. The PSC remained seven members, with Xi Jinping, who had exceeded retirement age, as the eldest. The protégés of Jiang and Hu had been completely pushed out, so all of the members remained were considered Xi's men. For example, 13 new members of the Politburo had all connected to Xi's life experiences.[73] Xi secured his third term of the General Secretary of the Party and "holds all the reigns—he controls the agenda, key people and institutions."[74]

For junior cadres, the anti-corruption campaign has opened up a fast channel for vertical mobility, allowing Xi's protégés to receive "helicopter" promotions. As a result, out of the total 281 standing committee members in the 20th Party Congress, only seven (2.5 percent) had held vice-ministerial positions prior to Xi's leadership. This means that 97.5 percent of the elite members were promoted to provincial party committee positions by Xi. Such a high turnover rate indicates the extensive cadre replacement that has taken place under Xi's leadership.[75] Over the decade, Xi has established a powerful personnel base at his disposal, penetrating deep to the Party ranks.

The 20th Party Congress once again enshrined Xi Jinping Thought and highlighted the importance of Party discipline and loyalty to the Party's leadership. The "two safeguards" were added to the new party constitution, calling for greater unity within the Party and emphasizing the importance of "staying true to the original aspiration and founding mission" of the Party. In December 2023, the Politburo convened a criticism and self-criticism meeting on the study of Xi Jinping Thought, presided over by Xi Jinping.[76]

Xi did not slow down ideological control. A few days after the conclusion of the 20th Party Congress, Xi led the members of PSC to visit Yan'an, and pledged to carry forward the Party's revolutionary legacy and fighting spirit. Particularly, he paid tribute to the Yan'an Rectification Movement and the Seventh Party Congress. To escape the historical cycle of rise and fall, Xi emphasized the need to carry out Party's

[73] Wu, "New Faces."

[74] Merics, "Special Issue."

[75] Wu, "Killing."

[76] Xinhua. "CCP leadership."

self-reform.[77] Xi continued to wage his own rectification campaigns. The most recent one was themed education on studying and implementing Xi Jinping's Thought on Socialism with Chinese Characteristics for a New Era. On March 30, 2023, the CCP decided to launch the program, covering the entire party from top to bottom. To set an example, on the same afternoon, the committee conducted its own study session. Quickly the education activities spread over the nation.[78] Lately, in December 2023, in commemorating the 130th anniversary of Mao's birth, Xi stressed "Mao Zedong Thought is an invaluable spiritual wealth for our Party and will guide our action in the long term," and called to stimulate the historical initiative of the people.[79]

Recently, the "Chinese Dream" has further evolved into the vision of "China Solution" for global governance.[80] For example, the concept of "discourse power" has become increasingly crucial for the CCP to "lead in ideological policy."[81] As explained by the *People's Daily*, "China's discourse system is fundamentally a theoretical expression and linguistic manifestation of China's path," and "we must be able to explain how China's path will succeed in the world and what its significance is for the world."[82] Scholars, media and diplomats are all engaged in the discussion and practice of building discourse power.[83] This development is becoming a critical component of building new ideology that can compete with western ideas and find more legitimacy for the CCP.

In March 2023, the 14th NPC convened and once again unanimously elected Xi as the president of China. It appointed the new State Council, which was considered "surprisingly lightweight."[84] The Executive Committee, composed of ten officials, was entirely made up of first-timers to this post, marking the largest turnover in its history. They were all "yes-men" to Xi.[85] The State Council released its quintennial restricting plan called the "State Council Institutional Reform Plan" (*guowuyuan jigou gaige fang'an*). The plan reshuffled several organizations within the council with a focus on streamlining the state's control over science and technology and overhauling the state's supervision of the entire financial industry.[86]

At the same time, the Party acknowledged the need to "deepen institutional reform in key areas and ensure that the Party's leadership over socialist

77 Xinhua. "Xi urges."
78 Li, "Politics of Anticorruption."
79 Xinhua, "CCP Central Committee."
80 Blanchette, "Xi Jinping's."
81 Eto, "Xi Jinping Administration."
82 Wang, "buduanzengqiang" (Continuously Enhance).
83 For discussions on the topic, see Atlantic Council, "Chinese Discourse Power."
84 Katsuji, "Heavyweight Xi."
85 Li, "China's New State Council."
86 Merics, "Special Issue."

modernization," and thus announced its own reform plan.[87] A Central Commission for Finance will be established to strengthen the Party's centralized and unified leadership over financial work, and a Central Commission for Science and Technology will be set up to enhance the Party's centralized leadership over the work of science and technology. Several other commissions also correspond to the newly formed state ministries.[88] In addition, each commission has its own staff, providing Xi with a power base distinct from that of the governmental bureaucracy. Through the Party commissions, Xi could manage and coordinate the overall direction of the most important policy arenas.[89] Xi's concept of "self-reform" astonishingly reminds us of Mao's "continuous revolution."

Former Prime Minister of Australia, Kevin Rudd, commented that Xi Jinping's ascent to power signifies the resurgence of ideological influence and control.[90] Today, it is unlikely that Xi will encounter any direct challenge from within; rather, everyone else will compete for Xi's favor to advance his or her careers. Nevertheless, it is likely that Xi's rule will encounter similar problems as Mao had.

In the political arena, the first challenge is how to gain access to accurate information and policy options. In Mao's era, information was filtered, data inflated, communications manipulated.[91] As a scholar points out, "the more coercive the regime, the more what passes upward is what leaders want to hear. Negative information is suppressed and its agents repressed."[92] As reliable information fails to ascend the bureaucratic hierarchy, Xi Jinping will find that he is formulating policies with a growing lack of insight and awareness. The Xi administration has not found solutions for this.

Xi's top-down campaigns have reduced the productivity of bureaucrats. For example, qualitative evidence suggests that the anti-corruption campaign has resulted in "administrative slack" among bureaucrats.[93] Xi Jinping will face the challenge of balancing his aspiration for the CCP to exert control over politics and policymaking with the escalating requirement for a capable administrative state to effectively address China's diverse developmental complexities.[94]

87 Xinhua, "China Releases."

88 Ibid.

89 Economy, *The Third Revolution.*

90 Rudd, "The World."

91 Hou. *Negotiating Socialism.*

92 Apter, *Revolutionary Discourse*, p 27.

93 Wang," Frightened Mandarins."

94 Blanchette, "Xi Jinping's."

Another uncertainty is succession. Xi has not signaled any intention to select an heir. By breaking the Party norm on the transition process, creating a new one will become a daunting task, as Mao had eternally faced.[95]

Xi, wearing the shiniest crown, walks on a precarious path.

Dr. **Xiaojia Hou** received her Ph.D. in history from Cornell University in 2008, and her undergraduate and master's degrees in history from Peking University. Her book, *Negotiating Socialism in Rural China: Mao, Peasants, and Local Cadres in Shanxi 1949—1953*, was published by the Cornell East Asian Series (Ithaca, New York) in 2016. She has also published multiple book chapters, articles, and book reviews. Her research agenda centers on China's socialist transformation in the 1950s, particularly on the daily life under Mao Zedong and how nature interacted with politics. She is currently an Associate Professor at the Department of History, San Jose State University.

Bibliography

Ang, Yuen Yuen. *China's Gilded Age: The Paradox of Economic Boom and Vast Corruption*. Cambridge: Cambridge University Press, 2020.

Apter, David and Tony Saich. *Revolutionary Discourse in Mao's Republic*. Cambridge: Harvard University Press, 1998.

Atlantic Council. "Chinese Discourse Power: China's Use of Information Manipulation in Regional and Global Competition." December 2020. Available at: https://www.atlanticcouncil.org/wp-content/uploads/2020/12/China-Discouse-Power-FINAL.pdf

Blanchette, Jude and Evan Medeiros. "Xi Jinping's Third Term." *Survival*, 64:5, 2022, 61–90. DOI: 10.1080/00396338.2022.2126179.

Bell, Daniel A. *The China Model: Political Meritocracy and the Limits of Democracy*. Princeton: Princeton University Press, 2016.

Borokh, O. "From Rethinking the Soviet Model to Searching for China's Path." *World Economy and International Relations*. Vol 65, no 9, 2021, 45–55.

Brown, Kerry. "Knowing and Feeling the 'China Dream': Logic and Rhetoric in the Political Language of Xi's China." *Journal of Current Chinese Affairs*. Vol 51 (3), 2022, 437–455.

Buckley, Chris. "An Interview with Xi, Long Before He Was China's Leader." June 12, 2014. Available at: https://archive.nytimes.com/sinosphere.blogs.nytimes.com/2014/06/12/an-interview-with-xi-long-before-he-was-chinas-leader/. Accessed June 1, 2023.

Buckley, Chris. "Chinese President Returns to Mao's (and His) Roots in Yan'an." February 13, 2015. Available at: https://archive.nytimes.com/sinosphere.blogs.nytimes.com/2015/02/13/chinese-president-returns-to-maos-and-his-roots-in-yanan/, Accessed June 2, 2023.

Carothers, Christopher. "Xi's Anti-Corruption Campaign: An All-Purpose Governing Tool." March 1, 2021. Available at: https://www.prcleader.org/carothers. Accessed June 13, 2023.

[95] Ibid.

Carothers, Christopher and Zhu Zhang. "From Corruption Control to Everything Control: The Widening Use of Inspections in Xi's China." *Journal of Contemporary China*, 32:140, 2023, 225–242. DOI: 10.1080/10670564.2022.2071885.

Cui Xiaosu. "Yinian nei sanci qinjin rujia, Xi jinping weihe ruci qiangdiao zhongshi chuantong wenhua" (Getting intimate with Confucianism: Why Xi Jinping has emphasized regaining traditional culture). September 25, 2014. Available at: http://cpc.people.com.cn/n/2014/0925/c164113-25731729.html, Accessed May 4, 2023.

China Daily. "Red tourism Reinforces Yan'an's Place in History." June 14, 2021. Available at: http://english.www.gov.cn/news/topnews/202106/14/content_WS60d2ce00c6d0df57f98dbb4d.html. Accessed May 20, 2023.

Doyon, Jérôme. "Clientelism by Design: Personnel Politics under Xi Jinping." *Journal of Current Chinese Affairs*. Vol 47, no 3, 2018, 87–110.

Economic and Security Review Commission. *2022 Report to Congress*. Nov 2022. Available at: https://www.uscc.gov/sites/default/files/2022-11/2022_Annual_Report_to_Congress.pdf. Accessed June 2, 2023.

Economy, Elizabeth. *The Third Revolution: Xi Jinping and the New Chinese State*. Cambridge: Oxford University Press, 2018.

European Council on Foreign Relations. "China's 'New Era' with Xi Jinping Characteristics." 2017. Available at: http://www.jstor.com/stable/resrep21567. Accessed June 2, 2023.

Fewsmith, J. "The 19th Party Congress: Rising in Xi Jinping's New Age." *China Leadership Monitor* 55 (Winter 2018): 1–22. Available at: https://www.hoover.org/sites/default/files/research/docs/clm55-jf-final.Pdf. Accessed May 20. 2023.

Grzywacz, Jarek. "How Xi Jinping Used the CCP Constitution to Cement His Power." Available at: https://thediplomat.com/2023/01/how-xi-jinping-used-the-ccp-constitution-to-cement-his-power/. Accessed June 15, 2023.

He, Alex. "Top-Level Design for Supremacy: Economic Policy Making in China under President Xi." *Centre for International Governance Innovation*. May 2020, 6–13.

Hou, Xiaojia. *Negotiating Socialism in Rural China: Mao, Peasants, and Local Cadres in Shanxi 1949–1953*. Ithaca, New York: Cornell East Asia Series, 2016.

Katsuji Nakazawa. "Heavyweight Xi Jinping gives himself a lightweight cabinet." *Nikkei Asia*. March 16, 2023. Available at: https://asia.nikkei.com/Editor-s-Picks/China-up-close/Analysis-Heavyweight-Xi-Jinping-gives-himself-a-lightweight-cabinet

Kojiam, Kazuko. "Politics under Xi Jinping: Centralization and its Implications." *Public Policy Review*. Vol.16, no.3, September 2020.

Introvigne, Massimo. "The Resolution on CCP History." March 15, 2022. Available at: https://bitterwinter.org/the-resolution-on-CPC-history/. Accessed June 5, 2023

Li, Cheng. *Chinese Politics in the Xi Jinping Era: Reassessing Collective Leadership*. Brookings Institution Press, 2016.

Li, Cheng and Mallie Prytherch. "China's new State Council: What analysts might have missed." March 7, 2023. Available at: https://www.brookings.edu/blog/order-from-chaos/2023/03/07/chinas-new-state-council-what-analysts-might-have-missed/. Accessed June 23, 2023.

Li, Ling. "Politics of Anticorruption in China: Paradigm Change of the Party's Disciplinary Regime 2012–2017." *Journal of Contemporary China*, 28:115, 47–63. DOI:10.1080/10670564.2018.1497911

Liu, Qibao. "zai 'shiyue geming yu zhongguo tese shehuizhuyi'lilun yantaohui shang de jianghua" (Speech at the Theoretical Seminar "October Revolution and Socialism with Chinese Characteristics"). *People's Daily*, September 26, 2017.

Minzner, Carl. *End of an Era: How China's Authoritarian Revival is Undermining Its Rise*. Cambridge, Oxford University Press, 2018.

Merics Briefs. "Special Issue: National People's Congress Digest." March 16, 2023. Available at: https://merics.org/en/merics-briefs/special-issue-national-peoples-congress-digest

Nathan, Andrew. "China: Back to the Future." May 10, 2018. Available at: https://www.nybooks.com/articles/2018/05/10/china-back-to-the-future/.

Naoko, Eto. "The Xi Jinping Administration's Desire for Legitimacy: the strategic implication of its 'new political party system.'" *Journal of Contemporary East Asia Studies*, 11:2, 2022, 214–228. DOI: 10.1080/24761028.2023.2197366

Pei, Minxin. *China's Crony Capitalism: The Dynamics of Regime Decay*. Cambridge: Harvard University Press, 2016.

Ren, Zhongwen ed. *Xuexi Guanche Xi Jinping zongshujii 7.26 zhongyao jianghua jingshen* (Studying and thoroughly implementing the spirit of the important speech held by General Secretary Xi Jinping on July 26). Beijing: Renmin Chubanshe, 2017.

Rudd, Kevin. "The World According to Xi Jinping: What China's Ideologue in Chief Really Believes." *Foreign Affairs*. Vol 101: 6–21. 2022.

Schubert, Gunter and Björn Alpermann. "Studying the Chinese Policy Process in the Era of 'Top-Level Design': the Contribution of 'Political Steering' Theory." *Journal of Chinese Political Science*. (2019) 24:199–224. https://doi.org/10.1007/s11366-018-09594-8. Accessed June 14, 2023.

Shirk, Susan L. "China in Xi's "New Era": The Return to Personalistic Rule." *Journal of Democracy*. Vol 29, issue 2, 22–36, 2018.

Stanzel, Angela, Jérôme Doyon, Heike Holbig, Jean Christopher Mittelstaedt and Yevgen Sautin. "China's 'New Era' with Xi Jinping Characteristics." 2017. Available at: http://www.jstor.com/stable/resrep21567

State Council Information Office, Central Policy Research Office of the Central Committee of the Chinese Communist Party) and China International Publishing Group eds. *The Governance of China*. Foreign Languages Press. 2014, 2017, 2020 and 2022.

Tatlow, Didi Kirsten. "China's Cosmological Communism: A Challenge to Liberal Democracies." July 18, 2018. Available at: https://merics.org/en/report/chinas-cosmological-communism-challenge-liberal-democracies. Accessed June 14, 2023.

Wang, Eric. "Frightened Mandarins: The adverse effects of fighting corruption on local bureaucracy." *Comparative Political Studies*. Vol 55 (11), 1807–1843. 2022. https://doi.org/10.1177/00104140211060276.

Wang, Mingchu and Zengzhi Wang. "buduan zengqiang zhongguo huayu tixi de ganzhaoli" (Continuously Enhance the Appeal of China's Discourse System). November 18, 2016. Available at: http://theory.people.com.cn/n1/2016/1118/c40531-28877902.html Accessed June 18, 2023.

World Socialism Research Center of Chinese Academy of Social Science. *Sulian wangdang wangguo ershinian ji:Eluosi ren zai sushuo* (20 years' reflection on Soviet Communist Party's Decline: In the words of the Russian people). Beijing: Dangjian duwu chubanshe, 2012.

Wu, Guoguang. "Killing the Different Dreams, Keeping the Same Regime: Xi Jinping's Ten-Year Struggle to Remake CCP Elite Politics." *China Leadership Monitor*. September 1, 2022. Available at: https://www.prcleader.org/wu-september-2022. Accessed May 14, 2023.

Wu, Guoguang. "New Faces of Leaders, New Factional Dynamics: CCP Leadership Politics Following the 20th Party Congress." *China Leadership Monitor*. December 1, 2022. Available at: https://www.prcleader.org/wu-december-2022. Accessed June 15, 2023.

Xi, Jinping. "2013 nian 1yue 5ri zai xinjin zhongyang weiyuanhui de weiyuan, houbu weiyuan xuexi Guanche dang d eshibada jingshen yantaoban shang de jianghua" (Speech given on January 5th, 2013 at the study seminar on learning and implementing the spirit of the 18th National Congress of the Communist Party of China, for newly elected members and alternate members of the Central

Committee). Available at: http://www.qstheory.cn/zhuanqu/2021-04/08/c_1127308462.htm accessed June 27, 2023.

Xi Jinping. "Secure a Decisive Victory in Building a Moderately Prosperous Society in All Respects and Strive for the Great Success of Socialism with Chinese Characteristics for a New Era." Oct 18, 2017. Available at: https://www.neac.gov.cn/seac/c103372/202201/1156519.shtml

Xi, Jinping. "guanyu jianchi he fazhan zhongguo tese shehuizhuyi de jige wenti" (Several Questions on Adhering to and Developing Socialism with Chinese Characteristics). *Qiushi*, no. 7, 2019. Available at: http:// www.qstheory.cn/dukan/qs/2019-04/01/c_1124307480.htm, Accessed June 3, 2023.

Xinhua. "Xi Jinping: Pursuing a dream for 1.3b Chinese." March 17, 2013. Available at: https://www.chinadaily.com.cn/china/2013npc/2013-03/17/content_16313950_2.htm. Accessed June 1, 2023.

Xinhua. "Chinese President Xi Underlines Morality during Confucius Site Visits." Nov 29, 2013. Available at: http://en.people.cn/102839/8470126.html, Accessed May 18, 2023.

Xinhua. "Xi Jinping zhuchi zhonggong zhongyang zhengzhiju changweihui huiyi" (Xi Jinping Chairs Meeting of the CCP Central Committee's Political Bureau Standing Committee). January 7, 2016. Available at: http://www.xinhuanet.com/politics/2016-01/07/c_1117705534.htm, Accessed June 11, 2023.

Xinhua. "Principal Contradiction Facing Chinese Society Has Evolved in New Era: Xi." October 18. 2017. Available at: http://www.xinhuanet.com/english/2017-10/18/c_136688132.htm

Xinhua. "Dang de shijiuda juxing diyichang jizhe zhaodaihui, jieshao jiaqiang dangjian gongzuo he quanmian congyan zhidang youguan qingkuang" (The 19th Party Congress held the first press conference to introduce the situation of strengthening party building work and comprehensively and strictly governing the party). October 19, 2017. Available at: http://www.xinhuanet.com//politics/19cpcnc/2017-10/19/c_1121828330.htm. Accessed June 17, 2023.

Xinhua. "Xi Stresses Implementation of Major Policies, Integrity of Leading Officials." December 27, 2017. Available at: www.xinhuanet.com/english/2017-12/27/c_136853671.htm. Accessed June 13. 2023.

Xinhua. "Xi Asks Officials to Remain Loyal to Party 'at Any Time, and Under Any Circumstance.'" January 11, 2018. Available at: www.xinhuanet.cothm/english/2018-01/11/c_136888644.htm. Accessed June 15, 2023.

Xinhua. "Resolution of the CCP Central Committee on the Major Achievements and Historical Experience of the Party over the Past Century." November 16, 2021. Available at: http://www.news.cn/english/2021-11/16/c_1310314611.htm. Accessed May 20, 2023.

Xinhua. "Xi Urges Efforts to Carry Forward Great Founding Spirit of CCP and Yan'an Spirit." October 29, 2022. Available at: http://english.www.gov.cn/news/topnews/202210/29/content_WS635c022ac6d0a757729e1e5a.html. Accessed June 20, 2023.

Xinhua. "China Releases Plan on Reforming Party and State Institutions." March 16, 2023. Available at: http://english.www.gov.cn/policies/latestreleases/202303/16/content_WS6413be82c6d0f528699db58e.html. Accessed June 21, 2023.

Xinhua. "CCP Leadership Convenes Criticism and Self-criticism Meeting, Xi Delivers Important Speech." December 24, 2023. Available at: https://english.www.gov.cn/news/202312/24/content_WS658766acc6d0868f4e8e2782.html, accessed January 3, 2024.

Xinhua. "CCP Central Committee Holds Symposium Commemorating 130th Anniversary of Mao's Birth." December 26, 2023. Available at: https://english.www.gov.cn/news/202312/26/content_WS658abd8fc6d0868f4e8e288e.html, accessed January 3, 2024.

Zhao Suisheng. "Xi Jinping's Maoist Revival." *Journal of Democracy*. Vol 27, no. 3, 2016, 83–97. Available at: https://factsanddetails.com/china/cat2/4sub5/entry-5542.html. Accessed June 27, 2023.

Zhou Xincheng. "buneng dui sulian shehui zhuyi moshi caiqu lishi xuwu zhuyi taidu – yu Zuo Fengrong jiaoshou shangque" (There should be no historical nihilistic attitude towards the Soviet model of socialism – discussion with Professor Zuo Fengrong). *Studies on Marxism*, no. 7, 2013, 120–129.

CHAPTER FOUR

Understanding the "Rule of Law" in Xi's China

Qiang Fang

UNIVERSITY OF MINNESOTA DULUTH

Abstract: *In early 2021, while the world was still struggling with Covid 19, Xi Jinping declared that China should construct the socialist "rule of law" with Chinese features. Why did he make such a proclamation? What was his authentic purpose behind his proclamation of the rule of law? To what extent does his notion of the socialist rule of law depart from or resemble the rule of law in previous periods? Addressing those questions will be the main aim of this chapter. While many students around the world have studied Xi's policies since he took the helm in late 2012, most of them have centered on his political, foreign, and economic policies, and only a handful have briefly examined his legal policies and practices. Zheng Yongnian, for example, went as far as to argue in 2016 that Xi genuinely aimed to establish the rule of law in China. However, as evidenced in numerous legal practices from 2014 to early 2023, Xi and Chinese law enforcements had often flouted law in campaigns against corrupt officials, rights lawyers, and dissidents. More important, human rights organizations have accused the Chinese government of exercising extra-legal means such as forced and arbitrary detention, beating, and incarceration navigating pro-democracy activists in Hong Kong. During the rage of the pandemic between 2019 and 2023, massive lockdowns were imposed and forced upon residents across the country, resulting in numerous law violations by police. This study will be the first serious one to delve into Xi Jinping's understandings of the rule of law via in-depth studies of prominent legal cases implicating abduction of Hong Kong booksellers, clampdown of rights lawyers, and the Hong Kong National Security Law. The chapter argues that the legal policies and practices of Xi Jinping's "rule of law" with Chinese features should better be referred to as "Rule of the Party Law" as the CCP and Xi would follow a law only if it fits their needs and create a law if existing laws do not serve their policy.*

Keywords: Xi Jinping; Pandemic; The Rule of Law; Legal traditions

Authors in previous chapters have discussed Xi Jinping's polices in invoking historical lessons, restricting media, and consolidating personal power. This chapter aims at examining Xi's understanding of the rule of law, a term arguably originating in the West. Since Xi Jinping became the head of the Chinese Communist Party (CCP) in late 2012, he has made many comments and emphases on the importance of the rule of law in the PRC. On January 8, 2014, for instance, Xi told cadres in judiciary, law enforcement, and procuratorate that they should unequivocally safeguard the Party's leadership. Echoing his predecessor Jiang Zemin's talk in 1997, Xi spelled out that the Party would not only "lead the people to promulgate the law, but also lead people to enforce the constitution and law." He urged judicial cadres to take the lead in abiding by the law and not to replace the law with their words, suppress the law with their power, and tailor the law for their relatives (*xunsi wangfa*). To demonstrate his belief in the rule of law, Xi emphasized the supremacy of constitution and law and equated them with the Party.[1] While it is Jiang Zemin who first called for the construction of a socialist rule of law in China at the Fifteenth Party Congress in 1997,[2] Xi in late 2014 went farther that China should establish a socialist rule of law with Chinese features.[3] In early 2019, however, Xi seemed to dial back from his 2014 claim that law was supreme in China. He now remarked that law had to be guided by the "socialist thought with Chinese features in the new era (lit. Xi's era)." He demanded that law be under the Party's "absolute leadership" without being aware that it might contradict his effort to fulfill the rule of law.[4] Xi's decision to boost the Party's role over the law showed that he had become more confident and powerful after seven years in power. By then, Xi had not only secured his supremacy inside the Party but also cleared the path for his third term, which had not been seen since the death of Mao Zedong.

In May 2021, about a year and a half after the outbreak of Covid-19, *Seeking Truth* (*qiushi*), one of the most important journals for the CCP, reported Xi's latest speech on the socialist rule of law in China. Xi first traced the history of CCP's efforts in constructing the rule of law and claimed that the Party had promulgated numerous laws and created the "Ma Xiwu Style" to solve peasant marriage cases before it took over China in 1949.[5] During the era of Mao, the Party had also led the people to enact laws such as the 1954 Constitution and Marriage Law and crafted a framework of the socialist legal system. After China reopened to the West in 1978, the Party stressed the rule of law as its basic strategy and method for state management. In addition to doubling down on the leadership of the Party in building a socialist rule of law, Xi touted the unique and excellent legal tradition of China including, among other "traditions," the *minben* (people as the root of the state) concept, the "ideal of no lawsuit (*tianxia wusong*)," "respecting rite and stressing law (*longli zhongfa*)," "virtue first, penalty second (*dezhu xingfu*)," and "promoting virtue and being

1 "Important Speech of Xi Jinping in Central Political and Legal Meeting."

2 Jiang, "Speech at the Fifteenth Party Congress."

3 Xi Jinping, *The Governance of China*, 119.

4 Xi Jinping, "Important Talk of Xi Jinping in Central Political and Legal Meeting."

5 For Ma Xiwu Style see Fang, *Communist Judicial System in China:* Chp 2.

prudent in punishment (*mingde shenfa*)." In the face of the increasingly strained relations between China and the West during the pandemic, Xi prodded the Party to unswervingly rebuke western constitutionalism, separation of power, and judicial independence. China's path toward the "rule of law" had to be based on China's superior national condition and its political institutions.[6]

At the 20th Party Congress in October 2022, the CCP formally endorsed the indefinite extension of Xi's presidency. Reeling from both internal economic downturn and external fraught tensions with the West amid the persistent pandemic and Russia's aggression against Ukraine, Xi appeared unscathed and remained assertive, and in the spring of 2023 laid out his blueprint for a modernization with Chinese characteristics. One of the seminal components of Xi's modernization is legal modernization. In the words of Gong Pixiang, a law professor and former president of Nanjing Normal University, the fundamental platform of a legal modernization with Chinese features proposed by Xi Jinping is to make "people as the center."[7] Feng Guo, president of Wuhan University, provides a more informative illustration of Xi's legal modernization. Quoting Xi's words as saying, "a modern nation must be a nation of the rule of law," Feng asserts that the rule of law is a vital component of modern state management. China's modernization epitomizes "striking logic of the rule of law" and the construction of the rule of law is "the internal request of China's modernization." In conclusion, Feng writes that China's modernization will have an indelible impact on the socialist rule of law in China and ensure that it will be unique as it differs from both the bottom-up model in the West and the top-down model in some East Asian countries. China's legal modernization under Xi will implicate both bottom-up and top-down interactions.[8]

Why does Xi Jinping believe the importance of the rule of law? What kind of rule of law does he mean in his speeches? To what extent is Xi's understanding of the rule of law similar or dissimilar to the classic notions and practice of the rule of law in both the West and China's imperial and republican periods? Why does Xi repeatedly push forward the rule of law with Chinese features? How does Xi's rule of law differ from other CCP leaders after the Cultural Revolution? In this chapter, I will try to answer those questions and the first step is to parse Xi's understanding of the rule of law. Then I will compare Xi's description of the rule of law with the classic notions of the rule of law in the West and from Chinese leaders in the imperial and republican periods. Third, by examining several well-known legal cases such as the kidnapping of Hong Kong booksellers, attacks on the rights lawyers, and the imposition of a national security law in Hong Kong, I want to probe into the nature

6 Xi Jinping, "Unswervingly Following the Path of Socialist Rule."

7 Gong, "People as the Center."

8 Feng, "Deepening Study on the Relations."

of Xi Jinping's rule of law. I argue that Xi Jinping's "rule of law" is not so much the conventional rule of law that has been taken for granted by Chinese legal scholars as Xi's personal understanding or interpretation of the rule of law. Emboldened by China's stunning rise of economic and military power, Xi has become increasingly assertive in imposing stringent laws on anyone against him and the Party in China and surrounding regions but, in the meantime, flatly rejects or flouts laws that are not in China's favor.

Xi's Definition of the Rule of Law

Ever since he became the paramount leader in China as a result of the "will and actions" of other senior leaders,[9] Xi has repeatedly proclaimed that China should establish the socialist rule of law with Chinese features. His understanding and definitions of the rule of law contain important implications that could be a far cry from what legal scholars in the West or in China's republican periods would agree or believe. Even Peng Zhen, former Beijing mayor and the top official overseeing the legal reform in the 1950s and 1980s, might not have agreed to some of Xi's definitions of the rule of law.

Xi's first definition of the rule of law is the ambiguity between the rule of law and legislation. In October 2014, Xi stated at the Fourth Plenary Session of the 18th CCP Central Committee that the plenary had made "comprehensive plans to advance the rule of law in China" because it had introduced more than 180 important measures covering all aspects of the rule of law.[10] Here, Xi, like the CCP in the 1950s, presumed that the scores of law-related "important measures" were on a par with the rule of law.[11] In another speech made during the pandemic in 2021, Xi went over the history of CCP's rule of law construction in which he claimed that the Party had since its inception stressed the rule of law. Prior to 1949, the Party had enacted laws such as The Constitutional Guideline of the Chinese Soviet Republic in 1934 among many other laws and regulations. During the Yan'an era (1935–1947), the Party created the "Ma Xiwu Style" to deal with difficult marriage cases in remote villages. After the founding of the PRC, the Party had led the people to promulgate the 1954 Constitution and numerous other laws including The State Organizational Law and Organic Law of the Court. Since China launched the market-oriented reform in 1978, the Party has made the rule of law a basic strategy of its effort to manage the country. In addition, Xi had lumped other law-related activities and

[9] Baranvitch, "A Strong Leader for a Time of Crisis."

[10] Xi Jinping, 2017: 126.

[11] People's Daily Editorial, "There is Still Grave Struggles."

policies such as enhancing the legal consciousness among the people, promoting the construction of a professional legal team, and lawfully correcting a bevy of falsely-charged cases into the rule of law. As he did in 2014, Xi continued to treat legislation per se the same as the rule of law in China.[12]

Unlike some earlier Party leaders such as Liu Shaoqi and Peng Zhen who somewhat embraced certain notions of the rule of law in the West, Xi clearly rejects Western rule of law and judicial independence.[13] He instead turns to China's legal traditions for the source and model for the rule of law with Chinese features, a move many previous CCP leaders since Mao's death had refrained to take.[14] In October 2014, Xi, like his predecessor Jiang Zemin,[15] said that it was important to "integrate the rule of law with the rule of virtue" because "laws are ethics that have been written down, while ethics are laws that we follow in our hearts." The combination of law and virtue is a concept that can hark back to the Tang Code. Even republican leaders like Yuan Shikai whose imperial ambition was unsuccessful also believed that virtue was substance while law was instrumental.[16] Xi went further to argue that laws "must conform to ethics and have deep moral foundations that will be conscientiously observed by the majority of the people." In Xi's words, Chinese law "serves to safeguard ethics." But Xi fell short to elaborate to which ethics Chinese law should conform, say filial piety, royal power, people as the root, or parental officials (*fumuguan*). He went on to remind officials that if China wanted to advance the rule of law, "we must promote the core socialist values and carry forward traditional Chinese virtues."

To justify his rationale on the virtue and ethics, Xi quoted the words of Lord Shang, a renowned legalist and reformer in the Warring State Era (475–221BCE), that "a wise ruler establishes laws through observing popular customs," namely the traditional values.[17] Xi's effort to replace Western rule of law with traditional Chinese law could best be fleshed out by official legal scholars in China. For example, in early 2023, Chen Xiangjian, Party Secretary of the Fujian Social Science Academy, wrote that the "excellent" traditional legal culture in Xi's argument could

[12] Xi Jinping, 2021.

[13] For the remarks of Liu Shaoqi and Peng Zheng on the law see *A Compendium of CCP's Important Historical Materials* (*zhonggong zhongyao lishi wenxian ziliao huibian*), No. 8. (Los Angeles: Zhongwen chubanwu fuwu zhongxin, 2000): 37.

[14] See, for example, Fang, "Chinese Media and the Rule of Law."

[15] For Jiang's talk on the rule of virtue see Jiang Zemin, Collected Works of Jiang Zemin (Beijing: Remin chubanshe, 2006): 91–2; also see Leigh K. Jenco, "'Rule of Man' and 'Rule by Law.'"

[16] The Tang Code reads "Virtue and rites are the basis of governmental teaching and punishments and chastisements are the instrument of governmental teaching" in Deborah Cao, *Chinese Language in Law: Code Red* (Lanham: Lexington Book, 2018): 25; for Yuan Shikai see Leigh K. Jenco, "'Rule by Man' and 'Rule by Law.'"

[17] Xi Jinping, 2017: 124.

convey "rich aspiration for the birth and development of the socialist rule-of-law thought, the rule-of-law mindset, and the rule-of-law principles with Chinese features." The "excellent" traditional legal culture would comprise both legalist and Confucian notions such as people as the root of the society, law's implementation is more important than law's making, and "states whose rulers can strictly follow the law will be strong." Yet, Chen was also aware that some Chinese traditional legal cultures were bad and should be cast off, but he failed to point them out.[18]

The person who best interprets Xi's view on traditional Chinese rule of law may be Li Cunpeng, a scholarly official in the Chinese Law Society. Li hails Xi's socialist thought in the new era as "modern Marxism," which is aligned with the Mao Zedong thought that was first coined by Liu Shaoqi in the 1940s. Invoking Xi's words that a state will be strong if its ruler can respect law, Li points out a litany of rulers including Qin Shihuang, Han Wudi, and Tang Taizong whose rigorous laws paved the way for their remarkable accomplishments. Li also cites Xi's emphasis on constitutional education and the legislation of "good laws (*shanfa*)" that are crucial for the national security, scientific creativity, ecological civilization, and the like. In this regard, the core of Xi's rule of law is legislation of laws for national security and practical purposes. Xi is keen on the enforcement and belief of law. In the words of ancient legalist Guan Zhong, "law must be just and squarely implemented" and Ming official Zhang Juzheng, "the most difficult thing under heaven is not legislation, but law's enforcement." Although Confucius appears to be suspicious to the rule of law and hostile to the legalists, Xi quoted Confucius as saying that "if a ruler is upright, people will obey him without [ruler's] order; if a ruler is dishonest, people will not follow him despite his orders."[19] We may extrapolate from Xi's comprehension of the rule of law in Chinese culture that it is a hodgepodge of legalist and Confucian comments on law that sometimes may contradict each other.[20]

The third definition of Xi Jinping's rule of law entails an explicit message that it must "uphold the leadership" of the CCP. As he put it, "Upholding the Party's leadership is the essential feature of China's socialism and a fundamental guarantee for socialist rule of law in the country." All efforts of the Party to promote the rule of law in China must be "conducive to strengthening and improving the Party's leadership, bolstering its position as the governing party, and accomplishing its mission in governing the country." Xi demands that all judicial and law-enforcement officials "unequivocally uphold the Party's rule." Only with the CCP as the leadership can the Chinese people become the master of the country and govern their country.

18 Chen, "Inheriting Excellent Chinese Legal Culture."

19 Xi Jinping, 2017: 146–47; Li Cunpeng, "Xi Jinping's Rule of Law."

20 For a detailed study on the rule of law in Chinese history see Fang and Roger Des Forges, "Were Chinese Rulers above the Law."

In this sense, the socialist rule of law in China is tantamount to the rule of the CCP. Xi has made several similar arguments on the Party's leadership in the rule of law from 2014 to 2021.[21]

To avert the Party and officials from violating the law, Xi who is in line with most of his predecessors, insists that "all [people] are equal before the law" and that the CCP should take the lead in abiding by the law. "Equality is a basic attribute of socialist law and a fundamental requirement of the socialist rule of law," Xi says, "all organizations and individuals must respect the authority of the Constitution and law, confine their activities to the boundaries prescribed by the Constitution and law, and exercise powers…" Xi chastises some Party members and officials for infringing the law and their false belief in the rule of man. He dictates that whoever "breaks the law must be held legally accountable for their actions."

However trenchant Xi's argument that the Party must follow the law, his other comments on the loyalty of judges, lawyers, and police to the Party could nonetheless undercut the credibility and sincerity of the rule of law in China. Like most previous Party leaders, Xi rebuts Western values of the rule of law and separation of power. The socialist rule of law envisioned by Xi Jinping should include two critical features: 1) All political and legal organs (i.e. police, procuratorate, and court) must believe in the law and uphold the rule of law; 2) All political and legal officials must be beholden to the Party. What seems paradox in a Western state that cherishes the rule of law has been seamlessly reconciled with two otherwise contradictory practices. As Xi said in October 2014, aside from the requirement that all legislative, law-enforcement, and judicial personnel be "upright and embrace the socialist rule of law," the Party should also educate and guide these people to ensure that they "are loyal to the Party, the country, the people, and the law."[22]

Instead of honing a forceful, stable, and independent mechanism to enforce the law and make sure that all governments, political parties (esp. the CCP), and officials follow nothing other than the law, Xi continues to view the law enforcement and judiciary as a necessary "knife hilt (*daobazi*)" that must be fully controlled by the CCP.[23] Even lawyers that mostly disappeared in the Mao era and were reinstituted after 1978 were told to "enhance their political integrity and uphold the Party's leadership and the socialist rule of law." Xi also remarks that officials "must remain ever mindful not to cross or challenge the line of the law and set a

[21] Xi Jinping, 2017: 119; Xi Jinping, 2021.

[22] Xi Jinping, 2017: 132.

[23] The term "knife hilt" first appeared in the 1950s referring to the judicial and law-enforcement organs in the PRC. The CCP regarded them as a tool of the Party to maintain its rule in China. See Qiang Fang, *Communist Judicial System in China*, Chp 3.

good example in observing and enforcing the law."[24] Yet, all Xi's talk cannot hide the elephant in the room: How does the "knife hilt" investigate and punish the Party and top government officials who have violated the law? Xi's answer is to demand that the Party and all levels of officials "set a good example in upholding the law and holding the law with reverence; set a good example in studying and understanding the law as well as in observing the law and defending the rule of law" in China. In other words, the success and enforcement of the socialist rule of law in China is reliant not so much on any forceful legal and judicial apparatus as on the self-consciousness and self-restraint of Party and government officials to respect and abide by the law.

Understanding the Rule of Law in the West

The socialist rule of law illustrated in Xi Jinping's talks and writings can be summarized into three elements: importance of legislation, drawing legal culture from China's past, and law's primary role to cement CCP's power. While Xi indicates that China needs to learn from other culture and legal practice, he makes it clear that China will not accept key Western legal concepts and institutions such as constitutional government, separation of power, and judicial independence.[25] To what extent does Xi's rule of law differ from Western rule of law? Do the two strikingly different rule-of-law paradigms share some commonalities?

In the West, the orthodox definition of the rule of law can boil down to at least two concepts: a ruler must not be above the law and the law must be applied equally or at least equitably to all people in the society.[26] Tom Bingham suggests that the core of the principles of the rule of law is that all persons and authorities within the state, "whether public or private, should be bound by and entitled to the benefit of laws publicly made, taking effect in the future and publicly administered in the courts."[27] The concept of the rule of law has a long history in the West, originating as early as in the ancient Greece and Roman Republic. After his master Socrates was condemned to death by Athenian democrats, Plato and his disciple Aristotle became increasingly worried about the tyranny of the rule of man in the name of a populist democracy and both stressed the importance of the rule of law. The two philosophers believed that law was the "reflection of a divine order and

[24] Xi Jinping, 2017: 137.

[25] Xi Jinping, 2021.

[26] See, among many other studies, Dicey, *Introduction to the Study of the Law of the Constitution*, 183–89, 207; Turner, "Sage Kings and Laws."

[27] Bingham, *The Rule of Law*: Chp 1; Peerenboom, *China's Long March Toward Rule of Law*: Ch1.

consistent with the Good." Aristotle also argued that the rule of law should include two elements: no one was above the law and the law itself should be good.[28] Yet, their views on the rule of law have their limitations as they flew in the face of any rebellion against the law even if it was unjust. By the same token, Tullius Cicero, a famed scholar and politician in the last days of the Roman Republic, argued that law was the "rule of reason" and it "should be just and good" to the community that had a supreme status. Harmful or unjust rules were not law at all and hence were not supreme. He lambasted rulers who did not obey the law, as a despot was "the foulest and most repellent creature imaginable."[29]

In the medieval era, the German customary law that had significant influence on German-speaking people, England, France, and Spain, believed in the supremacy of the law and therefore placed the king below it. Like Mencius who justified people's right to rebel if a ruler was brutal and despotic, the German law championed the "rightful resistance when a king breached the law."[30] In this period, the Magna Carta could be the most important and representative advocate of the rule of law. In the words of Brian Z, Tamanaha, the Magna Carta not only expressly forbade English rulers to detain, outlaw, or exile any free man without lawful judgment of his peer or the law of the land, but also initiated the notion of the due process of law, albeit its formal term appeared much later in 1354.[31] Enlightenment scholars such as John Locke and Montesquieu helped lay the foundation for the modern rule of law and separation of power. Believing that personal liberty is a natural right, and it should not be subject to the "inconstant, uncertain, unknown, and arbitrary will of another man," Locke strongly opposed absolute arbitrary power of a government or governing without "settled standing laws."[32]

Despite important contributions that Locke has made to the rule of law, he failed to mention judicial independence. It is Montesquieu who mapped out a distinct and crucial path for an independent judiciary to prevent the executive and legislative from imposing their powers, interests, and persecutive inclinations upon the judiciary. With an independent judiciary, people would have the best barrier against lawless government actions. Montesquieu cautioned: if any two of the three powers in a government (legislation, judiciary, administration) are not separated, there would be no liberty.[33]

28 Ji Weihong, "The Basic Characteristics."

29 Tamanaha, *On the Rule of Law:* 7–12.

30 Tamanaha, *On the Rule of Law*: 23–4; for Mencius see Zhu Xi, *Collective Connotation of Mencius*: 239.

31 Ibid: 26; also see Danziger and Gillingham, *1215: The Year of Magna Carta*: 245–60.

32 Tamanaha, *On the Rule of Law*: 48–9.

33 Tamanaha, *On the Rule of Law*: 52–3.

During the American Revolution, many renowned federalists like Alexander Hamilton and James Madison, the father of the American Constitution, echoed Plato and Aristotle's worries of a majority rule.[34] Aside from representative democracy and separating state from federal governments, the federalists also wanted to establish judicial review of legislation, namely the constitution. Knowing that judiciary had the least power among the three branches of government, Hamilton deemed it necessary to empower the judiciary with the interpretation of the laws. Later, Justice John Marshall fully exerted the power of judicial review in interpreting the constitution despite no mention in the constitution per se, successfully cementing the judicial role as an equal to the other two governmental powers.[35]

Today, although the enforcement of the rule of law varies from one nation to another and even in some western countries (e.g. the United States) is facing formidable challenges, the classic notions and principles of the rule of law that equality before the law, no one is above the law, and judicial independence have been entrenched in many Western countries.[36]

"Excellent Traditions of the Rule of Law" in China

In Chapter One, Patrick Shan correctly argues that Xi likes to look back at Chinese history for lessons and experiences and China's legal tradition is no doubt one of them. Xi, in one of his recent talks on the rule of law, applauds the Chinese legal traditions as they epitomized the great creativity of the Chinese nation and the profound roots of the Chinese legal traditions. The Chinese legal system originated in the Qin dynasty (221–206BCE), became more mature in the Sui and Tang dynasties as represented by the Tang Code, and was gradually diminishing after the Qing dynasty. Xi argued that the Chinese legal traditions contained numerous "excellent" thoughts and concepts that should be carried over. Xi highlights some excellent legal traditions like "*minben*," "emphasizing both rites and law," "attaining zero litigation," "stressing harmony," and "being clear on virtue and cautious on punishment." Xi blames generations of legal reformers since the late Qing for mimicking the Western legal systems. "History has spoken for itself," Xi claims, "that the only path to build a successful socialist rule of law is to pair excellent traditional legal culture and legal practices throughout CCP's revolution, construction, and reform periods, plus a conducive Western rule of law."[37]

[34] Gutzman, *James Madison and the Making of America*: 54.

[35] Tamanaha, *On the Rule of Law*: 54–56.

[36] Collinson, "Trump's Immunity Appeal."

[37] Xi Jinping, 2021.

How about Xi's summary of China's "excellent" rule-of-law traditions? To what degree is his definition of China's legal traditions complete and representative? What are the legal practices during CCP's revolution and reform periods that Xi deems instrumental to attain the rule of law in China?

In fact, the aforementioned "excellent" rule-of-law traditions in Xi's talks account for only a fraction of China's legal traditions. Many important schools have discussed law, law's role, and law's enforcement. Yet, no one has offered more detailed and comprehensive interpretations of the rule of law than the legalists, albeit the rule of law in most legalists' comments differs in many crucial aspects from what we know in the Greek and Roman periods. For instance, Lord Shang explicitly pointed out that everyone except the ruler would be subject to the same law and punishment. Any violators would be executed. After the heir-apparent of Duke Qin Xiao broke the law, Lord Shang insisted on mutilating his tutors, a rare practice in Chinese history. The heir-apparent was so scared that he largely confined himself to his palace until his father died eight years later. In this case, Lord Shang's insistence on applying the law evenly to all people below the ruler is very much synonymous with "equality before the law," a key orthodox principle of the modern rule of law. However, Lord Shang was unwilling or dared not take one step further to make the ruler below the law.[38] He instead trumpeted rulers' exclusive right and power to promulgate law, which prompts some modern scholars to dismiss Lord Shang's "rule of law" as "rule of punishment (*xingzhi*)."[39]

Han Fei, another renowned legalist in the Warring States Era, offered similar views on the law to Lord Shang. He suggested that "penalty and reward be applied equally to both officials and commoners." "Without law, even Yao and Shun, two legendary able rulers, could not govern a state well;" Han Fei wrote, "but a mediocre ruler could preside over a well-governed state so long as he could follow the law." Like Lord Shang and Thomas Aquinas who exempted rulers from legal liability,[40] Han Fei believed that rulers had the discretion to "act, listen, and judge independently," thus a ruler "is the king who can act independently."[41] In that regard, by placing rulers above the law, the "rule of law" or more actually the "rule by law" championed by Lord Shang and Han Fei and quoted in Xi Jinping's speeches runs the risk of undermining the equality and supremacy of law, two key principles of the

[38] Si Maqian, *Historical Records* (*shiji*) (Beijing: Zhonghua shuju, 2014): 2707–23.

[39] According to Herrlee G. Creel, the Book of Lord Shang may not be authored by Lord Shang. For Lord Shang see Dong Xin and Shi Lei, *The Book of Lord Shang*: 112 and Yang and Gen, *The Legal Thought of Confucius*: 58; for Creel see Herrelee G. Creel, "Legal Institutions and Procedures during the Chou Dynasty."

[40] Thomas Aquinas argued that sovereigns should be exempted from their own law, see Tamanaha, *On the Rule of Law*: 19.

[41] Yang and Gen, *The Legal Thought of Confucius*: 58.

rule of law. One of the few legalists who expressly placed rulers under the law may be Guang Zhong, a politician in the early Spring and Autumn Period.[42] According to *Guanzi*, a book bearing the name of Guan Zhong, "all people, whatever their political statuses are rulers, officials, upper-class people, lower-class people, nobles, or pariahs (*jianmin*), must abide by the law."[43] Flouted in Xi's talks, Guan's argument is somewhat in tandem with the principle of the rule of law in today's West.

However questionable, the concept of *minben* has long been associated with Confucianism.[44] In addition to the Confucian concept of *minben*, Xi also mentions several "excellent legal concepts" of Confucianism in his speeches such as "virtue first, penalty second," "harmony and rites are prized," and "zero litigation under heaven (*tianxia wusong*)." How close is Confucianism related to the rule of law? Some modern observers have argued that Confucius' understanding of law is mostly about the rule of man rather than the rule of law. Jiang Suhong, for instance, writes that Confucianism is legal nihilism (*falu xuwu zhuyi*) vis-à-vis Legalist legal instrumentalism (*falu gongjuzhuyi*).[45] In their research, Zhang Jinfan and Zeng Xianyi note that the focus of Confucianism is on man, which is the antithesis of the Legalist emphasis of law. Confucius believed that man was the "decisive factor in governance (*weizheng zairen*)." "If a person (i.e. ruler) lives, his policies will be implemented," Confucius said, "if the person dies, his policies will die." Another Confucian scholar Xun Zi rejected the rule of law and stressed the importance of the rule of man whose argument is reminiscent of what Plato had deemed, that the best government should be ruled by man because law could not "speak to all situations."[46] Additionally, Mencius questioned the independent role of law as "either law or rite cannot be relied on to govern independently."[47] Since the Han dynasty, the Confucian notion of rite had gained traction and dominance in what Ju Tongzu calls a "Confucianized law" in which officials and seniors enjoyed legal privileges, further compromising the rule of law.[48]

It can be concluded that neither Legalism nor Confucianism stands up for the supremacy of the law and equality before the law. A likely reason for Xi to cite Legalist and Confucian legal concepts is that both schools' arguments on the law

[42] Scholars have argued that the author/s of the book entitled *Guanzi* could be living in later periods. See Creel, 1980: 52–3.

[43] Liu and Li, *Guanzi*: 300.

[44] Many early works and schools such as the Book of Song, the Ancient Book, and scholars like Mo Di have mentioned and discussed *minben*.

[45] Jiang, "A Preliminary Study on the Rule of Law."

[46] Gao, *Xunzi*: 229; Tamanaha, *On the Rule of Law*: 10.

[47] Zhang and Zeng, "A Historical Review."

[48] For Confucianized Law see Qu Tongzu, *Law and Society in Traditional China.*

dovetail with the needs of Xi and the CCP. After all, a bona fide rule of law would not only restrict but also challenge the omnipotent power and policies of the Party.

Throughout the dynastic periods, there had been no monolithic or persistent tradition in terms of understanding and practicing the rule of law. Indeed, Chinese rulers in different dynasties or the same dynasty have displayed a good deal of varieties in navigating the law. Some rulers in the earlier periods have demonstrated exceptional respect for the rule of law and especially the supremacy of the law. For example, Han Wendi (r. 180–157BCE), a famed benevolent ruler in the early Han dynasty who attained the throne in the wake of political chaos, could follow the law even though his own life was at risk.

In 177 BCE, while Wendi and his entourage were riding past a bridge, a commoner suddenly jumped out and startled Wendi's horses. Wendi almost fell from the saddle. Outraged, Wendi asked Zhang Shizhi, chief officer of law enforcement, to execute the commoner. Yet, Zhang protested the order on grounds that the state statutes stipulated a mere fine for such an offense, and the imposition of capital punishment would violate the law. Zhang pointed out that "Laws are universal and public. If [Wendi] infringes the law, it will cause people not to trust in the law." Although Wendi was not pleased at this legal restraint on his actions, he acknowledged the supremacy of the law and withdrew his unlawful request.[49]

As one of the most enlightened law-abiding rulers in Chinese history, Tang Taizong (r. 626–649) was wary of the causes for the speedy fall of the Sui dynasty (581–617) that Taizong interpreted as Yangdi's negligence to official criticism.[50] Like Aristotle and Cicero, Taizong firmly believed in the close tie between law and heaven. When he stepped into a case attempting to protect a loyal general who had been sentenced to death for corruption, Taizong explained to his court: "Law is something rulers obtain from heaven and accordingly they cannot run afoul of it for personal reasons. If I pardoned Ren Hong (the corrupt official), I would violate the law and betray heaven."[51] In Chinese culture, rulers often claimed that they were sons of heaven. It is imperative for emperors like Tang Taizong to obey the law of heaven. Otherwise, the mandate of violators would be at stake. If Xi Jinping wished to invoke "excellent traditions" of the "authentic" rule of law, Tang Taizong would be one of the best "traditions."

To be sure, the anecdotes of Han Wendi and Tang Taizong's strong faith in law's divinity and inviolability are nonetheless unusual if not a sheer outlier. Many Chinese rulers, if not most, showed contempt rather than reverence for the law and

[49] Sima, *Comprehensive Mirror for Aid*: 461; also see Fang and Des Forges, "Were Chinese Rulers above the Law."

[50] Twitchett, "How to be an Emperor."

[51] Sima, *Comprehensive Mirror for Aid*.

regulations. Some rulers relied on nothing but their personal whims in penalizing or even executing officials as well as ordinary people who had lightly offended them or had wronged. To cite just one case, at the beginning of his reign, Sui Wendi (r. 581–604), the founder of the Sui dynasty, respected the law and removed some cruel punishments such as castration and dismemberment out of the new Sui code. But before long, his respect and leniency for the law were outweighed by his whim and anger. In addition to beating and killing officials for minor offenses in the court, Wendi, infuriated by criminals looting the capital, also made one of the harshest punishments in history that any person who had stolen just one dollar would be executed. In so doing, what Wendi had practiced was the rule by law or the "rule of will" and not the rule of law as there was no effective means to check his whimsical penal laws.[52]

One of two reportedly "lawless" periods in Chinese history are during the reign of empress Wu Zetian (r.690–705) and the Cultural Revolution.[53] Being the only empress in male-dominated Chinese politics, Wu was exceptionally capable. But her ruling from the very inception had been challenged by Tang loyalists. After a rebellion against her was suppressed in 683, Wu, in order to counteract political enemies and deter future uprisings, appointed cruel persecutors to track and ferret out suspicious dissenters. With nearly unchecked power, the tormentors could arrest, torture, and kill almost everyone. A simple note from a person's enemy could suffice to justify inhuman torture and death. Under the imperial terror, law and legal proceedings were completely flouted by law-enforcement officers.[54] Due to the nature of Empress Wu's lawless reign, Xi Jinping had better exclude it from the list of "excellent" rule-of-law tradition.

In the final days of the Qing dynasty (1644–1911), Empress Dowager Cixi was forced to mete out last-ditch reforms to save the dynasty. Many fields ranging from law, military, police to prison and political institutions had undergone wholesale westernization.[55] The legal reform was initiated in 1903 and reformers led by jurist Shen Jiaben and Governor Zhang Zhidong had no intention to preserve any "excellent legal tradition." On the contrary, they were overwhelmed by an urgent task to replace Chinese legal traditions with Western legal principles and laws including, among other things, the principle of the rule of law and judicial independence. When the last baby emperor Puyi abdicated in February 1912, the West-oriented

[52] For Sui Wendi see Wei, *History of the Sui Dynasty*: 714.

[53] Fang, *Communist Judicial System in China*: Chp.7.

[54] Sima, *Comprehensive Mirror for Aid.*

[55] For late Qing reform see Fang, *Chinese Complaint Systems*: Chp 2; Wright, ed., *China in Revolution;* Chesneaux, ed., *Popular Movements and Secret Societies*; Prazniak, *Of Camel Kings and Other Things.*

legal reform was still fledgling. In the early Republic of China, some judicial officials and judges were able to embrace and defend judicial independence and the rule of law against orders from political leaders. In March 1913, after Song Jiaoren, the victorious leader of the largest party GMD (Guomindang, aka, KMT), was assassinated in Shanghai, President Yuan Shikai who was allegedly behind the assassination, attempted to create an ad hoc court to tackle the case. Yet, Xu Shiying, the head of the Justice Department, insisted that the case be tried by a regular court in Shanghai lest a special court would not uphold the law. In this case, judicial officials in the early Republic were brave enough to defend judicial independence in defiance of presidential orders. If Xi Jinping plans to carry over "excellent legal traditions" of the rule of law in Chinese history, he may find no better practice of the rule-of-law traditions than in the early Republic.[56]

Unfortunately, the judicial independence under the GMD eroded significantly due to Chiang's policy of particization (*danghua*). Judges in the administrative court were required to have "deep comprehension of GMD's principles."[57] To clamp down on Communist activities, special agents led by spymaster Dai Li in the GMD employed extra-legal means such as assassination, arbitrary arrests, and torture with explicit or tacit approval from Chiang Kai-shek.[58] However, many judges in the later Republic continued to defend the rule of law and judicial independence. According to one official document, about 33 percent of the ninety-two government decisions in cases of Commoners v. Officials were either partially or fully reversed by the court; the successful percentage is much higher than the 11.7–21 percent in the 1990s after the CCP restored the administrative court in 1989.[59]

Scholars have long been critical of Mao's China especially the Cultural Revolution for its lack of law and tortures and killings. Recent studies find a more nuanced picture of the judicial system in Mao's era. Some judges and top judicial leaders in some periods could still defend judicial independence, a key notion of the rule of law that was denounced as capitalist and Western legal concept in the 1952 legal reform movement and beyond.[60] Shortly after the Korean War ended in 1953, Peng Zhen, head of the powerful Political and Legal Committee, spoke at a national conference for judges and procurators that law in the PRC belonged to workers and the masses. If the CCP "intended to maintain legal privileges," Peng remarked,

[56] Zhang, "The Independent System."; Fang, *A Short History of Chinese Petition*: Chp 8; Fang, *Chinese Complaint Systems*: Chp 3.

[57] Xu, *Trial of Modernity:* 90; also see Fang, *A Short History of Chinese Petition:* Chp 9.

[58] Wakeman Jr., *Spymaster Dai Li*: 146.

[59] See Fang, *Chinese Complaint Systems*: Chp 4.

[60] For a more detailed study on the law in Mao's China see Fang, *Communist Judicial System in China*; also see Yan, *Ten-Year History*; MacFarquhar and Schoenhals, *Mao's Last Revolution*; Esherick, Pickowicz, and Walder, *The Chinese Cultural Revolution*; Clark, *The Chinese Cultural Revolution.*

"[the Party] would destroy itself…" On November 15, 1962, when Mao retreated to the second line after being disgraced in the disastrous Great Leap Forward, Peng defended judicial independence from Party's intervention. He noted, "courts need to make rulings on each case. Why should the Party intervene? The Party should not meddle in the decisions of courts, police, and procuratorates." Liu Shaoqi, the PRC president who was in charge of the economy and daily government affairs, also underscored the independence of the court. "All four levels of courts should judge independently." Liu said, "If a case needs approval from the Supreme Court, then all four parties like the litigants, procuratorate, police, and judge can appeal to the appellate court."[61]

After Mao's death in 1976 and the ascendency of Deng Xiaoping, the CCP launched a massive wave of legal and economic reform whose scale and scope can only be paralleled by the late Qing reform. In 1982, Peng Zhen and a group of legal scholars promulgated a new Constitution that reiterated most provisions of the 1954 Constitution such as judicial independence, equality before the law, and the like. In the 1990s, President Jiang Zemin declared that China would construct a socialist market economy, which, as many scholars have argued, should line up to the rule of law. "The functional principles of a market economy are the rule of law…" Ma Changsheng and Wang Xiangxin wrote in 1998. Both authors worried that China's "tradition of the rule of man…" would hamper the development of the market economy. Unlike Xi Jinping who craves inheriting "excellent Chinese legal traditions of the rule of law," the authors raised eyebrows at China's traditional legal culture and dismissed it as being intertwined with authoritarianism. As a result, the Chinese legal culture abhorred litigations and preferred settling a case behind closed doors.[62]

To deepen China's market economy and speed up China's entry into the World Trade Organization, Jiang Zemin promised in 1997 that China would pursue the rule of law. Two years later, the rule of law was written into the new edition of the Constitution, the same year China was accepted by the United States to become a member of the WTO. Adding the rule of law into the Constitution just needs a few more words, but pulling off the rule of law and subjecting the CCP and top officials to the Constitution and other state laws are more daunting tasks that only a few rulers and officials in Chinese history have been able to fulfill. In the presidencies of both Jiang Zemin and Hu Jintao, it is the rule by law rather than the rule of law that dominated the judicial system and law enforcement. In some notable national cases such as the crackdown of the Falun Gong in 1999 and the forced demolition of

[61] *Compendium of Important CCP Historical Documents* 2000: 37; also see Peng, *The Political and Legal Work*: 111–12.

[62] Ma and Wang, *A Study on the Issue of the Rule of Law*: 5–13.

the Wuhan Waitan Garden in 2001, the Party and the government remained above the law and many people whose personal or collective rights had been violated by Party or government officials would find all their efforts seeking justice to no avail.[63] Liu Xiaobo, a leader in the 1989 democracy movement and a Nobel Peace Prize laurate, was sentenced to 11 years by Hu Jintao for his leading role in the 2008-Charter's Movement that called for the CCP to conduct serious political reform and to implement the rule of law. According to the *New York Times*, he was secretly tried by judges appointed by the Party Central whose mission was to follow order but not law.[64]

After a brief review of various practices of law in Chinese history, several takeaways are worth highlighting. First, none of the two influential schools in Chinese history, Confucianism and Legalism, upheld the orthodox or universal rule of law. While Legalist theorists required all people to be equally treated by the law, they deliberately exempted the ruler, which de facto removed the cornerstone of the rule of law. Like Confucianism that favored the rule of a capable man, both Lord Shang and Han Fei believed that the ruler should be the final say for everything, albeit Han Fei argued that a sound legal mechanism would run by itself regardless of the ability of the ruler. Accordingly, the principles of the rule of law lacked a solid theoretical foundation in China, resulting in many rulers' unchecked power and extensive violations of the law. Second, in Chinese history, only a few enlightened Chinese rulers such as Han Wendi and Tang Taizong revealed a strong legal consciousness and respect to the supremacy and holiness of the law that emperors should not violate. Another period witnessing the genuine practice of the rule of law was in the early Republic of China. With the introduction of modern Western notions like the rule of law and separation of power, many judges were emboldened to defend judicial independence against orders from political leaders. In the later Republic and particularly the PRC, crucial principles of the rule of law were either contaminated by GMD's demand for particization or completely denounced by the CCP as capitalist and Western legal concepts. Third, the norm of the practice and enforcement of law in Chinese history was the rule by law during which the law was inferior to individual rulers or a ruling party. In some extreme periods such as part of the reign of Wu Zetian and Sui Wendi and much of the Cultural Revolution, the ruler's whims and the "rule without law" prevailed, causing rampant punishments, torture, and killings. Fourth, the legal traditions in Chinese history are not singular and there are at least three forms of the practice of the law: the rule of

[63] For the Waitan Garden Case see Fang and Li, *Power versus Law in Modern China:* Chps 1–3; for Falun Gong see Amnesty International, PRC Crackdown on Falun Gong and Other So-called "Heretical Organizations."

[64] Buckley, "Liu Xiaobo, Chinese Dissident."

law, the rule by law, the rule of whim/will or the rule without law. If there exist any "excellent traditions" of the rule of law in Chinese history, I do not know what "traditions" could be more "excellent" and qualified than during the reigns of Han Wendi and Tang Taizong and the early Republic of China.

Practice of Law in Xi's Era

We have discussed Xi Jinping's definition of the rule of law, the orthodoxy rule of law in the West, and the complexity of the practice of law in China's long history. To better grasp Xi's understandings of the rule of law and the actual practice of the rule of law in his era, we need to examine several legal cases since 2012. These cases are well-known and a couple of them have sparked intense fear and protest across China and parts of the world.

1. The Case of Causeway Bay Bookstore

In contrast to the sea of mainland China, Hong Kong is like an oasis where residents enjoy more political, academic, judicial, and economic freedoms than their counterparts in mainland China. In December 1982, Article 31 of the PRC Constitution stipulated the creation of the Hong Kong Special Administrative Zone. In early 1983, the Chinese government pledged to allow Hong Kong's political, social, and judicial systems to remain the same for 50 years including, among others, an independent judiciary, Hong Kong's final judicial decision, and current laws, statutes, and regulations. Hong Kong residents would preserve their freedoms of speech, protest, meeting, and publication.[65] The CCP attempted to cast its takeover of Hong Kong as a boon to the local residents. With the aegis of the basic law and CCP's written undertakings, Hong Kong became the most free and active society in China after 1997. People continued to hold annual candle parties to commemorate the dead in the 1989 Tiananmen incident. Books, movies, and journals with touchy contents such as reporting or exposing power struggles among Party leaders and the private lives of top Party leaders could still be published and sold in Hong Kong. Publishers of such books had no fear of government crackdown or harassment that their counterparts in China would face.

In the summer of 2015, the Causeway Bay Bookstore (*tongluowan*) in Hong Kong was selling a book entitled *Xi Jinping and his Mistresses*, which was filled with gossip and rumors about the private lives of Xi. As in the past decades, the booksellers assumed that the book was just like other books exposing private lives and

[65] News Office of the State Council, "White Paper of The Practice of the One Country."

power games of top CCP leaders. However, the political spectrum had dramatically shifted since Xi Jinping took power. What awaited the booksellers was harrowing abductions executed by mainland secret police that would forever change the fate of Hong Kong. The episodes began in October 2015 when five booksellers from the Causeway Bay Bookstore were suddenly missing one after another. The wife of Li Bo, one of the five kidnapped booksellers, went to a local police station to report that her husband was missing even though his travel documents were left at home. A few days later, Li called his wife from mainland China to say he had visited China "voluntarily" and asked her to cancel the kidnapping report in a local police bureau. However, surveillance cameras and witnesses proved that Li had been dragged into a car by several men.[66]

When people around the world were still wondering what had happened to Li Bo, news exposed that four more booksellers from the same bookstore were also missing, one of them, Gui Minhai, was a key publisher behind the book about Xi's private lives. He was taken by Chinese agents from a seaside apartment in Thailand and spirited to China. Despite his Swedish citizenship, Gui could not get assistance from the Swedish government. Gui later was forced to appear on Chinese CCTV and repented with tears his "crimes" of publishing the book. To stave off protests from the Swedish government, a Chinese foreign spokesperson asserted that Gui had renounced his Swedish citizenship and hence he could be tried and punished by Chinese law.[67]

Most of the abducted booksellers refused to tell of their experience after returning to Hong Kong. The only bookseller who had the courage to speak up about his abduction was Lam Wing-kee, a local Hong Kong resident. According to Lam, he was taken by secret Chinese agents to the border between Hong Kong and mainland China. He had been kept in solitary custody in Ningbo, Zhejiang, for a few months before he "confessed his crimes." Lam later told reporters that he was not allowed to hire a lawyer and to call his family, two legal rights that the Chinese government had promised Hong Kong people in the 1990 Basic Law.[68] Lam recalled that what the Chinese police had done to him was a "mental torture" until he went mad. The police later ordered him to write a confession to condemn Gui Minhai for selling books that could harm the society. As the main publisher of Xi's private life, Gui was the only bookseller still in Chinese custody.[69]

Several months after the exposure of the abductions by Western media and NGOs such as Amnesty International, the Chinese government remained silent on

[66] Cohen, "Practices of Abduction and TV Confessions."

[67] Wong, "Hong Kong Bookseller."

[68] Basic Law of Hong Kong Special Administrative Zone."

[69] Jacob, "Defying China."

the issue and refused to provide any information. Jerome Cohen, a law professor at New York University and an outspoken critic of the Chinese legal system, condemns the Chinese government for the kidnapping of booksellers. He points out that Gui's forced confession on Chinese television violates China's Criminal Procedural Law, which is "very deplorable and is against human rights."[70] Who was behind the abductions? Were top Chinese leaders aware of the kidnapping, incarceration, and confession? While there is little tangible evidence that top leaders including Xi Jinping was implicated, the unprecedented outright and bold incursion of Hong Kong's political and legal independence and the attendant diplomatic clash between China and Sweden demonstrate that the police gambit of abduction might have direct approval from top leaders. According to Cohen, Xi and other top leaders had refrained from chastising those perpetrators of the kidnapping and firing them. But unfortunately, we have seen no response or action from Beijing. It is likely that "what the abductors have done is exactly what the top leaders want to do."[71] For Lam and the rest of Hong Kong, the death knell of Hong Kong's autonomy and judicial independence pledged by the Chinese government has been sounded. The abductions conducted by Chinese agents contradict both Article 37 of the Chinese Constitution that citizens' habeas corpus cannot be violated and the rule of law.[72] Lam joined the Hong Kong protests in 2019 calling for more civil rights and opposing the proposed extradition law that would allow Hong Kong residents to be sent to mainland China. Feeling no safety in Hong Kong especially after he publicly denounced the Chinese abduction of him and his co-workers, Lam decided to move to Taiwan, the last bastion of democracy in the Chinese-speaking world, where he is now running a small bookstore in Taipei selling books that are no longer allowed in Hong Kong.[73]

2. *The Case of Rights Lawyers*

In April 2023, a secret court in China sentenced rights lawyers and political activists Xu Zhiyong and Ding Jiaxi to fourteen and twelve years in prison respectively, a heavier punishment than that in the Hu Jintao era.[74] According to Amnesty International, both lawyers had been subjected to torture, longtime interrogation, and other ill-treatment during detention.[75] The severity and arbitrariness of the

[70] Cohen, "Practices of Abduction."

[71] Ibid.

[72] Constitution of the People's Republic of China, revised in 2018. http://www.npc.gov.cn/npc/c505/201803/e87e5cd7c1ce46ef866f4ec8e2d709ea.shtml. Accessed May 15, 2023.

[73] Hernandez and Chien, "A Bookstore that Shines."

[74] Gan, "'A Democratic China Must Be Realized."

[75] Amnesty International, April 10, 2023.

punishment shocked many people both within China and without. For Xu, this was not the first time in prison. In January 2014, a Beijing court incarcerated Xu to four years in prison for "gathering a crowd to disturb public order," a crime that has blurry but broad leeway for the government to punish any person deemed a threat. Xu's primary crimes were his leading role in urging officials to expose their properties and organizing the New Citizen Movement (*xingongmin yundong*), a grassroots movement to promote equal education rights.

During his trial at the Beijing court in 2014, Xu delivered a fiery statement defending his constitutional and legal rights. In Xu's words, the trial and imprisonment were not about disturbing public order, it was in fact the fears of the judges: fear of open trials, fear of citizens' freedom to attend the trials, and fear of an upcoming free society." Xu defied the court charges that he and his fellow rights lawyers had "political purposes." "Yes," Xu stated, "our political purpose is evident, which is a beautiful China embracing democracy, the rule of law, freedom, justice, and love." In an ideal society envisaged by Xu, it should have real democracy and the rule of law. A real democracy should have political checks and balances, judicial independence, and that the military and police should serve the public but not a single party or an interest group.[76]

According to his lawyer, Zhang Qingfang, when the guards at the Beijing court were dragging Xu away from the courthouse, he said that "the court today has completely destroyed the remnants of respect for the rule of law in China." After the Beijing court sentenced Xu to four years in prison, Jen Psaki, a spokeswoman in the US State Department, announced that the United States government "is concerned that Mr. Xu's prosecution is retribution for his public campaign to expose corruption and for the peaceful expression of his views."[77] Even though Article 35 of the PRC Constitution allows citizens to have freedom of speech and protests and Article 37 outlaws illegal detainment by police without permits of the procuratorate, Xu tapped the loss of his own freedom to test the reality of the rule of law in China.[78]

In the meantime, Xi was trying to "bring back strong-man politics" by launching an anti-corruption movement, rekindling a Mao-era mass-line campaign, and proposing the concept of a "Chinese Dream," echoing the American Dream.[79] Xi's anti-corruption movement was initially quite popular among the people, but some scholars questioned his real motive behind the campaign and dubbed it "selective

[76] Xu, "For Freedom, Justice, and Love: My Court Statement."

[77] Jacobs and Buckley, "China Sentences Xu Zhiyong."

[78] Article 35 of the PRC Constitution states that all citizens have the liberty of speech, publication, gathering, organization, protest, and demonstration. See PRC Constitution, 2018.

[79] Zheng and Gore, *China Entering the Xi Jinping Era*: 1.

anti-corruption punishment."[80] Since 2013, the Chinese government has banned talks of Western universal values such as judicial independence, separation of power, and constitutionalism on college campuses. The Party also gave a green light to the arrests of media leaders and imposed rigorous restrictions on public media. When a group of journalists from the Southern Weekend, a liberal-leaning newspaper, protested against police suppression in its new-year editorial, dozens of them were detained, causing a chill-effect among Chinese media.[81]

To snuff out rights lawyers and other dissenters, the NPC promulgated the National Security Act on July 1, 2015. Ten days later, the police and national security agents detained hundreds of rights lawyers and human rights activists. Among the detained lawyers was Gao Yu, a 71-year-old female lawyer and one of the International Press Institute's fifty world press heroes. Gao's crime was "leaking state secrets" because she allegedly disclosed Xi's 2013 directive that demanded Chinese colleges not to allow talks of seven Western or universal values. Despite her old age, a Chinese court sentenced Gao to seven years in prison, one year for each of the seven "talks."[82] Gao did not believe that Xi Jinping was a liberal reformer like Zhao Ziyang or Hu Yaobang in the 1980s, but rather a relentless red princeling and a "Red Guard." Yu Jie, a dissident writer and a friend of Gao, blames Xi Jinping for manipulating the rule of law in China. "The aim of Xi Jinping's rule of law is a mere slogan," Yu writes, "[for Xi], the rule of law is the same as a dough that he can squish at will."[83] It seems that both Gao and Yu are not familiar with Chinese legal history. They simply blame Xi for the lack of the rule of law in China, but are not aware that the rule of law has never had a solid foundation and enforcement in China's past.

3. *The Hong Kong National Security Law*

If the 2015 abductions of Hong Kong booksellers marked the outset of China's bold breach of Hong Kong's legal and political independence, the 2020 National Security Law would be a gut punch to its legal and political autonomy promised by the Chinese government in 1993. Since the summer of 2020, the CCP has tightened its grip over Hong Kong during Covid-19, prompting the exodus of thousands of Hong Kong residents who cherish their political and judicial rights.

The prelude to the 2020 national security law was the 2019 Extradition Law, which might have been triggered in part by the mass media coverage in the West of

[80] Murong, "Xi Jinping's Selective Punishment."

[81] Wong and Buckley, "Presses Roll at Storied Chinese Newspaper."

[82] France-Presse, "Jailed Chinese Journalist Gao Yu."

[83] Yu, *Walking toward Throne*: 107–14.

China's 2015 abduction and the exposition of the kidnapped bookseller Lam Wing-kee. In May 2019, the Hong Kong government, apparently backed by the Chinese government, promulgated an Extradition Law that would allow extradition to states (i.e. China) with no extradition agreement with Hong Kong. But this law was ephemeral as the Hong Kong government soon backed off after it sparked massive protests. Infuriated and alarmed by the defiance of the Hong Kong people, the central government in Beijing responded on June 30, 2020 with a more draconian law, the National Security Law by, in the words of Victoria Hui, allowing "China's security police and public security agents [to] come in to overturn [Hong Kong's] autonomous judiciary and criminal justice system."[84] A spokesman for the Chinese Foreign Ministry praised the law for enhancing Hong Kong's rule of law and restoring stability and security in the city.[85]

The vagueness and broad definition of the law immediately drew criticism from major West-based human rights organizations and media. According to a report of Amnesty International, the term "endangering national security can mean virtually anything." Any accusations of secession, subversion, or collusion with foreign forces could "incur maximum penalties of life imprisonment." Violators of the law could also be extradited to China for "unfair" trials and punishments as evidenced in the abductions of Lam and Gui. The law in theory also has the power to charge any person in the world.[86] Article 15 of the law allows the central government in Beijing to establish a special national security agency whose power is beyond the purview of the Hong Kong government.[87]

As soon as the law took effect, the Hong Kong police began to clamp down on peaceful protests and independent media critical of the government. Any political protests, slogans, T-shirts, flyers, or even white papers could face the risk of being accused of endangering national security and the perpetrators would be detained and imprisoned. To protect its journalists, foreign media such as the *New York Times* relocated them to South Korea.[88] A Human Rights Watch report wrote that in Hong Kong, once Asia's "protest center," political protests were prohibited and over 100 people had been arrested for violating the National Security Law. With the law, the Hong Kong police became the "Talons and Teeth" of Beijing rather than "enforcers of the rule of law," once the backbone of Hong Kong's prosperity and freedom.[89] By the same token, the human rights watchdog of the United Nations also raised concern

[84] Roundtable before the Congressional-Executive Commission on China, "One Year of the National Security Law's Repression of Fundamental Freedoms in Hong Kong."

[85] Questions and Answers of the Chinese Foreign Ministry.

[86] Amnesty International, "Hong Kong's National Security Law."

[87] National Security Law in Hong Kong Special District, June 30, 2020.

[88] Amnesty International, July 17, 2020.

[89] Human Rights Watch, "Dismantling a Free Society."

over the law's "lack of clarity and possibility of transferring cases from Hong Kong to China." Photini Pazartzis, chairperson of the United Nations Human Rights Committee, stepped up pressure on the Hong Kong government to "repeal the law and refrain from applying it." Arif Balkan, a vice chair of a panel in the committee, noted that over 200 people including 12 children in Hong Kong had been reportedly arrested since the security law passed. Ted Hui, a former member of the Hong Kong Legislative Council says the number of arrested activists whose ages range from 15 to 90 is 260.[90]

Some influential Western media also cast doubt on the motive of the national security law in Hong Kong. One day after the law was passed, the *New York Times* lamented the demise of Hong Kong's judicial independence, "a legacy of British colonial rule that stood in stark contrast to the secretive, party-controlled courts in mainland China." Some experts cautioned that the law would bring to Hong Kong "many harsh legal practices common in mainland China" because the police could incarcerate a person "as long as six months incommunicado, subject to torture, coerced confession, no access to counsel or family or friends" before the police decided whether to charge you for a crime.[91] On June 28, 2022, roughly two years after the law came to force, the *BBC News* calculated the impact of the law on Hong Kong. It reported that the law "gives Beijing powers to shape life in Hong Kong it has never had before." Several days after the passage of the law, hundreds of protesters, activists, and former opposition lawmakers were arrested. Invoking UK Foreign Secretary Liz Truss's recrimination on the law that "we have seen a systematic erosion of liberty and democracy in Hong Kong," the news giant reported that the subsequent arrests had "caused far more damaging impacts on freedom and way of life than many people had envisaged one year ago."[92]

Western scholars such as Jerome A. Cohen have been largely aligned with human rights organizations and public media. On June 29, 2021, Cohen talked about the Hong Kong National Security Law at a congressional roundtable, that the law immediately "brought…the police state in mainland China to Hong Kong." Cohen denounced the law for its reneging of China's promise to Hong Kong. In agreement with Cohen, Victoria Hui called Hong Kong a "formal installation of the police state" as the national security office in Hong Kong had all the resources it needed to "bring in all the practices of mistreatment of political prisoners and do that within Hong Kong." In that regard, Hui renamed the Hong Kong security law as "Beijing security law." What Beijing wanted was to kill Hong Kong freedom, Hui argued, "but not Hong Kong's capitalism." The central government still needed Hong Kong

[90] "Top Rights Experts Urge Repeal of Hong Kong's National Security Law"; Hui, "China Puts a Bounty on My Head."

[91] Hernandez, "Harsh Penalties, Vaguely Defined Crimes."

[92] "Hong Kong National Security Law: What is is and is it Wrong?"

to be a bridge between China and the West.[93] Both Lydia Wong and Thomas Kellogg at Georgetown University co-authored a report on the Hong Kong law in early 2021. They noted that the security law marked the beginning of Beijing's direct control over Hong Kong's internal affairs, which seriously "degrade Hong Kong's autonomy under the Basic Law." The authors also warned that the law "constitutes one of the greatest threats to human rights and the rule of law since the 1997 handover."[94]

While Article 5 of the security law guaranteed all alleged violators of the law the right of presumption of innocence and due process,[95] a *New York Times* report on February 7, 2023 estimated that over 200 people had been arrested since the law passed and over 3000 had been prosecuted on charges of antigovernment protests. Among them, forty-seven were indicted on one single day in 2021 for subversion who had not undergone formal trials for almost two years, further testifying the incongruity between the rhetoric of the law and government's arbitrary practice and disregard of the law.[96] Moreover, the security law weighs on Hong Kong's once admirable freedom of press. With the arrest and trial of Jimmy Lai, founder of the outspoken *Apple Daily,* in June 2021 and early 2024 respectively,[97] Hong Kong's rank of press freedom in the world was not far from that of China, which was only better than North Korea's.[98] In 2022, one NGO ranked Hong Kong's freedom of press 140th out of 180 countries, which was a staggering drop from 18th in 2002 and 80th in 2019, a year prior to the national security law.[99]

The Rule of "Party" Law

In Xi's era, the "rule of law" can be multifaceted and its boundaries with the rule by law, legislation, and the rule of will are sometimes blurred and obfuscated. In 2014, Xi Jinping believed the Party's promulgation of laws was part of the rule of law. He stressed the importance of equality before the law and that all people including the CCP "must respect the authority of the Constitution and law," which is akin to the orthodox notion of the rule of law since as early as the ancient Greek civilization. Yet Xi and his legal advisors who are probably unaware of the distinctions between

[93] Roundtable before the Congressional-Executive Commission on China, 2021.

[94] Wong and Kellogg, "Hong Kong's National Security Law."

[95] National Security Law in Hong Kong, June 30, 2020.

[96] May, "How China Dealt with a 'Knockout Blow.'"

[97] Amnesty International, June 17, 2021.

[98] The rank in 2023 was eight places higher than in 2022. For the 2023 rank see Chau, "Hong Kong Ranks 140th on 2023 International RSF Press Freedom Index."; for the 2022 rank see Lau, "Hong Kong Plunges to 148th in World Press Freedom Rankings."

[99] "Hong Kong's Press Freedom Ranking."

the rule of law and the rule by law firmly reject the Western concept of judicial independence, a key component in the rule of law, and argue instead that all political and legal officials "must be loyal to the CCP." Like most of his predecessors especially Mao, Xi wants the law enforcement and judicial organs to be powerful and reliable tools for the Party. In that regard, Xi's understanding of the rule of law is nothing but the rule by law.[100]

Indeed, when Xi Jinping discusses the rule of law, he pines for drawing aspirations of the rule of law from China's tradition and dismisses the Western and universally recognized concepts of the rule of law that would place him and the CCP under the state constitution and law and their power in a cage. Xi's favorite and often-cited "excellent" traditions of the rule of law are mostly arguments of legalists and Confucians such as Lord Shang, Han Feizi, Confucius, and Mencius. As I have pointed out in this chapter, some of the comments made by Lord Shang and Han Feizi were analogous to the concepts of the orthodox rule of law, but the nature of legalists' arguments was the rule by law because their ultimate aim was, in the words of Herrlee G. Creel, to beef up the power of the ruler amid a turbulent period.[101] Neither Confucius nor Mencius mentioned the rule of law. What they considered most important were such concepts as rituals, people as the root of the state, and gentleman's rule. The ideal society of Confucius was the one governed by a sage ruler whose integrity and exemplar were sufficient to rule a state. Mencius went a little further than Confucius in emphasizing the equal importance between law (i.e. regulations) and ritual.

To justify his theoretical definition of the rule of law, Xi Jinping labels his rule of law as the socialist rule of law with Chinese characteristics. Within that framework of Chinese characteristics, the definition of the rule of law is more malleable and it could be tweaked to suit the needs of the Party leader (i.e. Xi Jinping), so to speak. Since ascending to power, Xi has adopted a tough stance in implementing the law and crackdowns on political dissenters in both Hong Kong and mainland China. His practice of the law is in many aspects in tandem with most rulers in dynastic and republican periods with the exception of Han Wendi and Tang Taizong who subjected their power below the law, early Republican judges, and early PRC officials such as Peng Zhen who held beliefs in the supremacy of and equality before the law.

In contrast to his immediate predecessors, Xi's understandings of the "rule of law" such as the omnipotence of the CCP and the Party's firm grip over the legal mechanism are similar to those of Deng Xiaoping, Jiang Zemin, and Hu Jintao.[102]

[100] Fang, *Communist Judicial System in China*: Conclusion

[101] Creel, *Legal Institutions and Procedures*: 54.

[102] For Deng Xiaoping's grip on CCP's leadership and denying people political and human rights see Shambaugh, "Deng Xiaoping: The Politician"; for Jiang and Hu see Fang, *Jiang Zemin and the United States*: Chp. 9.

However, as epitomized in cases such as, inter alia, the abductions of Hong Kong booksellers, the severe punishment of rights lawyers, the revision of the constitution to prolong his presidential terms, and the forceful imposition of the Hong Kong National Security Law, Xi appears to be more assertive and more aggressive than Jiang and Hu. What lies behind Xi's aggressive approaches? I would argue that there are two reasons. In the first place, Xi's era has witnessed a golden age of China's comprehensive power. In 2010, China's GDP for the first time overtook that of Japan. In 2021, China's GDP outstripped that of the European Union and was barely trailing that of the United States.[103] The same year, the CNBC in the US even predicted that China was projected to surpass the US in economic terms in 2028.[104] Thanks to Xi's shift of military focus from army to navy, China has since 2012 built three aircraft-carriers. In 2017, the US believed that China's naval ships had become the world's largest, which could challenge the dominance of the US navy.[105] Moreover, in 2022, China was the largest trade partner to more than 120 countries due to its status as the world factory.[106] All of these took place during Xi's presidency.

During the eras of Jiang and Hu roughly between 1989 and 2012, both leaders were working hard to plug China further into the global economy. To join the WTO and to gain the US market and technologies, Jiang downplayed the fiery crisis in the Taiwan Strait in the mid-1990s. After NATO bombed China's embassy in Yugoslavia in May 1999 and the Sino-US plane collision near Hainan Island in 2001, Jiang's conciliatory stance paved the way for a speedy solution and rapprochement with the U.S. Hu Jintao largely continued Jiang's friendly approach, or more correctly Deng Xioaping's strategy of "hiding strength and biding time for revenge," to the West.[107] Hu took a permissive stance toward the US invasion of Iraq in 2003. In return, US president George W. Bush became one of the few world leaders to attend the opening ceremony of the Beijing Olympic Games. Although a Chinese court in 2011 sentenced Nobel Prize laurate Liu Xiaobo to eleven years in prison, some other less prominent dissidents like Teng Biao and Yu Jie were allowed to visit and exile to the United States at the end of Hu's term.[108] Hu was not ready to challenge the West, above all the United States.

Emboldened by China's fast-growing economic, military, and trade heft and the perception that the West was declining, Xi is confident that the age of China has come and that he does not need to care about Western responses and criticism. He

[103] Zhou, "China's Most Productive Provinces and Cities."

[104] Cheng and Lee, "New Chart Shows China could Overtake."

[105] Myers, "With Ships and Missiles."

[106] Green, "China is the Top Trading Partner."

[107] Fang, "Jiang Zemin and the United States."

[108] For Teng Biao see Sheridan, "Chinese Exiled Lawyer Teng Biao"; for Yu Jie see Yu, *Walking toward Throne.*

quickly embarks on flexing muscle in domestic and international politics. Not only does he increase the suppression of dissenters inside of China, but he also for the first time extends China's police power in Hong Kong, a practice his predecessors had refrained from doing.[109] Xi's aggressive policies have affected China's ties with its neighbors and the West. China's rising power and provocative diplomacy immediately spark countermeasures in East Asia, pushing China's neighbors to seek military alliance with the United States. The Philippines, in particular, has "radically shifted" its former lukewarm relations with the U.S. by inviting US military to build more bases on its territory as a counterweight to China's island taking and building in the South China Sea.[110] Xi also leverages China's immense trade power to inflame boycotts against countries such as South Korea, Japan, Australia, and some European states that are either siding with the US or opposing China's military takeover of Taiwan.[111]

Another reason for the aggressive governmental policies under Xi is his understanding of the rule of law and affection for China's "traditional" legal concepts and practice. The mix of his rejection of Western judicial independence, reemphasis of CCP's total control over the judicial "knife hilt," and insistence on the Party's legal impunity doubles down on the hubris of Chinese leadership in navigating domestic and even international legal issues. If we are aware of Xi and the Party's comprehension of the rule of law, it will not be difficult to figure out the harsh punishments of rights lawyers, the extraordinary revision of China's constitution, the bold kidnapping of Hong Kong booksellers, the fleeting passage of the Hong Kong National Security Law to rein in local protesters, and the total rejection of the ruling of an International Tribunal over the South China Sea islands.[112] All of these policies have taken place during Xi's presidency, and it is likely that Xi himself has endorsed most, if not all, of them. Accordingly, Xi's rule of law could be characterized as the "rule of Party (CCP) law" or, more correctly, the "rule of Party leader's law." In other words, if a law suits his rule and need, Party leaders (i.e. Xi) would strictly follow and enforce it (e.g. the crackdown on rights lawyers and perpetrators of Hong Kong National Security Law), which is not the "rule of man" as some scholars have argued.[113] If a law is not in the Party's favor or if there is no law to pull off CCP's purposes, Party leaders would be agnostic about it or opt to

[109] For Jiang's furor over Hong Kong journalists see Gittings, "Hong Kong Reporters."

[110] Mansoor and Shah, "Why the Philippines is Letting the U.S. Expand."

[111] After South Korea agreed to deploy US THAD missile defense system in early 2017, the Chinese media called for boycott threats against South Korea. See Diaz and Zhang, "Angered by U.S. Anti-Missile System."

[112] The ruling of the court favored the Philippines as it opposed China's claim of islands in the South China Sea. See Philips, "Beijing Rejects Tribunal's Ruling."

[113] Guo, "A Partocracy with Chinese Characteristics."

create a new one at will (e.g. Hong Kong National Security Law). Xi's understanding and attitude toward law are reminiscent of Mao's with a key difference between the two: Mao often disregarded the law, whereas China under Xi could either implement law whenever it favors the Party rule or create new laws whenever the situation requires. Had CCP leaders had a genuine understanding of and respect for the principles of the orthodox rule of law, Party leaders would not have authorized the crackdowns of civil and political liberties in China, let alone in Hong Kong and other places, which could compound Xi's "China dream" and national rejuvenation. Had that been the case, the ongoing decoupling with the West and key Asian neighbors and a looming new "cold war" between China and the United States and its allies could have been avoided. With potential enemies having amassed around China, it is time for Xi and the Party to batten down the hatches.

Qiang Fang is professor of East Asian History at the University of Minnesota Duluth and a visiting professor at China University of Geosciences in Wuhan. He is the current president of the Association of Chinese Professors in Social Science (ACPSS). He has authored several books such as *The Communist Judicial System in China, 1927–1976: Building on Fear (2021), Power Versus Law in Modern China: Cities, Courts, and the Communist Party (2017), Chinese Complaint Systems: Natural Resistance (2013), and Zhongguo shangfang zhidu shihua, 1100 BCE–1949* [A Short History of Chinese Petition] (2013). In addition, he has co-edited books including *Sino-American Relations: A New Cold War (2022), Corruption and Anti-Corruption in Modern China (2019), A Century of Student Movement in China: The Mountain Movers, 1919–2019 (2020); Oumei xuezhe yanjiu zhongguo falushi lunwenxuanyi* [Selected Translated Works of Western Studies on Chinese Legal History] (2015), and *Modern Chinese Legal Reform: New Perspectives (2013).*

Bibliography

A Compendium of CCP's Important Historical Materials (*zhonggong zhongyao lishi wenxian ziliao huibian*), No. 8. Los Angeles: Zhongwen chubanwu fuwu zhongxin, 2000.

Amnesty International, "Hong Kong's National Security Law: 10 Things Need to Know," July 17, 2020. https://www.amnesty.org/en/latest/news/2020/07/hong-kong-national-security-law-10-things-you-need-to-know/; Accessed, May 27, 2023.

______, "Hong Kong: Apple Daily Raid, Arrests a Brazen Attack on Press Freedom," in Amnesty International Report, June 17, 2021. http://www.amnesty.org. Accessed May 31, 2023.

______, PRC Crackdown on Falun Gong and Other So-called "Heretical Organizations." https://www.amnesty.org/en/wp-content/uploads/2021/12/ASA170112000ENGLISH.pdf. Accessed June 1, 2023.

______, April 10, 2023. http://amnesty.org. Accessed, May 18, 2023.

Basic Law of Hong Kong Special Administrative Zone in the PRC, April 4, 1990. https://www.gov.cn/test/2005-07/29/content_18298.htm. Accessed June 15, 2023.

Baranvitch, Nimrod. "A Strong Leader for a Time of Crisis: Xi Jinping's Strongman Politics as a Collective Response to Regime Weakness" in *Journal of Contemporary China*, 2021, Vol. 30, No. 128, pp. 249–265: 250.

Bingham, Tom. *The Rule of Law*. London: Penguin Books, 2010.

Buckley, Chris. "Liu Xiaobo, Chinese Dissident who Won Nobel While Jailed, Dies at 61" in *The New York Times*, July 13, 2017.

Cao, Deborah. *Chinese Language in Law: Code Red*. Lanham: Lexington Book, 2018.

Chau, Candice. "Hong Kong Ranks 140th on 2023 International RSF Press Freedom Index below Columbia, Cameroon" in *Hong Kong Free Press*, May 3, 2023.

Chen, Xiangjian. "Inheriting Excellent Chinese Legal Culture to Provide Comprehensive Rule of Law with Rich Nourishment" in *Guangming ribao*, January 12, 2023. http://theory.people.com.cn/n1/2023/0112/c40531-32604801.html; Accessed March 20, 2023.

Cheng, Evelyn and Yen Nee Lee. "New Chart Shows China could Overtake the US as the World's Largest Economy Earlier than Expected" in CNBC News, February 1, 2021. https://www.cnbc.com/2021/02/01/new-chart-shows-china-gdp-could-overtake-us-sooner-as-covid-took-its-toll.html. Accessed May 31, 2023.

Chesneaux, Jean. ed., *Popular Movements and Secret Societies in China, 1840–1950*. Stanford: Stanford University Press, 1972.

Clark, Paul. *The Chinese Cultural Revolution: A History*. Cambridge: Cambridge University Press, 2008.

Cohen, Jerome. "Practices of Abduction and TV Confessions Show China's Insistence in Despising the Rule of Law (bangjia hedianshi renzui dengzuofa xianshi zhongguo zhiyi mieshi fazhi)" in *Voice of America*, January 28, 2016. https://www.voachinese.com/a/cohen-abduction-20160128/3167841.html. Accessed May 15, 2022.

Collinson, Stephan. "Trump's Immunity Appeal Sends a Stark Message about His Plans for a Possible Second Term" in www.cnn.com, January 9, 2024. https://www.cnn.com/2024/01/09/politics/trump-immunity-appeal-2024-analysis/index.html. Accessed January 9, 2024.

Constitution of the People's Republic of China, revised in 2018. http://www.npc.gov.cn/npc/c505/201803/e87e5cd7c1ce46ef866f4ec8e2d709ea.shtml. Accessed May 15, 2023.

Creel, Herrelee G. "Legal Institutions and Procedures during the Chou Dynasty" in Jerome A. Cohen, R. Randle Edwards, and Fu-mei Chang Chen, eds., *Essays on China's Legal Traditions*. Princeton: Princeton University Press, 1980.

"Criticizing Materials Related to the Issue of Peng Zhou" in *Compendium of Important CCP Historical Documents* (zhonggong zhongyao lishi wenxian ziliao huibian), Vol. 19. Los Angeles, Zhongwen chubanwu fuwu zhongxin, 2000.

Danziger, Danny and John Gillingham. *1215: The Year of Magna Carta*. New York: Simon & Schuster, 2004.

Des Forges, Roger, *The Mythistorical Scholar-Rebel-Advisor Li Yan, A Global Perspective*. Leiden: Brill, 2020.

Diaz, Adriana and Shuai Zhang. "Angered by U.S. Anti-Missile System, China Takes Economic Revenge" in www.cbs.com, April 7, 2017. https://www.cbsnews.com/news/china-retaliates-south-korea-us-thaad-missile-defense-lotte-and-k-pop/. Accessed June 1, 2023.

Dicey, A.V. *Introduction to the Study of the Law of the Constitution*. New York: Macmillan, 1959.

Dong, Xin and Lei Shi. *The Book of Lord Shang* (*Shangjunshu*). Haerbing: Heilongjiang renmin chubanhse, 2003.

Esherick, Joseph, Pickowicz, Paul, and Andrew G. Walder, *The Chinese Cultural Revolution as History*. Stanford: Stanford University Press, 2006.

Fang, Qiang. *Communist Judicial System in China, 1927–1976: Building on Fear*. Amsterdam: Amsterdam University Press, 2021.

———. "Chinese Media and the Rule of Law: The Case of the China Youth Daily" in Xiaobing Li and Qiang Fang, eds., *Modern Chinese Legal Reform: A New Perspective*. Lexington: University Press of Kentucky, 2013a.

——— and Roger Des Forges, "Were Chinese Rulers above the Law: Toward a Theory of the Rule of Law in China from Early Times to 1949CE" in *Stanford Journal of International Law*, Winter 2008, Vol. 44, No. 1. pp. 101–46.

———. *Chinese Complaint Systems: Natural Resistance*. U.K.: Routledge, 2013b.

———. *A Short History of Chinese Petition (zhongguo shangfang zhidu shihua)*. Beijing: China Youth Press, 2013c.

——— and Xiaobing Li, *Power versus Law in Modern China: Cities, Courts, and the Communist Party*. Lexington: University Press of Kentucky, 2017.

———. "Jiang Zemin and the United States: Hiding Hatred and Biding Time for Revenge" in Xiaobing Li and Qiang Fang, eds., *Sino-American Relations: A New Cold War* (Amsterdam: Amsterdam University Press, 2022), pp. 261–292.

Feng, Guo. "Deepening Study on the Relations between China's Modernization and the Construction of the Rule of Law (*shenru yanjiu zhongguoshi xiandaihua yufazhi jianshe deguanxi*)" in *The People's Daily*, March 20, 2023.

France-Presse, Agence. "Jailed Chinese Journalist Gao Yu Appeals Sentence for 'Leaking State Secrets'" in *The Guardian*, November 24, 2015.

Gan, Nectar. "'A Democratic China Must Be Realized in Our Time:' Beijing Jails Two Prominent Legal Activists for Subversion" in www.cnn.com, April 11, 2023. https://www.cnn.com/2023/04/10/china/china-lawyers-xu-zhiyong-ding-jiaxi-sentences-intl-hnk/index.html. Accessed May 11, 2023.

Gao, Changshan. *Xunzi*. Haerbing: Heilongjiang renmin chubanshe, 2003.

Gittings, John. "Hong Kong Reporters Make Jiang See Red" in *The Guardians*, November 1, 2000. https://www.theguardian.com/world/2000/nov/01/china.johngittings. Accessed May 23, 2023.

Gong, Pixiang. "People as the Center is the Fundamental Platform of the Legal Modernization with Chinese Features (*yirenmin weizhongxin shizhonguoshi fazhixiandaihua degenben lichang*)" in *Xinhua yuebao*, July, 2022. Vol.13. pp. 80–82.

Green, Mark A. "China is the Top Trading Partner to More Than 120 Countries" in Wilson Center, January 17, 2023. https://www.wilsoncenter.org/blog. Accessed May 31, 2023.

Guo, Baogang. "A Partocracy with Chinese Characteristics: Governance System Reform under Xi Jinping" in *Journal of Contemporary China*, Vol. 29, No. 126, Nov 2020, pp. 809–23: 821–22.

Gutzman, Kevin R.C. *James Madison and the Making of America*. New York: St. Martin's Press, 2012.

Hernandez, Javier C. "Harsh Penalties, Vaguely Defined Crimes: Hong Kong's Security Law Explained" in *The New York Times*, July 1, 2020.

Hernandez Javier C. and Amy Chang Chien. "A Bookstore that Shines as a 'Lighthouse of a Free Soviety'" in *The New York Times*, August 9, 2020.

"Hong Kong's Press Freedom Ranking" in *Reuters*, May 30, 2023. http://www.reuters.com. Accessed May 31, 2023.

"Hong Kong National Security Law: What is it and is it Wrong?" in *The BBC News*, June 28, 2022. https://www.bbc.com/news/world-asia-china-52765838. Accessed June 22, 2023.

Hui, Ted. "China Puts a Bounty on My Head" in *Wall Street Journal*, July 10, 2023.

Human Rights Watch, "Dismantling a Free Society: Hong Kong One Year After National Security Law," June 25, 2021. https://www.hrw.org/feature/2021/06/25/dismantling-free-society/hong-kong-one-year-after-national-security-law. Accessed May 22, 2023.

"Important Speech of Xi Jinping in Central Political and Legal Meeting (*Xi Jinping chuxi Zhongyang zhengfa gognzuo huiyi bingfabiao zhongyao jianghua*)" in *The People's Daily*, January 9, 2014.

Jacob, Andrew. "Defying China, Hong Kong Bookseller Describes Detention" in *The New York Times*, June 16, 2016.

——— and Chris Buckley. "China Sentences Xu Zhiyong, Legal Activist, to 4 Years in Prison" in *The New York Times*, January 26, 2014.

Jenco, Leigh K. "'Rule of Man' and 'Rule by Law' in Early Republican China: Contributions to a Theoretical Debate" in *The Journal of Asian Studies*, Vol. 69, No. 1 (February) 2010: 181–203: 182.

Ji, Weihong. "The Basic Characteristics of the Rule of Law in Aristotle's Rule of Law Concept (*Cong Yalisiduode defazhiguan kanfazhi dejiben biaozhi*)" in Ma Changsheng and Wang Xiangxin, eds., *A Study on the Rule of Law* (*fazhi wenti yanjiu*). Beijing: Falv chubanshe, 1998.

Jiang, Suhong. "A Preliminary Study on the Rule of Law Consciousness (*fazhi yishi qianlun*)" in Ma Changsheng and Wang Xiangxin, eds., *A Study on the Rule of Law* (*fazhi wenti yanjiu*). Beijing: Falv chubanshe, 1998.

Jiang, Zemin. "Speech at the Fifteenth Party Congress (shiwuda baogao)" in *Selected Works of Jiang Zemin* (*Jiang Zemin wenxuan*). Beijing: Renmin chubanshe, 2006.

Lau, Chris. "Hong Kong Plunges to 148th in World Press Freedom Rankings" in *South China Morning Post*, May 3, 2022.

Li, Cunpeng. "Xi Jinping's Rule of Law Thought is the Essence of Chinese Culture and Spirit of our Time (Xi Jinping sixiang szhonghua wenhua hezhongguo jingshen deshidai jinghua)" in The Law Institute of China Law Society, May 12, 2022. https://fzyjs.chinalaw.org.cn/portal/article/index/id/1153.html; Accessed March 25, 2023.

Liu, Ke and Kehe Li. *Guanzi*. Haerbing: Heilongjiang renmin chubanshe, 2003.

Mansoor, Sanya and Simmone Shah. "Why the Philippines is Letting the U.S. Expand its Miliatry Footprint in the Country Again" in *The Time Magazine*, February 3, 2023. https://time.com/6252750/philippines-us-military-agreement-china/. Accessed June 1, 2023.

Ma, Changsheng and Xiangxin Wang. *A Study on the Issue of the Rule of Law* (*fazhi wenti yanjiu*). Beijing: Falu chubanshe, 1998.

MacFarquhar, Roderick and Michael Schoenhals. *Mao's Last Revolution*. Harvard: Harvard University Press, 2006.

May, Tiffany. "How China Dealt with a 'Knockout Blow' to its Opponents in Hong Kong" in *The New York Times*, February 7, 2023.

Murong, Chunxue. "Xi Jinping's Selective Punishment" in *The New York Times*, January 19, 2015.

Myers, Steven L. "With Ships and Missiles, China is Ready to Challenge US Navy in Pacific" in *The New York Times*, August 29, 2018.

National Security Law in Hong Kong Special District, June 30, 2020. http://www.npc.gov.cn/npc/c30834/202007/3ae94fae8aec4468868b32f8cf8e02ad.shtml. Accessed May 27, 2023.

News Office of the State Council, "White Paper of The Practice of the One Country, Two Systems in Hong Kong Special Administrative Zone," June 10, 2014. http://www.scio.gov.cn/zfbps/ndhf/2014/Document/1373164/1373164.htm. Accessed May 30, 2023.

Peerenboom, Randle. *China's Long March Toward Rule of Law*. Cambridge: Cambridge University Press, 2000.

Peng, Zhen. *The Political and Legal Work in the People's Republic of China* (*lunxinz hongguo dezhengfa gongzuo*). Beijing: Zhongyang wenxian chubanshe, 1991.

People's Daily Editorial, "There is Still Grave Struggles in the Political and Legal Battle Line (*zai zhengfa zhanxian shanghaiyou yanzhong dedouzheng*)" in *Renmin jingcha*, Vol. 13. Oct 9, 1957.

Philips, Tom. "Beijing Rejects Tribunal's Ruling in South China Sea Case" in The Guardian, July 12, 2016. https://www.theguardian.com/world/2016/jul/12/philippines-wins-south-china-sea-case-against-china. Accessed May 31, 2023.

Prazniak, Roxann. *Of Camel Kings and Other Things: Rural Rebels against Modernity in Late Imperial China*. Lanham: Rowman & Littlefield Publishers, 1999.

Qian, Zhou. "China's Most Productive Provinces and Cities as per 2021 GDP Statistics" in China Briefing, February 7, 2022. https://www.china-briefing.com/news/chinas-2021-gdp-performance-a-look-at-major-provinces-and-cities/. Accessed May 31, 2023.

Qu, Tongzu, *Law and Society in Traditional China*. Paris: Mouton, 1961.

Questions and Answers of the Chinese Foreign Ministry, September 24, 2021. https://www.gov.cn/xinwen/2021-09/24/content_5639132.htm. Accessed May 30, 2023.

Roundtable before the Congressional-Executive Commission on China, "One Year of the National Security Law's Repression of Fundamental Freedoms in Hong Kong," June 29, 2021. www.cecc.gov or www.govinfo.gov. Accessed May 22, 2023.

Shambaugh, David. "Deng Xiaoping: The Politician" in *The China Quarterly*, No. 135, Special Issue, Sep. 1993.

Sheridan, Nina. "Chinese Exiled Lawyer Teng Biao wants to become the Lightning in the Dark (*zhongguo liuwang lvshi Teng Biao,yaozuo heianzhong deshandian*)" in *The New York Times*, August 1, 2017. https://cn.nytimes.com/china/20170801/where-are-you-teng-biao/. Accessed May 31, 2023.

Sima, Guang. *Comprehensive Mirror for Aid in Governance* (*zizhi tongjian*). Bejing: Zhonghua shuju, 1956.

Sima, Qian, *Historical Records* (*shiji*). Beijing: Zhonghua shuju, 2014.

Tamanaha, Brian Z. *On the Rule of Law: History, Politics, Theory*. Cambridge: Cambridge University Press. 2004.

"Top Rights Experts Urge Repeal of Hong Kong's National Security Law" in *UN News*, July 27, 2022. https://news.un.org/en/story/2022/07/1123432. Accessed May 20, 2023.

Turner, Karen. "Sage Kings and Laws in the Chinese and Greek Traditions" in Paul S. Ropp, ed., *Heritage of China: Contemporary Perspectives on Chinese Civilization*. Berkeley: University of California Press, 1990.

Twitchett, Denis. "How to be an Emperor: T'ang T'ai-tsung's Vision of his Role" *Asia Major* 1–3, 92–97. 3rd ed., 1996.

Wakeman, Frederic. Jr. *Spymaster Dai Li and the Chinese Secret Service*. Berkeley: University of California Press, 2003.

Wei, Zhengshou. *History of the Sui Dynasty* (*sui shu*). Beijing: Zhonghua shuju, 1973.

Wong, Alan. "Hong Kong Bookseller Says He Was Detained by China" in *The New York Times*, June 17, 2023.

Wong, Lydia and Thomas E. Kellogg. "Hong Kong's National Security Law: A Human Rights and Rule of Law Analysis," February 2021. Center for Asian Law, Georgetown Law.

Wong, Edward and Chris Buckley. "Presses Roll at Storied Chinese Newspaper but Frustration Remains" in *The New York Times*, January 11, 2013.

Wright, Mary C. ed., *China in Revolution: the First Phase, 1900–1913*. New Haven: Yale University Press, 1968.

Xi, Jinping. *The Governance of China*. Beijing: Foreign Language Press, 2017.

———. "Important Talk of Xi Jinping in Central Political and Legal Meeting (Xi Jinping chuxi Zhongyang zhengfa gognzuo huiyi bingfabiao zhongyao jianghua)" in *Xinhua News Agency*, January 16, 2019. http://politics.people.com.cn/n1/2019/0116/c1024-30559256.html; Accessed March 24, 2023.

———. "Unswervingly Following the Path of Socialist Rule of Law with Chinese Features (*jianding buyi zou zhongguo tesede shehui zhuyi fazhi daolu*)" in *Qiushi*, May, 2021.

Xu, Xiaoqun. *Trial of Modernity: Judicial Reform in Early Twentieth-Century China, 1901–1937*. Stanford: Stanford University Press. 2008.

Xu Zhiyong, "For Freedom, Justice, and Love: My Court Statement" in https://www.rfi.fr/cn/%E9%A6%96%E9%A1%B5/20140122-%E8%AE%B8%E5%BF%97%E6%B0%B8%E6%B3%95%E5%BA%AD%E9%99%88%E8%AF%8D%EF%BC%9A%E6%9C%80%E5%90%8E%E4%B8%BA%E4%BA%86%E8%87%AA%E7%94%B1%C2%B7%E5%85%AC%E4%B9%89%C2%B7%E7%88%B1. Accessed June 2014.

Yan, Jiaqi. *Ten-Year History of the Chinese Cultural Revolution*. Hong Kong: Hong Kong Dagongbaoshe, 1987.

Yang, Rongjing and Yurong Gen. *The Legal Thought of Confucius* (kongzi defalu sixiang). Beijing: Qunzhong chubanshe, 1984.

Yu, Jie, *Walking toward Throne: Xi Jinping and his China Dream* (*zouxiang dizhi, Xi Jinping hetade zhongguomeng*). Taipei: Qianwei chubanshe, 2016.

Zhang, Jinfan and Xianyi Zeng. "A Historical Review of the Rule of Man and the Rule of Law (*renzhi hefazhi delishi pouxi*)" in *A Collection of Discussions on the Rule of Law and the Rule of Man* (*fazhi yurenzhi wenti taolunji*). Beijing: Qunzhong chubanshe, 1981.

Zhang, Sheng. "*The Independent System and Practice of Supreme Court Jurisdiction in the Early Republic* (*minchu daliyuan shenpan duli de zhidu yu shijian*)" in *Zhongguo zhengfa daxue xuebao* pp.146–152, 2002.

Zheng, Yongnian and Lance Gore, L.P. *China Entering the Xi Jinping Era*. U.K.: Routledge, 2015.

"Zhongyang zhengfa gognzuo huiyi bingfabiao zhongyao jianghua)" in *Xinhua News Agency*, January 16, 2019. http://politics.people.com.cn/n1/2019/0116/c1024-30559256.html; Accessed March 24, 2023.

Zhu, Xi. *Collective Connotation of Mencius* (*Sishu zhangju jizhu*). Shengyang: Liaoning jiaoyu chubanshe, 1998.

PART TWO

Global Ambitions and Social Stability

CHAPTER FIVE

Necessitated by Geopolitics: China's Economic and Cultural Initiatives in Central Asia

Yi Sun

University of San Diego

Abstract: *This chapter examines the development of the complex relationship between China and the five Central Asian republics since the early 1990s. Although diplomatic activities initially focused on resolving the border disputes and tackling the uncertainties stemming from the new-found independence of these republics, China's relations with Central Asia have increasingly reflected a desire to protect its economic and security interests in that region since Xi Jinping became Chinese leader. Xi's One Belt One Road Initiative has created a vast infrastructure and network of trade, transportation, and communication, linking China to Central Asia. From 2012–2022, Beijing's economic programs have been accompanied by the practice of cultural diplomacy, evidenced by the establishment of many Confucius Institutes and the provision of scholarships to Central Asian students, thus deepening China's economic and cultural influence in the area. Beset by diplomatic woes elsewhere in the world, China sees Central Asia as a bright spot in a dramatically changed geopolitical environment.*

Keywords: Geopolitics; Central Asian republics; Foreign relations

From May 18–19, 2023, Chinese President Xi Jinping and his counterparts from the five Central Asian republics—Kazakhstan, Kyrgyzstan, Tajikistan, Turkmenistan, and Uzbekistan—held a summit in China's ancient capital Xian with much grandeur and pageantry. Greeting the Central Asian leaders with lavish dances and banquets, and dazzling them with extraordinary Chinese hospitality, the occasion was designed to celebrate the joint accomplishments between China and the Central Asian states in infrastructure building, trade expansion, and overall economic development while demonstrating their continued commitments to furthering their multifaceted economic collaboration, security cooperation, and cultural exchanges.[1]

1 "Xi'an Declaration of the China-Central Asia Summit," *News Central Asia* May 20, 2023; Zhuang, "China pulls on Tang dynasty Silk Road ties."

Cast in a glowing light, this event was the culmination of many high-level visits between Beijing and its Central Asian neighbors in recent years. Even during the COVID-19 pandemic, a video summit was organized in January 2022, marking the 30th anniversary of the establishment of diplomatic relations between China and the five republics and affirming their collective desire for sustained economic progress. They pledged to create a "common community of destiny" by "joining hands for a shared future" with the promise of mutual respect and friendship.[2] Largely overshadowed by other international news at the time, that video conference nonetheless denoted an important milestone in China's relationship with Central Asia, an area to which Beijing has strategically pivoted as a new frontier of economic engagement and cultural diplomacy while the world has been consumed with other tensions and conflicts. Beset by diplomatic woes and mishaps elsewhere, especially in East Asia and the Indo-Pacific, the Chinese government has become all the more keenly aware of the growing significance of Central Asia, featuring prominently in the formulation and execution of its foreign policy. Arguably, Central Asia is a bright spot in China's increasingly challenging geopolitical landscape.

It is no coincidence that Kazakhstan, the largest Central Asian country, was the site of both President Xi Jinping's announcement of China's One Belt One Road Initiative (BRI) in September 2013 and the destination of his first state visit abroad nine years later after reemerging from his COVID-19 isolation. During the same trip, Xi also visited Uzbekistan, where he was received with considerable fanfare and effusive praise for his statesmanship.[3] Both the video summit and Xi's September 2022 visit were widely reported in the Chinese state media and detailed on the Chinese Foreign Ministry website,[4] as was the Xian Summit this past May, because these events signaled China's persistent efforts at cultivating the good will and cooperation of the Central Asian republics since the early 1990s. This chapter examines the contour of the Chinese economic and cultural policies toward Central Asia during the past three decades, particularly during the Xi administration, as part of Beijing's broader geopolitical strategies.

Needless to say, China's interest in Central Asia is not a contemporary phenomenon; it dates back to the Han Dynasty over 2,000 years ago. After all, the Belt and Road blueprint that was articulated in President Xi's speech has its ancient roots in the famed Silk Road that evinced the prominence of Central Asia where

[2] Ministry of Foreign Affairs of the People's Republic of China, "Xi Jinping Chairs the Virtual Summit."

[3] Bradsher, "In the 'Great Game' of Central Asia."

[4] There was pervasive reporting on both Xi's 2013 BRI speech and Xi's visit to Central Asia in September 2022 by both government agencies and the media. Two examples include Wu and Zhang, "Xi proposes a 'new Silk Road' with Central Asia,", and Ministry of Foreign Affairs, "President Xi Jinping Makes a State Visit."

the caravan routes connected China and the West through vibrant trade of goods along with the flow of cultures and ideas. A dynamic and fluid network, the routes were traversed by "traders, diplomats, ... and proselytizers."[5] However, despite its vital role in facilitating trade and cultural exchanges centuries ago, Central Asia was largely eclipsed in importance by other developments across the world. After experiencing the historical vicissitudes from the mid-19th century to the late 20th century (1860–1991), in which the region underwent periods of Russian domination, short-lived semi-independence, incorporation into the Soviet Union, and full independence after the latter's dissolution, its reemergence on the global stage coincided with the rise of China.[6] Its proximity to Xinjiang with their shared ethnic and religious traditions and the resultant security concerns to the Chinese government, its coveted energy and natural resources, not to mention its geographical connections to Russia, India, and a number of major Islamic countries, have increasingly rendered Central Asia a significant player in global geopolitics.[7] Indeed, China's growing clout in that region has caused alarm in the United States, whose leaders have in recent years made strenuous efforts in countering and diluting Beijing's influence.[8]

Following the collapse of the Soviet Union, China's foreign policies toward the five newly-independent republics initially focused on tackling the uncertainties and border disputes. In 1997, China and Kazakhstan signed an agreement that resolved the majority of their quarrels with the transfer of some land to each side. Around the same time, a previously disputed border with Kyrgyzstan was settled with the signing of a bilateral accord. Similarly, Beijing dealt with its territorial contests with Tajikistan through diplomatic negotiations and peaceful means, which in turn clarified boundaries, promoted stability, and fostered cooperation. China conducted dialogues with each of its Central Asian neighbors separately, discussing their respective historical claims, assessing the needs and interests of both parties, and working towards an equitable solution. To achieve a greater strategic goal, China showed flexibility and willingness to compromise, including making certain territorial concessions.[9] It is worth noting that Beijing's tactfulness in settling border claims in Central Asia was premised on a more comprehensive objective of building and strengthening their economic ties. Regular communications and consultations were accompanied with cultural exchanges and the simultaneous

[5] Pradt, *The Prequel to China's New Silk Road*: 19.

[6] Roudik, *The History of the Central Asian Republics*: 7.

[7] Ibid., 10.

[8] United States Institute of Peace, "Blinken Debuts New U.S. Approach in Central Asia"; "America is at last getting serious about countering China in Asia."

[9] For a detailed explanation of the border agreements, see Kondapalli, "China's Role in Central Asia."

offering of various forms of economic cooperation and development projects, all of which aided in cultivating good will, building trust, and facilitating smoother resolutions. It stands to reason that the ways in which the Chinese government tackled the border issues in Central Asia could serve as models for its handling of territorial disputes with other countries in the Asian Pacific.

China's earnest desire for extensive economic relations and safeguarding its energy and geostrategic security compelled it to not only seek amicable territorial solutions with Central Asia countries but also adopt both economic initiatives and cultural diplomacy that began long before the onset of BRI. A substantial network of trade, transportation, and communication, including roads, railroads, as well as oil and gas pipelines, had already materialized during the two decades from 1993 to 2013. Meanwhile, security concerns due to Central Asia's geographical proximity to Xinjiang, where ethnic strife has posed persistent challenges to the Han Chinese government, also figured conspicuously in China's dealings with the five republics.[10]

Naturally, any analysis of Sino-Central Asian relations has to begin with Xinjiang, which not only has the longest border line with three of the five countries but also shares cultural identities and religious traditions with its neighbors. Historically, Xinjiang's geographic location often made it the focal point of territorial contention between the Han Chinese and the nomadic tribes in Central Asia. During the Han Dynasty (circa 121BCE), the Chinese forces defeated the powerful Xiongnu who had by then dominated the area for almost a century, and the subsequent opening of the Silk Road during the 100s BCE led to the infiltration of Chinese economic and cultural influences into that region. With Xinjiang as their sphere of influence, the various ensuing Chinese dynasties alternated between policies of confrontation and pacification in exercising their power through both military conquests and trade.[11]

Translated into English as the "New Frontier", Xinjiang was officially incorporated into the China Proper during the Qing Dynasty in the mid-18th century and formally became a province following the 1911 Republican Revolution. Designated as the Uighur Autonomous Region by the PRC government during the mid-1950s, Xinjiang has undergone tremendous changes during the past (nearly) seventy years. In the midst of their long-standing ethnic tensions with the Han Chinese and resistance against Beijing's heavy-handed control, residents in Xinjiang nonetheless saw notable improvement in their economic conditions even during the early stages of China's economic reforms. According to the famed historian A. Doak Barnett, Urumqi, the capital of Xinjiang, changed from "a large, sprawling, dusty

10 Ibid., 138–145.

11 Xie, ed. *Xinjiang Weiwuer Zizhiqu Jingji Dili* [The Economic Geography of the Xinjiang Uighurs Autonomous Region].

town, consisting mainly of one-story shops and residences" in 1948 to "a modern metropolis" four decades later.[12]

Still, Xinjiang lagged woefully behind other regions in China. With the possession of natural resources, including an estimated 30 billion tons of oil and gas reserves and 27 billion tons of coal deposits (about 35 percent and 40 percent of the total national reserves, respectively),[13] residents in Xinjiang were dubbed "beggars with a gold bowl in hand."[14] More than a decade into the reforms, the Chinese government decided to transform the region from simply a support base of raw materials into another front post of development.[15] By the early 1990s, a total of 19 billion yuan was spent on a series of large and medium-sized industrial projects with emphasis on building a modern transportation and communication system along with the oil and textile industries in Xinjiang.[16] The accelerated economic changes led to China's own "westward movement" in the 1990s, when the coastal areas were becoming saturated with new industrial and commercial establishments while the vast northwest assumed growing importance as a market, a resource center, and a trading post.[17] Early in the Jiang Zemin administration (1993–2003), the central government expressed its determination to make Xinjiang a "true new frontier".[18] It was at that critical juncture when the Central Asian republics gained their independence from the former Soviet Union, providing a timely outlet for China's growing economic ambitions.

The blueprint and prototype of the BRI were conceived during the early 1990s, though the plan was not formally articulated by President Xi until two decades later. Already, the Jiang Zemin administration made clear its intention to build a new Silk Road to connect China's inland with Central Asia through Xinjiang. Specifically, the government adopted a policy of *wai yin nei lian, dong lian xi chu,* (外引内联, 东连西出 attract external investment, ally with other interior regions, link with the east and export to the west). The region's phenomenal deposits of natural resources and its 200-billion-dollar market incentivized China to create a Central Asian Economic Circle anchored around Xinjiang.[19]

Starting in the 1980s, the regional government began to devote considerable resources to the development of Xinjiang, with some 7.2 billion yuan (equivalent to

[12] Barnett, *China's Far West: Four Decades of Change*: 352. This book provides a detailed study of the changes in Xinjiang during China's economic reforms up to the early 1990s.

[13] Wang, ed. *Encyclopedia of Xinjiang's Society and Economy*: 3.

[14] Bao and He, *The Opening of the Frontier and the Economic Development of Xinjiang*: 71.

[15] Guo and Jin, *The Socialist Market Economy*: 7.

[16] Abulaiti and Han, *Xinjiang's trading posts*: 8–9.

[17] 7 Xu, ed. *Strategies for Developing China's Northwestern Economy*: 209.

[18] *Tianjin Evening News* (*Tianjin Jinwanbao*) July 17, 1998.

[19] 9 Bao and He, *The Opening of the Frontier*: 47.

$870 million at the time) to new road construction and repair in order to meet the growing industrial and commercial demands. Within a decade, a much-improved transportation system became evident in the several direct rail lines connecting Urumqi to Beijing, Shanghai, Chengdu, Zhengzhou, Xian, and several other major cities. A 283-kilometer Turpan-Urumqi-Dahuangshan Expressway was completed in 1998 with the support of a $150 million loan from the World Bank, effectively reaching several key areas within the province. Another railroad linking Urumqi with Lianyun Harbor along the Yellow Sea and with Rotterdam in Holland, referred to as the "Eurasia transcontinental bridge" came into existence.[20] In July 1997, long before BRI's inception, a 26,000-kilometer road system, including the Uzbek-Kirghiz-Chinese Highway, became operational.[21] Furthermore, "efforts were launched for building a rail/road bridge between China and Europe through Central Asia" to connect "the developed regions of Europe on the one end and Japan, China, and Southeast Asia on the other end" along with other "railways, expressways, air routes and optical fiber, oil and gas pipelines."[22] In addition, a new postal and tele-communications network joined Xinjiang with over 140 countries and regions in the world, including Central Asia, with its service magnified by more than 10 times the level in 1978.[23]

The well-timed independence of the five republics in 1992 provided China with a much-needed external impetus to further develop the Xinjiang-Central Asia Economic Circle. Beijing lost no time in establishing diplomatic relations with all the five new countries. In the following year, thirty-three counties and major cities in Xinjiang along the border were opened to trade while direct flights between Urumqi and Kazakhstan and Uzbekistan came into existence. Trade relations between Xinjiang with the two countries quickly grew, from 40 enterprises of various sizes in 1991 to 260 within six years.[24] By 2012, the total trade volume jumped 78 times from $460 million to $36.45 billion.[25] As the economic hub, Xinjiang's historical connections and shared cultural traditions, languages, customs and religions proved to be highly conducive to advancing China's economic and trade relations with Central Asia, enabling Beijing to pursue a so-called "black and white" policy, one that emphasized the importance of both the oil and cotton industries. As the largest commercial cotton production site in China, Xinjiang became the chief exporter of China's cotton materials, both retail and non-retail, to Central Asia.

20 Ibid., 22.

21 Abulaiti and Han, *Xinjiang's trading posts*: 11.

22 Singh, "Sino-Central Asian Ties: Problems and Prospects."

23 Bao and He, *The Opening of the Frontier*: 71.

24 Ibid., 21, 71.

25 Li, *The Stable Economic and Trade Growth.*"

During 1995–96, its border trade constituted 48.7 percent of all its foreign trade, and over eighty different kinds of products were exported annually.[26]

Aside from trade, concerns with its energy security drove China to seek productive engagements with Central Asia whose significant energy resources, including oil, natural gas, and other minerals, were critical in helping China meet its increasing demands for industrialization.[27] It is rather telling that when Premier Li Peng visited four of the five Central Asian countries in the spring of 1994, he touted the appeal of China's inexpensive consumer goods while four years later, President Jiang Zemin during his Central Asia trip spoke more on China's energy needs and the mutually beneficial nature of their relationship. Jiang offered Central Asian countries opportunities to expand their trade with others in East Asia and the Pacific by using Chinese ports, an offer that was enthusiastically embraced. As a result, the port of Tianjin served as one of the main conduits through which Central Asian exports were shipped to Japan and Korea in exchange for electronic appliances through the same port.[28]

These aforementioned achievements from 1992 to 2012 laid the foundation for the relatively smooth implementation of BRI, which has further intensified China's investment in infrastructure building and deepening its trade relations with Central Asia. With its promise to "increase connectivity, expand regional trade, and modernize their obsolete transport infrastructure" without laying any demands for political and ideological changes, BRI proved to be highly appealing to most Central Asian leaders, who found the Chinese hybrid model of economic liberalism and political centralism more palatable in contrast to that of the West.[29]

Building upon their earlier successes, the Central Asian countries have collectively played a critical role in China's BRI achievements, including constructing a dynamic system of infrastructure, drawing direct Chinese investments in their large numbers of economic projects, and carrying out trade expansion. With only about 0.3 percent of the world economy in the 1990s, Central Asia at that time attracted less than $1 billion of Chinese investment limited to the oil and gas sector. However, with $40 billion Chinese investments by the end of 2020,[30] BRI has achieved impressive results, seen in "The China-Kazakhstan crude oil pipeline, the China-Central Asia natural gas pipeline, and the China-Kyrgyzstan-Uzbekistan road-rail transport corridor." Additionally, "China-Europe freight trains via Central Asia

[26] For a detailed account of the productivity levels of Xinjiang's various products, see Bao and He, *The Opening of the Frontier*: 22–24.

[27] Singh, "Sino-Central Asian Ties," 2.

[28] Ibid., 4.

[29] Nurgoshayeva, "How Is China's Belt and Road Changing Central Asia?"

[30] Khitakhunov, "Economic Cooperation between Central Asia and China."

have made over 25,000 trips … . China and Central Asian countries implemented a large number of new projects in such fields as water conservancy, electricity, textile and chemical industry. Agriculture, digital economy, artificial intelligence and new energy have become new highlights of cooperation."[31]

China is not the only party that has celebrated its accomplishments; Central Asian leaders have also voiced their strong support of BRI. According to a *Radio Free Europe* report on September 10, 2019, Deputy Prime Minister Zhenis Kasymbek lauded the completion of 15 joint Kazakh-Chinese projects worth $3.9 billion in "several sectors, including agriculture, the chemical industry, oil and gas, [and] transport generating 4,000 new jobs, 95% of which went to the Kazaks."[32] With its rich deposits of oil, coal, and other metals such as iron, copper, gold, and silver, as well as uranium and rare earths, Kazakhstan is a major geostrategic partner and has thus drawn increasing investments from China in exchange for its exports of energy resources and raw materials. Among other momentous developments is the fact that now "China is the owner of PetroKazakhstan, the largest oil company of the former USSR" and controls 30 percent of Kazakhstan's oil extraction.[33] During the two-year period (2015–17), Kazakhstan and China signed five agreements to "create cooperation zones in transport infrastructure, trade, processing industries, construction, agriculture, and other areas."[34] By 2020, China's investment in Kazakhstan had increased even more dramatically. Bilateral trade and Chinese direct investments in Central Asia have been mutually reinforcing. A coveted market, China is the second largest importer of raw materials from Uzbekistan, where heavy Chinese investments have created nearly 600 Chinese-Uzbek joint enterprises. Similarly, "China has signed about 200 agreements in the field of trade, health, agriculture, and education" with Tajikistan.[35] Three years into the BRI adventure, approximately one-third of Kyrgyzstan's imports and its largest foreign investments (about 37 percent) were already coming from China. As for Tajikistan, 58 percent of its foreign direct investment came from China two years after BRI's implementation.[36]

In addition to initiating a wide range of infrastructure projects, BRI has further advanced China-Central Asian bilateral trade, the overall volume of which grew 100 times from approximately $460 million in 1992 to more than $50 billion in 2021.[37] According to the Observatory of Economic Complexity (OEC) that provides

31 Liu, "China-Central Asia Relations Entering a New Era."
32 Najibullah, "Anti-Chinese Protests Don't Deter Kazakh President."
33 Kobushkina and Soloshcheva, "The Role of Central Asia."
34 Toktogulova and Zhuang, "A Critical Analysis of the Belt."
35 Kobushkina and Soloshcheva, "The Role of Central Asia."
36 Toktogulova and Zhuang, "A Critical Analysis of the Belt and Road."
37 Liu, "China-Central Asia Relations."

the most detailed data on global trade, China's trade with the five countries grew at an annual average rate ranging from 21.8 percent to 13.7 percent, respectively from 1995 to 2020—Kazakhstan (21.8 percent: $75.4 million to $10.3 billion); Uzbekistan (20.4 percent: $47.5 million to $4.88 billion); Tajikistan (18.4 percent: 14.6 million to 998 million); Turkmenistan (15.8 percent: $11.3 million to $445 million), and 13.7 percent with Kyrgyzstan ($105 million to $2.6 billion). China's main exports consisted primarily of coated flat-rolled iron, rubber footwear, broadcasting equipment, non-knit women's coats, and synthetic filament yarn woven fabric, and retail or non-retail cotton.[38]

Correspondingly, the exports from most of the Central Asian countries to China have also gone up dramatically during the past twenty-five years with the exception of Kyrgyzstan. Turkmenistan saw a dramatic annual increase of 31.4 percent ($5.79 million to $5.32 billion); Kazakhstan's exports rose by 14.9 percent ($292 million to $9.42 billion); Uzbekistan's by 12.8 percent ($64 million to $1.29 billion); and Tajikistan's by 6.05 percent ($8.63 million to $37.4 million). Kyrgyzstan's exports to China fell by an annual average of 3.49 percent (114 million to 47 million) largely due to the decreased export of copper ore and precious metal ore. However, with its membership in the World Trade Organization, the country has served as a "major trade and re-export hub for the rest of the region" by offering "important transit routes for affordable Chinese consumer goods."[39] Overall, the Central Asian products comprised mainly petroleum gas, crude petroleum, refined copper, ethylene polymers, ore, slag and ash, rawhide and leather, mineral fuels, mineral oil, wool and other animal hair, and fruit.[40]

Needless to say, Sino-Central Asian relations are multi-dimensional. The positive developments of trade and infrastructure building have been punctuated with China's security concerns largely related to Xinjiang. Fueled by resentment against economic disparities, Han Chinese infiltration, political crackdowns, and civil rights violations, ethnic tensions and conflicts have persisted for decades,

[38] The Observatory of Economic Complexity, https://oec.world/en/profile/bilateral-country/chn/partner/kaz). To access the information on a given country, it is necessary to write its name in the "search" box. Also see "China and Kyrgyzstan: Bilateral Trade and Future Outlook, *China Briefing*, August 27, 2021.

[39] Toktogulova and Zhuang, "A Critical Analysis of the Belt and Road."

[40] The Observatory of Economic Complexity, https://oec.world/en/profile/bilateral-country/chn/partner/kaz). To access the information on a given country, it is necessary to write its name in the "search" box. Also see "China and Kyrgyzstan: Bilateral Trade and Future Outlook, *China Briefing*, August 27, 2021. For the most comprehensive information and analysis of the different economic landscapes in the five Central Asian republics, including the various resources—energy, agriculture, manufacturing, and other fields— see Eric Balan's published dissertation "China-Central Asia's Regiocentric Strategies of Integration and Geoeconomics Perspectives" (available from Amazon, 2021).

sometimes simmering under the surface, other times erupting into the open.[41] Several well-publicized acts of violence attributed to the Uighurs were committed during 2013–2014. The Chinese Ministry of Public Security categorized these events as terrorist attacks perpetrated by Uighur separates who may have received support from Kazakhstan-based Uighur organizations that have in the past expressed support for an independent East Turkestan within Xinjiang.[42]

In recent years, much has been written by Western journalists and academics about the history of Xinjiang as the crossroads in Central Asia as well as the government's abusive treatments of the Uighurs as a way of suppressing political dissension and separatism.[43] It goes without saying that the stability of Xinjiang plays a determining role in shaping China's policy towards Central Asia where over half a million Uighurs reside, and where leaders have generally supported Islam while attempting to maintain a secular governing apparatus.[44] To fend off external

[41] Heightened ethnic tensions were evident in several incidents. In February 1997, anti-Han Chinese riots in Yining, a town located near the Chinese-Kazakh border, resulted in the deaths of nine people and the wounding of nearly 200. Afterwards, three people were executed and twenty-seven were sentenced to prison terms ranging from seven years to life after the riot. Uighur nationalist groups in Kazakhstan claimed that 57,000 Uighurs had been arrested by the Chinese authorities in Xinjiang since April 1996, and that 150 Uighurs activists were executed while attempting to escape from jail in Xinjiang, though the Chinese government strenuously denied the report. According to *The Voice of Eastern Turkestan*, a newspaper published in the Russian language by the United Eastern Turkestan National Front in Almaty, the Chinese armed police detained many suspected separatists in Xinjiang in the summer of 1997. (This information is derived from the notes that I took after reading online news articles on Chinese News Digest dated March 26, 1997 and July 23, 1997 http://www.cnd.org). Concerns with terrorism related to Uighur separatism mounted after 9/11. "On January 21, 2002 Beijing released a lengthy article on East Turkestan activities in Xinjiang, which identified six major actions of the terrorists in the region—explosions, assassinations, attacks on police and government organs, crimes of poison and arson, secret training bases and plotting and organizing riots and disturbances. China has succeeded in getting some of the East Turkestan groups included in the internationally sanctioned list of terrorist groups,"; Kondapalli, "China's Role in Central Asia."

[42] On October 28, 2013, a group of five Uighurs allegedly drove a jeep into Tiananmen Square in Beijing, set the gas tank on fire, killed two civilians, and injured another forty bystanders. There was evidence that the attackers had jihadist flags and probably had ties to the East Turkestan Islamic Movement. See Jiang and Hunt, "Five Arrested in Tiananmen Square Incident." On March 2, 2014, eight Uighurs, reportedly armed with knives, attacked civilians in a train station in southern China, killing thirty-three individuals and wounding another 143 (See *Jiang and Hunt, October 30, CNN)* At the site of the "Kunming Attack," a jihadist East Turkestan Flag was purportedly found. On May 31, 2014, several Uighurs crashed two cars into an Urumqi market and killed thirty-one people (see "China Blames Uighur Separatists for Knife Attack.")

[43] See Starr, *Xinjiang: China's Muslim Borderland*; Mackerras and Clarke, eds., *China, Xinjiang and Central Asia*; Betts, Vicziany, and Weiming Jia, eds., *The Cultures of Ancient Xinjiang*.

[44] Roudik, *The History of the Central Asian Republics*, 162. Also see Niquet, "China and Central Asia, China Perspectives."

encouragements from Central Asia to the pro-independence sentiment and activities in Xinjiang, the Chinese government has made strenuous efforts at incentivizing people in those republics to lessen their affinity with the Uighurs and refrain from criticizing the latter's treatment. Addressing its security concerns while striving to build trust, strengthen economic cooperation and broaden regional cooperation, Beijing took the lead in founding the Shanghai Five in April 1996, with China, Russia, Kazakhstan, Kyrgyzstan, and Tajikistan as its original members. Seeking promises from the signatories not to provide sanctuary for Uighur separatists, China signed agreements with both Kazakhstan and Tajikistan to oppose all forms of separatism. At the Shanghai Five Summit in 1998, "China succeeded in getting through a resolution where all agreed to reject all manifestations of national separatism and religious extremism and to ban on their territories activities harmful to the sovereignty, security and public order of any of the five countries."[45] The ensuing annual summits, held in the member nations on a rotating basis, reaffirmed such commitments.

The Shanghai Five also pledged to "oppose intervention in other countries' internal affairs on the pretexts of 'humanitarianism' and 'protecting human rights'" while supporting their member countries' "national independence, sovereignty, territorial integrity, and social stability." In general, the Central Asian countries have taken a cautious approach and have resisted uttering sharp criticisms of Beijing. When voicing concerns with the crackdown of Uighurs, for instance, the Kazakhstan spokesman conceded that it was an internal problem of China's.[46] Beijing has conveyed appreciation for the "Central Asian regimes' reluctance in supporting Uighur nationalism ... and their refusal to provide outside support to Muslim separatists in Xinjiang."[47] The Shanghai Five later morphed into the Shanghai Cooperation Organization (SCO) in 1997 with Uzbekistan as its new member and subsequently expanded its membership in 2001 to include India and Pakistan and more recently, Iran. During the first decade of the 21st century, the SCO added to its chief agenda the urgency of combating terrorism."[48] At SCO's most recent meeting in Uzbekistan in September 2022, President Xi once again called for its members to enhance security cooperation in combating terrorism, separatism, extremism, drug trafficking and transnational organized crime.[49]

[45] Singh, "Sino-Central Asian Ties: Problems and Prospects."

[46] Gill, "Shanghai Five: An Attempt to Counter U.S."

[47] Roudik, *The History of the Central Asian Republics*, 10.

[48] Kondapalli, "China's Role in Central Asia."

[49] Shanghai Cooperation Organization website: https://odi.org/en/insights/shanghai-cooperation-organisation-summit-2022-keytakeaways/#:~:text=The%20SCO%2C%20a%20Eurasian%20political,with%20Iran%20soon%20to%20join). Accessed July 10, 2023.

Meanwhile, to bolster trade and economic relations, tackle security concerns, facilitate the smooth operation of BRI projects, and alleviate Central Asians' anxieties over excessive dependence on China or the loss of their natural resources, Beijing has increasingly employed cultural and education diplomacy to exercise its "soft power" in the region.[50] A two-prong approach has been adopted—setting up Confucius Institutes in Central Asian countries to promote the learning of the Chinese language, arts, and culture while simultaneously offering scholarships to their students for pursuing college or advanced studies in China. In his 2013 BRI speech in Kazakhstan, President Xi announced a ten-year plan to provide 30,000 government-sponsored scholarships to SCO members in addition to inviting students and teachers at their Confucius Institutes to visit China.[51] These policies and practices aimed to project positive Chinese images, tell a compelling "China Story" about its cultural heritage, historical vicissitudes, and contemporary achievements while assuaging Central Asians' resentments against the perceived Chinese dominance and, perhaps most importantly, to allay their pro-Uighur sentiment.[52]

In less than two decades since the early 2000s, thirteen Confucius Institutes have been established, including five in Kazakhstan, four in Kyrgyzstan, two in Uzbekistan, and two in Tajikistan. Most of these Institutes have formed partnerships with universities in Xinjiang and serve as hubs for promoting Chinese language, history, and culture to thousands of Central Asian students in the Confucius classrooms. Furthermore, the Chinese embassies in the five republics have organized "cultural and humanitarian events, information tours for journalists and media representatives, and offered affordable treatment with Chinese traditional medicine."[53] Despite the current absence of a Confucius Institute in Turkmenistan, the Chinese language is now in the education curriculum at schools and universities in several parts of the country, along with English, German, and French.[54]

Convinced that "Chinese language promotion is the most effective way of encouraging a Chinese voice in global affairs,"[55] the Confucius Institutes have organized cultural activities and academic exchanges along with other opportunities for the locals to learn about China. Many exhibitions, festivals, and workshops have regularly taken place, showcasing China's historical artifacts, artworks, highlighting its rich history, and enhancing the people-to-people connectivity as part of Beijing's cultural diplomacy in Central Asia, where a positive presentation

[50] Aliyev, "China and Central Asia."

[51] Li, " 'One Belt One Road' and Central Asia."

[52] Sorbello, "Cultural Diplomacy as a Key Instrument."

[53] Aliyev, "China and Central Asia."

[54] Izimov, "China and Turkmenistan: A Regional Dimension."

[55] Yau, "China Polishes Its Image in Central Asia."

of China's international image is deemed crucial in boosting its power and prestige. Various Chinese organizations also frequently send performing arts groups to Central Asia to put on display traditional Chinese music, dance, opera, and martial arts for the purpose of popularizing Chinese cultural and artistic expressions. They provide an effective platform for Chinese artists and practitioners and participants in the host countries to interact, share their experiences, and engage in productive conversations. These programs and activities have served to heighten mutual understandings and strengthen China's overall diplomatic and economic relations with Central Asian countries. Moreover, China has invested in the development of a cultural infrastructure in that region, seen in the building of cultural centers, museums, and libraries that also aid in fostering an appreciation of Chinese tradition and providing avenues of exchange. Likewise, as part of a grand design to propel its "soft power," China has played an increasingly dynamic role in energizing the Intangible Cultural Heritage Cooperation, a program aimed at restoring, preserving, and refining cultural heritage sites. To such an end, Beijing has engaged in joint research projects, workshops, training programs, and exhibitions with Central Asian countries in safeguarding and revitalizing traditional arts, crafts, rituals, and practices.[56] It is noteworthy that, for all its geo-economic importance, BRI has also dramatically changed "the political impetus for cultural sector cooperation," leading to experts from China and Kazakhstan alone cooperating in more than thirty cultural and historical sites. "Given dozens of Silk Road corridors potentially linking more than five hundred sites across the region have been identified, the Silk Road is likely to emerge as the most ambitious and expansive international cooperation program for heritage preservation ever undertaken."[57]

Interestingly though not surprisingly, the identified sites also helped to justify the construction of tangible infrastructure such as roads, airports, and other urban accommodations. In other words, "heritage diplomacy," billed as way of exercising soft power, has increasingly become the vehicle for carrying out "hard power" in light of the fact that the "Central Asian heritage corridor" involves four of the republics (with the exception of Turkmenistan).[58]

Aside from "exporting" its cultural influences, the Chinese government has focused on "inviting in" Central Asian students as a way of cultivating the good will of the younger generations. It has subsidized scholarships and educational programs to selected students from the five countries, enabling them to study at

[56] For China's increasingly active role in promoting the Intangible Cultural Heritage, see the United Nations Educational, Scientific, and Cultural Organization website: https://ich.unesco.org/en/state/china-CN?info=periodic-reporting. Accessed July 1, 2023.

[57] Winter, "Heritage Diplomacy along the One Belt One Road."

[58] Ibid.

Chinese universities and institutions, thereby facilitating academic cooperation and providing opportunities for these students to immerse in Chinese culture and society. There are several different types of scholarships, both official and private in nature. The ones sponsored by the Chinese Ministry of Education cover full or partial tuition and provide accommodations, medical insurance, and a monthly living allowance to undergraduate and graduate students in various fields. The Silk Road Scholarship is specially geared towards students from the Belt and Road participating countries as part of a broader agenda to advance academic and cultural cooperation between China and the BRI partaking countries. Additionally, some Chinese universities offer their own scholarships for outstanding international students.[59]

According to the Chinese Ministry of Education, Kazakhstan, with close to 120,000 students studying in China in 2018 and one-third of them on Chinese scholarships, ranked among the top ten countries across the world in terms of its number of students in China.[60] The Silk Road Scholarship also contributes a generous stipend for Kazak students to complete their undergraduate or graduate degrees at Chinese universities. The practice of cultural and education diplomacy has yielded impressive results, as the “soft indoctrination” has apparently been quite successful in “building a pro-China elite in Kazakhstan.”[61] Those with a Chinese education and now in leadership positions have generally adopted a pro-China stance. For instance, Kazakhstan’s President Kassym-Jomart Tokayev, who studied in China and is a fluent Mandarin speaker, made his first trip to Beijing in September 2019 to celebrate the close Kazak-Chinese alliance. Like his predecessor, Tokayev has embraced stronger ties with China, now Kazakhstan’s most important trade partner and foreign investor.[62] Similarly, Dariga Nazarbayev, Kazakhstan’s former deputy prime minister and daughter of its former president, “extolled the virtue of learning Chinese, arguing that closer ties to China is the destiny of Kazakhstan.”[63] Overall, Kazakhstan maintains a rather positive attitude toward China. Despite the fact that there is a sizable population of ethnic Kazaks in Xinjiang who may have been affected by Beijing’s repressive policies toward the Uighurs, Astana has abstained from publicly criticizing China’s actions.

The same can be said of Kyrgyzstan that relies on Chinese investment and assistance for infrastructure development and other economic projects. While harboring certain anxieties about the BRI-induced influx of Chinese goods and labor, Bishkek has nonetheless worked to preserve a friendly relationship with

59 Sorbello, “Cultural Diplomacy as a Key Instrument.”
60 Jiang, “China’s Education Diplomacy in Central Asia.”
61 Plakhina, “Chinese Higher Education Programs.”
62 Albert, “Kazakh President Yokayev Goes to Beijing.”
63 Jiang, “China’s Education Diplomacy in Central Asia.”

its influential neighbor. In fact, President Sadyr Japarov, whose father was born and educated in China,[64] and who personally harbors strong pro-China sentiment, recently proclaimed that "The China-Kyrgyzstan relationship is now at its best in history," and the China-Kyrgyzstan partnership agreements "promise to combat 'East Turkestan terrorist forces,' including through 'suspect repatriation.'"[65]

As for Tajikistan, a shared border with Xinjiang together with many economic considerations have also persuaded Dushanbe to seek a constructive relationship with China for the sake of domestic development and regional stability. As "the largest investor and creditor in Tajikistan," China has exercised vigorous "education diplomacy" in the country. Several agreements on academic, scientific, and overall educational cooperation have been signed since the early 1990s, including "special quotas allocated to applicants from Tajikistan to Chinese universities," increasing the number of Tajik students in China from fewer than 300 to more than 3,000 from the early 1990s to the mid-2010s. Among the nearly 10,000 Tajik students who have studied at the Confucius Institutes, some were prepared to work in Chinese enterprises in their country and others have become leaders in the area of national education.[66]

China's application of cultural diplomacy in Uzbekistan has been even more active. In 2013, China and Uzbekistan signed a cultural exchange agreement, under which the two countries began their engagements in areas of culture, education, science, and technology. The successful first China-Uzbekistan cultural exchange week in 2017, during which seminars, exhibitions, and performances took place, was replicated in the following years. In addition, China has provided Uzbekistan with a variety of cultural assistances, including support for the restoration and preservation of cultural heritage sites in Uzbekistan. Deeming the media sector as essential in helping to "tell the China Story well," China has also begun to solicit the help of some Central Asian journalists.[67] China Central Television (CCTV) and Uzbekistan's National Television and Radio Corporation (UzTRK) have been cooperating to produce joint programs and documentaries. Nonetheless, Uzbek leaders remain cautious and pragmatic, trying to strike a balance between cooperating with China on economic, cultural, and security issues and avoiding placing all their eggs in the China basket to fend off excessive dependency.

Among the five republics, Turkmenistan has made more conscious efforts at diversifying its connections with other regional powers while remaining collaborative with China, including considering exporting its gas to Europe and South

[64] Jiang, "Central Asian elites choose China over Russia."

[65] Colville, "The China-Kyrgyzstan Close Embrace and the Threat to it."

[66] Rashdov, Mullojonov, Rashidova, and Lemon, "Academic Diplomacy."

[67] Sorbello, "Cultural Diplomacy as a Key Instrument."

Asia. Notably, known for its policy of neutrality, Turkmenistan is the only Central Asian republic that does not have a Confucius Institute. Despite these efforts, however, "China's share in the strategic sector of the Turkmen economy continues to grow."[68] The so-called "gas connection"—that is, Turkmenistan supplies about half of China's natural gas imports to fuel the latter's industrial growth—is a primary factor that seems to overshadow Ashgabat's concerns with its over-dependency on China. Moreover, anxieties over Afghan terrorism spilling across the border have compelled the Turkmenistan government to seek some level of security guarantee from China, thus further coagulating its connections to Beijing, and further weakening its resistance to China's cultural infiltration.[69]

Interestingly, the COVID-19 pandemic played a dual role of both limiting and expanding China's cultural activities and outreach efforts, as digital tools have come into play due to travel restrictions. Videos and other visual conveyors of information about China have found their way into various media outlets.[70] Arguably, China's cultural diplomacy in Central Asia has fulfilled its desired outcomes. Generally speaking, the five countries have prioritized economic cooperation, stability, and maintaining good relations with China over responding to growing public sentiments against unchecked growth of Chinese presence. They have stayed away from decrying the human rights violations of the Uighurs, the most serious of which took place under the leadership of Chen Quanguo, who governed Xinjiang as the Party Secretary from 2016 to 2021, despite the shared ethnic and cultural ties between their respective populations and their counterparts in Xinjiang.

Central Asia, with its historical connections to Xinjiang and its strategic location, has been one of the focal points of geopolitical preoccupation for China's foreign policy makers. The economic development of Xinjiang during the early stages of China's economic reforms in the 1980s and early 1990s was ready for an outlet, one that was provided by the independence of the five Central Asian republics in 1992. The concept of a Xinjiang-Central Asia Economic Circle had been conceived and put into motion a decade before the onset of the Belt and Road Initiative in 2013, evidenced in the roads and bridges, along with communication systems connecting Xinjiang to Eurasia.

China's strategic pivot to Central Asia was prompted by two main factors. First of all, it was eager to embrace the enormous economic opportunities that only Central Asia could accord with its rich and diverse natural resources, chiefly oil, gas, and other minerals, as well as the massive potential for bilateral trade and markets. At the same time, Beijing was also compelled by security concerns over the stability of Xinjiang, where ethnic conflicts between the Uighurs and the

68 Izimov, "China and Turkmenistan: A regional Dimension."

69 Ibid.

70 Ibid.

Han Chinese had continued for decades, and where government oppression and mistreatment of the Muslims had intensified the latter's resistance. Consequently, the Chinese government has been keenly aware of the necessity to cultivate the goodwill of the Central Asian countries, where over half a million Uighurs live and where organizations supporting the separatist movement in Xinjiang are located, in order to mitigate pro-Uighur sympathies and minimize risks for a destabilized Xinjiang with external support. The dual and intertwining interests in deriving economic benefits and safeguarding its national security have motivated the Chinese government to adopt a "good neighbor" policy toward Central Asia.

The BRI has been an effective vehicle for China to deepen its economic engagement with Central Asia by providing massive investment, loans, and labor for the construction and updating of transportation and communication infrastructure in that region, and by gaining access to its vast energy reserves and market. Meanwhile, cultural and education diplomacy has propelled the Chinese "soft power" through the use of Confucius Institutes and generous scholarships for Central Asian students. Both approaches have yielded impressive results, as they have generated pro-China sentiment among the general public and the educated elite, doubts of China's intentions and anxieties over its dominance notwithstanding.

In addition to serving its intricately linked and mutually reinforcing economic and security interests, China's policy toward Central Asia seems to have an added layer of benefit, namely, the ability to use the Beijing-led strategic alliance as a counterweight against Washington's policy of containing China in East Asia and the Pacific. Simultaneously, despite the symbolic gesture of friendship, as projected by Xi and Putin at the SCO summit in Uzbekistan, a weakened Russia due to its invasion of Ukraine gives China a wider window of opportunity to strengthen its involvement in Central Asia.[71] Having replaced Russia as the most important trade partner and investor in Central Asia, not to mention as the more popular destination for its students, China is poised to exert further influence in a critical region of the world by cementing a regional alliance while advancing globalization. Indeed, in navigating a troubling and troubled world with many self-inflicted injuries, Central Asia appears to be the much-coveted oasis to the Chinese leadership, at least for now.

Dr. **Yi Sun** is professor of history at the University of San Diego, where she teaches courses on Asian histories, Asian Women and U.S.-East Asia Relations. She is co-author of two books, *East Asia and the West: An Entangled History*, published by Cognella in 2019. The other book deals with the historical experiences of Chinese Americans. Professor Sun has published a number of articles on topics ranging

71 Yang, "China leading the race for influence in Central Asia."

from Chinese women and modernization to Sino-American Relations. She is working on her manuscript on the changing political culture and the experiences of women in contemporary China. She has served on the executive board of several academic organizations, including the ASIANetwork, Chinese Historians in the United States and the Association of Third World Studies, and is presently the associate editor of the Asian section of the *Journal of Third World Studies*. She is the President of the Chinese Historians in the United States (CHUS). Sun is the recipient of the prestigious University Professorship for research accomplishments and the Davies Teaching Excellence Award at her university.

Bibliography

Aliyev, Nurlan. "China and Central Asia," *The Central Asia-Caucasus Analyst*, December 12, 2019. https://www.cacianalyst.org/publications/analytical-articles/item/13599-chinas-soft-power-in-central-asia.html.

Abudurexiti, Abulaiti and Xueqi Han. *Xinjiang's Trading Posts That Are Open to the Outside World* (*Duiwai Kaifang de Xinjiang Kouan*). Xinjiang Renmin Chubanshe, 1994.

Albert, Eleanor. "Kazakh President Yokayev Goes to Beijing," *The Diplomat*, September 12, 2019. https://thediplomat.com/2019/09/kazakh-president-tokayev-goes-to-beijing/

"America is at last getting serious about countering China in Asia," *The Economist*, September 25, 2011.

Bao, Dunquan and He, *The Opening of the Frontier and the Economic Development of Xinjiang* (lunzhi, *Yanbian Kaifang yu Xinjiang Jingji Fazhan Yanjiu*). Urumqi, Xinjiang: Xinjiang University Press, 1997.

Betts, Alison, Vicziany, Marika, and Peter Weiming Jia. eds., *The Cultures of Ancient Xinjiang, Western China: Crossroads of the Silk Roads.* Oxford: Archaeopress Archaeology, 2020.

Balan, Eric. "China-Central Asia's Regiocentric Strategies of Integration and Geoeconomics Perspectives" (available from Amazon, 2021).

Barnett, A. Doak. *China's Far West: Four Decades of Change.* Boulder, CO: Westview Press, 1993.

Bradsher, Keith. "In the 'Great Game' of Central Asia, China's Leader Seeks the Advantage," *New York Times*, September 16, 2022. https://www.nytimes.com/2022/09/16/world/asia/china-xi-central-asia.html

"China Blames Uighur Separatists for Knife Attack at Train Station That Leaves 33 People Dead," Associated Press, March 2, 2014, Print.

"China and Kyrgyzstan: Bilateral Trade and Future Outlook, *China Briefing*, August 27, 2021. (https://www.china-briefing.com/news/china-and-kyrgyzstan-bilateral-trade-and-future-outlook/).

Chinese News Digest. March 26, 1997 and July 23, 1997 http://www.cnd.org.

Colville, Alex. "The China-Kyrgyzstan Close Embrace and the Threat to it," *The China Project* May 30, 2023. https://thechinaproject.com/2023/05/30/china-and-kyrgyzstan-enter-a-new-era-of-strategic-cooperation/

Gill, Bates. "Shanghai Five: An Attempt to Counter U.S. Influence in Asia?" *Brookings*, May 4, 2001. https://www.brookings.edu/opinions/shanghai-five-an-attempt-to-counter-u-s-influence-in-asia/

Guo, Hongsheng and Jin Binggao. *The Socialist Market Economy and Ethnic Problems in China* (*Shehuizhuyi Shichang Jingji yu Zhongguo Minzu Wenti*). Beijing: Zhongyang Minzu Daxue Chubanshe, 1997.

Izimov, Rushlan. "China and Turkmenistan: A Regional Dimension," Central Asian Bureau for Analytical Reporting, nd. file:///Users/drsun/Downloads/China%20and%20Turkmenistan%20%E2%80%93%20a%20Regional%20Dimension.pdf

Jiang, Jon Yuan. "Central Asian elites choose China over Russia," *East Asia Forum* 25 November 2021. https://www.eastasiaforum.org/2021/11/25/central-asian-elites-choose-china-over-russia/

Jiang, Jon Yuan. "China's Education Diplomacy in Central Asia," *The Interpreter*, October 28, 2021. https://www.lowyinstitute.org/the-interpreter/china-s-education-diplomacy-central-asia

Jiang, Steven and Kacie Hunt. "Five Arrested in Tiananmen Square Incident, Deemed a Terrorist Attack," *CNN*, October 30, 2013: n. Print.

Khitakhunov, Azimzhan. "Economic Cooperation between Central Asia and China," Eurasian Research Institute, n.d. https://www.eurasian-research.org/publication/economic-cooperation-between-central-asia-and-china/

Kondapalli, Srikanth. "China's Role in Central Asia," *World Affairs: The Journal of International Issues* Vol. 13, No. 3 (Autumn, 2009), 139.

Kondapalli, Srikanth. "China's Role in Central Asia," *World Affairs: The Journal of International Issues* Vol. 13, No. 3 (Autumn, 2009), 143.

Kondapalli, Srikanth. "China's Role in Central Asia," *World Affairs: The Journal of International Issues* Vol. 13, No. 3 (Autumn, 2009), 145.

Kobushkina, Irina V. and Maria A. Soloshcheva. "The Role of Central Asia in the 'One Belt-One Road' Initiative," *Iran and the Caucasus* 23 (2019): 292.

Li, Aisi. "'One Belt One Road' and Central Asia: A New Trend in Internationalization of Higher Education?" The Boston College Center for International Higher Education, November 92, Winter 2018. https://ejournals.bc.edu/index.php/ihe/article/view/10279.

Li, Cuifa, *The Stable Economic and Trade Growth between China and Central Asian Countries* (*Woguo yu zhongyaguojia jingmaohezuo wenbufazhan*) in *Chinese Economics Daily* June 6, 2012. http://intl.ce.cn/specials/zxgjzh/201206/06/t20120606_23384119.shtml

Liu, Bin. "China-Central Asia Relations Entering a New Era," *Journal of the Chinese People's Institute of Foreign Affairs*, nd. http://www.cpifa.org/en/cms/book/354.

Mackerras, Colin and Michael Clarke eds., *China, Xinjiang and Central Asia: History, Transition and Crossborder Interaction into the 21st Century*. New York: Routledge, 2011.

Ministry of Foreign Affairs of the People's Republic of China, "Xi Jinping Chairs the Virtual Summit to Commemorate the 30th Anniversary of Diplomatic Relations Between China and Central Asian Countries," January 25, 2022. https://www.fmprc.gov.cn/eng/zxxx_662805/202201/t20220126_10634121.html#:~:text=On%20the%20afternoon%20of%20January,Central%20Asian%20Countries%20in%20Beijing

Ministry of Foreign Affairs, "President Xi Jinping Makes a State Visit to the Republic of Kazakhstan," September 12, 2022. https://www.fmprc.gov.cn/eng/zxxx_662805/202209/t20220915_10766191.html.

Najibullah, Farangis. "Anti-Chinese Protests Don't Deter Kazakh President from Visiting Beijing," *Radio Free Europe*, September 10, 2019. https://www.rferl.org/a/anti-chinese-protests-don-t-deter-kazakh-president-from-visiting-beijing/30157466.html

Nurgoshayeva, Roza. "How Is China's Belt and Road Changing Central Asia?" *The Diplomat*, July 9, 2020. https://thediplomat.com/2020/07/how-is-chinas-belt-and-road-changing-central-asia/

The Observatory of Economic Complexity, https://oec.world/en/profile/bilateral-country/chn/partner/kaz).

Plakjina, Yevgeniya. "Chinese higher education programs attract increasing numbers of students for Kazakhstan." September 15, 2021. https://globalvoices.org/2021/09/15/chinese-higher-education-programs-attract-increasing-numbers-of-students-from-kazakhstan/

Pradt, Tilman. *The Prequel to China's New Silk Road: Preparing the Ground in Central Asia.* Singapore: Palgrave Macmillan, 2020.

Rashdov, Tuychi, Mullojonov, Parviz, Rashidova, Umayra, and Edward Lemon. "Academic Diplomacy: The Educational Aspects of Chinese and Russian Soft Power in Tajikistan," published online by Cambridge University Press, July 24, 2023. https://www.cambridge.org/core/journals/nationalities-papers/article/academic-diplomacy-the-educational-aspects-of-chinese-and-russian-soft-power-in-tajikistan/A30B69D4A7825F8F72EA2545128B3C33

Roudik, Peter L. *The History of the Central Asian Republics.* Westport, CT: Greenwood Press, 2007.

Shanghai Cooperation Organization website: https://odi.org/en/insights/shanghai-cooperation-organisation-summit-2022-keytakeaways/#:~:text=The%20SCO%2C%20a%20Eurasian%20political,with%20Iran%20soon%20to%20join).

Singh, Swaran. "Sino-Central Asian Ties: Problems and Prospects," *Strategic Analysis: A Monthly Journal of the IDSA*, September 2000 (Vol. XXIV, No 6), p.5 https://ciaotest.cc.columbia.edu/olj/sa/sa_sep00sis01.html

Sorbello, Paolo. "Cultural Diplomacy as a Key Instrument of China-Central Asia Cooperation," *The Diplomat*, June 14, 2023.

Starr, S. Frederick, *Xinjiang: China's Muslim Borderland.* New York: Routledge, 2004.

Tianjin Evening News (*Tianjin Jinwanbao*) July 17, 1998.

Toktogulova, Diana and Weiqing Zhuang. "A Critical Analysis of the Belt and Road Initiative in Central Asia," *n* Vol. 8, Issue 8, August 2020, 45–46.

United Nations Educational, Scientific, and Cultural Organization website: https://ich.unesco.org/en/state/china-CN?info=periodic-reporting

United States Institute of Peace, "Blinken Debuts New U.S. Approach in Central Asia." https://www.usip.org/publications/2023/03/blinken-debuts-new-us-approach-central-asia;

Wang, Qiao, ed. *Encyclopedia of Xinjiang's Society and Economy.* Urumqi: Xinjiang People's Press, 1994.

Winter, Tim. "Heritage Diplomacy along the One Belt One Road," *International Institute for Asian Studies Newsletter*, Summer 2016, https://www.iias.asia/the-newsletter/article/heritage-diplomacy-along-one-belt-one-road

Wu Jiao and Yunbi Zhang. "Xi proposes a 'new Silk Road' with Central Asia," *China Daily*, September 8, 2013. https://www.chinadaily.com.cn/china/2013xivisitcenterasia/2013-09/08/content_16952228.htm

"Xi'an Declaration of the China-Central Asia Summit," *News Central Asia May* 20, 2023. https://www.newscentralasia.net/2023/05/20/xian-declaration-of-the-china-central-asia-summit/

Xie, Xiangfang, ed. *Xinjiang Weiwuer Zizhiqu Jingji Dili* [The Economic Geography of the Xinjiang Uighurs Autonomous Region]. Beijing: Xinhua Publishing House, 1991.

Xu, Bingwen, ed. *Strategies for Developing China's Northwestern Economy* (*Zhongguo Xibei Diqu Jingji Fazhan Zhanlue Gailun*). Beijing: Jingji Guanli Chubanshe, 1994.

Yau, Niva. "China polishes its image in Central Asia through the soft power of language," *Open Democracy*, March 23, 2021. https://www.opendemocracy.net/en/odr/china-central-asia-soft-power-language/.

Yang, Jiang, "China leading the race for influence in Central Asia," Danish Institute for International Studies, October 10, 2022. https://www.diis.dk/en/research/china-leading-the-race-influence-in-central-asia

Zhuang, Sylvie. "China pulls on Tang dynasty Silk Road ties to help secure central Asian future," *South China Morning Post*, May 19, 2023. https://www.scmp.com/news/china/diplomacy/article/3221147/china-pulls-tang-dynasty-silk-road-ties-help-secure-central-asian-future

CHAPTER SIX

Confucius Institutes in the Xi Jinping Era: From Peak to Demise in the United States[1]

Shuhua Fan

UNIVERSITY OF SCRANTON

Abstract: *This chapter examines the Confucius Institutes (CI) in the Xi Jinping era, focusing on their expansion and demise in the United States. In 2004, the People's Republic of China (PRC) established its first CI to export Chinese language and culture overseas. Under Xi, CIs expanded significantly across the globe, with about 118 CIs in the U.S. However, when China became more assertive and combative in both domestic and foreign policies and when U.S.-China relations deteriorated, U.S. leaders urged the closure of CIs. As of May 2023, there were only a handful of CIs still in operation. Why did the Chinese government initiate CIs? What caused the stunning CI expansion during the early Xi era? Why did mounting hostility to CIs rise in Western nations and especially in the U.S. from the mid-2010s? Why and how did CIs' mass closure take place in the U.S. in the past few years? This chapter argues that CIs are a part of China's cultural diplomacy to expand its cultural/educational influence and promote its international image overseas, thus serving the country's national interests. China's vigorous campaigns to project its soft power abroad via CIs and the U.S.' soaring resistance are both driven by national interests. CIs' mass closure in the U.S. is a result of the confrontation of the two countries' national interests.*

Keywords: Confucius Institutes; Cultural diplomacy; Chinese cultural nationalism; U.S.-China relations; Language and culture; CI demise

Introduction

In the Introduction of this book, Qiang Fang and Xiaobing Li have discussed the increasingly strained relations between China and the United States in the wake of Covid-19. The deteriorating tensions have weighed on Confucius Institutes in

[1] This paper uses some information from an unpublished paper I drafted in 2011 to compare the rise of Confucius Institutes in the U.S. and Harvard's first Chinese class (1877–1882). I would like to express my heartfelt thanks to professors Qiang Fang, Roger Des Forges, Charles Hayford, Madeline Levine, Steve Levine, Xiaobing Li, Patrick Shan, Kristin Stapleton, and Iris Xu for their support.

the United States. In early February 2023, I learned from Dr. Iris Xu, CI dean at Troy University in Alabama, that the CI at her institution had just closed. I had heard about the possibility of its closure in 2023 when I attended an international conference in late October 2022 at the Troy campus in Phenix City. However, the news of the CI closure at Troy still came as a surprise. I was shocked by the rapid process, with the closure taking place about three months after the conference.

The closure of Troy's CI is one of numerous CI closures in the U.S. in early 2023. As one of more than 110 CIs in the U.S., this closure is a snapshot of CIs' mass closure from the late Trump era to the Biden years. The development portends CIs' tragic fate in the U.S. and perhaps in the entire Western world after about two decades of existence. In 2004, the PRC established its first CI in South Korea and at the University of Maryland in America respectively to export Chinese language and culture overseas. Under Xi Jinping, CIs expanded significantly across the globe and especially in America, with about 118 CIs and many more Confucius Classrooms (CC, K-12 equivalents of CIs, but on a smaller scale) operating on U.S. campuses.[2] However, when China became more assertive and combative in both domestic and foreign policies and when U.S.-China relations deteriorated, CIs encountered enormous opposition in America. U.S. political leaders put huge pressure on universities hosting CIs and urged them to close their CIs. By May 2023, there were only about ten functioning CIs in the U.S, and by early August, at the time of writing this chapter, probably only a handful of CIs are still in operation.

This chapter addresses a number of important questions regarding the rise and fall of CIs with an emphasis on their history in the United States. Why did the Chinese government spend enormous sums of money to establish CIs worldwide in the early 2000s? Why were CI programs popular in their early stage? What are the reasons for the rapid CI expansion during the early Xi era? Why did CIs encounter mounting hostility in the West and especially in the U.S. from the mid-2010s? Why and how did the mass closure of CIs take place in the U.S. in the past few years?

There is rich scholarship on China's Confucius Institute project. Scholars have examined the CI project from multi-disciplinary perspectives, focusing either on a theoretic framework of China's soft power projection or on the practice and impact of CI programs.[3] However, there is no adequate scholarly writings on the rapid decline and mass closure of CIs in the U.S. Building on the existing scholarship on this controversial topic, this chapter fills a gap in the literature by analyzing the process of CI's stunning expansion and the ensuing rapid mass closure of CIs in the U.S. during the Xi Jinping era. It highlights the impact of the changing domestic

[2] Peterson, et al., 2022, p. 7.

[3] The works cited throughout this paper (also shown in the bibliography) offer a glimpse of the rich literature on CI programs. Excellent examples include Hartig, 2016 and Hubbert, 2019.

and international factors on the fate of these Chinese language and culture centers. Among these factors are China's response to foreign interests in Chinese language and to foreign fears about China's rapid rise, and Chinese cultural nationalism and cultural diplomacy intended to project soft power abroad. The chapter also looks at CI's objectives, management/operation, and programs, which reveal the Chinese government's control of CIs, raising concerns among Western and especially U.S. leaders. The chapter also explores the factors leading to CIs' mass closure in America, notably the impact of soaring tensions in U.S.-China relations and strong resistance to CIs expressed by U.S. political leaders.

The chapter argues that CIs are a part of China's cultural diplomacy intended to expand its cultural influence and promote China's international image overseas, thereby serving the country's national interests. China's intensive campaigns to project soft power via CIs combined with Xi's more assertive and aggressive domestic and foreign policies elicited increasing resistance from U.S. political leaders and educators. Both China's vast investment in CI initiatives in America and the strong U.S. resistance was driven by national interests. As both the U.S. and China increasingly perceived that their national interests were in conflict, the position of CIs in the U.S. became increasingly imperiled, culminating in CIs' mass closure, a result of the confrontation of the two countries' national interests.

Part 1. Confucius Institutes: Rapid Expansion and Driving Forces

Overview of CIs' Rise and Growth in Number

The rapid rise of CIs across the globe over the first fifteen years of the twenty-first century is quite a phenomenon. The first CI was established in Seoul, South Korea in 2004. Then CIs spread quickly to North America, Japan, Australia, and Europe. According to Chinese official data, about 322 CIs and 369 CCs in primary and secondary schools had opened in 96 countries worldwide by October 2010, and about 250 institutions from over 50 countries "expressed requirements for establishing Confucius Institutes or Classrooms, amongst them some of the world's top universities."[4]

The U.S., China's biggest strategic rival, became the main target of China's CI and CC initiatives. By April 2011, there were about 103 CIs in twelve nations and 240 CCs in six nations in the Americas. The U.S. hosted the largest number of both CIs and CCs in America. In 2005 alone, three CIs were opened in the U.S., at the University of Maryland (the founding process started in 2004), Chicago Public Schools, and the

[4] It is possible that some CIs and CCs were not in operation after being founded. See Jensen, 2012, p. 280.

China Institute in New York City. By 2007, there were 31 CIs in the U.S.[5] By 2011, over 80 CIs and about 100 CCs were operating in 44 states in the U.S.[6]

The stunning expansion of CIs and CCs was partly a result of the increasing popularity of the Chinese language. China's changing status as the second largest world economy in 2010 and its winning bids to host the 2008 Olympic Games in Beijing and the 2010 World Expo in Shanghai have made Chinese language increasingly popular. These developments/events looked like China's coming-out party to showcase its booming economy and resurgent national pride and attracted many foreigners to learn the Chinese language and culture. According to a 2010 report, "approximately 40 million non-Chinese worldwide have learned Chinese as a foreign language."[7] The United Nations held its first Chinese Day in November 2010 and second Chinese Day in April 2011.[8]

In America, a December 2010 survey showed that Chinese ranked "seventh among the most studied languages on U.S. college campuses, and has registered an increase of 18.2 percent in enrollments since 2006."[9] Edward Park, headmaster of Barnard Elementary School in San Diego, California, said that Chinese has become by 2011 "one of the most important foreign languages Americans are studying," and the U.S. "has witnessed a consistent increase in Chinese language learners across the education system," with Chinese classes mushrooming across America.[10] Dennis Richardson, the state representative who authored the bill to provide resources for public schools in Oregon to teach Chinese, predicted that "Chinese will be the global language of the 21st century."[11]

After Xi Jinping became the leader of China in late 2012/early 2013, CI and CC expansion reached a peak across the globe, with their strongest presence in the U.S. In 2014 alone, about 35 CIs and 205 CCs were founded worldwide. By late 2014, there were 475 CIs and some 850 CCs in 126 nations.[12] By 2017, more than 500 CIs and over 1,000 CCs have been founded in 142 nations throughout the world.[13]

[5] Peterson, et al., 2022, p. 30. James Paradise lists US CI number as 32, see Paradise, 2009, p. 653.

[6] "An Epic Tale of Two Peoples across the Pacific," *People's Daily*, Apr. 13, 2011; Chinese MOE website, "Constitution and By-Laws of the Confucius Institutes," Oct. 2006; Hartig, 2016, pp. 2–3.

[7] Tang, 2010.

[8] UN News, 2011, "UN Celebrates Chinese Language Day with Art abd Exhibitions"; China.org.cn news, "Chinese Language Play Invaluable Role in Bringing Chinese Culture to World," Xinhua News Agency, Apr. 21, 2011; and UN website, 2011, "About the Chinese Language Day."

[9] China.org.cn news, 2011, "More Foreigners Gung-ho about Learning Chinese."

[10] "Growing International Stature Spurs Boom in Chinese Language Learning in U.S.," *People's Daily*, Apr. 15, 2011.

[11] "Growing International Stature Spurs Boom in Chinese Language Learning in U.S.," *People's Daily*, Apr. 15, 2011.

[12] Hartig, 2016, p. 2.

[13] Pong, et al., 2017.

The U.S., China's strongest geopolitical competitor, became a particular focus of Xi Jinping's cultural diplomacy, and had far more CIs and CCs than any other nation.[14] In the early Xi era, there was an explosive CI expansion in the U.S., peaking in 2015, with the total number reaching 109.[15] In 2016, CI and CC numbers rose by almost 40 percent in the world and about 35 percent in the U.S. By late 2016 and early 2017, there were more than 100 CIs and over 500 CCs in the U.S., comprising about 38 percent of China's 1579 CIs and CCs worldwide.[16]

After a peak, several more CIs and CCs were opened in the U.S., with roughly 110 CIs located in 44 states by January 2019.[17] By spring 2022, about 500 American K-12 schools hosted CCs.[18] As various sources reveal, China intended to pump about $10 billion annually into the CI and CC projects, and China's plan has "only been bolstered by growing interest in China among American college students."[19]

CIs: Goals, Administration, and Programs

CIs are cultural centers overseas aiming to teach Chinese language and culture to foreigners. They are administered by the Office of Chinese Language Council International, also known as Hanban, located in Beijing. Established in 1987, Hanban is the executive body of the State Leading Group for Teaching Chinese as a Foreign Language. Although it is listed as a non-profit and non-governmental public organization affiliated with the Ministry of Education, Hanban is operated by a committee consisting of senior party members/representatives from twelve state ministries and commissions, including the State Council.[20] Based on the member source of its overseeing committee, Hanban is affiliated with, staffed, and even controlled by high-ranking officials of the Chinese government and the Chinese Communist Party (CCP).

With the rapid rise of CIs since the formation of the first one in 2004, Confucius Institute Headquarters was officially opened in Beijing on April 9, 2007. Governed by its own council, the Beijing CI Headquarters administers and supervises the formation, developments, and operations of CIs worldwide.[21] After Xi Jinping became the paramount leader of China, Hanban opened the Confucius Institute U.S. (CIUS) Center in Washington, D.C. in 2013 due to the explosive expansion of CIs and CCs

[14] Pong, et al., 2017; Peterson, 2017, p. 24.

[15] Peterson, et al., 2022, p. 30.

[16] Peterson, 2017, p. 15.

[17] The U.S. Senate PSI report, 2019.

[18] Peterson, et al., 2022, p. 13.

[19] Epstein, 2018.

[20] "Hanban" and "Han Ban – Chinese Language Council."

[21] Chinese MOE website, "Constitution and By-Laws of the Confucius Institutes," Oct. 2006.

in America and the strategic importance of the U.S. The CIUS Center organizes and supports Chinese language programs in America.[22]

Not only do CI objectives and leadership show the control by the Chinese government, but the models of CI partnership also reveal China's domination of these cultural centers. There are five main models of CI management: Through a partnership between a Chinese university and a foreign university, between a Chinese secondary school and a foreign secondary school, between a foreign non-governmental organization and a Chinese university, between a foreign government and the Chinese government, or between a Chinese university and a foreign enterprise.[23]

The most common model is through a partnership between a Chinese university and a foreign university. The foreign host university needs to sign a contract/agreement with Hanban, usually for a term of five years, with automatic renewal unless one side cancels the agreement 90 days before the expiration date.[24]

In this most popular model, the two sides of the partnership have different obligations regarding the operation of CI programs. The Chinese university sends teaching materials, one co-director/dean and teachers while the foreign host institution provides space, facilities, and staff. Hanban oversees the selection of textbooks, selection of Chinese director/dean, and recruitment and training of teachers who, usually recommended by their Chinese university, need to pass the examinations administered by Hanban.[25] Most teachers are from the English Departments while some from the Chinese Departments. Contracted with and paid by Hanban, these teachers are not university employees in the host country, thus not enjoying standard academic freedom protections.[26]

Most CIs are "physically located" on the campuses of foreign host universities, with a plaque of Confucius Institute (孔子学院) from Hanban, but without its own office and classroom building. Some CIs have cooperation with existing Chinese studies programs on the same campuses while others operate independently, thus causing tensions between the existing and new Chinese programs at some schools because of competition for resources.[27]

[22] Chinese Embassy in Sri Lanka website, 2013, "China Inaugurates Confucius Institute U.S. Center in Washington."

[23] Chinese MOE website, "Constitution and By-Laws of the Confucius Institutes," Oct. 2006; Zhang, 2010.

[24] Chinese MOE website, "Constitution and By-Laws of the Confucius Institutes," Oct. 2006; Also see Starr, 2009, pp. 70–72.

[25] Chinese MOE website, "Constitution and By-Laws of the Confucius Institutes," Oct. 2006.

[26] Pong et al., 2017.

[27] Chinese MOE website, "Constitution and By-Laws of the Confucius Institutes," Oct. 2006; Starr, 2009, pp. 71–72.

Besides getting teachers, a Chinese co-director/dean and free textbooks and other teaching materials from China selected by Hanban, and receiving supervision/ guidance from Hanban/CI Headquarters in Beijing, each CI receives a start-up fund of about $100,000–150,000 U.S. dollars and an annual appropriation in the range of $100,000 to $150,000 from Hanban. Occasionally Hanban provides a substantial amount to a host university such as Stanford.[28]

As conditions for receiving all these types of support from Hanban, CIs need to abide by the CI constitution and by-laws. They "shall not contravene the laws and regulations of China" and "shall not involve or participate in any activities that are not consistent with the missions of Confucius Institutes." Furthermore, CIs should furnish annual reports to Hanban/CI Beijing Headquarters, including detailed information on teaching and other academic activities, budget and financial statements, and future plans, etc. Of course, CIs "shall abide by the laws and regulations of the countries in which they are located, respect local cultural and educational traditions and social customs."[29]

The CI constitution and by-laws also stipulate specific obligations for these cultural centers: CIs should "be dedicated to pursuing their functions, including teaching Chinese language and culture to people from all walks of life, offering Chinese teachers training programs, administering all kinds of Chinese proficiency tests and Chinese teachers qualification authentication, providing Chinese teaching resources and other information and consultation services about Chinese education, culture and economy, developing study programs about modern China, and conducting language and cultural exchange activities between China and other countries."[30] It seems that conspicuously absent from this list of specific obligations is information about the PRC political system and the Chinese society.

Accordingly, most CIs focus primarily on language teaching and community outreach programs, while prestigious host universities may operate research-oriented CIs.[31] The majority of CIs offer for-credit or not-for-credit courses on Chinese language and culture. In addition, they frequently host a variety of extracurricular cultural activities, such as Chinese New Year Festival, Mid-Autumn Festival, Chinese

[28] Chinanews.com, 2010, "Director of Hanban: The Global Upsurge of People in Learning Chinese an Unstoppable Momentum"; Zhang, 2010. Also see Redden, 2012, and Sahlins, 2013.

[29] Chinese MOE website, "Constitution and By-Laws of the Confucius Institutes." There are changes in the wording and tone in the new constitution and by-laws in response to foreign concerns about interference from the Chinese government and especially from Hanban. See Paradise, 2009, p. 659, footnote 51.

[30] Chinese MOE website, "Constitution and By-Laws of the Confucius Institutes"; Liu Yandong, 2009; CCTV website, "The 4th Confucius Institute Conference Held in Beijing, Dec. 11-13, 2009," Dec. 27, 2009; Tang, 2010.

[31] Redden, 2010.

tea ceremony, art exhibitions, musical performances, film screenings, guest lectures, and/or conferences. Some community outreach programs have become an important part of CI functions to promote Chinese culture to the public overseas.[32]

In addition to administering CIs, Hanban also supports the creation and operation of CCs at K-12 primary and secondary schools, usually offshoots of a CI at a local college or university. As a smaller equivalent of CIs, CCs mainly offer Chinese language courses to elementary and secondary school students.[33]

The above analysis reveals that CIs and CCs are operated and supervised by the Chinese party-state, which is a unique feature of China's CI project and may doom it to failure under certain circumstances. CIs' main goals, administration/management, and programs show that these cultural centers serve China's national interests.[34]

CIs: Instrument of China's Cultural Diplomacy

The thrust for the establishment of CIs also shows that these cultural centers clearly serve China's national interests. Furthermore, Chinese leaders' official statements confirm that CIs are a part of China's cultural diplomacy to project its soft power by using language and culture to promote China's image overseas, create a friendly international environment for China, and expand China's global influence.

China started CI initiatives in the early 2000s partly as a response both to foreigners' increasing interest in Chinese language and to their concerns/fears about China's rapid rise. On the one hand, China's miraculous economic accomplishments and increasing international stature have made Chinese language and culture more attractive to foreigners, leading to the rise of a "China frenzy" and "Chinese language craze" among foreigners, and an "awakening of language consciousness" at home.[35]

Milestone events such as the 2008 Beijing Olympic Games, the 2010 Shanghai World Expo, and China's rise to the second largest world economy in 2010 have also created a modern-day "China market myth," attracting more and more foreigners and especially young people. These foreigners saw lucrative business and job opportunities in China and realized the importance of learning the Chinese language. Francisco Todd, foreign language coordinator at the International Language Institute in Washington, described this vividly: "China has opened its doors on a plethora of opportunities to be taken. Government jobs, as well as private industry,

[32] Tang, 2010; Hartig, 2012, pp. 63–64.

[33] Peterson, et al., 2022, pp.19, 71.

[34] Hartig, 2016, p. 2; Hartig, 2012, pp. 60–63.

[35] "Growing International Stature Spurs Boom in Chinese Language Learning in U.S.," *People's Daily*, Apr. 15, 2011; China.org.cn news, 2011, "More Foreigners Gung-ho about Learning Chinese," June 17, 2011; Guo, 2008.

from English teaching jobs to manufacturing, etc."[36] Americans had started working or doing business in China to pursue their American dream there, and more wanted to come to China.[37]

On the other hand, China's economic miracle and increasing international influence has caused concerns and even fears abroad and especially in the U.S. because of ideological differences and strategic competition between the two nations. "Threat from a rising China," "Red China," "Red Storm," and similar subjects have often become the topics of conferences, research publications, and media reports on China.[38]

In response to the surging foreign demand to learn Chinese language and culture and to ease international concerns/fears about China's phenomenal rise, the Chinese government attempted to pursue a new strategy, i.e., a cultural diplomacy, by integrating "Chinese hard power and soft power to create a soft rise for China."[39] Using CIs and other "charm offensive" campaigns as instruments of soft power would make China's rapid rise look less threatening and would help attract rather than intimidate foreigners in the long run, thus winning their hearts and minds to create a favorable international image of China.[40] One report summarizes this strategy very well: Chinese leaders have decided to "ride the wave, not just capitalizing on the newfound chic that surrounds the language but also determined to perpetuate it as a way of extending Chinese international influence and good will toward the country."[41]

China's rising cultural nationalism is another push behind China's new cultural diplomacy to project its soft power overseas via CIs, which also serves the country's national interests. Since the late 1990s, Chinese leaders and the public had gradually become more confident and nationalistic, wanting China to play a larger role on the international stage.[42] Given China's economic power, extensive business exchanges, and increasing international influence, Chinese leaders recognized that it was necessary for the country to expand its cultural and educational exchanges with the outside world to make China a cultural power. They realized that China had an enormous cultural deficit in its relations with the West, especially with the U.S. China had imported much more U.S. cultural products such as movies/TV series, books, and newspapers/magazines/journals than exporting similar Chinese

[36] China.org.cn news, 2011, "More Foreigners Gung-ho about Learning Chinese"; "Growing international stature spurs boom in Chinese language learning in U.S.," *People's Daily*, Apr. 15, 2011.

[37] French, 2006; Ye, 2011; MacLeod, 2011.

[38] Bill, 2000; Yee, et al., 2004; Menges, 2005; Timperlak, et al., 1999.

[39] Wang, Mar. 2008, p. 257. Also see Paradise, 2009, pp. 647–648, 655; and Hartig, 2010, p. 3.

[40] Kurlantzick, 2007; Liu, 2019, p. 82.

[41] French, 2006. Also see Hartig, 2010, p. 3.

[42] Cho, et al., 2008, p. 459.

items abroad. They believed it was the right time to pursue a new cultural diplomacy to spread Chinese culture abroad.[43]

The surge of cultural nationalism motivated China to pursue a cultural diplomacy to promote its comprehensive national power, including its cultural power, to serve the country's national interests in an age of rapid globalization.[44] According to Nicholas Cull, cultural diplomacy is "an actor's attempt to manage the international environment through making its cultural resources and achievements known overseas and/or facilitating cultural transmission abroad."[45] Chinese scholars, leaders, and media reports have publicly used the terms "cultural diplomacy" and "public diplomacy." For example, one 2011 report on CIs in *People's Daily* stated: "The establishment of Confucius Institutes is actually a form of public diplomacy. The Confucius Institute can enhance the international influence of China as well as foreigners' understanding towards China."[46] Cai Wu, China's Minister of Culture (2008–2013), stressed in 2009 in his assessment of China's 60-year cultural exchanges with foreign countries: "Entering the new century, China's cultural diplomacy has become increasingly active, becoming a beautiful scene in the international arena."[47]

This cultural diplomacy serves as an instrument for China to wield and enhance its soft power by promoting its international image and creating a favorable global environment to aid the nation's economic rise and continuing development. This is a part of China's new "grand strategy," i.e., to portray the country as a peace-loving, responsible, and welcome global power.[48] Joseph Nye, Jr., a distinguished professor at Harvard, introduced the idea of "soft power" in 1990, and later further developed the term. He defined soft power as "the ability to get what you want through attraction rather than coercion or payments," and described its three main resources/elements as culture, political values/ideas, and foreign policies.[49]

Soon after the concept of soft power was introduced into China, it gained currency there.[50] Chinese scholars and top policymakers realized the value of

[43] Chinese government website, 2006, "Be Wary of Enormous Cultural Deficits, Representatives Calling for Enhancing 'China's Soft Power'"; "Confucius Institutes Become 'Brand' for Disseminating Chinese Culture," *People's Daily*, Mar. 13, 2009.

[44] More scholars have regarded CIs as a part of China's cultural diplomacy. Examples include French, 2006; Hartig, 2010, 2012, and 2016.

[45] Cull, 2008, p. 33.

[46] "Confucius Institutes Face Uphill Battle in Development," *People's Daily*, June 2, 2011.

[47] Chinese government website, 2009, "Cai Wu Talks about the Development of China's 60-Year Cultural Exchanges with Foreign Countries."

[48] Hartig, 2010, p. 11; Paradise, 2009, p. 649. Also see Goldstein, 2005, pp.18–19, 30–32.

[49] Nye, 1990a, pp. 153–171; 1990b; 2004, pp. x, 7, 18–19, 30–32; and 2008.

[50] Wang, et al., Aug. 2008, pp. 427–431. Also see Paradise, 2009, pp. 657–658.

China's soft power and especially the dynamic relationship between the use and enhancement of soft power, and started to apply it to China's domestic and foreign policies, with an emphasis on culture and foreign policy as the instruments. It was not clear whether these scholars and leaders realized that there can be and often is a disjuncture between China's soft power (cultural diplomacy) and its hard power (military and economic power). Cultural diplomacy is a way to soften the reality that the hard instruments of power are the dominant ones and that soft power is a means of trying to disguise that reality.

Chinese scholars and leaders believed that projecting China's soft power and promoting China's international cultural influence is not only a historical duty to enrich and strengthen the country, but also a solemn mission to rejuvenate the Chinese nation and culture. They highlighted on many occasions that culture is a key part of China's soft power, interacting with political and economic developments and playing an increasingly important role in international competitions of comprehensive national power.[51]

For example, several representatives at the 2006 Political Consultative Conference stressed that culture was the soft power of China's comprehensive national power, and the rejuvenation of the Chinese nation (中华民族的复兴) included not only the economic rise, but also the rejuvenation of Chinese culture. They pointed out that culture was now becoming a sharp weapon for nations to compete in international arenas, and competition in cultural strategy has become the fifth wave of international competitions, following those for resources, management/governance, science and technology, and talented people. They emphasized that rejuvenation and international promotion of Chinese culture was of vital importance to a powerful China and to the future of the Chinese nation.[52] These views reveal conference representatives' national pride and mission to promote Chinese language and culture overseas, which is, in Don Starr's words, "one of the more benign manifestations" of Chinese nationalism.[53]

In his keynote speech at the 17th CCP National Congress in 2007, President Hu Jintao (term: 2002–2013; CCP's General Secretary, 2002–2012, and top leader of the military, 2004–2012) highlighted the need to enhance Chinese culture as China's "soft power." Hu said: "In the present era, culture has become a more and more important source of national cohesion and creativity and a factor of growing significance in the competition in overall national strength." He stressed, "The great

[51] Wang, et al., Aug. 2008, pp. 438–441; Cho, et al., 2008, p. 459.

[52] Chinese government website, 2006, "Be Wary of Enormous Cultural Deficits, Representatives Calling for Enhancing 'China's Soft Power.'"

[53] Starr, 2009, pp. 66, 79–80.

rejuvenation of the Chinese nation will definitely be accompanied by the thriving of Chinese culture."[54]

Hu Jintao emphasized again in late 2011 and early January 2012 the key role of culture as soft power, especially in fighting ideological battles. He pointed out: "We must clearly see that international hostile forces are intensifying the strategic plot of Westernizing and dividing China, and ideological and cultural fields are the focal areas of their long-term infiltration." Hu added, "We should deeply understand the seriousness and complexity of the ideological struggle, always sound the alarms and remain vigilant, and take forceful measures to be on guard and respond."[55]

One main way to carry out China's new cultural diplomacy to project its "soft power" is the creation of CIs for international promotion of Chinese language and culture. Chinese leaders and scholars have repeatedly highlighted CIs as a part of China's "soft power" in the new century.[56] Xu Lin, top leader at Hanban, pointed out in 2007 that CIs "have become the brightest brand to reflect China's 'soft power.'"[57]

Liu Yandong, Chair of the Council of CI Headquarters in Beijing, member of the CCP's Central Politburo and State Councilor, emphasized on many occasions the importance of cultural diplomacy in an age of economic globalization, the role of "soft power," and especially of the Chinese language. In her keynote speech at the Third World Confucius Institute Conference in Beijing in 2008, with more than 500 scholars and university presidents from 78 nations and regions worldwide attending, Liu stated that cultural cooperation has an irreplaceable role in promoting political trust and strengthening economic and trade exchanges, and language is a key tool for cultural exchange, communication, and cooperation.[58]

In her keynote speech at the 2009 fourth Confucius Institute Conference, Liu Yandong highlighted the role of CIs. She said: "Confucius Institutes belong to China, but more to the world"; and the Chinese government and people "have attached great importance to the cause of Chinese international education and promotion, and will provide long-term, stable support."[59]

[54] Hu Jintao, 2007a; and China.org.cn news, 2007, "Hu Jintao Calls for Enhancing 'Soft Power' of Chinese Culture."

[55] Wong, 2012.

[56] Some Chinese educators and educational officials involved in CIs have not regarded CI programs as a part of China's soft power offensive. Instead, they viewed CIs as academic rather than political programs, with an aim to promote academic exchanges and mutual understanding. See Paradise, 2009, pp. 657, 659.

[57] Chinese government website, 2007, "2006: Confucius Institutes Have Become the Brightest Brand of China's 'Soft Power.'"

[58] Liu, 2008; CCTV news, 2008, "Liu Yandong Emphasizes: Working Together and Cooperating on an Equal Footing to Make Confucius Institutes Better and Better."

[59] Liu, 2009. Liu repeated her positions on many other occasions such at the 10th "Chinese Bridge" competition, an international Chinese proficiency competition held in July 2011 in China for foreign

Liu Yunshan, then a member of the CCP Politburo Standing Committee and minister of the CCP Central Propaganda Department, also highly valued CIs as a part of China's overseas propaganda. He wrote in a January 2010 article for *People's Daily*: "Coordinate the efforts of overseas and domestic propaganda, further create a favorable international environment for us." Liu emphasized that overseas propaganda should be "comprehensive, multilevel, and wide-ranging ... Our strategy is to proactively take our culture abroad ... We should do well in establishing and operating overseas cultural centers and Confucius Institutes."[60]

Li Changchun, then the head of the CCP propaganda system and a member of the CCP Politburo Standing Committee, also called CIs "an important part of China's overseas propaganda set-up."[61]

The above sample official statements show that Chinese leaders have realized and highlighted the role of language and culture as China's soft power and the role of CIs as an ideal instrument of China's cultural diplomacy to project soft power overseas. Furthermore, as analyzed earlier, CI's objectives, administration/management, and programs/activities also reveal that these cultural centers, under the control of the Chinese government, serve China's national interests.

Scholarly writings have illustrated and summarized well Chinese leaders' statements on cultural soft power strategy and the functions of CIs to tell "a good story of China." Howard French describes CIs as an instrument of China's cultural diplomacy, "competing intensely for international prestige and influence." Xiaolin Guo treats CIs as a part of China's "soft power building" and "an image management project" to "promote the greatness of Chinese culture" while counterattacking "China threat" rhetoric in the international community," which is one of China's new diplomatic offensives to tell a good story of China. James F. Paradise interprets CIs as a "part of a broader soft power projection in which China is attempting to win hearts and minds for political purposes" by creating a more favorable image of China. Tony Tai-ting Liu views CIs as a part of China's newest charm offensive to "reduce the anxieties surrounding China" and to promote the nation's image as a benevolent and peaceful power abroad.[62] It is clear that Chinese leaders' statements show that, as analyzed by scholars, CIs and China's cultural diplomacy serves the country's national interests.

college students and in her 2011 visit to the U.S. See Liu Yandong, "Speech at Opening Ceremony of Fourth National Chinese Language Conference," Apr. 14, 2011, San Francisco; and "Chinese Official Calls for More Language, Culture Exchanges with Foreign Countries, " *People's Daily*, July 18, 2011.

60 Liu Yunshan, Minister of Propaganda, Jan. 2010, Yongning government website, cited from Sahlins, 2015, p. 6; and Sahlins, 2018.

61 *The Economist*, 2009.

62 French, 2006; Guo, 2008, pp. 13, 34; Paradise, 2009, pp. 647, 649; Liu, 2019, p. 82.

Besides their official purpose as shown in the statements of Chinese leaders, CI programs have serious limitations. Lionel Jensen argues that Hanban and CIs have reduced "the diverse cultures of Chinese tradition to a uniform, quaint commodity," and CI programming can be most appropriately termed "culturetainment." Falk Hartig emphasized that CIs, as the star and instrument of China's public/cultural diplomacy to wield and bolster soft power globally, "tend to present a politically correct version of China," rather than "the *real* China" to the world.[63] Indeed, the version of Chinese culture presented by CIs is limited, superficial, and banal as to be a caricature of the richness and complexity of China.

These limitations did not create problems in the early stage but would later cause concerns among U.S. leaders. During the peak of globalization when China and the U.S. were more open to the outside world and when U.S.-China relations were relatively stable, both sides mainly saw CIs and even China's cultural diplomacy as a means to promote cultural and educational exchanges and mutual understanding, thus serving rather than hurting their respective national interests.

In the early stage of CI initiatives, China in general encountered no serious resistance from the U.S. government and political and educational leaders in conducting its cultural diplomacy, including the operation and expansion of CIs. The U.S. federal and state governments even supported the promotion of Chinese language study. According to a 2009 article, the Pentagon "has been helping to fund some language courses at Confucius Institutes under the National Security Language Initiative, launched by George Bush in 2006 to promote the study of 'critical-need' languages."[64] In October 2009, the U.S. House of Representatives passed a resolution to honor the 2560th anniversary of Confucius' birth to recognize his "invaluable contributions to philosophy and social and political thought."[65] In November 2009, the Obama administration announced the "100,000 Strong Initiative" to send 100,000 American students to study in China over the next four years, with the objective to prepare the next generation of American Chinese experts who "will be charged with managing the growing political, economic, and cultural ties between the United States and China."[66] Hillary Clinton, then U.S. Secretary of State, officially launched the initiative in Beijing in May 2010.[67]

Oregon represents one example of state-level efforts to promote Chinese language studies in the U.S. In early 2010, the Superintendent of Public Instruction in Oregon was authorized to enter into an agreement with China/Hanban for the purpose of

[63] Jensen, 2012, p. 293; Hartig, 2016, pp. 185–187; Hartig, 2012, p. 57.

[64] *The Economist*, 2009.

[65] CCTV website, 2009, "U.S. House Honors Ancient Chinese Philosopher Confucius."

[66] U.S. State Department website, n.d., "100,000 Strong Educational Exchange Initiatives."

[67] U.S. State Department website, n.d., "100,000 Strong Educational Exchange Initiatives."

ensuring that the instruction of Mandarin Chinese was available to public school students in Oregon by facilitating the placement of teachers in statewide public schools.[68] Eduardo M. Ochoa, Assistant Secretary for Postsecondary Education at the U.S. Department of Education, explained the rationales: "Given the increasingly important role that China will play in the world in the years to come, it makes sense if we want our students to be well-educated so as to be globally competitive."[69]

Part 2. Demise of Confucius Institutes in the United States

Against the background of this very promising growth of CIs in the United States, China's new cultural diplomacy of using CIs to project soft power and especially its leaders' official statements explicitly stating their thinking about this strategy portended potential conflicts of national interests with Western nations and especially with the U.S. when domestic and international situations changed for both China and the U.S.

After Xi Jinping became the leader of China in 2012, the relatively open and favorable international environment for China to pursue its cultural diplomacy changed significantly, a change which may doom China's CI project. The change was partly caused by new situation in China. After consolidating power at home, Xi adopted an increasingly assertive and bellicose domestic and foreign policy. He gradually abandoned Deng Xiaoping's low-profile foreign policy and Hu Jintao's peaceful rise policy, and followed a proactive and belligerent foreign policy, often referred to as wolf-warrior diplomacy, which is partly reflected in his uncompromising policy toward Xinjiang, Tibet, Hong Kong, Taiwan, other sensitive issues and the U.S.[70]

Xi's hardline domestic and foreign policy has caused concerns among American leaders and led to increasing conflicts with the U.S., especially after Donald Trump took office in 2017. Trump discarded a relatively more cosmopolitan policy of his immediate predecessor and turned inward to "keep America great." Trump's "isolationist," non-interventionist, and protectionist policy and the rise of a new wave of nationalism in America caused new concerns and vigilance among U.S. leaders about China's domestic authoritarian trends and its hawkish foreign policy. In particular, China's cultural diplomacy and especially the establishment of CIs came

[68] "Growing International Stature Spurs Boom in Chinese Language Learning in U.S.," *People's Daily*, Apr. 15, 2011; Oregon state government website, 2010, "Agreement by Superintendent to Ensure Availability of Instruction of Chinese Language."

[69] China.org.cn news, 2011, "More U.S. Students Encouraged to Study in China."

[70] Guo, 2008, pp. 13, 34; Glaser et al., 2007, pp. 291–310; Sun, 2023, pp. 52–68; Ding, et al., 2020; Dai, et al., 2022, pp. 253–283; Huang, 2022, pp. 37–40.

to be seen as an effort to infiltrate American universities to spread Chinese propaganda and potentially engage in intelligence gathering. Furthermore, the domestic American discourse about the Chinese origins of Covid-19 added fuel to the fire. After Joe Biden became the president in early 2021, more tensions rose between the U.S. and China in various areas, and the bilateral relationship approached an historic low, completely different from that during the Obama era when Biden served as vice-president.[71]

U.S. leaders came to the conclusion that China's domestic and foreign policies, including using CIs to carry out its cultural diplomacy, threatened American national security and national interests. They realized that China under Xi was moving fast in a different direction, unlike what they had expected earlier. China became the second largest world economy in 2010,[72] but did not conduct political reforms or import Western democracy and other values, instead becoming more authoritarian at home and more belligerent in foreign policy. U.S. leaders believed that what China has exported via CIs and other "charm offensives" served only China's national interests and conflicted with and threatened American values and ideas such as democracy, freedom, and human rights.

Thus, fierce conflicts of national interests between the U.S. and China rose due to China's assertive, uncompromising, and even aggressive domestic and foreign policy and American leaders' increasing realization of potential serious threats from a rapidly rising and more authoritarian China. Under the new circumstances, China faced increasing opposition and hostility in America and other Western nations. In particular, its CI project in the U.S. encountered enormous and unprecedented pressures from the federal and state governments, educators/professors, college students, various scholarly associations, media, and other organizations. The strong resistance has led to mass closure of CIs in the U.S. in the past few years, which portends the failure of China's entire CI project and perhaps other Chinese cultural programs in America as well.

Resistance from Professors, Students, and Scholarly Associations

A number of university professors and scholarly associations took the lead to protest China's CI programs in the U.S. They were mainly concerned about what they perceived as China's interference in the U.S. educational system and especially in higher education. In their view, CIs have threatened academic freedom and academic integrity, and led to a climate of self-censorship on American campuses.

[71] Nye, 2023; Ashbee, et al., 2021, pp. 720–737; Copper, 2021, pp. 101–116; Wang, et al., 2021, pp. 315–320; Song, 2022, pp. 132–151.

[72] Barboza, 2010.

Dr. Marshall Sahlins (1930–2021), professor emeritus of anthropology at the University of Chicago, was perhaps one of the earliest and most famous protestors among educators. Sahlins was one of the main leaders of a faculty petition drive in early June 2010 against the University of Chicago's decision to start a CI. Chicago submitted its CI proposal to Hanban in September 2009, and signed an agreement with Hanban on September 29, 2009. Three days after Chicago formally opened its CI on June 1, 2010, 174 faculty members signed a petition protesting the "corporatization" of the university, of which its CI was a prime example, and other developments on campus.[73]

Later Sahlins authored an article titled "China U" for *The Nation* in late 2013 to outline his position on CIs. The article recalled details about the June 2010 Chicago faculty petition drive. He regarded CIs as a critical component of China's "politics of cultural conquest" and "an important part of China's overseas propaganda set-up," the latter being the words of Li Changchun, a CCP Politburo member. Sahlins pointed out that routinely and assiduously, Hanban wanted CIs to conduct activities to "put the PRC in a good light." In Sahlins' view, CIs function as an ideal tool to tell a good story about China: "A beautiful and peaceful China, harmonious and generous: These are major themes of Confucius Institutes."[74]

Sahlins believed that CIs lacked transparency and threatened academic freedom. For example, the model agreement between the two partner institutions was subject to non-disclosure. Its article 5 requires that CI activities "conform to the customs, laws and regulations of China as well as those of the host institution's country." Furthermore, CIs "censor political discussions and restrain the free exchange of ideas." Sahlins stressed that by hosting CIs, universities "have become engaged in the political and propaganda efforts of a foreign government in a way that contradicts the values of free inquiry and human welfare to which they are otherwise committed."[75]

In late April 2014, Sahlins and his colleagues led a second petition at the University of Chicago before it was time for the university to renew its contract with Hanban (the contract for the first 5-year term would expire in September 2014 and application for renewal should be submitted 90 days before the expiration date). More than 100 faculty members, including several department chairs, joined the petition to renew their opposition to the CI on their campus. They demanded that Chicago terminate its contract with Hanban.[76]

73 Sahlins, 2013.

74 Sahlins, 2013.

75 Sahlins, 2013.

76 Redden, 2014. Also see Epstein, 2018.

In September 2014, Chicago announced a major decision to close its CI, about five months after the second faculty petition against contract renewal with Hanban.[77] Sahlins was regarded as a major player behind the termination: "Sahlins' criticisms helped sway his institution ... to cancel its Confucius Institute in 2014, the first major CI closure in the United States."[78]

Sahlins developed his ideas on CIs and published an article in *The Asia-Pacific Journal: Japan Focus* in late 2014 and then published it in 2015 as a booklet with the same title *Confucius Institutes: Academic Malware*. In this piece, Sahlins analyzed official Chinese statements on the politics of culture and especially on CIs, which show clearly that CIs and CCs are China's ideal instruments to project soft power overseas. Sahlins also chronicled incidents in which CIs played a key role in extending Chinese political influence and interference in American higher education, and examined the conflicts among the faculties in either installing or rejecting CIs.[79]

In 2018, Sahlins published an article with an almost similar title in *Inside Higher Education*. He stressed again that CIs are China's instrument to project soft power abroad. He stated that Hanban and the CI Beijing headquarters are "controlled by high officials of the Chinese party-state implementing the policies of the PRC propaganda apparatus." He concluded, "insofar as Confucius Institutes and classrooms are installed in colleges and K-12 schools the world around, these educational institutions function as peripheral propaganda branches of the Chinese party-state," and as academic malware threatening academic freedom and free inquiry.[80]

Scholarly/educational associations soon joined the fight to resist CI programs in America. The American Association of University Professors (AAUP) was one of the leaders in the campaigns. AAUP issued a statement in June 2014, calling on universities across the U.S to reconsider their partnerships with Hanban to uphold principles of academic freedom and academic integrity. The AAUP statement stressed that CIs "function as an arm of the Chinese state and are allowed to ignore academic freedom." The statement also pointed out the lack of transparency in CI programs. For example, most CI agreements "feature nondisclosure clauses" and "unacceptable concessions to the political aims and practices" of the Chinese government. The statement highlighted the serious problems in the U.S.: "Specifically, North American universities permit Confucius Institutes to advance a state agenda in the recruitment and control of academic staff, in the choice of curriculum, and in the restriction of debate."[81]

[77] University of Chicago, 2014, "Statement on the Confucius Institute at the University of Chicago."

[78] Peterson, et al., 2022, p. 20.

[79] Sahlins, 2014 and 2015.

[80] Sahlins, 2018.

[81] AAUP report, 2014, "On Partnerships with Foreign Governments: The Case of Confucius Institutes."

The AAUP statement concluded that "allowing any third-party control of academic matters is inconsistent with principles of academic freedom, shared governance, and the institutional autonomy of colleges and universities."[82] It recommended that universities cease their involvement in CIs unless the agreement between the university and Hanban is renegotiated to meet certain conditions so as to guarantee academic freedom, academic integrity, and greater transparency, etc.[83]

Another example of scholarly associations that has been dedicated to resisting CI programs is the National Association of Scholars (NAS), a right-leaning educational campaign group in the U.S. NAS launched an investigation of twelve CIs in New Jersey and New York and published a detailed report in 2017. The report identified the main causes for concern about CI programs as lack of transparency, restrictive contractual languages, threats to academic freedom, pressure for self-censorship, and use of soft power. For example, the report described CIs as "a textbook example of a soft power initiative," tending to "present China in a positive light and to focus on anodyne aspects of Chinese culture."[84]

The 2017 NAS report criticized the US educational institutions hosting CIs for being naïve and indifferent to the consequences due to "a combination of greed and vanity."[85] The report recommended that universities immediately sever their contracts with Hanban and close their CIs, and also urged federal and state legislative bodies to exercise oversight over CIs.[86]

NAS was determined to advocate the closure of all CI programs until none remained in the United States. Even after many CIs closed, NAS made enormous efforts to track down what happened after the mass closure and so to eliminate those that remained or operated in an alternative format. In June 2022, NAS issued a thorough report to document CIs' enduring threat to American higher education even after their closure. The report analyzed in detail China's initiatives to seek alternative means of influencing American colleges and universities after CI closure, especially "the effort to rebrand Confucius Institute-like programs under other names."[87]

The 2022 NAS report suggested that "all universities not only close their remaining Confucius Institutes, but also withdraw from CI-replacement programs, including sister university relationships with Chinese universities."[88] The report also provided four recommendations for the U.S. federal government: short-term

[82] Ibid.

[83] Ibid.

[84] Peterson, 2017, pp. 12, 20.

[85] Peterson, 2017, p. 13.

[86] Peterson, 2017, pp. 10-11.

[87] Peterson, et al., 2022, p. 7.

[88] Peterson, et al., 2022, p.10.

efforts against post-CI influence campaigns, long-term efforts against Chinese government influence operations, commissioning a study of CCs, and strengthening transparency requirements.[89]

One more example is the alerts from a report released in April 2018 by the Wilson Center's Kissinger Institute on China and the United States. This preliminary report examined China's general political influence and interference activities in American higher education. Although the report did not focus specifically on CIs and CCs, its findings suggested "a worrisome trend in which faculty, students, administrators, and staff across a range of disciplines within American universities are encountering pressure to align their academic activities with PRC political preferences." The report pointed out that the concerns laid "largely in Beijing's framing of its strategic ambitions." Under Xi Jinping, China made "explicit its quest for comprehensive national power," which included military, economic, technological, normative, and cultural power. As the CCP consolidated its control over every aspect of domestic society under Xi, the party "increasingly seeks to shape the world in its image." The report stressed, "ensuring that American higher educational institutions remain champions of free thought is crucial to the health of democratic society, and by extension, the security of the United States."[90]

College students also protested CI programs to safeguard academic freedom and academic integrity. For example, one group of students and alumni at UMass Boston joined faculty and outside advocates to submit a petition letter to the university administration in early 2018. They expressed deep concerns that the university was "unwittingly assisting the Chinese government to promote censorship abroad, while undermining human rights and academic freedom."[91]

College Republicans and Democrats, including students, scholars, and others, also "teamed up to establish a non-profit to combat Chinese government influence on American campuses."[92] In mid-May 2020, the leadership of College Republican National Committee and the College Democrats of America worked together, issuing an open letter to show their strong support for academic freedom and opposition against authoritarianism. The letter stated that "the Chinese government's flagrant attempts to coerce and control discourse at universities in the United States and around the world pose an existential threat to academic freedom."[93]

The open letter stressed that "immediate action in defense of academic freedom is necessitated" not only by the concerns about threats to academic freedom, "but

[89] Ibid.

[90] Lloyd-Damnjanovic, 2018.

[91] Epstein, 2018. Also see Krantz, 2018.

[92] Evans, 2020.

[93] College Republicans and College Democrats, 2020. Also see Evans, 2020.

by a long and growing list of offenses adding up to a long-term campaign undeniably aimed at expanding the reach and power of the Chinese state's apparatus of oppression."[94] The letter pointed out that part of that long list included China's efforts to infiltrate the American campuses via CIs, which are "proprietary outlets of soft power that promote self-censorship and arbitrarily censor discussion of issues 'sensitive'" to the CCP.[95] The letter called for "the immediate and permanent closure" of all CIs in the U.S. and also called for "full and public disclosure of all ties, both financial and academic, between centers of higher learning and all Chinese state agencies and proxies."[96]

Actions of the U.S. Government and Leaders

Urged by scholarly associations, members of Congress and various bodies of the U.S. federal government have worked together to raise alarms about threats from China and especially its CI programs. Keith Krach, Under Secretary of the U.S. State Department, said that the perception of the increasing threat of China's political influence, particularly the infiltration of American university campuses, "has become one of the most passionately unifying bipartisan issues of our time," which has united various sections of the government and especially the two branches of the Congress.[97]

For example, the U.S. Congress commissioned committee hearings to conduct investigations of CI programs and other threats from China. In February 2018, the U.S. Senate Committee on Intelligence held hearings on worldwide threats to the U.S., including those from China. Christopher Wray, director of the Federal Bureau of Investigation (FBI), testified before this hearing. In response to Florida senator Marco Rubio's questions about China's use of non-traditional espionage approach such as CIs, Wray stressed that "it's across basically every discipline" around the country. He said that the FBI has shared concerns about CIs, not only "watching warily" that development, but also even developing "appropriate investigative steps" in certain instances.[98]

On July 23, 2019, Wray testified again, this time before the U.S. Senate Judiciary Committee. He emphasized that CIs were "a source of concern," for they were a "part of China's soft power strategy and influence," offering "a platform to

[94] College Republicans and College Democrats, 2020. Also see Evans, 2020.

[95] College Republicans and College Democrats, 2020.

[96] College Republicans and College Democrats, 2020. Also see Evans, 2020.

[97] U.S. State Department website, 2020, "Letter from Under Secretary Keith Krach."

[98] Wray, 2018, Testimony before the U.S. Senate Committee.

disseminate Chinese government or Chinese Communist Party propaganda, to encourage censorship, to restrict academic freedom, etc."[99]

In 2019, two federal bodies—The U.S. Senate Permanent Subcommittee on Investigations (PSI) and the Government Accountability Office (GAO), commissioned by the Congress—conducted investigations and issued reports on CI programs in America. The PSI report described CIs as China's soft power instrument and "one part of China's broader, long-term strategy." The report stressed that the Chinese government has controlled nearly every aspect of CIs at U.S. schools, and its funding "comes with strings that can compromise academic freedom." For example, certain limitations on CIs "attempt to export China's censorship of political debate and prevent discussion of potentially politically sensitive topics." The report recommended that CIs "should not continue" in the U.S. due to various problems and potential threats. It also put forward specific measures for the Congress, the Departments of State, Justice and Education, and schools to take to deal with the CI threat.[100]

GAO reviewed 90 agreements establishing CIs in the U.S. and interviewed officials operating CIs, and issued a report, dated February 28, 2019. The report identified both benefits and concerns and suggested ways to improve CI programs. Concerns included a possible climate of self-censorship for campus activities and classroom content, "so as to not offend Chinese partners." However, the report seemed to show that U.S. universities had control over curriculum and teaching materials in most cases, and downplayed concerns about CIs.[101]

In addition to hearings and investigations, the U.S. government took other steps to apply pressure on universities operating CIs. For example, the Congress amended the National Defense Authorization Act (NDAA) in 2018 and 2020 respectively to prohibit universities hosting CIs from receiving U.S. government funding. Introduced and signed into law in 2018, the 2019 NDAA banned the Department of Defense (DOD) funding to universities hosting CIs: "Sec. 1091. Prohibition of funds for Chinese language instruction provided by a Confucius Institute."[102] Introduced in 2020, the 2021 NDAA broadened the ban of funding for any program at universities hosting CIs if without DOD waivers: "Sec. 1062. Limitation on provision of funds to institutions of higher education hosting Confucius Institutes."[103]

The U.S. Congress also discussed and passed other bills, introduced by senators, to increase oversight over CIs. For example, the Congress passed in March 2020 the "Transparency for Confucius Institute" Act, introduced by Senators Marsha

[99] Hawley, 2019, YouTube video posting.

[100] The U.S. Senate PSI report, 2019.

[101] Bair, 2019.

[102] U.S. Congress website, 2019, NDAA.

[103] U.S. Congress website, 2021, NDAA, and 2021, "Public Law 116–283."

Blackburn (R-TN), Ted Cruz (R-TX), Josh Hawley (R-MO), etc. and strongly supported by Senator Marco Rubio (R-FL) and other senators.[104] The Act aimed to amend the Higher Education Act of 1965, requiring program participation agreements between Hanban/CIs and American institutions of higher education participating in U.S. federal student-aid programs. An educational institution hosting CI on its campus "shall enter into a program participation agreement" with Hanban regarding the separation of CI programs and the institution's Chinese language, history, and cultural programs, CI administration, staff, and teachers, transparency, decision-making authority, etc.[105] Rubio said: "For far too long, the Communist Chinese government has attempted to infiltrate American universities through the disguise of the government-run Confucius Institute." He believed that the Transparency for Confucius Institute Act "adds needed pressure on Confucius Institutes and pushes universities to take responsibility in a way that's consistent with American and democratic values."[106]

Congresspeople like Rubio and others also wrote their constituent universities, urging the institutions to close their CIs. Rubio sent a letter to several universities and one high school in Florida, asking them to sever their relationship with Hanban and CIs. Rubio said in a letter dated early 2018: "There is mounting concern about the Chinese government's increasingly aggressive attempts to use 'Confucius Institutes' and other means to influence foreign academic institutions."[107]

Another example, Texas Congressmen Michael McCaul (Republican) and Henry Cuellar (Democrat) sent a bipartisan letter, dated March 23, 2018, to Texas universities hosting CIs, and also issued a joint statement. They strongly urged the universities *to "consider terminating their partnerships" with CIs and other Chinese government supported organizations. They viewed these organizations as "a threat to our nation's security by serving as a platform for China's intelligence collection and political agenda."*[108]

The Department of State (DOS) also took actions to warn universities about China's political influence and to pressure them to close their CIs. On August 13, 2020, Michael Pompeo, Secretary of State, designated the Confucius Institute U.S. Center (CIUS) in Washington, D.C. as a foreign mission controlled by the Chinese government. He described CIUS as "an entity advancing Beijing's global propaganda and malign influence campaign on U.S. campuses and K-12 classrooms," and

104 Cruz, 2021.

105 U.S. Congress website, 2020, "Transparency for Confucius Institutes Act."

106 Rubio, 2020.

107 Amos, 2018.

108 McCaul, 2018.

regarded China-funded CIs as a part of the CCP's "global influence and propaganda apparatus."[109]

Pompeo and Betsy DeVos, Secretary of Education, stated in a joint letter: "This designation will provide much-needed transparency by requiring CIUS to provide information about its operations to the State Department, including regarding its relationship with individual Confucius Classrooms across the United States. As a result, U.S. stakeholders, including primary and secondary schools, will be able to make more informed choices about PRC government influence being exerted on their communities."[110]

On August 18, 2020, Keith Krach, Under Secretary of DOS, sent a letter to the governing boards of U.S. institutions of higher education. Representing the State Department, Krach warned the boards of the serious and malign challenges imposed by the CCP's authoritarian influence. Krach stressed that this was "a real and urgent threat that has broad implications for ensuring academic freedom, honoring human dignity, protecting university endowments, and safeguarding intellectual property." Krach also identified specific challenges from CIs, which, he believed, "exert malign influence on U.S. campuses and disseminate CCP propaganda." Krach urged universities to increase oversight over CI activities on their campuses to "ensure that academic freedom, institutional autonomy, transparency, and clean financial practices are being upheld."[111]

DOS also worked with the Department of Education (DOE) to manage the perceived threats from China's CI project. Pompeo and DeVos sent a joint letter, dated October 9, 2020, to school districts hosting CCs, alerting U.S. educators of "a real and increasing threat to U.S. classrooms" from China's infiltration. They pointed out that CCs "are in reality an important element of the PRC's global influence campaign, now reaching tens of thousands of U.S. schoolchildren every day." They warned state educational commissioners that "the presence of an authoritarian slant in curriculum and teaching has never been more concerning, nor more consequential," and urged the commissioners and school staff to carefully examine any CC activities in their educational programming.[112]

DOS and DOE also sent a joint letter to presidents of American institutions of higher education and affiliates, with similar content to the letter to primary and secondary school districts. Also dated October 9, 2020, and signed by DeVos and Pompeo, the joint letter warned higher education leaders "about a real and growing threat" and the "malign influence" of the authoritarian Chinese government

[109] Pompeo, 2020.

[110] Quoted from DeVos and Pompeo, 2020a.

[111] U.S. State Department website, 2020, "Letter from Under Secretary Keith Krach."

[112] DeVos and Pompeo, 2020a.

on U.S. campuses via CI programs. Pompeo and DeVos pointed out that CIs "are branded as Chinese language and cultural learning centers, but there is increasing evidence that they are also tools of malign PRC influence and disseminators of CCP propaganda on U.S. campuses." In their view, the presence of China's authoritarian influence on U.S. campuses "has never been more concerning, nor more consequential." They asked university boards and staff "to examine carefully all PRC regime-related activities" associated with their campuses and "consider whether student physical safety, academic freedom, institutional autonomy, and appropriate governance and transparency are upheld."[113]

In addition to working with DOS, DOE made separate efforts, particularly to put restraints on receiving foreign funding. After conducting investigations and analyzing the February 2019 Senate PSI report, DOE released its report in October 2020 and launched an initiative to enforce foreign fund reporting requirements. The 2020 DOE report emphasized the necessity of enforcing foreign fund reporting requirements. It stressed that "there is a very real reason for concern that foreign money buys influence or control over teaching and research."[114] The report pointed out that CIs have been established "at alarmingly exponential rates since 2004"; however, the 2019 Senate PSI report shows that nearly 70 percent of the schools failed to report Hanban gifts, contracts, or contributions in excess of $250,000 to DOE. The DOE report emphasized that "incomplete and inaccurate understandings of institutions' foreign funding hinder timely assessment of how these gifts and contracts could undermine U.S. academic and security interests."[115] DOE felt compelled to take steps to address the findings of the 2019 Senate PSI report, including correcting "a historically nonexistent record of compliance" and creating a new reporting portal for foreign fund reporting.[116]

Just like the PSI report, the letter from DOS Under Secretary Krach, and the DOS/DOE joint letters to public school districts and leaders of higher education, the 2020 DOE report aimed mainly to give warnings about potential dangers perceived by these leaders, without providing adequate concrete evidence supporting the charges they made about CIs.

State governments took similar steps to urge school districts to carefully examine their CC programs perhaps due to pressure from DOS and DOE. For example, the superintendent of Alabama Department of Education sent a letter, dated October 9, 2020, to local school systems in the state, asking them to carefully examine their CCs. The superintendent wrote: "Based on the information provided

113 DeVos and Pompeo, 2020b.

114 U.S. DOE report, 2020.

115 U.S. DOE report, 2020.

116 Horsley, 2021.

by the U.S. Departments of State and Education, I would encourage you to end any such Confucius Classroom experience as soon as practicable, with a goal to end them at the conclusion of this semester."[117]

Some of these actions and measures by the Congress, DOS, DOE, and other federal and state bodies might have been, to some extent, due to fervent desire to win over voters for the 2020 presidential election given the timing of these efforts, just shortly before the election. Some of the Congresspeople leading these efforts to resist CIs were among the most conservative supporters of President Trump whose administration had adopted a very critical and hostile policy toward the PRC. However, the various statements of the U.S. leaders seem to indicate that perceptions and concerns about real and serious threats from a rising and more authoritarian China to U.S. national security and national interests, via CIs and CCs, are among the main reasons for them taking action.

This partly explains why even more oversight measures and restrictions over CIs were put in place after the 2020 presidential election. Soon after Joe Biden started his presidency, the U.S. Senate passed on March 4, 2021 a bill titled the Confucius Act. Introduced by Senator John Kennedy (R-LA), a conservative pro-Trump Republican, the bill banned DOE funding to universities hosting CIs that do not comply with new oversight requirements. The bill stated: "An institution of higher education or other postsecondary educational institution ... shall not be eligible to receive federal funds" from DOE (except certain funds) unless oversight requirements are met, especially regarding the protection of academic freedom and integrity.[118] Kennedy believed that CIs "are under the control of the Chinese Communist Party in all but name." In his view, the Confucius Act would give universities full control over their CIs and "restore freedom of thought" on their campuses.[119]

Mass Closure of CIs in the United States

All these criticisms and actions, especially those by policymakers, contributed to building up unprecedented pressures on universities hosting CIs. Concerns about CIs' infringements of academic freedom, the problem of censorship/self-censorship, and particularly about threats to U.S. national security and national interests have become some of the common concerns unifying various sections of the government. And the 2019 and 2021 NDAA and the 2021 Confucius Act have added fuel to the fire and probably played the most significant role in forcing universities to close their CIs in the past several years. The Acts barred DOD and DOE funding respectively to

117 Mackey, 2020.

118 U.S. Congress website, 2021, "The Confucius Act."

119 Cited from Nunley, 2021.

universities with CIs on their campuses unless they met relevant federal oversight rules and regulations, which offered the institutions no other choice than closing CIs if they wanted to receive funding from the U.S. federal government.

All these pressures led to the swift wave of CI closures and other related developments in the past few years. The College Board, a non-profit organization that administers SAT and AP tests, announced on October 30, 2020 that it would sever ties with Hanban. It had received an annual grant from Hanban from 2006 to 2020 to support the teaching and learning of Chinese language and culture in U.S. schools. Now as a response to a joint letter from seven senators, including Marsha Blackburn, the College Board decided that 2020 was the final year to receive or pursue any grant funding from Hanban.[120]

Among institutions of higher education, the University of Chicago and Penn State University were the first two to close their CIs (in 2014). And mass closure of CIs has mainly taken place in the past four years. According to the NAS June 2022 report, three CIs were closed in 2017, followed by ten in 2018, 23 in 2019, 27 in 2020, and 34 in 2021. By the end of 2021 and early 2022, 104 out of 118 American institutions had closed their CIs or "were in the process of doing so." By May 2023, there were probably fewer than ten CIs open in the U.S., and by late July and early August at the time of writing this chapter, perhaps only three or more CIs are still in operation.

However, it seems that many CCs have survived the closure of their sponsoring CIs so far.[121] Given the determination of such organizations as NAS to eliminate China's cultural and political influence in the U.S. educational system, it is not clear whether CCs would become U.S. political and education leaders' next target for closure if the U.S.-China relationship continues to deteriorate.

One might say that the actions of the U.S. federal and state governments were greater infringements on academic freedom in the United States than anything CIs have done. However, U.S. political leaders believe that their efforts aim to safeguard American national security and national interests. Using the protection of national interests or even pursuit of personal interests/ambitions as a means to contravene the principle of academic freedom is a dangerous trend in any country, either the U.S. or China.

120 Bisht, 2020.

121 Peterson, et al., 2022, pp. 7–8, 13, 33.

Conclusion

Dr. Dan Mote, former President of the University of Maryland (term: 1998–2010), worked with the Chinese government to establish the first Confucius Institute in the U.S. on his campus, with a goal to promote a better understanding of China after the country joined the World Trade Organization in 2001. Dr. Mote explained the rationale in a documentary video: "Culture was the right topic because it's clear. It is not controversial."[122]

This is only a scientist's hope or wish. Culture is not neutral, for language and culture always serve national interests. Imitating international counterparts such as the British Council, the German Goethe Institute, and the Alliance Francaise, CIs have shared some similar fundamental tasks and services. The 2014 AAUP report stated that the three earlier cultural programs "are clearly connected to imperial pasts, ongoing geopolitical agendas, and the objectives of 'soft power.'"[123] As Falk Hartig has pointed out, these language/cultural programs, including CIs, work "for their governments and their government's foreign policy goals."[124]

As examined earlier, CIs are a part of China's new cultural diplomacy to project its soft power overseas. Chinese leaders' official statements clearly illustrate this. For example, the words of Li Changchun, a CCP Politburo Standing Committee member in charge of ideology and propaganda, fully summarizes CIs' main functions: "The Confucius Institute is an appealing brand for expanding our culture abroad," and "it has made an important contribution toward improving our soft power."[125] In addition, CIs' objectives, management/operation, and programs all serve China's national interests by expanding China's cultural influence worldwide and promoting a favorable international environment for China's continuing domestic development. Chinese leaders' frank statements, CIs' goals and administration/operation, and the lack of transparency have gradually caused concerns and strong resistance among U.S. leaders.

Furthermore, other developments both in China and in U.S.-China relations worked to doom CIs. Xi Jinping's authoritarian rule at home and assertive and combative foreign policy alerted U.S. policymakers of new dangers to U.S. national security and national interests. Under both Trump and Biden, the extremely tense U.S.-China relationship has added further fuel, eventually undermining CIs and perhaps CCs too in America. As analyzed above, U.S. leaders and educators

[122] "Episode 5: *Standing on a Riverbank, Confucius Said,*" *People's Daily*, Jan. 20, 2020.

[123] AAUP report, 2014, "On Partnerships with Foreign Governments: The Case of Confucius Institutes."

[124] Hartig, 2016, p. 2 and 2012, p. 68.

[125] Epstein, 2018. Also see Wachter, 2007.

have increasingly realized that CIs are a part and also an instrument of China's cultural diplomacy to project its soft power and to shape Westerners and especially Americans' views of China. U.S. leaders believed that CIs have threatened U.S. national security and national interests by infiltrating American campuses at an alarming speed to promote a favorable Chinese image during the Xi era, thus launching initiatives to pressure U.S. universities to close CIs. These unprecedented pressures led to CIs' mass closure in the past several years, almost leading to the end of CI history in America by summer 2023.

The recent CI closures in the U.S. and other Western countries have shown that scholars' caution about the outcomes of CIs or even China's cultural diplomacy is reasonable. For example, James Paradise has assumed that "only time will tell whether the Confucius Institutes can help spark a more sympathetic understanding of China and usher in a more benign view of it."[126] Jeffrey Gil has argued that although China has successfully established CIs at an amazing speed, the actual influence and benefits China can derive from this project are currently limited to shaping preferences in language learning and attitudes towards China.[127]

One 2009 special report in *The Economist* wrote: "The late Samuel Huntington, in his 1996 bestseller *The Clash of Civilisations and the Remaking of World Order*, describes a Confucian world, with China at its centre, that will find itself in growing conflict with the West. This is the kind of view that the Confucius Institutes are intended to dispel."[128] The recent CI mass closure in America shows that CIs might have failed to achieve this goal to promote a favorable image of a peaceful, harmonious, and beautiful China overseas to avoid conflict.

Hartig's comments on one significant difference between CIs and their international counterparts/predecessors such as the British Council or the German Goethe Institute perhaps reveal the most important reason for CIs' failure in America. He wrote: "The fundamental difference ... is in the nature of the political system Confucius Institutes represent and the way they are structured and organized," while CIs' counterparts follow "the principle of non-intervention by the government."[129] Thus, CIs' unique feature "as a tool of cultural diplomacy with Chinese characteristics" perhaps helps partly explain their failure or eventual demise in America and other Western nations.[130]

However, the disappearance forever of CIs in the U.S. is probably not a foregone conclusion. CIs may be welcomed back to America in the future in alternative

[126] Paradise, 2009, p. 67.

[127] Gil, 2009, p. 67.

[128] *The Economist*, 2009.

[129] Hartig, 2016, p. 2 and 2012, p. 70.

[130] Hartig, 2010, p. 11.

forms, perhaps under a different name when the U.S. welcomes them to advance its national interests and/or when China adopts some form of Western democracy in the distant future. Language and culture always serve national interests, and cross-cultural/educational exchanges always continue between countries, sometime even without diplomatic relations.

Dr. **Shuhua Fan** is professor of history at the University of Scranton, Scranton, Pennsylvania. She received her BA from Sichuan Normal University, her MA from Jilin University, and her MA and PhD from the University of North Carolina at Chapel Hill. She is a visiting scholar at the Harvard-Yenching Institute. She published her book, *The Harvard-Yenching Institute and Cultural Engineering: Remaking the Humanities in China, 1924–1951*, in 2014. Her current book project is titled "Empire, Commerce, Language, and Sino-American Interactions: Francis Kinght, Ko Kunhua, and the Origins of Sinology at Harvard (1877–1882)."

Bibliography

AAUP Committee A on Academic Freedom and Tenure Report. "On Partnerships with Foreign Governments: The Case of Confucius Institutes," American Association of University Professors, June 2014. https://www.aaup.org/report/confucius-institutes, accessed June 5, 2023.

Amos, Denise. "Rubio Asks Florida Colleges to End Deals with Confucius Institutes," *The Florida Times-Union*, Feb. 6, 2018. https://www.jacksonville.com/story/news/2018/02/06/rubio-asks-florida-colleges-to-end-deals-with-confucius-institutes/15296836007/, accessed June 6, 2023.

"An Epic Tale of Two Peoples across the Pacific," *People's Daily*, Apr. 13, 2011.

Ashbee, Edward and Steven Hurst. "The Trump Administration and China: Policy Continuity or Transformation?" *Policy Studies*, Sept.-Nov. 2021, 42.5/6: 720–737.

Bair, Jason. "Observations on Confucius Institutes in the United States and U.S. Universities in China," Testimony Before the Permanent Subcommittee on Investigations, Committee on Homeland Security and Governmental Affairs, U.S. Senate, Feb. 28, 2019. https://www.gao.gov/assets/gao-19-401t.pdf, accessed June 16, 2023.

Barboza, David. "China Overtakes Japan to Become No. 2 Global Economic Power," *New York Times*, Aug. 15, 2010. http://www.nytimes.com/2010/08/16/business/global/16yuan.html, accessed June 26, 2011.

Bill, Gertz. *The China Threat: How the People's Republic Targets America.* Washington, DC: Regnery Publishing, 2000.

Bisht, Inder Singh. "College Board to Sever Ties with Chinese Institute after Senators' Letter," Nov. 5, 2020. https://thecollegepost.com/college-board-sever-ties-confucius-institute/, accessed June 8, 2023.

CCTV website. "Liu Yandong Emphasizes: Working Together and Cooperating on an Equal Footing to Make Confucius Institutes Better and Better," Dec. 10, 2008. https://cctvenchiridion.cctv.com/special/C22950/20081210/102614.shtml, accessed Mar. 23, 2024.

CCTV website. "The 4th Confucius Institute Conference Held in Beijing, Dec. 11-13, 2009," Dec. 27, 2009. https://news.cctv.com/china/20091227/102700.shtml, accessed Mar. 26, 2024.

Chinanews.com. "Director of Hanban: The Global Upsurge of People in Learning Chinese an Unstoppable Momentum," July 12, 2010. http://www.chinanews.com/hwjy/2010/07-12/2395169.shtml, accessed July 6, 2011.

China.org.cn news. "Hu Jintao Calls for Enhancing 'Soft Power' of Chinese Culture," Oct. 15, 2007. www.china.org.cn/english/congress/228142.htm, accessed Mar. 26, 2024.

China.org.cn news. "Chinese language Play Invaluable Role in Bringing Chinese Culture to World," Xinhua News Agency, Apr. 21, 2011. http://www.china.org.cn/learning_chinese/news/2011-04/21/content_22411292.htm, accessed Mar. 27, 2024.

China.org.cn news. "More Foreigners Gung-ho about Learning Chinese," Xinhua News Agency, June 17, 2011. http://www.china.org.cn/learning_chinese/news/2011-06/17/content_22806293.htm, accessed Mar. 26, 2024.

China.org.cn news. "More U.S. Students Encouraged to Study in China," Xinhua News Agency, July 11, 2011. http://www.china.org.cn/learning_chinese/news/2011-07/11/content_22962616.htm, accessed Mar. 24, 2024.

Chinese Embassy in Sri Lanka website. "China Inaugurates Confucius Institute U.S. Center in Washington," Nov. 20, 2013. http://lk.china-embassy.gov.cn/eng/zgxw/201311/t20131122_1421848.htm, accessed June 8, 2023.

Chinese government website. "Be Wary of Enormous Cultural Deficits, Representatives Calling for Enhancing 'China's Soft Power,'" Mar. 11, 2006. http://www.gov.cn/ztzl/2006-03/11/content_224682.htm, accessed July 6, 2011.

Chinese government website. "2006: Confucius Institutes Have Become the Brightest Brand of China's 'Soft Power,'" Jan. 1, 2007. http://www.gov.cn/jrzg/2007-01/01/content_485693.htm, accessed June 16, 2011.

Chinese government website. "Opening Ceremony for CI Headquarters in Beijing," April 9, 2007. http://www.gov.cn/ldhd/2007-04/09/content_576207.htm, accessed July 20, 2011.

Chinese government website. "Cai Wu Talks about the Development of China's 60-Year Cultural Exchanges with Foreign Countries," July 30, 2009. http://www.gov.cn/gzdt/2009-07/30/content_1379485.htm, accessed July 20, 2011.

Chinese Ministry of Education (MOE) website. "Constitution and By-Laws of the Confucius Institutes," Oct. 2006. http://www.moe.gov.cn/srcsite/zsdwxxgk/200610/t20061001_62461.html, accessed Mar. 25, 2024.

"Chinese Official Calls for More Language, Culture Exchanges with Foreign Countries," *People's Daily*, July 18, 2011.

Cho, Young Nam and Jong Ho Jeong. "China's Soft Power: Discussions, Resources, and Prospects," *Asian Survey*, May/June 2008, 48.3: 453–472.

College Republicans and College Democrats. Open Letter: "Concerning the Threat of Authoritarian Influence and the Defense of Public Institutions," May 13, 2020. https://ded2c2d3-2166-446c-a941-a2344cb88920.filesusr.com/ugd/d5a0ea_441a6671c13b4720b2d9f39ceb9e1208.pdf, accessed June 9, 2023.

"Confucius Institutes Become 'Brand' for Disseminating Chinese Culture," press conference of the 2nd Plenary Session of the 11th National People's Congress, *People's Daily*, Mar. 13, 2009.

"Confucius Institutes Face Uphill Battle in Development," *People's Daily*, June 2, 2011.

Copper, John F. "The Biden Administration's China and Taiwan Policies: Connecting the Dots," *East Asian Policy*, July-Sept. 2021, 13.3: 101–116.

Cruz, Ted. "Sens. Cruz, Blackburn Introduce Bill Targeting Beijing's Influence at American Colleges," news release. Apr. 6, 2021. https://www.cruz.senate.gov/newsroom/press-releases/sens-cruz-blackburn-introduce-bill-targeting-beijing-and-146s-influence-at-american-colleges, accessed June 8, 2023.

Cull, Nicholas J. "Public Diplomacy: Taxonomies and Histories," *The Annals of the American Academy of Political and Social Science*, Mar 2008, 616: 31–54.

Dai, Yaoyao and Luwei Rose Luqiu. "Wolf Warriors and Diplomacy in the New Era: An Empirical Analysis of China's Diplomatic Language," *China Review*, May 2022, 22.2: 253–283.

DeVos, Betsy and Michael R. Pompeo. "Joint Letter to Commissioners of Education about China's Confucius Classrooms Program," Oct. 9, 2020a, available at USC U.S.-China Institute website, Oct. 14, 2020. https://china.usc.edu/mike-pompeo-and-betsy-devos-joint-letter-commissioners-education-about-chinas-confucius-classrooms, accessed June 8, 2023 and also available at Office of Elementary and Secondary Education website, https://oese.ed.gov/files/2020/10/State-ED-Joint-Letter-to-Chief-State-School-Officers-re-PRC-Influence-Oct.-9-2020.pdf, accessed June 8, 2023.

DeVos, Betsy and Michael R. Pompeo. "Joint Letter to Presidents of American Institutions of Higher Education and Affiliates regarding the People's Republic of China," Oct. 9, 2020b. https://2017-2021.state.gov/joint-letter-to-presidents-of-american-institutions-of-higher-education-and-affiliates-regarding-the-peoples-republic-of-china/index.html and https://www2.ed.gov/about/offices/list/ope/state-edjointltrreprcinfluence1092020.pdf, accessed June 8, 2023.

Ding, Arthur S. and Jagannath P. Panda, eds. *Chinese Politics and Foreign Policy under Xi Jinping: The Future Political Trajectory*. London: Routledge, 2020.

"Episode 5: Standing on a Riverbank, Confucius Said" (第五集: "子在川上日") (Dr. Clayton Daniel Mote, Jr.), *People's Daily*, Jan. 20, 2020. http://world.people.com.cn/n1/2020/0120/c1002-31557106.html, accessed June 3, 2023.

Epstein, Ethan. "How China Infiltrated U.S. Classrooms," *Politico Magazine*, Jan. 16, 2018. https://www.politico.com/magazine/story/2018/01/16/how-china-infiltrated-us-classrooms-216327/, accessed June 11, 2023.

Evans, Zachary. "Leading College Republicans and Dems Draft Open Letter Urging American Universities to Combat Chinese Influence," *National Review*, May 14, 2020. https://www.nationalreview.com/news/leading-college-republicans-and-dems-draft-open-letter-urging-american-universities-to-combat-chinese-influence/, accessed June 9, 2023.

French, Howard W. "Another Chinese Export Is All the Rage: China's Language," *New York Times*, Jan. 11, 2006. http://www.nytimes.com/2006/01/11/international/asia/11china.html, accessed June 16, 2011.

Gil, Jeffrey. "China's Confucius Institute Project: Language and Soft Power in World Politics," *The Global Studies Journal*, July 2009. 2.1: 59–72.

Glaser, Bonnie S. and Evan S. Medeiros. "The Changing Ecology of Foreign Policymaking in China: The Ascension and Demise of the Theory of 'Peaceful Rise,'" *The China Quarterly*, June 2007, 190: 291–310.

Goldstein, Avery. *Rising to the Challenge: China's Grand Strategy and International Security*. Stanford: Stanford University Press, 2005.

"Growing International Stature Spurs Boom in Chinese Language Learning in U.S.," *People's Daily*, Apr. 15, 2011.

Guo, Xiaolin. "Repackaging Confucius: PRC Public Diplomacy and the Rise of Soft Power," *Asia Papers*, published by the Institute for Security and Development Policy, Sweden, Jan. 2008. https://isdp.eu/content/uploads/publications/2008_guo_repackaging-confucius.pdf, 50pp, accessed June 18, 2023.

"Hanban." https://hanban.ca/hanban.php?lang=en, accessed Mar. 26, 2024.

"Han Ban – Chinese Language Council." https://www.gvaschools.org/apps/pages/index.jsp?uREC_ID=219810&type=d&pREC_ID=482867, accessed Mar. 26, 2024.

Hartig, Falk. "Confusion About Confucius Institutes: Soft Power Push or Conspiracy? – A Case Study of Confucius Institutes in Germany," paper presented at the 18th Biennial Conference of the Asian Studies Association of Australia in Adelaide, July 5–8, 2010.

Hartig, Falk. "Confucius Institutes and the Rise of China," *Journal of Chinese Political Science*, Mar. 2012, 17.1: 53–76.

Hartig, Falk. *Chinese Public Diplomacy: The Rise of the Confucius Institute*. London and New York: Routledge, 2016.

Hawley, Josh (Poster). YouTube video – "Sen. Hawley Questions FBI Director Wray Over Chinese Espionage through Confucius Institute," July 24, 2019-posting date. https://www.youtube.com/watch?v=WnlSKZoDrzo, accessed June 22, 2023.

Horsley, Jamie P. "It's Time for a New Policy on Confucius Institutes," *Lawfare*, Apr. 1, 2021. https://www.lawfareblog.com/its-time-new-policy-confucius-institutes, accessed June 6, 2023.

Hu, Jintao. "Hold High the Great Banner of Socialism with Chinese Characteristics and Strive for New Victories in Building a Moderately Prosperous Society in All Respects." Report at the 17th National Congress of the Communist Party of China, Xinhua News Agency, Oct. 15, 2007. 2007a. http://www.china.org.cn/english/congress/229611.htm, accessed July 16, 2011.

Hu, Jintao. Report to the 17th National Congress of the Communist Party of China on Oct. 15, 2007, Xinhua News Agency, 2007b. http://www.china.org.cn/english/congress/229611.htm, accessed July 16, 2011.

Huang, Zhao Alexandre. "'Wolf Warrior' and China's Digital Public Diplomacy during the COVID-19 Crisis," *Place Branding and Public Diplomacy*, 2022, 18: 37–40. https://doi-org.ezp.scranton.edu/10.1057/s41254-021-00241-3, accessed June 6, 2023.

Hubbert, Jennifer Ann. *China in the World: An Anthropology of Confucius Institutes, Soft Power, and Globalization*. University of Hawaii Press, 2019.

Jensen, Lionel M. "Culture Industry, Power, and the Spectacle of China's 'Confucius Institutes,'" in Timothy B. Weston and Lionel M. Jensen, eds., *China in and Beyond Headlines*. Rowman and Littlefield, 2012. pp. 271–299.

Krantz, Laura. "Chinese Institute at UMass Boston Is Accused of Promoting Censorship," *The Boston Globe*, Jan. 15, 2018. https://www.bostonglobe.com/metro/2018/01/15/chinese-institute-umass-boston-accused-promoting-censorship/U5nL824cIpKTFF7h186TSP/story.html, accessed June 16, 2023.

Kurlantzick, Joshua. *Charm Offensive: How China's Soft Power Is Transforming the World* (e-book). New Haven: Yale University Press, 2007.

Liu, Tony Tai-Ting. "Public Diplomacy: China's Newest Charm Offensive," in Daniel Johanson, Jie Li, and Tsunghan Wu, eds., *New Perspectives on China's Relations with the World: National, Transnational, and International*. E-International Relations Publishing, 2019. pp.77–87.

Liu, Yandong. Keynote Speech at the 3rd World Confucius Institute Conference, Dec. 9, 2008. http://www.gov.cn/ldhd/2008-12/09/content_1173203.htm, accessed June 25, 2011.

Liu, Yandong. "Operate CIs Successfully to Promote Sino-Foreign Cultural Exchange and Cooperation," speech at the 4th CI Conference, Dec. 11–13, 2009, Beijing. http://www.gov.cn/ldhd/2009-12/11/content_1485517.htm, accessed July 10, 2011.

Liu Yandong. "Speech at Opening Ceremony of Fourth National Chinese Language Conference," Apr. 14, 2011, San Francisco. http://nl.china-embassy.gov.cn/eng/zgyw/201108/t20110801_2645062.htm, accessed Mar. 23, 2024.

Lloyd-Damnjanovic, Anastasya. "A Preliminary Study of PRC Political Influence and Interference Activities in American Higher Education," Wilson Center, Aug. 2018. https://www.wilsoncenter.org/sites/default/files/media/documents/publication/prc_political_influence_full_report.pdf, accessed June 11, 2023.

Mackey, Eric G. (Alabama State Superintendent of Education). Letter to City and County Superintendents of Education, Oct 9. 2020. https://www.scribd.com/document/479535117/Confucius-Classrooms-In-Alabama-pdf#, accessed June 1, 2023.

MacLeod, Calum. "U.S. Expatriates Pursue American Dream in China," *USA Today*, July 12, 2011. http://www.usatoday.com/news/world/2011-07-12-Americans-China-dreams-transplants_n.htm, accessed Aug. 20, 2011.

McCaul, Michael. "McCaul, Cuellar Send Letter to Texas Universities Hosting Confucius Institutes," press release, Apr. 5, 2018. https://mccaul.house.gov/media-center/press-releases/mccaul-cuellar-send-letter-to-texas-universities-hosting-confucius, accessed June 8, 2023.

Menges, Constantine C. *China: The Gathering Threat*. Nashville, TN: Nelson Current, 2005.

Nunley, Christian. "Senate Approves Bill to Tighten Controls on China-funded Confucius Institutes on U.S. University Campuses," CNBC, Mar. 5, 2021. https://www.cnbc.com/2021/03/05/us-senate-approves-bill-against-china-funded-confucius-institutes.html, accessed June 18, 2023.

Nye, Joseph S. Jr. "Soft Power," *Foreign Policy*, Autumn 1990a, 80 (Twentieth Anniversary): 153-171.

Nye, Joseph S. Jr. *Bound to Lead: The Changing Nature of American Power*. New York: Basic Books, 1990b.

Nye, Joseph S. Jr. *Soft Power: The Means to Success in World Politics*. New York: Public Affairs, 2004.

Nye, Joseph S. Jr. "Public Diplomacy and Soft Power," *The Annals of the American Academy of Political and Social Science*, Mar. 2008, 616: 94–109.

Nye, Joseph S. Jr. *Soft Power and Great-Power Competition: Shifting Sands in the Balance of Power Between the United States and China*. Springer, Singapore, 2023.

Oregon state government website. "Section 326.327: Agreement by Superintendent to Ensure Availability of Instruction of Chinese Language," *Oregon Revised Statutes*, Vol. 9, Title 30, Chap. 326, State Admin of Edu, Feb. 2010. https://www.oregonlegislature.gov/bills_laws/ors/ors326.html and https://oregon.public.law/statutes/ors_326.327, accessed July 30, 2023.

Paradise, James. "China and International Harmony: The Role of Confucius Institutes in Bolstering Beijing's Soft Power," *Asian Survey*, July/Aug. 2009, 49.4: 647–669.

Peterson, Rachelle. *Outsourced to China: Confucius Institutes and Soft Power in American Higher Education.* National Association of Scholars. Apr. 2017.

Peterson, Rachelle. "Senator Josh Hawley Reveals the Nasty Truth Behind Confucius Institutes," *National Review*, Aug. 2, 2019. https://www.nationalreview.com/2019/08/senator-josh-hawley-reveals-the-nasty-truth-behind-confucius-institutes/, accessed June 9, 2023.

Peterson, Rachelle, Flora Yan, and Ian Oxnevad. *After Confucius Institutes: China's Enduring Influence on American Higher Education*. National Association of Scholars. June 2022.

Pompeo, Michael. "Designation of the Confucius Institute U.S. Center as a Foreign Mission of the PRC," press statement, Aug. 13, 2020. https://2017-2021.state.gov/designation-of-the-confucius-institute-u-s-center-as-a-foreign-mission-of-the-prc/index.html, accessed June 5, 2023.

Pong, Jane Pong and Emily Feng. "Confucius Institutes: Cultural Asset or Campus Threat?," *Financial Times*, Oct. 26, 2007. https://ig.ft.com/confucius-institutes/, accessed June 9, 2023.

Redden, Elizabeth. "Debate Over Chinese-Funded Institutes," *Inside Higher Education*, Jan. 3, 2012. https://www.insidehighered.com/news/2012/01/04/debate-over-chinese-funded-institutes-american-universities#sthash.1XrPR3mX.9wWDPAi7.dpbs, accessed June 6, 2023.

Redden, Elizabeth. "Rejecting Confucius Funding," *Inside Higher Education*, Apr. 29, 2014. https://www.insidehighered.com/news/2014/04/29/chicago-faculty-object-their-campuss-confucius-institute, accessed June 5, 2023.

Rubio, Marco. "Rubio Joins Blackburn and Colleagues in Introducing Bill to Ensure Confucius Institutes Abide by Standards of Transparency," press release, Mar.12, 2020. https://www.rubio.senate.gov/public/index.cfm/2020/3/rubio-joins-blackburn-and-colleagues-in-introducing-bill-to-ensure-confucius-institutes-abide-by-standards-of-transparency, accessed June 8, 2023.

Sahlins, Marshall. "China U.," *The Nation*, Oct. 30, 2013. https://www.thenation.com/article/archive/china-u/, accessed June 12, 2023.

Sahlins, Marshall. "Confucius Institutes: Academic Malware," *The Asia-Pacific Journal/Japan Focus*, Oct. 30, 2013, 12.46.1. https://apjjf.org/2014/12/46/Marshall-Sahlins/4220.html, accessed June 12, 2023.

Sahlins, Marshall. *Confucius Institutes: Academic Malware*. Chicago: Prickly Paradigm Press, 2015.

Sahlins, Marshall. "Confucius Institutes: Academic Malware and Cold Warfare," *Inside Higher Education*, July 25, 2018. https://www.insidehighered.com/views/2018/07/26/confucius-institutes-function-propaganda-arms-chinese-government-opinion, accessed June 11, 2023.

Song, Guoyou. "The Biden Administration's Economic Policy toward China: Readjustment and New Areas of Competition," *China International Studies*, Nov./Dec. 2022, 97: 132–151.

Starr, Don. "Chinese Language Education in Europe: Confucius Institutes," *European Journal of Education*, Mar. 2009, 44.1 (2009): 65–82.

Tang, Yuankai. "Education: Confucius Teaching Chinese Abroad: An Expanding Network of Institutes Teaches the Chinese Language Overseas," *Beijing Review*, Jan. 4, 2010. http://www.bjreview.com.cn/life/txt/2010-01/04/content_237885.htm, accessed June 17, 2011.

The Economist. Special report (Anonymous). "A Message from Confucius" (New Ways of Projecting Soft Power), Oct. 24, 2009, 393.8654. https://www.economist.com/special-report/2009/10/24/a-message-from-confucius, accessed June 18, 2023.

Timperlake, Edward and William C. Triplett II. *Red Dragon Rising: Communist China's Military Threat to America*. Washington, DC: Regnery Publishing, 1999.

"Top Advisory Body Holds Seminar on 'Soft Power,'" *China Daily*, July 25, 2007.

UN website. "About the Chinese Language Day – 20 Apr. 2011," Apr. 20, 2011. http://www.un.org/zh/events/chineselanguageday/english.shtml, accessed July 15, 2011.

UN website. "UN Celebrates Chinese Language Day with Art and Exhibitions," Apr 20, 2011. https://news.un.org/en/story/2011/04/372852, accessed Mar. 28, 2024.

University of Chicago. "Statement on the Confucius Institute at the University of Chicago," Sept. 25, 2014. https://news.uchicago.edu/story/statement-confucius-institute-university-chicago, accessed June 12, 2023.

U.S. Congress website. 115th Congress (2017–2018). "H.R.5515 – John S. McCain National Defense Authorization Act for Fiscal Year 2019," 2019. https://www.congress.gov/bill/115th-congress/house-bill/5515/text, accessed June 16, 2023.

U.S. Congress website. "Transparency for Confucius Institutes Act," introduced by Senator Marsha Blackburn to Senate, 116th Congress, 2D session, Mar. 2020. https://www.congress.gov/bill/117th-congress/senate-bill/822?s=1&r=32#:~:text=This%20bill%20requires%20an%20institution,operates%20on%20the%20IHE's%20campus, accessed June 8, 2023.

U.S. Congress website. 116th Congress (2019–2020). "H.R.6395 – William M. (Mac) Thornberry National Defense Authorization Act for Fiscal Year 2021," 2021. https://www.congress.gov/bill/116th-congress/house-bill/6395, accessed June 16, 2023.

U.S. Congress website. "S. 590 – Confucius Act," considered and passed U.S. Senate, Mar. 4, 2021. https://www.congress.gov/bill/117th-congress/senate-bill/590/text, or https://www.congress.gov/117/bills/s590/BILLS-117s590cps.pdf, accessed June 6, 2013.

U.S. Congress website. "Public Law 116–283 – Jan. 1, 2021 William M. (Mac) Thornberry National Defense Authorization Act for Fiscal Year 2021," 2021. https://www.congress.gov/116/plaws/publ283/PLAW-116publ283.pdf, accessed June 16, 2023.

U.S. Department of Education report. "Institutional Compliance with Section 117 of the Higher Education Act of 1965," Oct. 2020. https://www2.ed.gov/policy/highered/leg/institutional-compliance-section-117.pdf, accessed June 6, 2023.

U.S. Senate Permanent Subcommittee on Investigations (PSI), Committee on Homeland Security and Governmental Affairs. Report on Confucius Institutes – *China's Impact on the U.S. Education System*, 2019. https://www.hsgac.senate.gov/wp-content/uploads/imo/media/doc/PSI%20Report%20China's%20Impact%20on%20the%20US%20Education%20System.pdf, accessed June 16, 2023.

U.S. State Department website. "100,000 Strong Educational Exchange Initiatives," n.d. https://2009-2017.state.gov/100k/, accessed June 10, 2023.

U.S. State Department website. "Letter from Under Secretary Keith Krach to the Governing Boards of American Universities," U.S. Department of State, Aug. 18, 2020. https://2017-2021.state.gov/letter-from-under-secretary-keith-krach-to-the-governing-boards-of-american-universities/, accessed Mar. 26, 2024.

USC US-China Institute newsletter. "Confucius Institutes in The United States," Nov. 8, 2021. https://china.usc.edu/confucius-institutes-united-states, accessed June 3, 2023.

Wang, Hongying and Lu Yeh-chung. "The Conception of Soft Power and Its Policy Implications: A Comparative Study of China and Taiwan," *Journal of Contemporary China*, Nov. 8, 2021, 17.56: 425–447.

Wang, Jiangyu and Dawn Yamane Hewett. "U.S.-China Trade Relations in the Biden Era: Trade War, Industrial Policy, and Rule-Based International Order," *American Society of International Law: Proceedings of the Annual Meeting*, 2021, 115: 315–320.

Wang, Yiwei. "Public Diplomacy and the Rise of Chinese Soft Power," *The Annals of the American Academy of Political and Social Science*, Mar. 2008, 616: 257–273.

Wachter, Will. "The Language of Chinese Soft Power in the US," *Asia Times*, May 24, 2007. http://www.atimes.com/atimes/China/IE24Ad02.html, accessed June 18, 2011.

Wong, Edward. "China's President Lashes Out at Western Culture," *The New York Times*, Jan. 3, 2012. https://www.nytimes.com/2012/01/04/world/asia/chinas-president-pushes-back-against-western-culture.html, accessed June 26, 2023.

Wray, Christopher. Testimony before the U.S. Senate Committee on Intelligence, Hearing on "Worldwide Threats," Feb. 13, 2018. https://www.intelligence.senate.gov/hearings/open-hearing-worldwide-threats-0#, accessed June 5, 2023.

Ye, Xin. "Expats Seeking Opportunities in China," *People's Daily*, May 3, 2011.

Yee, Herbert and Ian Storey, eds. *China Threat: Perceptions, Myths, and Reality.* London: Routledge, 2004.

Zhang, Zhiping. "Spreading the Word Overseas," *Beijing Review*, July 27, 2010. http://www.bjreview.com.cn/print/txt/2010-07/26/content_287040.htm, accessed July 6, 2011.

CHAPTER SEVEN

Belt and Road by the Sea: 21st Century Maritime Silk Road

Ting Jiang

METROPOLITAN STATE UNIVERSITY OF DENVER

Abstract: *Until the 14th century, the terrestrial Silk Road had been the artery between the East and the West, contributing to international trade and cultural diffusion. Around the same period, there was an equally important trade route by sea, later known as the Maritime Silk Road, connecting Southeast China to West Asia, Africa, and Europe via the Indian Ocean and the Red Sea. This chapter compares China's 21st Century Maritime Silk Road with the ancient Maritime Silk Road to clarify its conceptual framework and to demystify some of the concerns around this integral component of China's Belt and Road Initiative. Findings shed light on how temporal dimensions of social life of the past could leave profound marks on the current conditions of life, for example, Xi's framing and operationalization of the 21st century Maritime Silk Road.*

Keywords: Belt and Road Initiative; 21st century Maritime Silk Road; Ancient Maritime Silk Road legacies; China's global investment

Introduction

In Chapter Five, Yi Sun has traced the history of the Silk Road. Indeed, for years, the terrestrial Silk Road was of great interest to the public and academia. The public awareness of the Silk Road was largely shaped by Hollywood motion pictures, which are marked by exoticism, adventure, nostalgia, deserts, and camels. Inside academia, the Silk Road is a popular topic in humanities and social sciences. The consensus is that the term Silk Road was coined by German geographer Ferdinand von Richthoften around 1877.[131] Though the formal conceptualization of the terrestrial Silk Road did not occur until the late 19th century, its spirit and legacy, which is characterized by innovation, prosperity, diversity, and inclusiveness has been extensively documented by folklore, ancient texts, archeological discoveries, and collective memories. The consensus in literature emphasizes its connectivity

131 Billé, Mehendale, and Lankton, *The Maritime Silk Road*: 11.

between the East and the West, as well as its contribution to international trade, cultural and technological diffusion.

Around the same period as the terrestrial Silk Road, another important trade route by the sea was acting as the artery that connects Southeast China to West Asia, Africa, and Europe via the Indian Ocean and the Red Sea. This maritime trade route laid the foundation for China's 21st Century Maritime Silk Road, a term making its debut on October 3, 2013, during President Xi Jinping's keynote speech at the Indonesia Congress during his state visit. In his speech, President Xi proposed to jointly build a China-ASEAN community with a shared future. This 21st Century Maritime Silk Road has since become an integral component of China's Belt and Road Initiative, a China-led model of global cooperation and mutual development driven by large-scale infrastructure projects funded by China's outward direct investments. Since its inception, the 21st Century Maritime Silk Road has been laden with geopolitical implications, causing skepticism and criticism questioning China's legitimacy to utilize the Silk Road to frame this initiative as well as its capability to wield its growing power in a responsible manner, in particular the financial sustainability and commitment to green projects to avoid potential environmental disruption.

Historical context of the 21st Century Maritime Silk Road

Beginning: Han Dynasty

China's recorded international maritime adventures can be traced back to the Han Dynasty (BC 206–AD 220). These expeditions were endorsed and dispatched by the emperors to build trade networks, source exotic treasures, and establish diplomatic relationships with faraway places. The first trade route for this purpose was documented in the *Book of Han*,[132] which was completed in AD 111, covering the period from 206 BC to AD 23. According to this book, sail boats would depart from ports of Xuwen and Hepu to reach the Indian Ocean via the waters of the South China Sea, the Gulf of Thailand, and Bay of Bengal.[133] These boats would stop at India and Sri Lanka to trade exotic items like pearls, colored glazes, rare stones, gold, and Chinese silk. Chinese silk would later be transported to Rome. On the way back, sail boats would navigate through the Malacca Strait to make another stop in Malaysia before heading back to China.

[132] Gu, *Book of Han*. (https://ctext.org/han-shu/ens?searchu=%E5%BE%90%E9%97%BB. – accessed on June 10, 2023).

[133] Xuwen is located in today's Guangdong province. Hepu is located in today's Guangxi Zhuang Autonomous Region.

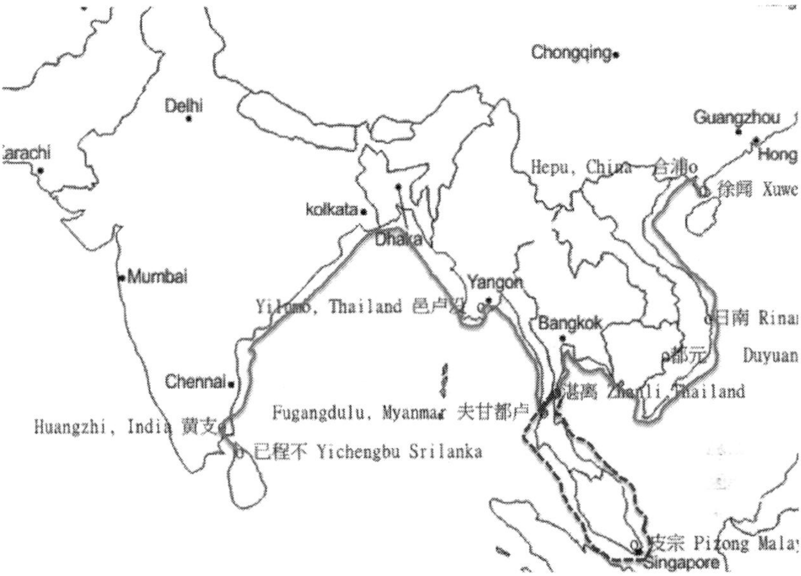

Figure 7.1: Maritime Trade route in Han Dynasty
Source: *Book of Han Vol. 28 Geography Record* 8. 1671. 2–9; Zhionghua Shuju 1962. (https://ctext.org/han-shu/ens?searchu=%E5%BE%90%E9%97%BB – accessed on May 1, 2023)
Note: The map is directly from dmaps.com, a free map resource.[134] The solid line and the dotted lines, as well as English notations and Chinese pinyin are added by the author.

Perhaps the most notable narration of the *Book of Han* is the vivid depiction of this sea adventure, which helps us get a glimpse of the countries and regions along this early maritime trade route. In Figure 7.1, the solid line denotes the westward trade route from China to India. The dotted line represents the detour on the way back. As the book reads: "From Xuwen and Hepu, (to travel along the Indo-China Peninsula) for five months to reach Duyuan Kingdom (in today's Vietnam); another four months to reach Yilumo Kingdom (in today's Thailand). From Yilumo Kingdom, it takes twenty days to get to Zhanli Kingdom (in today's Thailand). Once landed, hike on foot westward for ten days to reach Fugandulu Kingdom (which is on the other side of the south end of the Indochina peninsula) and then travel by the sea for about two months (along the Bay of Bengal taking advantage of the monsoon wind) to reach Huangzhi Kingdom (today's India) ...... On the way home, sail boats

134 Web address for the map: https://d-maps.com/carte.php?num_car=32159&lang=zh. Per dmaps disclaimer, these maps "are modifiable, free for any use—even commercial—under the following conditions: The exact URL where the original map comes from must be mentioned; the number of maps is limited to 10 per publication (website, DVD, Book ...) (https://d-maps.com/conditions.php?lang=en)

will travel eight months (and navigate through the Malacca Strait) to reach Pizong (today's Malaysia), and another two months to Rinan and the border of Xianglin (in today's Vietnam). South of Pizong is Yichengbu (today's Sri Lanka), where the return voyage of Han delegates begins."[135]

Growth: Tang Dynasty

In the following 400 years, this maritime trade route continued to grow in length and coverage. Toward the Sui and Tang dynasties (6th to 7th centuries), the terrestrial Silk Road could no longer guarantee safe and timely passage due to regional conflicts and instability west of China's territories. Roadblocks and forced detours were common. Under such circumstances, the maritime trade route became the logical alternative to sustain international trade from the East to the East. In the *New Book of Tang* compiled by Ouyang Xiu and his colleagues around 1080, during the Tang dynasty, a maritime trade route was recorded as the "Guangzhou tonghai yidao" (广州通海夷道/Guangzhou sea passage to foreign countries).[136] It begins from the city of Guangzhou, travels throughout the waters of Southeast Asia, Bay of Bengal, the Indian Ocean, and continues westward to the Red Sea, reaching North and East Africa, Persian Gulf, and the Arab Empire.[137] Numerous archeological and shipwreck discoveries of ceramic trade have been discovered in the Indian Ocean and Southeast Asian waters,[138] some as far as the Lamu archipelagos of Kenya.[139]

[135] "自日南障塞、徐闻、合浦船行可五月, 有都元国; 又船行可四月, 有邑卢没国; 又船行可二十馀日, 有谌离国; 步行可十馀日, 有夫甘都卢国。自夫甘都卢国船行可二月馀, 有黄支国, 民俗略与珠砀相类。其州广大, 户口多, 多异物, 自武帝以来皆献见。有译长, 属黄门, 与应募者俱入海市明珠、璧流离、奇石异物, 赍黄金杂缯而往。所至国皆禀食为耦, 蛮夷贾船, 转送致之。亦利交易, 剽杀人。又苦逢风波溺死, 不者数年来还。大珠至围二寸以下。平帝元始中, 王莽辅政, 欲耀威德, 厚遗黄支王, 令遣使献生犀牛。自黄支船行可八月, 到皮宗; 船行可二月, 到日南、象林界云。黄支之南, 有已程不国, 汉之译使自此还矣。"

[136] Ouyang, *Xintangshu.*

"其入四夷之路与关戍走集最要者七: 一曰营州入安东道, 二曰登州海行入高丽渤海道, 三曰夏州塞外通大同云中道, 四曰中受降城入回鹘道, 五曰安西入西域道, 六曰安南通天竺道, 七曰广州通海夷道。90. 「广州东南海行, 二百里至屯门山, 乃帆风西行, 二日至九州石。又南二日至象石。又西南三日行, 至占不劳山, 山在环王国东二百里海中。又南二日行至陵山。又一日行, 至门毒国。又一日行, 至古笪国。又半日行, 至奔陀浪洲。又两日行, 到军突弄山。又五日行至海硖, 蕃人谓之「质」, 南北百里, 北岸则罗越国, 南岸则佛逝国。」

[137] Wu, "*Guangzhou tonghai yidao.*"

[138] Kimura, "Archaeological Evidence of Shipping and Shipbuilding"; Tai et al. "The Impact of Ming and Qing Dynasty."

[139] Zhao, "Chinese-Style Ceramics in East Africa."

Peak: Song Dynasty

The Song dynasty witnessed the heyday of this maritime trade route. Widespread use of the compass coupled with mature shipping building and navigation technology contributed to an exponential growth in maritime trade volumes and trade networks covering almost every continent. During this period, we see an increasing governmental involvement to regulate and promote international trade. Such effort is epitomized by the Song government's creation of the "Shibo Si" (市舶司/Bureau of Maritime Commerce) in 977, a specialized governmental apparatus for overseeing trade administration.[140] The Bureau of Maritime Commerce performed the following functions: 1) taking care of tributary envoys and encouraging foreign merchants to come to China; 2) inspection of incoming and outgoing ships; 3) collection of duties; 4) sale and distribution of goods; 5) administrating the sale of foreign goods by foreign and Chinese merchants; 6) administration of seafaring Chinese merchants 7) enforcement of laws on restrictions and smuggling; 8) supervision and administration of foreign settlements; 9) supervision of rescue of wrecked ships and disposal of property left by foreign merchants.[141] Another milestone came shortly after in 1080, when the Song government enacted the "Guangzhou Shibo Tiaofa" (广州市舶条法/Guangzhou Maritime Trade and Commerce Law). It is China's first official legal document to regulate international trade and commerce.[142] Maritime trade became an essential source of revenue during the Song dynasty. In 1162, taxation from Fujian Bureau of Maritime Commerce alone was 2 million min, which comprised 5 percent of the national revenue.[143]

140 Wang, "T'ang Maritime Trade Administration."

141 Sen, "Administration of Maritime Trade."

142 Liao, "Shilun Songdai shibosi guanzhi de yanbian."

143 Li, *Jianyan yilai chaoye zaji*, Vol. 15, No. 1, line 34.

"福建市舶司言自建炎二年至绍兴四年收息钱九十八万缗.诏官其纲首十二月乙巳十四年命蕃商之以香药至者十取其四。十七年诏于沈香豆蔻龙脑之属号细香药者十取其一。至绍兴末两舶司抽分及和买岁得息钱二百万缗。"

Decline: Ming and Qing Dynasties

The first sign of decline appeared during the Ming dynasty when the first maritime ban was implemented during 1371–1529, followed by a second ban during 1521–1529.[144] These bans were an effort to combat piracy, and most importantly to institutionalize government control of foreign trade. For example, these bans would not apply to "tributary trade" (exchange of goods and services between China and its vassal states),[145] but strictly prohibiting private trading between Chinese and foreign merchants.[146] Such a decline accelerated following another ban in the Qing Dynasty (1654–1684),[147] and came to a stop after the Qing government's defeat in the 1840 Opium War, marking the end of China-led and China-centric maritime international trade and expeditions.

Legacies of the Ancient Maritime Silk Road

The ancient Maritime Silk Road connected China with faraway places, and resulted not only in trade volume of goods and treasures but also encounters with diverse cultures and peoples. Innovation, pragmatism, multiculturalism, and collaborative development are the common themes of these early maritime explorations. These maritime legacies accentuate the primacy of human interactions in the formation of diverse cultures and societies along this ancient trade route. Commercial exchange produced profits, revenues, job opportunities, as well as a culture of inclusion and openness that are conducive for sustainable growth.

In addition, heavily influenced by Confucianism, these maritime expeditions were invariably peaceful in nature, demonstrating an effective model of collaborative and constructive interactions between different cultures, peoples, cities, and kingdoms. This is in drastic contrast to the violent and exploitive maritime expeditions led by western explorers.

144 Tai et al.,"The Impact of Ming and Qing Dynasty."

145 Fairbank, "Tributary Trade and China's Relations with the West."

146 Liu and Hu, "Dierjie Mingdai qianqi de haijin ji chaogong tizhi."

147 Tai et al.,"The Impact of Ming and Qing Dynasty."

Conceptualizing the 21st Century Maritime Silk Road (MSR)

Vision and Mission

According to "Vision and actions on jointly building Belt and Road" (2015),[148] the 21st Century Maritime Silk Road "emphasized the need to build the Maritime Silk Road oriented towards ASEAN, and to create strategic propellers for hinterland development. Accelerating the building of the Belt and Road can help promote the economic prosperity of the countries along the Belt and Road and regional economic cooperation, strengthen exchanges and mutual learning between different civilizations, and promote world peace and development." It continues to call for concerted effort from all parties to implement the Initiative, and to "instill vigor and vitality into the ancient Silk Road, connect Asian, European and African countries more closely and promote mutually beneficial cooperation to a new high and in new forms."

In short, the 21st Century Maritime Silk Road underscores interconnectivity via trade and financial investment, which prioritize bilateral and multilateral cooperation. Infrastructure building and sustainable growth are the two major propellers of this undertaking.

Building on the Ancient Maritime Silk Road

This vision statement explicitly mentioned the ancient Silk Road and the ambition to revitalize it to serve the 21st century's needs. In addition to utilizing and building on the historical maritime trade routes, the 21st Century Maritime Silk Road also champions the values resonating with the ancient maritime legacies: economic prosperity, cooperation, exchange and mutual learning, world peace and development.

Innovative Model of Development and International Collaboration

Comparing the ancient Maritime Silk Road phenomenon, this 21st century version is unique in its innovative model of international development collaboration, which heavily relies on large scale cross-border infrastructure building. According to the vision statement, to put the new Silk Road to effective use, a robust and functional infrastructure is a necessity.[149] While the terrestrial silk road prioritizes railway and highway building, the Maritime Silk Road focuses on acquiring and building

148 Ministry of Foreign Affairs, "Vision and actions on jointly building Silk Road."
149 Ibid.

seaports and trade routes to optimize shipping efficiency and minimize capricious conditions like weather, regional conflicts, and terrorism.

The construction of the Doraleh Multipurpose Port (DMP), an affiliate of the Port of Djibouti city, is a prime example of this new model of development and collaboration. Situated at the Horn of Africa, Djibouti's strategic location has made it an ideal hub for the new Maritime Silk Road. This seaport links Addis Ababa (Ethiopia) with Djibouti's newly constructed international free-trade zone via Addis Ababa–Djibouti Railway (both the DMP and the railway are financed and constructed by China's state-owned enterprises),[150] providing valuable seaport access to landlocked countries like Ethiopia. It is a viable model to convert landlocked countries to land-linked countries, providing equitable logistic conditions for economic development and growth.

In January 2016, China and Djibouti signed an MOU to lease Port of Djibouti for a length of 10 years. In July 2017, The People's Liberation Army Support Base adjacent to the DMP was officially opened in Djibouti, whose task is to conduct anti-piracy operations off the coast of Djibouti and around the Horn of Africa, as well as safeguarding China's security interests in Africa, the Middle East, and the Indian Ocean.[151]

Define Maritime Silk Road Countries

According to Xinhua Silk Road Information Service, the major port cities along China's 21st Century Maritime Silk Road include Quanzhou/Zeitun, Fuzhou/Foochow, Guangzhou/Canton, Haikou, Beihai, Hanoi, Kuala Lumpur, Jakarta, Calcutta, Nairobi, Athens, and Venice. According to the Belt and Road Portal, as of June 2023, China has signed over 200 MOUs and cooperation documents for joint construction of the "Belt and Road" with 152 countries and 32 international organizations. In this chapter, any non-landlocked country that has signed the Belt and Road MOU and cooperation documents with China is considered a participating country of the 21st Century Maritime Silk Road. According to this definition, altogether 72 countries are active participants of China's 21st Century Maritime Silk Road.[152]

[150] Styan, "Doraleh Multipurpose Port (I)."

[151] Cabestan, "China's Military Base in Djibouti."

[152] Landlocked Belt and Road participating countries connected to seaports via China build infrastructure are also considered as participants of the 21st Century Maritime Silkroad.

Participating Countries and Regions

Ancient Maritime Silk Road

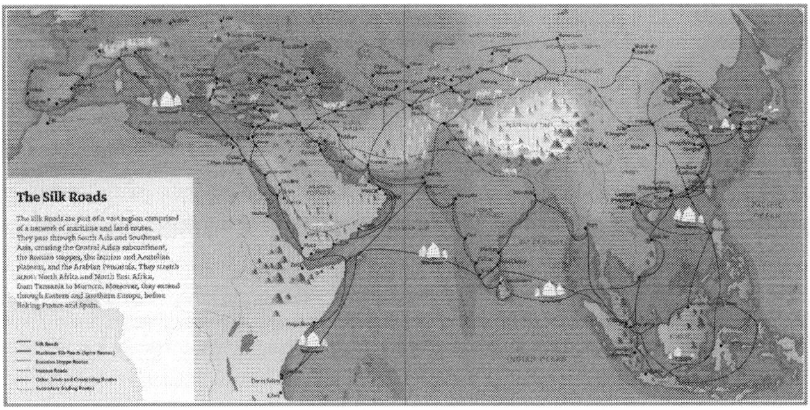

Figure 7.2: The Silk Roads
Source: UNESCO https://en.unesco.org/silkroad/about-silk-roads

According to UNESCO's mapping in Figure 7.2, the ancient Maritime Silk Road travelled through the waters of the Pacific Ocean, Yellow Sea, South China Sea, Gulf of Thailand, Bay of Bengal, Indian Ocean, Arabian Sea, Gulf of Oman, Persian Gulf, Red Sea, and Mediterranean Sea, putting a long list of port cities on the map, including those in today's Japan (Nara, Osaka, Nagasaki Fukuoka), South Korea (Gyengju, Busan, Seoul), China (Penglai, Qingdao, Liangyungang, Nanjing, Hangzhou, Ningbo, Fuzhou/Foodchow, Quanzhou/Zaitun, Guangzhou/Canton, Haiphong/Cattigara, Macau), Vietnam (Hanoi, Hội An, Óc Eo), Myanmar (Pegu), the Philippines (Bolinao), Brunei (Bandar Seri Begawan), Indonesia (Sulawesi, Jakarta, Sriwijaya/Palembang), Malaysia (Malacca), Singapore, India (Tamralipta, Madras, Pondicherry, Kochi, Calicut, Goa, Barygaza, Barbaricon, Karachi), Sri Lanka (Anuradhapura), Oman (Qalhat, Muscat, Sohar, Sohar, Hormuz Strait,[153] Qalhat, Salalah), Iran (Siraf, Susa), Iraq (Apologou), Yemen (Cana, Aden, Muza), Saudi Arabia (Jeddah, Leuce Come), Egypt (Qusair/Myos-Hormos, Cairo, Alexandria), Palestine (Gaza), Sudan (Suakin), Somalia (Zeila, Mogadishu), and Tanzania (Zanzibar, Dar es Salaam, Kilwa).

[153] Hormuz Strait is shared with the United Arab Emirates.

Past and Present Link

Regions	Ancient Maritime Silk Road	21st Century Maritime Silk Road
East Asia	China	China
	Japan	
	Korea	South Korea
Southeast Asia	Brunei	Brunei
	Indonesia	Indonesia
	Malaysia	Malaysia
	Myanmar	Myanmar
	Singapore	Singapore
	The Philippines	The Philippines
	Vietnam	Vietnam
		Cambodia
		Laos*
		Maldives
		Samoa
		Thailand
South Asia	India	
	Sri Lanka	Sri Lanka
		Bangladesh
		East Timor
		Maldives
		Pakistan
Arab & Middle East	Iran	Iran
	Iraq	Iraq
	Oman	Oman
	Palestine	Palestine
	Saudi Arabia	Saudi Arabia
	Yemen	Yemen
	United Arab Emirates	United Arab Emirates
		Israel
		Kuwait
		Qatar

Regions	Ancient Maritime Silk Road	21st Century Maritime Silk Road
Africa	Egypt	Egypt
	Kenya	Kenya
	Somalia	Somalia
	Sudan	Sudan
	Tanzania	Tanzania
		Angola
		Algeria
		Djibouti
		Eritrea
		Ethiopia**
		Ghana
		Guinea
		Guinea Bissau
		Ivory Coast
		Jamaica
		Liberia
		Madagascar
		Mozambique
		Namibia
		Niger
		Nigeria
		Rwanda
		Sao Tome
		South Africa
Europe	Portugal	Portugal
		Croatia
		Greece
		Italy
		Malta
		Poland
		Slovenia
		Türkiye
		Ukraine

Regions	Ancient Maritime Silk Road	21st Century Maritime Silk Road
South America		Panama
		Peru
		Suriname
		Venezuela
		Antigua and Barbuda
		Argentina
		Ecuador
Oceania		New Zealand
		Papua New Guinea
		Solomon Islands

Table 7.1: Participant countries and regions of the Maritime Silk Road (past and present).
* Laos is a landlocked country connected to ASEAN port cities via China-Laos Railway.
** Ethiopia is a landlocked country connected to a seaport via Addis Ababa–Djibouti Railway.
Sources: The table is compiled based on information from the following sources:
1. Wei, Xiaohui, and Feng Zheng, "Zhongguo yu 21 shiji haishang sichou zhilu gongjian guojia gaodeng jiaoyu hezuo baogao" [Report on China's collaboration with 21st Century Maritime Silk Road countries in higher education], in Liu, Xiaoping, and Chunsheng Zheng (editors) *Gaodeng jiaoyu lanpishu: Zhongguo gaodeng jiaoyu fazhan baogao* (2020-2021) [Higher education blue book: Report on China's higher education development (2020–2021)], Beijing: Shehuikexuewenxianchubanshe, 2021, 205–227.
2. Belt and Road Portal. "Yitong zhongguo qianding gongjian 'yidaiyilu' hezuo wenjian deguojiayilan" [List of countries having already signed Belt and Road cooperation documents with China] (https://www.yidaiyilu.gov.cn/p/77298.html, accessed May 31, 2023)
3. Rui, Feng, "21 shiji haishang sichouzilu yanxian guojia younaxie" [What are the countries along the 21st Century Maritime Silk Road], Xinhua Silk Road Information Service. 2021. (https://www.imsilkroad.com/news/p/397932.html –accessed July 26, 2023)

Table 7.1 is a comparison of participant countries, presenting convincing evidence that China's 21st Maritime Silk Road is built upon the historical maritime trade route as shown from the overlapping countries and regions. At the same time, it is also quite obvious the 21st century network has expanded to a great extent. With 72 participating countries, it has tripled in size. A closer look at the new membership suggests a growth pattern that is characterized by innovation, pragmatism, diversity, and inclusiveness. These are all legacies of the ancient Maritime Silk Road.

For example, Greece and Italy, two European countries previously connected by other maritime trade routes in the Mediterranean are now active members of China's 21st Century Maritime Silk Road. Other notable additions include incorporating South America and Oceania in the 21st century network, as well as embracing almost all coastal countries on the African continent, a clear commitment to equity and inclusiveness.

Incorporation of Laos and Ethiopia, two landlocked countries, into the 21st century network exemplifies the pragmatism and innovative strategy to maximize interconnectivity via infrastructure building. As discussed earlier, Addis Ababa (Ethiopia) is connected to Djibouti's seaport via Addis Ababa–Djibouti Railway. Similarly, with the completion of China-Laos Railway, Laos, a landlocked country has reemerged as a land-linked country with access to port cities in Asia. This railway connects Laos with China, Thailand, Malaysia, and Singapore and is expected to greatly promote the country's economic and social development due to enhanced connectivity.[154] Its significance is well captured during a recent interview with Lattanamany Khounnyvong, vice minister of public works and transport: "Once completed, the railway will help facilitate people-to-people exchanges, reduce traveling time and costs ... the railway will also help promote agricultural production in Laos, increase income, attract more foreign investment and provide more employment opportunities... . The railway will not only be the major railway line in Laos, but also connects China and ASEAN countries."[155] These are all keywords in the vision statement of China's Belt and Road Initiative.[156]

However, it is also hard not to notice the two glaring absences from the 21st century network: Japan and India. According to the World Bank country snapshots in 2023, even though China remains a top trading partner with India (ranked no. 2 in 2021) and Japan (ranked no. 1 in 2022), neither country has officially signed cooperation agreements with China's Belt and Road Initiative.

Visualize China's 21st Century Maritime Silk Road (2013–2023)

The most direct approach to visualize China's commitment to the 21st Century Maritime Silk Road is via its investment in participating countries. According to China's Global Investment Tracker,[157] between 2013 to 2023, worldwide Chinese investments and construction had reached a cumulative record of $1016.49 billion with 1524 projects in Asia, Africa, Arabia and the Middle East, South America, Europe, and Oceania. Almost half of it ($401.63 billion) is marked as Belt and Road

[154] Kelly and Lu. *Critical Landscape Planning*: 37.

[155] Xinhua News. "Belt and Road Initiative."

[156] Ministry of Foreign Affairs, "Vision and actions."

[157] China Global Investment Tracker – American Enterprise Institute (AEI), accessed August 26, 2023, https://www.aei.org/china-global-investment-tracker/.

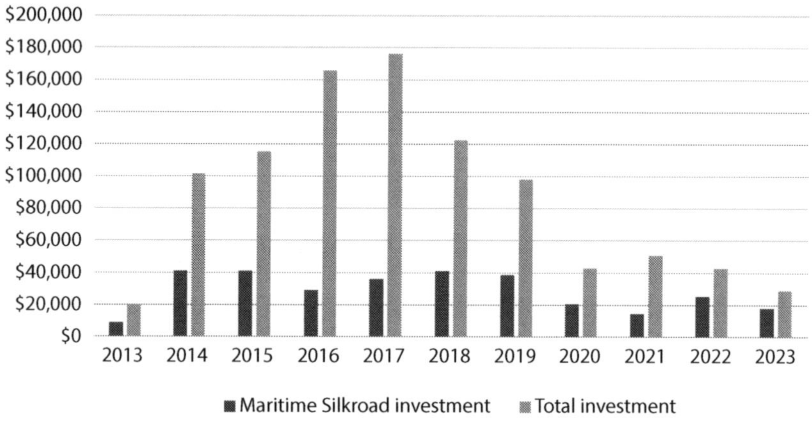

Figure 7.3: China's global investments in $100 million (2013–2023)
Data source: China Global Investment Tracker (https://www.aei.org/china-global-investment-tracker/)

projects. Among them, the majority of the investments ($315.99 billion) goes directly to the 521 Maritime Silk Road projects across various industrial sectors.

Figure 7.3 is a visual representation of China's global investment endeavors at the 10-year anniversary of the Belt and Road Initiative. It had a modest beginning in 2013 and then quickly took off between 2014 and 2015. 2016 and 2107 witnessed the highest volume of China's global investment followed by a gradual and then a drastic decline amid the global pandemic. It reached its lowest point in 2023, with less than 1/5 of its peak day in investment volumes. On the other hand, Maritime Silk Road investments remained relatively steady and rose to 60 percent of the total investment during 2022 and 2023. This steady growth of investments in Maritime Silk Road projects in spite of adverse global economic conditions is a clear indication of the financial sustainability and China's commitment to follow through its mission and vision.

Figure 7.4 summarizes the destinations of China's 21st Century Maritime Silk Road projects in the past 10 years. Southeast Asia is by far the most popular destination with 41.5 percent of the investments, followed by Europe (12.5 percent), South Asia (12.3 percent), Africa (11.6 percent), and Arabia and the Middle East (9.5 percent). East Asia and Oceania ranked bottom at 3.1 percent and 1.8 percent, respectively.

Figure 7.5 illustrates the type of industrial sectors of China's 21st Century Maritime Silk Road. The energy sector stands out as the most heavily invested with 161 projects across Asia, Africa, the Middle East, South America, and Europe. Over

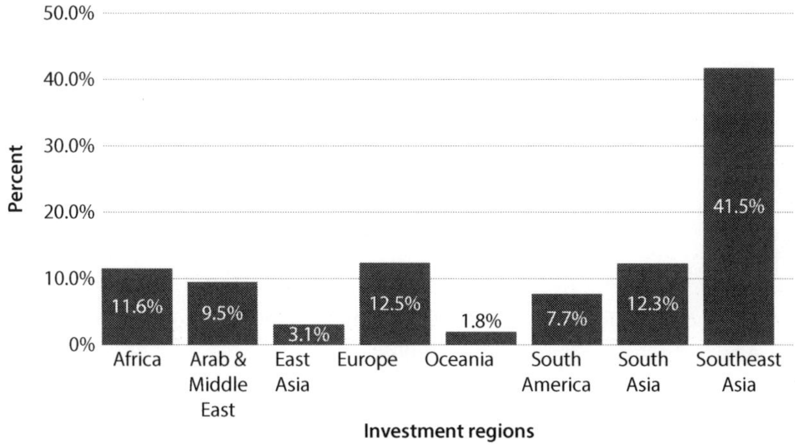

Figure 7.4. China's 21st Century Maritime Silk Road investment regions
Data source: China Global Investment Tracker (https://www.aei.org/china-global-investment-tracker/)

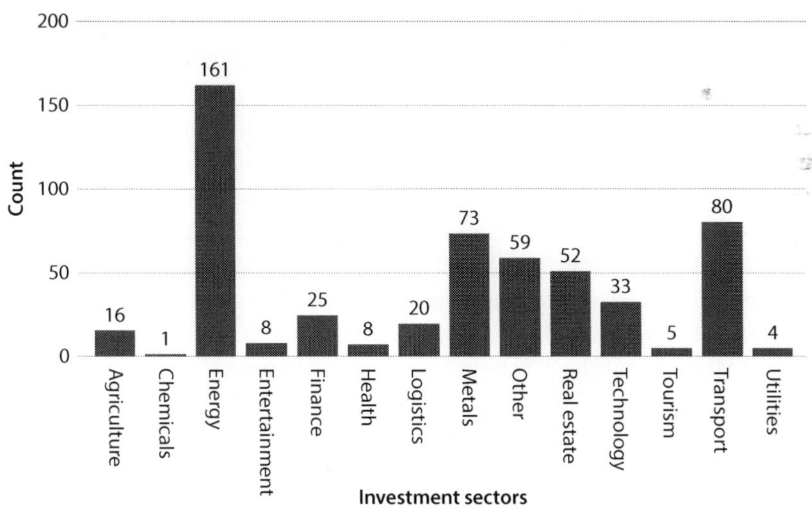

Figure 7.5: Investment Sectors of China's 21st Century Maritime Silk Road
Data source: China Global Investment Tracker (https://www.aei.org/china-global-investment-tracker/)

half of these projects (54 percent) are in the subsectors of clean and alternative energy. This is a prime example of "green investment" that refutes the skepticism towards China's capability to utilize its power in a responsible manner.

Transport is the second largest investment sector with 80 projects ($168.50 billion) in infrastructure building: $86.40 billion in railway constructions in Indonesia, Laos, the Philippines, Thailand, and Nigeria; and the remaining $82.10 billion to support shipping infrastructure construction in Sri Lanka, Pakistan, Myanmar, Singapore, Indonesia, Greece, Italy, Panama, Peru, Israel, Nigeria, Djibouti, and Sao Tome. China's continued investment in transport projects resonates with the essence of the Belt and Road Initiative, a China led model of global development driven by large-scale infrastructure building.

Challenges

The primary challenge of the 21st Century Maritime Silk Road is maintaining sustainable growth. The list of participating countries remains dynamic. Addition and attrition are common. India and Japan might join the project later, while existing members could opt not to renew MOUs and cooperation documents at the time of expiration. For example, Italy has explicitly expressed unwillingness to renew its Belt and Road Initiative (BRI) deal with China, which is set to expire in March 2024.[158]

Other challenges are caused by regional instability in an increasingly volatile and even hostile geopolitical backdrop, including piracy and terrorism. Such a challenge is a daily reality even in countries like Pakistan where China's flagship investment projects are hosted. Since 2017, a series of violent attacks have been targeted against Chinese consulate, Chinese nationals and facilitates linked to China's investment.[159] These attacks hindered bilateral collaborations and overshadowed the prospect of advancing China's Belt and Road Initiative.

Piracy is another unique challenge to the 21st Century Maritime Silk Road.[160] It was the leading cause of the sea bans which contributed to the decline of the ancient Maritime Silk Road. The opening of China's first overseas military base at Djibouti is a direct response to address such a challenge. The People's Liberation Army is poised to provide regional security and support the implementation of the 21st Century Maritime Silk Road at the confluence of the Red Sea and the Indian Ocean.

158 Balmer, "Italy Unlikely to Renew China Deal, but Needs Time, Official Says."

159 Cullen, "Chinese Nationals Have Become Targets."

160 Bilal et al.,"China's Maritime Silk Road and Security in the Red Sea Region."

Conclusion

This chapter has compared the ancient Maritime Silk Road with its 21st century counterpart. Findings suggest a clear inheritance of ideas, values, and practices from the past. There is no doubt China's 21st century version is built upon the existing physical and ideological framework of the ancient Maritime Silk Road, which remained active for over 2000 years. The term "Maritime Silk Road" thus effectively contextualizes China's cross border developmental efforts within the context of 21st century geopolitical realities. Legacies of the ancient Maritime Silk Road, namely, innovation, mutual understanding, openness, and inclusiveness continue to be at the core of China's 21st Century Maritime Silk Road visions and mission. It is a perfect example to demonstrate how temporal dimensions of the past could leave profound marks on the current conditions of social life.

At the same time, China's 21st Century Maritime Silk Road differs from its ancient prototype due to the "vigor and vitality" brought forth by its emphasis on cross-border infrastructure building. Solid foundations of infrastructure eliminate physical and geographic barriers that prevent free flow of products, capital flows, and people. Cross-border infrastructure building of ports and railways greatly enhances regional connectivity. It converts landlocked countries into land-linked countries, thus setting the stage for inclusive growth: economic growth that is distributed fairly across society and creates opportunities for all (OECD, 2023).

Dr. **Ting Jiang** is a professor of Sociology and the Associate Dean of Curriculum, Accreditation, and Program Review at the College of Letters, Arts and Sciences at the Metropolitan State University of Denver. She received her Ph.D. in Sociology from the University of California, Irvine. Her long-term research interest resides in the interactions between domestic and globalization processes along the themes of inequality, cultural dissemination, social welfare, and public policies. Her current research focuses on the sociocultural and geopolitical significance of China's Belt and Road Initiative in the 21st century.

Bibliography

American Enterprise Institute (AEI). China Global Investment Tracker. https://www.aei.org/china-global-investment-tracker/, accessed August 17, 2023.

Belt and Road Portal. "Yitong zhongguo qianding gongjian 'yidaiyilu' hezuo wenjian deguojiayilan" [List of countries already signed Belt and Road cooperation documents with China]. https://www.yidaiyilu.gov.cn/p/77298.html, accessed May 31, 2023.

Balmer, Crispian. "Italy Unlikely to Renew China Deal, but Needs Time, Official Says." *Reuters*, May 4, 2023. https://www.reuters.com/world/italy-unlikely-renew-china-deal-needs-time-official-says-2023-05-04/, accessed August 20, 2023.

Bilal Y. Saab, Yahya Alqahtani, and Danny Makki, "China's Maritime Silk Road and Security in the Red Sea Region," Middle East Institute, May 18, 2021, https://www.mei.edu/publications/chinas-maritime-silk-road-and-security-red-sea-region, accessed August 21, 2023.

Billé, Franck, Sanjyot Mehendale, and James W. Lankton, *The Maritime Silk Road: Global Connectivities, Regional Nodes, Localities*. Amsterdam: Amsterdam University Press, 2022.

Cabestan, Jean-Pierre. "China's Military Base in Djibouti: A Microcosm of China's Growing Competition with the United States and New Bipolarity." *The Journal of Contemporary China,* Vol. 29, no. 125, 2020, 731–747.

Cullen S. Hendrix, "Chinese Nationals Have Become Targets for Violence as China Deepens Its International Reach," PIIE, June 15, 2022. https://www.piie.com/blogs/realtime-economic-issues-watch/chinese-nationals-have-become-targets-violence-china-deepens, accessed August 18, 2023.

Fairbank, J. K. "Tributary Trade and China's Relations with the West," *The Far Eastern Quarterly*, Vol 1, no. 2, February 1942, 129–149.

Gu, Ban. *Book of Han*. https://ctext.org/han-shu/ens?searchu=%E5%BE%90%E9%97%BB, accessed on June 10, 2023.

Kelly, Ashley Scott and Xiaoxuan Lu. *Critical Landscape Planning during the Belt and Road Initiative*. Singapore: Springer Nature, 2021.

Kimura, Jun. "Archaeological Evidence of Shipping and Shipbuilding Along the Maritime Silk Road." *In The Maritime Silk Road: Global Connectivities, Regional Nodes, Localities*, edited by Franck Billé, Sanjyot Mehendale, and James W. Lankton. Amsterdam University Press, 2022, 97–127.

Li, Xinchuan, *Jianyan yilai chaoye zaji*, Vol. 15, No. 1, line 34. https://ctext.org/wiki.pl?if=gb&chapter=706156&remap=gb, accessed June 23, 2023.

Liao, Dake. "Shilun Songdai shibosi guanzhi de yanbian" [Exploring the evolution of Shibosi officials' rank in Song Dynasty], *Lishiyanjiu,* No. 3, 1998, 38–48. https://core.ac.uk/download/41451161.pdf, accessed July 28, 2023.

Liu, Niao, and Shuyang Hu, "Dierjie Mingdai qianqi de haijin ji chaogong tizhi" [Chapter 2 The Sea Ban policy and tributary system during early Ming Dynasty] in *Chenchuan, ciqi yu haishang sichouzhiliu* [Shipwreck, porcelain and Maritime Silkroad], Beijing: Shehuikexuewenxian chubanshe,122–123.

Ministry of Foreign Affairs, "Vision and Actions on Jointly Building Silk Road Economic Belt and 21st-century Maritime Silk Road," March 28, 2015. https://www.fmprc.gov.cn/eng/topics_665678/2015zt/xjpcxbayzlt2015nnh/201503/t20150328_705553.html, accessed May 1, 2023.

OECD. "Inclusive Growth – Economic Growth That Is Distributed Fairly ... – OECD." What Is Inclusive Growth? https://www.oecd.org/inclusive-growth/, accessed July 31, 2023.

Ouyang, Xiu. *Xintangshu* Vol. 33, no. 2, *Geography* Vol. 7, no. 2. https://ctext.org/wiki.pl?if=gb&chapter=400563&remap=gb#p85, accessed July 25, 2023.

Rui, Feng, "21 shiji haishang sichouzilu yanxian guojia younaxie" [What are the countries along the 21st Century Maritime Silkroad], Xinhua Silk Road Information Service. 2021. https://www.imsilkroad.com/news/p/397932.html, accessed July 26, 2023.

Sen, Tansen. "Administration of Maritime Trade during Tang and Song Dynasties." *China Report (New Delhi),* Vol. 32, no. 3, 1996, 251–265.

Styan, David. "Doraleh Multipurpose Port (I)." The People's Map of Global China, March 4, 2022. https://thepeoplesmap.net/project/doraleh-multipurpose-port-phase-i/, accessed July 31, 2023.

Tai, Yew Seng, Patrick Daly, E. Edwards Mckinnon, Andrew Parnell, R. Michael Feener, Jedrzej Majewski, Nazli Ismail, and Kerry Sieh. "The Impact of Ming and Qing Dynasty Maritime Bans on Trade

Ceramics Recovered from Coastal Settlements in Northern Sumatra, Indonesia." *Archaeological Research in Asia,* Vol. 21, March 2020, 100174.

UNESCO "Did You Know?: The Great Silk Roads." Silk Roads Programme. https://en.unesco.org/silkroad/content/did-you-know-great-silk-roads, accessed July 30, 2023.

Wang, Zhenping. "T'ang Maritime Trade Administration." *Asia Major*, Vol. 4, no. 1–2, 1991: 7–38. https://www2.ihp.sinica.edu.tw/file/1576mxCnVHB.pdf, accessed July 28, 2023.

Wei, Xiaohui, and Feng Zheng, "Zhongguo yu 21 shiji haishang sichou zhilu gongjian guojia gaodeng jiaoyu hezuo baogao" [Report on China's collaboration with 21st Century Maritime Silkroad countries in higher education], in Liu, Xiaoping, Zheng Chunsheng (editors) *Gaodeng jiaoyu lanpishu: Zhongguo gaodeng jiaoyu fazhan baogao* (2020–2021) [Higher education blue book: Report on China's higher education development (2020–2021)], Beijing: Shehuikexuewenxianchubanshe, 2021, 205–227.

World Bank. *World Integrated Trade Solution*. "Country Snap Shots." https://wits.worldbank.org/countrysnapshot/en/JPN, accessed July 27, 2023; https://wits.worldbank.org/countrysnapshot/en/IND, accessed July 27, 2023.

Wu, Yan. "*Guangzhou tonghai yidao*" [Guangzhou's pathway to foreign countries], in Zhongguo dabaike quanshu, 2022. https://www.zgbk.com/ecph/words?SiteID=1&ID=674694&Type=bkztb&SubID=1080, accessed July 28, 2023.

Xinhua News. "Belt and Road Initiative Bringing Tangible Benefits to Laos: Official," May 2, 2017. https://www.chinadaily.com.cn/beltandroadinitiative/2017-05/02/content_29172984.htm, accessed August 29, 2023.

Zhao, Bing. "Chinese-Style Ceramics in East Africa from the 9th to 16th Century: A Case of Changing Value and Symbols in the Multi-Partner Global Trade." *Afriques,* Vol. 6, no. 6, 2015.

PART THREE

Military Outreach and Geopolitical Strategy

CHAPTER EIGHT

Xi Jinping and the Derailment of the KMT-CCP "1992 Consensus"

Dean P. Chen

RAMAPO COLLEGE OF NEW JERSEY

Abstract: *Having suffered consecutively from two national electoral losses in 2016 and 2020 to the Democratic Progressive Party (DPP), the Kuomintang (KMT or GMD) has been unable to settle on a strategically sound position to cope with the People's Republic of China (PRC)'s determination to unify with Taiwan, instead opting to grapple with a near-moribund formula known as the "1992 consensus" to maintain ties with the Chinese Communist Party (CCP). At the time of writing, the KMT's prospects to recover Taiwan's presidency in 2024 remain uncertain. If it does, however, the party's relatively more conciliatory position on China may still place Taiwan at odds with the strategic interests of the island democracy's chief security backer, the United States, which is now locked in an intense struggle for power with the PRC. Since 2016, though the KMT has strived to redefine its framing of the "1992 consensus," it has failed to escape from its "one-China" precept that has become so sensitive given that China's President Xi Jinping had equated, in 2019, the political formulation with the PRC (as well as the "one country, two systems"). This chapter sets out to analyze the changing KMT and CCP stances on the "1992 consensus," as conceived by both Xi and successive KMT leaders since 2013 and attempts to illustrate how a domestic security imaginary that is deeply rooted in history, culture, and identity has prevented KMT-CCP from adopting a pragmatic arrangement, hence exacerbating the overarching cross-strait relationship as well the U.S.-PRC ties.*

Keywords: KMT; CCP; 1992 Consensus

Introduction

As both editors of this book have noted, ties between Washington and Beijing have in recent years become more competitive and adversarial over a range of divergent issues, including trade, military, espionage, human rights, governance, and high technologies that are pivotal in determining the global distributions of power of the twenty-first century.[1] The world also pays greater attention to the security and

[1] For an in-depth discussion on the history and changing strategic circumstances driving this growing competition between Washington and Beijing, see Evan Medeiros, "Explaining and Understanding Competition in US-China Relations."

freedom of Taiwan (also known as the Republic of China, ROC), a self-governing democracy which is claimed by the People's Republic of China (PRC) as an inalienable part of its national territory. The PRC's paramount ruler, Xi Jinping, had vowed that the Taiwan issue "cannot be dragged on generation after generation,"[2] implying a sense of urgency on China's longstanding reunification goal.[3] The Chinese leader has stepped up military coercive campaigns[4] to pressure Taiwan while accusing Washington of implementing "all-round containment, encirclement and suppression against China."[5] Indeed, commanding the production of cutting-edge semiconductor chips, Taiwan becomes front and center of U.S.-Chinese rivalry.[6] The island's two major political parties—the Chinese Nationalist Party or the Kuomintang (KMT or GMD) and Democratic Progressive Party (DPP)—prioritize deepening relations with the United States, which has been the ROC's chief security backer for more than 70 years. Moreover, since 1979, Washington has based its Taiwan Strait policy on an ambiguously defined "one-China policy" that rests upon the Taiwan Relations Act, Three Joint U.S.-PRC Communiqués, and the Six Assurances.[7] While the U.S. does not support Taiwan independence,[8] Washington also does not take a stance on Taiwan's sovereignty. Any cross-strait resolutions, the U.S. insists, must be reached peacefully and "consistent with the wishes and best interests of the people on Taiwan."[9]

Nonetheless, on January 2, 2019, in an address marking Beijing's "40th anniversary of issuance of messages to the compatriots of Taiwan," which announced the shift from a policy of forceful liberation to one of peaceful unification, Xi appeared to suggest that the "1992 consensus" is synonymous with the PRC's "one China principle" and advancement of "national reunification" based on the "one country, two systems" formula,[10] hence leaving no space for the so-called "one China,

[2] "Xi says 'China Must Be, Will Be Reunified' As Key Anniversary Marked," *Xinhua News* (January 2, 2019), http://www.xinhuanet.com/english/2019-01/02/c_137714898.htm.

[3] Wong, *Party of One.* pp. 199–200.

[4] Wu, "China Flies 38 Warplanes Near Taiwan, 6 Navy Vessels in Area."

[5] Chun, Zhai, and Areddy, "China's Xi Jinping Takes Rare Direct Aim at U.S. in Speech."

[6] Miller, *Chip War: The Fight for the World's Most Critical Technology.*

[7] The U.S. Department of State, "Fact Sheet: U.S. Relations with Taiwan," May 28, 2022, https://www.state.gov/u-s-relations-with-taiwan/.

[8] The U.S. Department of State, "The Biden Administration's Approach to the People's Republic of China, by Secretary of State Antony Blinken," May 26, 2022, https://www.state.gov/the-administrations-approach-to-the-peoples-republic-of-china/.

[9] Hass, Glaser, and Bush, *U.S.-Taiwan Relations.* pp. 80–81.

[10] The Taiwan Affairs Office of the State Council, "Xi Jinping's Speech Marking the 40th Anniversary of the Issuance of the Message to Compatriots to Taiwan: Working Together to Realize Rejuvenation of the Chinese Nation and Advance China's National Reunification," January 2, 2019, http://www.gwytb.gov.cn/wyly/201904/t20190412_12155687.htm.

respective interpretations," as espoused by the KMT regarding the consensus.[11] As will be discussed in greater detail later, for the KMT, "one China" stands unequivocally as the ROC.[12] Thus, the KMT's cross-strait position has been significantly discredited in Taiwan's electoral arena, where voters have identified the PRC as a growing national security threat and firmly rejected Beijing's unification ambition. These attitudes were duly reflected by the KMT's two consecutive major losses in Taiwan's 2016 and 2020 presidential elections. The DPP under the Tsai Ing-wen administration has underscored how the KMT was inept at defending the ROC and even coopted by the Chinese Communist Party (CCP)'s version of the "one China" principle. The KMT's relatively more China-friendly platform has also made the party a less attractive strategic partner for the United States in its ongoing global power contest with the PRC.

This chapter will briefly examine the origins of the "1992 consensus" and the more flexible interpretations of the term that Beijing was willing to accommodate, albeit briefly and tacitly, between 2008 and 2016, when the KMT's Ma Ying-jeou was Taiwan's president. Then, as cross-strait relations deteriorated after Tsai's election in 2016, and coincided with the rising tensions between the United States and PRC, Xi's 2019 Taiwan speech not only undermined the KMT's position, but also inadvertently empowered Tsai's re-election bid in 2020. Meanwhile, in the light of a more robust relationship between Washington and Taipei, the KMT is in a bind as the party continues to grapple with creating a new definition for the "1992 consensus," whose one-China element can be better justified to placate the angst of Taiwan's electorates and reassure Washington that the KMT, if it wins the 2024 presidential election, isn't going to erode or concede Taiwan's democracy, freedom and security at the expense of improving relations with Beijing. Indeed, public opinion surveys in Taiwan have consistently found that a great majority of the island's citizens are opposed to Beijing's "one country, two systems" and the notion of unification under the PRC's one China principle. The Taiwanese people, in contrast, have communicated their "greatest consensus" is to support and defend the continued existence of the ROC.[13]

Following the 20th CCP Party Congress in October 2022 and the 14th National People's Congress in March 2023, Xi Jinping has successfully secured and consolidated an unprecedented third term in office as the CCP general secretary, president of the PRC, and chairman of the Central Military Affairs Commission. Such has been

[11] Wong, *Party of One*, p. 201.

[12] Chen, "Security, Domestic Divisions."

[13] Mainland Affairs Council, Republic of China (Taiwan), "Defending ROC's Sovereignty and Dignity is the Greatest Consensus among Taiwanese People," February 8, 2019, https://www.mac.gov.tw/en/News_Content.aspx?n=2BA0753CBE348412&sms=E828F60C4AFBAF90&s=4BB376D86553B326.

the norm-breaking in the post-Mao reform and opening era.[14] Indeed, being arguably the most powerful PRC leader since Chairman Mao Zedong, Xi has promised the "rejuvenation of the Chinese nation," which sits at the heart of his "Chinese Dream." This requires, as one of the highest priorities, recovering China's lost glory, dignity, and prestige from the hands of Western and Japanese imperialists during the "century of humiliation." Consequently, Taiwan, for Xi and the CCP, remains the final piece of territory that needs to be brought back to vindicate that shameful period of Chinese history and complete their national unity and sovereignty. Since coming to power, President Xi has on numerous occasions talked about the imperative of reunifying with Taiwan, which is "an inevitable course of development."[15] He clearly showed no patience to wait indefinitely, stressing that a resolution must come eventually. For Xi, if he can resolve the Taiwan issue, not only would the CCP's ruling legitimacy be further enhanced along with China's global power status, but he would surely be remembered as the greatest leader since the founding of the PRC—a legacy which would surpass that of Mao. In November 2023, Xi told U.S. president Joe Biden during their summit meeting in San Francisco that China must "reunify with Taiwan." Though the Chinese leader expressed a preference to do so through peaceful means and refrained from setting a timeline, he did not rule out using military actions if necessary.[16]

However, for the sake of cross-strait peace and stability, recognizing objectively the ROC's contributions to the state building and national development of modern China, and respecting the Taiwanese people's wishes today for their liberal democratic self-governance, Xi should consider facing up to the reality of the continued presence of the Republic of China, which was founded and established by Dr. Sun Yat-sen in 1912 and that has persisted ever since. Notwithstanding all of their shortcomings and corruption while governing the Chinese mainland, the ROC fought hard and endured huge sacrifices in their military resistance against Imperial Japan during the Second World War. Under the ROC's national flag and central command, both the KMT and CCP cooperated, albeit half-heartedly, to confront a common enemy, even though a former U.S. national security advisor reported in his memoir that the "Chinese Communists had spent most of the war ducking Japan and trying to undercut the Chinese Nationalists."[17] In the decades following

[14] Wong, *Party of One*, pp. 14–15.

[15] Simone McCarthy, "China's Xi Claims 'Reunification' with Taiwan Is 'Inevitable' as Crucial Election Looms," *CNN* (December 26, 2023), https://www.cnn.com/2023/12/27/china/china-xi-jinping-taiwan-reunification-intl-hnk/index.html.

[16] Kristen Welker, Courtney Kube, Carol E. Lee and Andrea Mitchell, "Xi warned Biden during summit that Beijing will reunify Taiwan with China," *NBC News* (December 20, 2023), https://www.nbcnews.com/news/china/xi-warned-biden-summit-beijing-will-reunify-taiwan-china-rcna130087.

[17] Bolton, *The Room Where It Happened:* p. 302.

the KMT's loss of the Chinese civil war and retreat to Taiwan in 1949, the ROC has gone through strenuous decades of struggles, paving the way for state building, economic development, and political liberalization and transformation, prompting Taiwan to become an affluent and leading Chinese constitutional democracy today in the Asia-Pacific region. Accordingly, unless the Xi administration is willing to temper some of their hawkish nationalist impulses and be more accommodating in their handling of cross-strait relations by recognizing the ROC's formal existence, the "1992 consensus" will continue to be a contentious concept between Taiwan and China and, more critically, unlikely to be endorsed by the people of Taiwan. In other words, Xi's "overreaching" nationalist ambition as well as high concentration of political power in his own hands can cloud his rational judgement and banish informed perspectives and deliberations within his policymaking circles.[18] This could lead to misperception and a cross-strait policy that would only drive away the Taiwanese people and undermine peaceful relations between the two sides.

Origins and Development of the "1992 Consensus"

Between 2008 and 2016, cross-strait interactions between Taiwan and the PRC were mostly amicable and smooth. The relaxation of cross-strait tensions in those years resulted from Taipei's acceptance (under the then-president Ma Ying-jeou of the KMT) of the "1992 consensus"—a nebulously-defined verbal formula referring to the November 1992 Hong Kong meeting between the Chinese Communist Party and Kuomintang, which agreed that both sides of the Taiwan Strait belong to one and the same Chinese nation.[19] Nonetheless, the KMT construed the framework as "one China, respective interpretations" (OCRI), where "China" stands for the Republic of China that was established by Dr. Sun Yat-sen in 1912. Beijing, on the other hand, has focused on the formulation of both Taiwan and the Chinese mainland "respectively expressing a 'one-China' principle," and "China" is the People's Republic of China founded in October 1949.[20] Yet, Beijing never chose to object publicly to Taipei's position, at least when the KMT was in power. The following subsections offer a

[18] Shirk, *Overreach: How China Derailed Its Peaceful Rise.*

[19] Su Chi, who served as President Ma's secretary-general of the National Security Council from 2008 to 2010, coined the term "1992 consensus" in April 2000 when he was the head of Taiwan's Mainland Affairs Council. The context then was during the political transition of Taiwan's first political party rotation of power from the KMT to DPP. Su was hoping that his creation of the term—ambiguous enough to accommodate differences and flexibility—would allow the PRC and the incoming DPP administration under Chen Shui-bian to continue negotiations and stabilize cross-strait relations. See Su, *Taiwan's Relations with Mainland China.*

[20] Ho, "Cross-Strait Relations."

concise summary on the evolution of "one China" between the KMT and CCP since 1949, giving rise to the "1992 consensus."[21]

1. Beijing's Rigid Identity and Interest in "One China," 1949–1992

Despite its defeat in China's civil war and retreat to Taiwan in 1949, the KMT government continued to regard Mao's PRC as merely a "rebellious bandit group" whereas Taipei, China's sole legal government. Until the 1970s, the ROC enjoyed international recognition and support from most countries, including the United States, and represented China in the UN until 1971. On the other hand, Beijing also saw Chiang Kai-shek's forces as lackey to American imperialism and that the CCP must wipe out the KMT remnants to "liberate" Taiwan. Nonetheless, after Beijing replaced Taipei in the United Nations and normalized relations with Washington, the CCP leaders began to extend more conciliatory gestures. Instead of calling Taiwan "Chiang's clique" and that the CCP would "liberate Taiwan," Beijing began to address the ROC as "Taiwan authorities" and stressed "peaceful reunification."[22] In the "New Year Day's Message to Taiwan Compatriots," issued on January 1, 1979, the NPC's Standing Committee pledged to "take present realities into account in accomplishing the great cause of reunifying the motherland and respect the status quo on Taiwan and the opinions of people in all walks of life there and adopt reasonable policies and measures in settling the question of reunification so as not to cause the people of Taiwan any losses."[23]

Then, on September 30, 1981, Ye Jianying, the chairman of the NPC's Standing Committee, elaborated on peaceful reunification under his "Nine Points Proposal," in which Taiwan is promised a "high degree of autonomy" after reunification. This statement also brought up the notion of "three links" across the Taiwan Strait in trade, transportation, and postal exchanges as well as "four exchanges" in culture, academics, economics, and sports.[24] Ye essentially underscored Deng's "one country, two systems" principle.[25] Notwithstanding the more conciliatory attitudes in these statements, the "one China" is always defined as the PRC and Taiwan its local administrative unit. Deng said, "We are pursuing a policy of 'one country, two systems.' More specifically, this means that within the People's Republic of China, the mainland...will maintain the socialist system while Hong Kong and Taiwan

[21] On a fuller discussion of the KMT-CCP's changing interpretations of "one China" and creation of the "1992 consensus," see Chen, "Constructing Peaceful Development."

[22] Zhao, "Chinese Nationalism and Beijing's Taiwan Policy."

[23] "Qtd. in Chen, "Constructing Peaceful Development," p. 33.

[24] Ibid.

[25] Ibid.

continue under the capitalist system."[26] Reunification, according to the CCP leader, is the "aspiration of the whole nation."[27]

2. *The "1992 Consensus" and KMT's "One China, Respective Interpretations"*

In 1987, responding to an increasing demand for liberalization and democratization, President Chiang Ching-kuo decided to lift Taiwan's martial law and permitted political parties to freely assemble and compete in elections. He also opened up cross-strait economic and cultural contacts, marking the "beginning of the current cross strait relations."[28] Between the end of 1987 and June 1995, Taipei and Beijing worked incessantly to dispatch secret envoys and construct formal and informal institutions and agencies, including Taiwan's Mainland Affairs Council (MAC) and Strait Exchange Foundation (SEF) and the PRC's Taiwan Affairs Office (TAO) and Association for Relations Across the Strait (ARATS), to promote trust and constructive dialogues. Notwithstanding their differences, both the KMT and CCP concurred on China's territorial integrity and national unification with Taiwan. The only question is whose China. On August 1, 1992, Taipei provided an answer, as the ROC's National Unification Council (NUC) passed the "Definition of One China Resolution," which stipulated:

> The two sides of the Taiwan Strait uphold the one China principle, but the interpretations of the two sides are different.... Our side believes that one China should mean the Republic of China, established in 1912 and existing today, and its sovereignty extends throughout China, but its current governing authority is only over Taiwan, Penghu, Kinmen, and Matzu. Admittedly, Taiwan is a part of China, but the mainland is also a part of China.[29]

The NUC resolution furnished the basis for the quasi-governmental SEF-ARATS negotiations in October-November 1992. The SEF stated, in a press release on November 3, that "each side expresses its own interpretation *verbally* in order to solve this sticky problem of [one China] and thereby reaffirmed the August 1st NUC resolution as SEF's interpretation of one China."[30] In response, ARATS, on the same day, telephoned SEF, informing that the former "fully respected and accepted" Taipei's proposal to use a verbal declaration of each side's position on the matter. On November 16, ARATS sent a formal letter to SEF, stating that ARATS "fully

[26] Ibid.

[27] Ibid.

[28] Su, *Taiwan's Relations with Mainland China*, p.1.

[29] Ibid., p. 13.

[30] Ibid.

respect and accept your Foundation's suggestion" and, simultaneously, affirming the content of its own interpretation, which was that "both sides of the strait uphold the principle of one China, and actively seek national unification, but the political interpretation of the one China will not be referred to in the cross-strait negotiations on functional issues."[31] This is the so-called "1992 consensus," which was coined by Su Chi in early 2000 to describe that verbal arrangement made between the KMT and CCP. In the KMT's view, the consensus is about "one China, respective interpretations" (OCRI), with the ROC being that "one China."

By late November, both SEF and ARATS had moved on to focus on the preparation works for the upcoming meeting between Koo Chen-fu, chairman of SEF, and Wang Daohan, head of ARATS, which took place in April 1993 in Singapore. The Koo-Wang talks launched rounds of negotiations and sub-meetings, centering on technical issues including fishing disputes, hijacking, cross-strait document notarization, express mailings, and other civil matters. In the words of Su Chi, former secretary general of Taiwan's National Security Council, OCRI was not "coined by either government but by the Taipei media in nearly unanimous fashion, which the Taipei government later adopted. [Thus], the mainland had never fully accepted this characterization since 1992, but it never completely rejected it either."[32] While Beijing emphasized the part that "both sides of the strait uphold the principle of one China," and that Taiwan is part of China, Taipei construed that both Taiwan and the mainland belonged to China, which, based on the ROC Constitution and the NUC resolution, is the Republic of China. The "creative ambiguity" inherent in such a formulation allowed cross-strait relations to move forward in the early 1990s. However, as President Lee Teng-hui opted for a more independence-oriented policy in the mid-1990s onward, Beijing began to criticize OCRI as "deliberate distortion," a mere disguise utilized by independence advocates to promote either "two Chinas" or Taiwan's formal separation.[33] Indeed, in July 1999, in an interview with Germany's *Radio Deutsche Welle* at Taipei, Lee declared that cross-strait relations were in fact "special state-to-state relations." The "two states theory" invoked consternation in both Washington and Beijing just three years after the 1995–96 Taiwan Strait crisis. The PRC not only launched incessant recriminations and polemical attacks against the Taiwan leader but also canceled ARATS chairman Wang Dao-han's scheduled visit to Taiwan in the fall of 1999. After that, SEF-ARATS talks ceased, even though limited pacts were negotiated between Beijing and Taipei to facilitate economic and culture exchanges. In August 2002, President Chen Shui-bian also became more

[31] Ibid., p. 14. See also ARATS eds., *Jiuer Gongshi Lishi Cunzheng [The Historical Documents of the 1992 Consensus]* (Beijing: Jiuzhou Press, 2005), p. 11.

[32] ARATS, eds., *Jiuer Gongshi Lishi Cunzheng*, p. 14.

[33] Ibid., pp. 12–15; Chen, "The Taiwan Straits Situation."

vocal on the independence issue when proclaiming that "Taiwan and China are each one country on each side of the strait." Up to May 2008, cross-strait relations severely worsened and all SEF-ARATS talks were effectively suspended. Chen and the DPP further denounced the existence of the "1992 consensus" and OCRI altogether as they sought to move Taiwan further away from China.[34]

3. Beijing's Reconceptualization in the Late 1990s: Both Mainland and Taiwan Belong to One China

By the mid to late 1990s, the Jiang Zemin administration, responding to Taiwan's greater tilt toward independence, took a more flexible approach on the "one China" issue. In essence, Jiang's so-called "Eight-Point Proposal," announced in January 1995, suggested a gradualist and "phased" process of rapprochement and negotiations leading eventually to reunification.[35] While building his pronouncement on the "one country, two systems" formula, Jiang emphasized more on maintaining the status quo, facilitating cross-strait economic exchanges and the "three links," and deterring Taiwan's attempt to separate from the mainland. More importantly, as long as the island accepts the one-China principle, Beijing would consider and address all of Taiwan's concerns, including renouncing the use of force, treating Taipei as an equal political entity, and allowing Taiwan greater international space.[36] On the other hand, Jiang's initiative also encompasses a clear hardline dimension in order to prevent Taiwan independence.[37] As a result of the Taiwan Strait crisis of 1995–96 and the growing influence of the pro-independence political forces in Taiwan, Beijing's focus on a more coercive measure intensified in the latter half of the 1990s. Chinese military modernization increased rapidly to prepare for a possible Taiwan Strait contingency and to prevent, delay, and deter America's timely involvement in the region. Moreover, the policies of Lee and Chen further reinforced Chinese pessimism regarding Taiwan's future. In fact, Beijing issued *The One-China Principle and Taiwan Issue White Paper* in February 2000 to sternly warn against Taiwan separatism and to state explicitly that the PRC would consider the use of force if Taipei continued to avoid meaningful talks with China indefinitely.[38]

Nonetheless, an even more notable change in Beijing's Taiwan policy had emerged by the end of Jiang's tenure, that is, top CCP elites have begun to identify

[34] Hickey, *Foreign Policy Making in Taiwan;* Su, *Taiwan's Relations with Mainland China*, and Rigger, *Why Taiwan Matters*, especially Ch. 4.

[35] Chen, "Constructing Peaceful Development," p. 35.

[36] Swaine, "Decision-Making Regarding Taiwan." pp. 313–314

[37] Chen, "Comparing Jiang Zemin's Impatience."

[38] Chen, "Constructing Peaceful Development," p. 35.

both sides as "equal political entities." This important shift, from the previous principal-subordinate relationship, has made a lasting impact on the cross-strait policy discourse and reconceptualized Beijing's identity and interests on "one China." To reconcile with Taipei after the 1995–96 strait crisis, the Chinese foreign minister Qian Qichen, in September 1997, suggested resuming the stalled cross-strait negotiations under the condition of the one-China principle. But, he did not make the usual reference to the PRC as the sole legitimate government of all of China. This explicit omission of any reference to the PRC in the standard definition of one China by a senior Chinese official was unprecedented.[39] Beijing also became increasingly explicit that it would treat Taipei as equal in cross-strait negotiations. The then-TAO director Chen Yunlin posited that "cross-strait negotiations are equal talks based on the principle of one China, not in the name of talks between the central government and a local government."[40]

In 1998, Wang Daohan said that "one China" does not refer to "either the ROC or the PRC. [It] indicates a unified China that will be created by the Chinese people of the two sides in the future."[41] On January 4, 2001, Qian, in an interview with the *Washington Post* at Zhongnnanhai, advanced a more inclusive and conciliatory definition of Beijing's "one China" principle. While reaffirming Beijing's goal in national unification, he stated:

> In the past, Chinese officials said "one China" meant Communist China, that Taiwan was a breakaway province and the Beijing government was the only legal government. When Taiwan's leaders thought of one China, "they were trapped." In order to ease their doubts, we said "one China" not only includes the mainland, but also Taiwan. We think of this China as an integral whole which can't be separated in sovereignty or territory. This is the true meaning of "one China." And they had another doubt.... They think that Taiwan being part of Chinese territory means Taiwan and China are not equal.... To ease this doubt, we said the mainland and Taiwan belong to the same one China. At least, it shows some kind of equality. I think it can help ease their doubt.[42]

Another Chinese official was quoted in the same report, stressing: "Once we said we would liberate Taiwan, then we said Taiwan was just a province of China, now we are saying Taiwan can be our equal.... For the mainland to make these kinds of

[39] Swaine, "Decision-Making Regarding Taiwan," p. 330.

[40] Zhao, "Chinese Nationalism and Beijing's Taiwan Policy," p. 96.

[41] Ibid.

[42] John Pomfret, "Beijing Signals New Flexibility on Taiwan: Comments Appear Aimed at Bush," *The Washington Post* (January 5, 2001), https://www.washingtonpost.com/archive/politics/2001/01/05/beijing-signals-new-flexibility-on-taiwan/989f803c-1be3-41c5-8a58-b8e0fbcf9154/.

adjustments in policy is not an easy thing."[43] This broader understanding of "one China" has become more similar to the KMT's OCRI interpretation of the "1992 consensus." In a speech delivered on January 24, 2002, Qian noted that "both the mainland and Taiwan belong to one China. Despite the absence of reunification at present, the two sides should work hard to create conditions for it by reducing contentions, improving cross-straits relations and breaking the political deadlock.... The importance of the '1992 consensus' lies in the fact that, under the prerequisite of adhering to the 'one-China' principle, both sides seek common ground while reserving differences in a flexible way and take the interests of both sides into consideration with a view to building mutual trust, negotiating matters in a practical manner and always looking towards the future."[44]

4. Beijing's Pragmatic and Broader Treatment of "One China," 2008–16

Hence, when Hu Jintao came to power in 2002–03, he urged Taiwan's DPP administration to resume cross-strait dialogues on the basis of the "1992 consensus."[45] However, by the mid-2000s, Chen Shui-bian had taken a more radical turn, abolishing the NUC, calling to draft a new Taiwanese Constitution to replace the ROC, and pushing Taiwan to rejoin the UN. He aimed at severing any ties between the mainland and Taiwan. Had the Bush administration not intervened to restrain Taipei, a new round of Taiwan Strait crisis would have erupted. Witnessing Taiwan's rising independence sentiments, Hu sought to promote greater peaceful development across the strait. Thus, at the 17th CCP Party Congress in October 2007, he raised the idea of a "common destiny community," implying a reorientation of the political status across the Taiwan Strait, in which the "one China does not

[43] Ibid.

[44] Qtd. in Chen, "Constructing Peaceful Development," p. 36. See the full transcript: Embassy of the PRC in the Republic of the Philippines, "Speech by Vice Premier Qian Qichen at the Forum to Commemorate the Seventh Anniversary of President Jiang Zemin's Important Speech entitled 'Continuing to endeavor for the accomplishment of the grand cause of reunification of the motherland,'" January 24, 2002, http://ph.china-embassy.gov.cn/eng/zt/twwt/zxxx/200404/t20040408_1334934.htm.

[45] Su, *Taiwan's Relations with Mainland China*, p. 122. On April 29, 2005, in their first meeting since 1945 between the heads of the KMT and CCP, Lien Chan and Hu Jintao issued a joint statement on the "peaceful development" of cross-strait relationships, outlining five major goals: (1) resume cross-strait negotiations on the basis of the "1992 consensus"; (2) cease hostilities, conclude a peace agreement, and launch confidence building measures (CBMs); (3) comprehensively expand economic engagements; (4) negotiate Taiwan's international participation; and (5) set up party-to-party platform. See Kan, "China/Taiwan: Evolution of the 'one China' Policy". p. 75. For the full press communique on Lien-Hu's five major goals, see: http://www.cctv.com/english/20050430/100193.shtml. On Hu's patient policy, see Chen, "Comparing Jiang Zemin's Impatience." p.4.

mean PRC's China, but [simply] a common homeland for both sides."[46] After the KMT returned to power in May 2008, Beijing showed more tolerance to the Ma administration's more literal and explicit interpretation of China as the ROC.[47] In essence, "Ma's unambiguous adherence to the one-China principle provided the fundamental dynamic for Beijing's policy shift."[48]

Three sets of discourse from Hu Jintao suggested Beijing's greater receptivity of the ROC. First, shortly after Ma's electoral victory on March 22, 2008, Hu, in a telephone conversation with the then U.S. president George W. Bush, expressed that both China and Taiwan should "restore consultation and talks on the basis of the '1992 consensus,' which sees both sides recognize there is only one China, but agree to differ on its definition."[49] Bush welcomed the Chinese leader's flexibility.[50] Second, on December 31, 2008, Hu formally described that "both the mainland and Taiwan belong to one China" and urged both sides to "make *pragmatic explorations* in their political relations under the *special circumstances* where the country has not yet been reunified."[51] Lastly, in March 2012, when meeting with the then KMT's honorary chairman Wu Poh-hsiung, the Chinese president remarked that the CCP should view cross-strait situations "objectively," that is, the "fact that [both] the mainland and Taiwan belong to one China [is] in line with the *current cross-strait rules and regulations* and should be observed by both sides."[52] The remarks that "one China is in line with current cross-strait rules and regulations" seemed to imply that both the ROC and PRC Constitutions agree on "one China" though differ on what that China is.[53]

Moreover, in April 2012, while expressing the hope of eventually creating conditions conducive for a cross-strait political agreement, the then TAO director Wang Yi acknowledged that more time is needed to overcome difficulties and differences

[46] Xin, "Beyond Power Politics," p. 529.

[47] Su, *Taiwan's Relations with Mainland China*: p. 14.

[48] Xin, *Mainland China's Taiwan Policy:* p. 19.

[49] The Permanent Mission of the People's Republic of China to the UN, "Chinese, U.S. Presidents Hold Telephone Talks on Taiwan, Tibet," March 26, 2008, http://un.china-mission.gov.cn/eng/gyzg/xizang/200803/t20080326_8410854.htm.

[50] Chen, "Constructing Peaceful Development," p. 37.

[51] The USC US-China Institute, "Let Us Join Hands to Promote the Peaceful Development of Cross-Straits Relations and Strive with a United Resolve for the Great Rejuvenation of the Chinese Nation Speech at the Forum Marking the 30th Anniversary of the Issuance of the Message to Compatriots in Taiwan," December 31, 2008, https://china.usc.edu/hu-jintao-let-us-join-hands-promote-peaceful-development-cross-straits-relations-and-strive-united. *Emphasis added.*

[52] Qtd. in Chen, "Constructing Peaceful Development," p. 37. Hu already raised the idea as early as March 2005. The Embassy of the PRC in the Kingdom of Denmark, "Four-point guideline on cross-Straits relations set forth by President Hu Jintao," March 14, 2005, http://dk.china-embassy.gov.cn/eng//zdgx/200503/t20050314_2555985.htm.

[53] Huang, *Liangan Da Jiagou:* pp. 17–18.

between the two sides. The "1992 consensus" was referred to as the political foundation, in which both sides "adhered to the common ground of one China and setting aside political differences."[54] After 2008, President Ma has more frequently stipulated that "one China" refers to the ROC which incorporates the mainland region and Taiwan.[55] During his second inaugural address on May 20, 2012, Ma maintained:

> When we speak of "one China," naturally it is the Republic of China. According to our Constitution, the sovereign territory of the Republic of China includes Taiwan and the mainland. At present, the ROC government has authority to govern only in Taiwan, Penghu, Kinmin, and Matsu. In other words, over the past two decades [since 1992], the two sides of the Taiwan Strait have been defined as "one Republic of China, two areas." This status has remained unchanged throughout the administrations of the [past] three presidents.... [One ROC, two areas] is an eminently rational and pragmatic definition and constitutes the basis for assuring the ROC's long-term development and safeguarding Taiwan's security. Both sides of the Taiwan Strait ought to squarely face up to this reality, seek common ground while respecting differences, and establish a consensus regarding "mutual non-recognition of sovereignty and mutual non-denial of authority to govern." Only in this way can the two sides move forward with confidence.[56]

In sum, during Ma's two terms in office, he engaged Beijing by reassuring the latter of his administration's commitment to the "1992 consensus," albeit based on the stance of "one China, respective interpretations" or "one Republic of China, two areas" in line with the ROC Constitution.[57] Beijing did not openly reject Ma's ROC position. Xi Jinping's first five years in office (2012–17) corresponded almost exactly with Ma's second term presidency. As a result, Xi showed some flexibility towards Ma's OCRI. For instance, Xi agreed that "both Taipei and Beijing base their legal and government systems on the one-China principle, under which Taiwan is a part of China, as is the Chinese mainland."[58] He said: "We also are soberly aware that historical problems remain in cross-strait relations, and that there will be issues in the future that will require time, patience, and joint effort to resolve."[59]

[54] Qtd. in Chen, "Constructing Peaceful Development," p. 37.

[55] Office of the President, Republic of China (Taiwan), "總統出席「中華民國釋憲60年」研討會," December 21, 2008); https://www.president.gov.tw/NEWS/12920.

[56] Office of the President of Republic of China (Taiwan), "Full Text of President Ma Ying-jeou's Second Inaugural Address," May 20, 2012, https://english.president.gov.tw/NEWS/3887.

[57] Chen, "The Strategic Implications."

[58] Qtd. in Chen, "Constructing Peaceful Development," p. 40.

[59] "China's Xi to Tread Peaceful Patient Path on Taiwan," *Reuters* (Feb 25, 2013), https://www.reuters.com/article/uk-china-taiwan/chinas-xi-to-tread-peaceful-patient-path-on-taiwan-idUKBRE91O0CA20130225/.

In this context, both the KMT and CCP governments deepened cross-strait ties, building an intricate web of economic, social, and institutional linkages that led to 23 agreements signed between the SEF and ARATS, representative bodies of Taipei and Beijing, respectively as well as the historic Singapore summit meeting between Ma and Xi Jinping in November 2015.[60] "Cross-strait political engagement peaked on November 7, 2015, when Xi and Ma shook hands in Singapore addressing each other as 'mister' within their capacity as 'leader of mainland China' and 'leader of Taiwan,' respectively, marking the first meeting between top leaders of both sides in 66 years, since the end of the Chinese civil war in 1949. This historic meeting, as the culmination of mutual efforts to replace confrontation and conflict with dialogue and reconciliation, highlighted the political trust and delivered goodwill to maintain cross-strait peace and development."[61]

The Growing Cross-Strait Tensions since 2016

Nonetheless, the DPP and a significant segment of the Taiwanese public remained largely distrustful of the KMT-CCP détente, fearing that greater socioeconomic liberalization and closer contact between the two sides would allow too much Chinese influence into Taiwan that could potentially undermine the latter's democracy, freedom, and security. Even the United States, then under the Barack Obama administrations, voiced concerns on the KMT's deepening tilt towards the PRC and the potentially pernicious effects on America's national interests in the region amidst Xi's more expansionist endeavors in the South China Sea.[62] Taiwan's strong public anxiety culminated in the Sunflower student demonstrations in Taiwan in the spring of 2014 that not only halted Ma's attempt to further push for a services trade agreement with Beijing but also sparked an anti-KMT campaign that gave the party a series of stinging defeats in the island's major elections, especially in the last two presidential contests in 2016 and 2020.

Thus, the cross-strait relationship under Ma was far from smooth and stable as seen from its superficial appearance. Beijing's underlying intent to coerce and promote unification has always been clear to the Taiwanese civil society and the younger generation, whose angst regarding the PRC's ambitious encroachment toward Taiwan, using a combination of military pressure campaign, economic coercion, and grey-zone tactics in the forms of cognitive warfare and misinformation initiatives, has only amplified their hostility towards Beijing and skepticism of the

[60] Ho, "Cross-Strait Relations," pp. 349–351.

[61] Xin, *Mainland China's Taiwan Policy*, p. 22.

[62] Chen, *U.S.-China Rivalry*; Hass, Glaser, and Bush, U.S.-Taiwan Relations, pp. 46–48.

KMT's rapprochement policy.[63] In the words of Syaru Shirley Lin, Taiwan clearly faces a "China dilemma, and the key to understanding it lies in "the emergence and consolidation of Taiwanese national identity and the relationship between identity and Taiwan's most important national economic interests, namely growth, stability, equity, and security." Taiwan has been facing these economic opportunities and challenges under the "threat of a militarily hostile neighbor that seeks to absorb it politically and on which it has become dependent economically."[64]

Between the KMT and DPP, China certainly prefers the former given that both the KMT and CCP share a common Chinese heritage and agree on the same Chinese national identity. The DPP, in contrast, is viewed by the PRC as the more dangerous opponent because of its pro-independence platform. Yet, according to Richard Bush, there is a "mismatch" between Beijing's preconceived notion or assumptions about the DPP's cross-strait position and the political pragmatism chartered by the Tsai Ing-wen administration since May 2016. Beijing has largely perceived the strategy employed by Taiwan presidents Lee Teng-hui (though a KMT), Chen Shui-bian, and Tsai as similarly geared toward "achieving independence by moving incrementally and covertly, to create a fait accompli, to which Beijing would find harder to respond."[65] Lee's eagerness to expand Taiwan's international space and push for the Two States Theory in 1999, and Chen's attempted efforts, through several referendum initiatives, to transform Taiwan's legal status in the 2000s had confirmed this worst fear for the PRC leadership. As for Tsai, who rose to prominence as a consultant to Lee's Mainland Affairs Council (MAC) in the late 1990s, she is believed by many in Taiwan and China as the "brains" behind the Two States Theory. She also served as the minister of MAC under Chen Shui-bian's first term and was credited for revitalizing and ultimately leading the DPP back to power after the party's stinging electoral setbacks in 2008 and 2012.[66]

Since Tsai, as president, has refused to embrace the "1992 consensus," in the manner Ma Ying-jeou and the KMT politicians did, the Xi administration has criticized the DPP administration for taking a pro-independence route. According to analysts of cross-strait relations, however, China's depiction misrepresented the reality and failed to recognize Tsai's more moderate approaches given the domestic political constraints she faced.[67] Even without explicitly endorsing the "1992 consensus," Tsai affirmed in her first inauguration address on May 20, 2016:

[63] Bush, *Difficult Choices: Taiwan's Quest for Security."*

[64] Lin, *Taiwan's China Dilemma:* p. 208.

[65] Bush, *Difficult Choices*: p. 130.

[66] Rigger, "The 2012 Elections," p. 42.

[67] Hass, Glaser, and Bush, *U.S.-Taiwan Relations*, pp. 75–77.

> We will also work to maintain the existing mechanisms for dialogue and communication across the Taiwan Strait. In 1992, the two institutions representing each side across the Strait (SEF & ARATS), through communication and negotiations, arrived at various joint acknowledgements and understandings. It was done in a spirit of mutual understanding and a political attitude of seeking common ground while setting aside differences. I respect this historical fact. Since 1992, over twenty years of interactions and negotiations across the Strait have enabled and accumulated outcomes which both sides must collectively cherish and sustain; and it is based on such existing realities and political foundations that the stable and peaceful development of the cross-Strait relationship must be continuously promoted. The new government will conduct cross-Strait affairs in accordance with the Republic of China Constitution, the Act Governing Relations Between the People of Taiwan Area and the Mainland Area, and other relevant legislation. The two governing parties across the Strait must set aside the baggage of history, and engage in positive dialogue, for the benefit of the people on both sides. By existing political foundations, I refer to a number of key elements. The first element is the fact of the 1992 talks between the two institutions representing each side across the Strait (SEF & ARATS), when there was joint acknowledgement of setting aside differences to seek common ground. This is a historical fact. The second element is the existing Republic of China constitutional order. The third element pertains to the outcomes of over twenty years of negotiations and interactions across the Strait. And the fourth relates to the democratic principle and prevalent will of the people of Taiwan.[68]

To a great extent, Tsai used her speech to reassure Beijing that her administration was neither going to change the cross-strait status quo nor promote Taiwan's de jure independence. Notably, Tsai pledged that her government would conduct cross-strait policies on the basis of the "ROC constitutional order" and the "Act Governing Relations between the People of the Taiwan Area and the Mainland Area," both of which are one-China documents that essentially imply both Taiwan and the Chinese mainland are parts of the same nation.[69]

Indeed, in July 2016, I had an invaluable opportunity to interview a high authority in the Tsai government responsible for handling mainland affairs, who stated that "we seek to show greater flexibility than the previous Chen Shui-bian and Ma Ying-jeou administrations." The official continued, "President Tsai wants to avoid getting into the debates on whether Taiwan and mainland are regions under one China, as Ma noted in his 'one ROC, two areas' characterization. While following the ROC Constitution, we can't say One-China. People can interpret our position freely

[68] Office of the President, Republic of China (Taiwan), "Inaugural Address of ROC 14th-Term President Tsai Ing-wen," May 20, 2016. Accessible at: https://english.president.gov.tw/News/4893.

[69] Bush, *Difficult Choices*, p. 153.

on their own.... [President Tsai's] mentioning of the 'ROC constitutional order' and the 'Act Governing Relations between the People of Taiwan Area and the Mainland Area' [implicitly] echoes the point that mainland China and Taiwan are not international but cross-strait relations."[70] Moreover, they added, "by respecting the historical fact of various joint acknowledgements and understandings arrived [in 1992] and done in a spirit of mutual understanding and a political attitude of seeking common ground while setting aside differences," and "cherishing the over 20 years of interactions and negotiations across the strait [and] accumulated outcomes," Tsai practically expressed the "1992 consensus," akin to Ma's "one China, respective interpretations," in a more "qualitative way." At the same time, the president also insisted that any cross-strait resolutions must reflect the democratic preferences of the Taiwanese people.[71]

Xi Jinping's 2019 Taiwan Speech

Nevertheless, Beijing was unwilling to give the DPP leader the benefit of the doubt. The Chinese government has suspected that Tsai's genuine intention is to promote de jure Taiwan independence in the long run, though for the time-being her separatist proclivity is merely cloaked in the ROC cover. For instance, the Chinese side has pointed out how the DPP administration has engaged in the "de-Sinicization" agenda across the social, cultural and educational spectrums in Taiwan, by denigrating the KMT as an "alien authority" or a "foreign regime" while commemorating Japanese colonialism in Taiwan in order to undercut, if not nullify, the relations between Taiwan and China.[72] Yet, in the light of the DPP platform's longstanding objection to one China (regardless of whether that China is the ROC or PRC), especially coming from its Deep Green faction, Tsai has her hands tied. Her winning coalition also consisted of political and civil societal groups in favor of Taiwan independence. Furthermore, as U.S-PRC relations grew more confrontational over the past several years under both the Trump and Biden administrations, Washington has also become more skeptical of the KMT's China-friendly position, which could potentially compromise Taiwan's democracy and security. U.S. national interests, therefore, have welcomed Tsai's more centrist bent on cross-strait relations. Thus, Tsai, in the opinion of many, is actually doing her

[70] This author's interview with a high authority in the Tsai administration responsible for handling cross-strait policy, July 26, 2016, Taipei, Taiwan. The interviewee requested to remain anonymous. See also Chen, *U.S.-China Rivalry and Taiwan's Mainland Policy*, pp. 174–175.

[71] Ibid.

[72] Xin, *Mainland China's Taiwan Policy*, pp. 37–38.

best to address Beijing's demands, without undermining her domestic political legitimacy as well as international support.[73]

Bush, as a longtime observer of the Taiwan Strait issue, has provided an interesting insight:

> My own view is that the PRC leaders cannot afford to accept the reality that the mainstream of the DPP recognizes that independence is not an option. To do so would be to legitimize the DPP and require Beijing to creatively find a way to coexist with it, which, in turn would reduce even further the chances for unification and produce an outcome of permanent de facto separation. Beijing must therefore demonize the DPP and deliberately set the bar for coexistence higher than the DPP is willing to go. Moreover, in situations such as Taiwan, where the CCP exercises less control than it would like, the PRC seeks to ally with internal forces that share its goals in order to obstruct, constrain, and isolate adversaries that defy the CCP's interests. Having an enemy to demonize and oppose is an essential element of this Leninist, united-front strategy.[74]

Whatever the ambiguity China was willing to accommodate in the "1992 consensus" during the Ma era, Beijing has moved the goalposts and tightened its definition by unequivocally insisting that the Tsai government must endorse the "one-China" core connotation.[75] For Beijing, to be sure, the PRC government is always the one and only legitimate Chinese state that superseded the ROC state in 1949. The Chinese leadership was willing to entertain Ma's "respective interpretations" not because they agreed with him about the existence of ROC but because they trusted his intention and support for a one China.[76] Yet, when President Tsai brought up the ROC, Beijing refused to allow for any more wiggle room.

On January 2, 2019, in a speech commemorating the 40th anniversary of the issuance of the "Message to Compatriots in Taiwan"[77] by the Standing Committee of the PRC's National People's Congress, President Xi Jinping called for a "peaceful reunification with Taiwan" in accordance with the "One-China principle" of the "1992 consensus." The Chinese leader explained that the Taiwan issue originally emerged from China's internal weaknesses dating back to the Opium Wars of the mid-nineteenth century. After WWII, "[the] two sides of the Taiwan Straits fell into a special state of protracted political confrontation due to the civil war in China and

[73] Ho, "Cross-Strait Relations," p. 355; Bush, *Difficult Choices*, pp. 153–154; Hass, Glaser, and Bush, *U.S.-Taiwan Relations*, pp. 86–87. See also deLisle, "United States-Taiwan Relations."

[74] Bush, *Difficult Choices*, p. 131.

[75] Cole, *Cross-Strait Relations since 2016*, pp. 11–12.

[76] Bush, *Difficult Choices*, p. 152.

[77] The Standing Committee of the Fifth National People's Congress, "Message to Compatriots in Taiwan," January 1, 1979. Accessible at: http://www.china.org.cn/english/7943.htm.

interferences of foreign forces." Since 1949, he said, "the Communist Party of China, the Chinese government, and the Chinese people have endeavored to pursue the historic mission of resolving the Taiwan question and realizing China's complete reunification." "On this basis," Xi continued, "we have formulated a fundamental strategy of upholding the principle of 'one country, two systems' and promoting national reunification. With this, we have responded to the call of our time, namely to promote, in the new era, the peaceful development of cross-strait relations and unite our compatriots in Taiwan to strive for our country's rejuvenation and peaceful reunification."[78]

Xi's address has been widely interpreted as setting Beijing's record straight on what the "1992 consensus" prescribes—that is both Taiwan and mainland China belong to the same country under the PRC sovereign jurisdiction, and the blueprint for achieving unification is through the "one country, two systems" model that has been applied to Hong Kong and Macau. In other words, Taiwan would become a special administrative region (SAR) of the PRC. Though Taiwan is promised a high degree of political and socioeconomic autonomy, Beijing would decide ultimately how much latitude and freedom to delegate to its subordinate units, be they provinces, autonomous regions, or special administrative regions.[79] Xi also devoted a great proportion of his remarks denouncing and "resolutely opposing" Taiwan independence, which, he warned, would bring "disaster." He said that the PRC would "not renounce the use of force and reserve the option of taking all necessary measures" to fight against "external interference" and "Taiwan's separatists and their separatist activities."[80] The Taiwanese public opinion has been firmly against China's "one country, two systems" model, especially in the light of Beijing's stricter and more repressive control over Hong Kong. Moreover, by erasing the ROC from the "1992 consensus," Xi's 2019 New Year Day address not only discredited the KMT's "one China, respective interpretations," alienated its Pan-Blue supporters, but also blunted Tsai's concession to handle cross-strait ties on the basis of the ROC constitutional framework. The campaign against the unpopular "one country, two systems" (and, by extension, the "1992 consensus") and Hong Kong's massive democracy demonstration movements throughout 2019–20 emboldened President Tsai's reelection prospects in January 2020, propelling the DPP incumbent to a

[78] Taiwan Work Office of the CPC Central Committee and the Taiwan Affairs Office of the State Council, "Working Together to Realize Rejuvenation of the Chinese Nation and Advance China's Peaceful Reunification by Xi Jinping," January 2, 2019. Accessible at: http://www.gwytb.gov.cn/wyly/201904/t20190412_12155687.htm.

[79] Bush, *Difficult Choices*, p. 211.

[80] "Working Together to Realize Rejuvenation of the Chinese Nation and Advance China's Peaceful Reunification."

landslide victory over the populist KMT candidate Han Kuo-yu (who was also the then Kaohsiung mayor).[81]

As the DPP appears to have become well-entrenched in a robust one-party dominance of Taiwan's national politics since 2016—prompting some analysts to describe that year's election as constituting a "critical realignment" in which the younger voters have been motivated to vote for the DPP due to the China threats—Beijing has embarked upon a series of punitive acts to combat the Tsai government.[82] The PRC, never a fan of the ROC which the CCP defeated and expelled from the Chinese mainland, feels more compelled to expunge the old regime in order to deny the DPP government any means of escaping from recognizing the one-China principle on Beijing's terms.[83] In her second-term inauguration address on May 20, 2020, Tsai underscored the words "peace, parity, democracy, and dialogue,'" stating that "we will not accept the Beijing authorities' use of 'one country, two systems' to downgrade Taiwan and undermine the cross-strait status quo. We stand fast by this principle." Yet, Taiwan's president reiterated her 2016 pledge to "handle cross-strait affairs according to the Constitution of the Republic of China and the Act Governing Relations between the People of the Taiwan Area and the Mainland Area. This has been our consistent position for maintaining the peaceful and stable status quo in the Taiwan Strait."[84] Beijing has bluntly denied the existence of the ROC. On April 14, 2021, the Taiwan Affairs Office of the PRC's State Council, in response to a question on the removal of the "Republic of China government" from Hong Kong's textbook revision, stressed, "It's an indisputable historical fact that in 1949, the Kuomintang regime lost the civil war it launched against the people and retreated to the island of Taiwan, thus losing its status as the legal government representing the whole of China."[85]

Meanwhile, the CCP has stepped up its military pressure and coercive campaigns around the air and maritime vicinities of Taiwan, while relying on economic incentives, social and cultural exchanges, and even disinformation tactics to penetrate into Taiwan's civil society, media, business, educational and political institutions to try to befriend individuals, groups, and communities who are opposed to Taiwan independence and against the cross-strait policies of the DPP/Tsai administration. For instance, the Chinese united front campaigns targeted Beijing-friendly political parties, including the New Party (which was originally from the pro-unification

[81] Wang and Cheng, "Threat Perception and Taiwan's 2020 Presidential Election," pp. 127–129.

[82] Clark, Tan, and Ho, "Was 2016 a Realigning Election in Taiwan?"

[83] Ho, "Cross-Strait Relations," p. 355.

[84] Office of the President, Republic of China (Taiwan), "Inaugural Address of ROC 15th Term President Tsai Ing-wen," May 20, 2020. Accessible at: https://english.president.gov.tw/News/6004.

[85] "China Says ROC Hasn't Existed since 1949," *FTV* (April 15, 2021), accessible at: https://www.ftvnews.com.tw/video/detail/NF4WvazUfZs.

wing of the KMT who decided to form its own party because of their disagreement with Lee Teng-hui in the mid-1990s) and the China Unification Promotion Party, headed by a former gangster, Chang An-le (also known as the "White Wolf").[86] KMT politicians and independent or centrist candidates, like the "White Force" represented by the former Taipei mayor Ko Wen-je, have also become optimal partners as they are supporters of either the "1992 consensus" or the notion "the two sides of the Taiwan Strait are one family."[87]

The KMT's China Quandary

The KMT, after losing two consecutive presidential contests in Taiwan in 2016 and 2020, is on the defensive and needs to convince a majority of skeptical Taiwanese electorates and Washington that the party fully appreciates what is possible given the prevailing strategic circumstances, not what the party thinks is desirable based on its pro-China ideational orientations. In that sense, the KMT wants to demonstrate it has the ability to effectively defend Taiwan's security, de facto independence, and self-governed democratic system from Beijing's unabated threats while reassuring Washington that a KMT administration would remain a dependable strategic partner in the maintenance of a stable and peaceful cross-strait equilibrium that not only stops short of unilaterally declaring Taiwan's de jure independence but also preventing the island from tilting towards the PRC's spheres of influence. In spite of the KMT's repeated pledges that it is a "pro-U.S., pro-democracy and close to U.S. party,"[88] their pro-China position has placed the party in a very difficult spot amidst the heightening U.S.-PRC competition.

Indeed, like many democracies worldwide, Taiwan faces a longstanding China conundrum. On the one hand, the island relies heavily on the PRC for commercial exchanges, with approximately 40 percent of Taiwanese exports going to Mainland China and Hong Kong while 20 percent of imports coming from them. On the other hand, Beijing's Leninist system and unrelenting coercive pressures on Taiwan have also put the democratically self-ruled island in grave danger. But, unlike Japan, South Korea, the Philippines, Vietnam, or other ASEAN states, to name just a few, which also have, simultaneously, extensive economic interdependence with China as well as their respective territorial, maritime, and political feuds with Beijing,

[86] Bush, *Difficult Choices*, pp. 241–242.

[87] Xin, *Mainland China's Taiwan Policy*, p. 36.

[88] "Taiwan's Path Forward: A Conversation with KMT Chairman Eric Chu," Keynote and Conversation at the Brookings Institution (June 6, 2022), https://www.brookings.edu/wp-content/uploads/2022/05/fp_20220606_taiwan_chu_transcript.pdf.

Taiwan cannot maintain a tenable hedging posture between Washington and Beijing. This is because the CCP government has never ceased claiming control over Taiwan, as Xi stressed in 2021: "Resolving the Taiwan question and realizing China's complete reunification is a historic mission and an unshakable commitment of the Communist Party of China. It is also a shared aspiration of all the sons and daughters of the Chinese nation."[89] During the early days of China's economic reform and opening period in the 1980s and 1990s, Beijing promised that its "one country, two systems" formula would ensure the people of Hong Kong (and, in the future, Taiwan, as well) continue with their liberal socioeconomic system and enjoy a high degree of unfettered and autonomous political freedom and democracy. Nonetheless, in recent years, as the Chinese government increasingly tightened its political grip and stepped-up censorship capacity over the former British colony, Taiwan's people have grown more repulsive towards any calls for a political accommodation within the PRC's authoritarian system, although that does not necessarily mean a rejection of identifying with Chinese culture.[90]

The KMT's Attempt to Reinvigorate the 1992 Consensus

As noted, having lost twice electorally to Tsai Ing-wen, the KMT has still not been able to settle on a strategically sound posture to cope with the PRC. Xi's 2019 remarks certainly derailed, to some extent, the KMT's confidence in the "1992 consensus," given the term is now treated as synonymous with unification on the PRC's terms and its "one country, two systems." Moreover, in March 2023, China's then foreign minister Qin Gang, reading out from the preamble of the PRC Constitution, stressed that "Taiwan is part of the sacred territory of the People's Republic of China."[91] Therefore, it becomes more difficult for the KMT to accord the ROC in its definition of "one China."

The KMT's substantial electoral success in the November 2022 local mayoral races boosted the party's morale. However, their similar victory in 2018 also demonstrated that municipal elections are less about national security/cross-strait

[89] Qtd. in David Sacks, "What Xi Jinping's Major Speech Means for Taiwan," Council on Foreign Relations: Asian Unbound (July 6, 2021), https://www.cfr.org/blog/what-xi-jinpings-major-speech-means-taiwan.

[90] Shelley Rigger, Lev Nachman, Chit Wai John Mok, and Nathan Kar Ming Chan, "Why Is Unification So Unpopular in Taiwan? It's the PRC Political System, Not Just Culture," Brookings Institution (February 7, 2022), https://www.brookings.edu/articles/why-is-unification-so-unpopular-in-taiwan-its-the-prc-political-system-not-just-culture/.

[91] The Ministry of Foreign Affairs, PRC, "Foreign Minister Qin Gang Meets the Press," March 7, 2023, https://www.fmprc.gov.cn/mfa_eng/zxxx_662805/202303/t20230307_11037190.html.

issues than domestic affairs.[92] Hence, the KMT's prospect of recovering Taiwan's presidency in 2024 is far from ensured. Over the past seven years, the KMT has been led by four chairpersons: Hung Hsiu-chu (2016–17); Wu Den-yih (2017–20), Johnny Chiang (2020–21), and Eric Chu (2021–present), and each had formulated and articulated their stances and interpretations regarding the "1992 consensus." None, however, has been genuinely satisfying to Taiwan's voters, Washington, or even Beijing. For instance, Hung is considered the most similar to Beijing's position, as she simply focused on "one China" downplaying the "respective interpretations" aspect.[93] Hung and her advisor, Chang Ya-chung (professor of political science at the National Taiwan University), advocated for a peace agreement with the mainland to mark an official end to their decades of antagonism.[94] A peace agreement is also laying down a more concrete way for future reunification. Thus, Hung's view is seen to reflect the extreme pro-unification faction within the KMT, as she embraces explicitly the ultimate reunification with mainland China, even under the PRC system. She expressed, when meeting with Chinese officials, that "people on both sides of the Strait should uphold the 1992 Consensus and oppose "Taiwan independence," promote exchanges, enhance mutual trust, and contribute to the integrated cross-Strait development and the realization of peaceful reunification."[95]

In contrast, Wu Den-yih prevailed over Hung in the race for the KMT chairmanship in May 2017. As the ROC's former vice-president during the second Ma Ying-jeou administration (2012–16), Wu's position was in line with his former boss, that is, "one China, respective interpretations."[96] Yet, the huge KMT loss in January 2020 led to Wu's resignation, and the party then elected Johnny Chiang as its new chairman in March 2020. Chiang set up the Cross-Strait Team of the KMT's Reform Committee to examine how the party should charter its mainland policy going forward. On June 19, 2020, the committee published its preliminary report, describing the "1992 consensus" in a historical context, suggesting that the party should eschew the term in any future handling of China affairs. Furthermore, the new cross-strait approach

[92] Brian Hioe, "Once Again, the KMT Scores Big in Taiwan's Local Elections," *The Diplomat* (November 28, 2022), https://thediplomat.com/2022/11/once-again-kmt-scores-big-in-taiwans-local-elections/.

[93] Shih Hsiao-kuang and Jonathan Chin, "KMT Congress Approves New Policy Platforms," *Taipei Times* (September 5, 2016), https://www.taipeitimes.com/News/front/archives/2016/09/05/2003654519.

[94] Amber Lin, "Does the KMT Still Have a Cross-Strait Role?" *Common Wealth Magazine* (July 20, 2018), https://english.cw.com.tw/article/article.action?id=2031.

[95] "Top political advisor meets with Taiwan delegation led by Hung Hsiu-chu," *Xinhua News* (May 14, 2019), https://www.xinhuanet.com/english/2019-05/14/c_138055563.htm.

[96] "中國國民黨主席當選人吳敦義同志回覆中共賀電," (May 20, 2017), http://www.kmt.org.tw/2017/05/blog-post_77.html; Shih Hsiao-kuang, "REPORTER'S NOTEBOOK: Wu Must Face KMT Factionalism over China Relations," *Taipei Times* (May 22, 2017), https://www.taipeitimes.com/News/taiwan/archives/2017/05/22/2003671072.

should include the four pillars: (1) adherence to the sovereignty of the Republic of China (2) protection of freedom, democracy, and human rights, (3) maintenance of Taiwan's security and priority, and (4) creation of a win-win situation and shared prosperity." After facing strong pushback from the KMT's senior leaders and past chairpersons, including Ma, Wu, Hung, and Lien Chan, Chiang clarified his positions, explaining that he certainly recognized the significant and positive contributions of the "1992 consensus" during the eight years of Ma's presidency. Yet, he noted, in recent years, the "1992 consensus was "stigmatized and distorted by the ruling Democratic Progressive Party as well as Xi's government in Beijing." "It seems that excessive interpretation of this discourse has instead led to more misunderstandings amongst the people of Taiwan." Consequently, Chiang wanted to unequivocally identify the most important tenet behind the 1992 consensus as the "Constitution of the Republic of China," and "when you (Beijing) do not look squarely at the Republic of China, the 92 Consensus cannot exist."[97]

Nevertheless, Chiang's reform attempt ultimately led to his downfall, as the KMT establishment rallied behind Eric Chu to be the new party chair in 2021 (Chu served once as the KMT chairman back in 2015–16). When at the Brookings Institution in Washington DC in June 2022, Chu reaffirmed that the "1992 consensus" remains the "key foundation" in dealing with Beijing. He defined it as a "non-consensus consensus," based on "creative ambiguity."[98] In any event, the KMT's quandary has shown how its "domestic security imaginary,"[99] which is deeply rooted in the history, culture, and identity of the Kuomintang, has led them to paint the CCP as merely an "intrastate" political rival, in contrast to the majority of Taiwanese voters who primarily perceive Beijing as an external foe. Therefore, the KMT's deeply entrenched historical baggage and identity as a China-centric party (created by Dr. Sun Yat-sen, the founder of the ROC, and later led by strong Chinese nationalists Chiang Kai-shek and Chiang Ching-kuo who pledged to restore the ROC back to China after they fled to Taiwan in 1949) has constrained the party from chartering a more assertive position on the PRC.

[97] "Amid Backlash, Chiang Affirms Contributions of 1992 Consensus," Fair Winds Foundation, http://fairwindsfoundation.org/en/event/Taiwan%20Weekly/8/Amid%20Backlash,%20Chiang%20Affirms%20Contributions%20of%201992%20Consensus/60. See also David Brown, "Pay Attention to the KMT's Chair Election," *The Diplomat* (September 15, 2021), https://thediplomat.com/2021/09/pay-attention-to-the-kmts-chair-election/; Jessica Drun, "The KMT Continues to Grapple with its "1992 Consensus," *Global Taiwan Institute* (September 22, 2022), https://globaltaiwan.org/2022/09/the-kmt-continues-to-grapple-with-its-1992-consensus/.

[98] "Taiwan's Path Forward: A Conversation with KMT Chairman Eric Chu," Keynote and Conversation at the Brookings Institution (June 6, 2022), https://www.brookings.edu/wp-content/uploads/2022/05/fp_20220606_taiwan_chu_transcript.pdf.

[99] Weldes, "Constructing National Interests."

Ma Ying-jeou's China Visit of Spring 2023

In spring 2023, former president Ma Ying-jeou went on a 12-day visit to China. Traveling as a private citizen, his office noted that the former president's trip was just to pay homage to his ancestors (in Hunan) and, with Taiwanese university students, visited historical sites of great significance to the KMT when it still ruled China. Ma in Nanjing, the former capital of the ROC when it ruled the Chinese mainland, emphasized the ethnic Chinese unity between the people of Taiwan and China. He also underscored that the ROC continues to have political legitimacy and sovereignty over both Taiwan and the Chinese mainland,[100] in accordance with the ROC Constitution, its Additional Articles, and the Taiwan's Act Governing Relations between the People of the Taiwan Area and Mainland Area.[101]

Ma's rationale might have worked when Beijing was willing to tolerate, albeit tacitly, the presence of the ROC, as what happened during the administration of Hu Jintao and early years of Xi's administration when they acknowledged, as discussed earlier, that both Taiwan and China have their different legal and constitutional systems. Today, however, Xi would have none of that. Ma's references to the ROC were all censored by China's news media outlets.[102] In that sense, the KMT cannot compellingly persuade Taiwan's voters and the international community that "one China" can be respectively interpreted as the ROC. Washington politicians again raised concerns that the KMT's idealism may inadvertently tie Taiwan into the PRC's "one China" principle.[103] Tsai also took a swipe at Ma, asserting that the ROC and PRC are "not subordinate to each other."[104]

Table 8.1 summarizes the KMT's intraparty disagreements over how the "1992 consensus" should be conceptualized, as well as the interest positions of Washington and Beijing, respectively, towards each KMT perspective. The United States has consistently stated that it does not interfere in Taiwan's domestic affairs

100 "Former President Ma Mentions 'ROC' During Ancestor Worship in China," *Focus Taiwan News* (April 1, 2023), https://focustaiwan.tw/cross-strait/202304010004.

101 "Ex-President Tells Chinese Students ROC Constitution Covers Taiwan, Mainland," *Focus Taiwan News* (April 2, 2023), https://focustaiwan.tw/cross-strait/202304020009.

102 "馬英九訪中提台灣總統和民國 北京喉舌全過濾," *UDN News* (April 7, 2023), https://udn.com/news/story/123435/7082584?from=udn-relatednews_ch2.

103 Lauren Sforza, "McCaul Says China Could Influence, Take Over Taiwan in Next Election 'Without a Shot Fired,'" *The Hill* (April 9, 2023), https://thehill.com/homenews/sunday-talk-shows/3941129-mc-caul-says-china-could-influence-take-over-taiwan-in-next-election-without-a-shot-fired/.

104 Office of the President, Republic of China (Taiwan), "President Tsai delivers remarks on the termination of diplomatic relations with the Republic of Honduras," March 26, 2023, https://english.president.gov.tw/News/6464.

or "register a preference in Taiwan's electoral process."[105] Yet, it is also undeniable that the Taiwan candidates/parties' cross-strait approach would inevitably affect Washington's national security interests towards the Taiwan Strait and the wider Indo-Pacific region, especially in a global/regional context of escalated contentious relations with Beijing in recent years. Thus, it may be reasonable to surmise that Washington would take an unpalatable stance towards the KMT position preferred by Beijing and a more receptive attitude towards platforms that are less supported by the PRC. Given that the U.S. one-China policy is an ambiguously created framework, it is not hard to imagine that Washington would be least interested in a KMT definition of one China that boxes Taiwan into the PRC orbit. Overall, the United States expressed concerns about China's potential interference in Taiwan's 2024 elections, lest that Beijing would provide support for candidates who are friendlier towards the PRC. Indeed, on November 15, 2023, Presidents Joe Biden and Xi Jinping held their second in-person meeting on the sidelines of the APEC summit in the San Francisco Bay Area. In their efforts to deaccelerate U.S.-PRC's fallen bilateral relations, both wanted to focus on areas where they can cooperate (such as resuming military communications, curbing fentanyl, and managing risks of AI) so as to manage their heightening competition. When discussing the Taiwan issue, Biden, though reiterating Washington's adherence to the U.S. one China policy, didn't oblige Xi's request in expressing a stronger opposition to Taiwanese independence. As Xi warned Biden that China will eventually "reunify Taiwan with mainland China," the U.S. leader cautioned his counterpart against interference in Taiwan's election.[106]

Meanwhile, Hou Yu-ih, the KMT's 2024 presidential nominee and the mayor of New Taipei City, has sought to convince the Taiwanese people and Washington that the KMT is clear-eyed about Beijing's intentions and sovereign claims with respect to Taiwan. Hou argued in the pages of *Foreign Affairs*, "I have no unrealistic expectations about Beijing's intentions of seeking unification, and if necessary, by force. Taiwan's most important priority should be to strengthen its national defense and deter the use of force by mainland China." He reassured Taiwan's "collaboration with the United States in various areas such as sharing intelligence and promoting regular joint training exercises."[107] He also sought to improve cross-strait relations

[105] Jude Blanchette and Ryan Hass, "How the United States Can Support Taiwan's Democracy," CSIS Analysis (June 15, 2023), https://www.csis.org/analysis/how-united-states-can-support-taiwans-democracy.

[106] Kristen Welker, Courtney Kube, Carol E. Lee and Andrea Mitchell, "Xi warned Biden during summit that Beijing will reunify Taiwan with China," *NBC News* (December 20, 2023), https://www.nbcnews.com/news/china/xi-warned-biden-summit-beijing-will-reunify-taiwan-china-rcna130087.

[107] Hou Yu-ih, "Taiwan's Path between Extremes," *Foreign Affairs* (September 18, 2023), https://www.foreignaffairs.com/taiwan/taiwans-path-between-extremes.

on the basis of the "1992 consensus," in accordance with the ROC constitution and its amendments, adding that his formulation is firmly opposed to both de-jure Taiwan independence and the PRC's "one country, two systems."[108] Hou promised to pursue a "3D" strategy—deterrence, dialogue, and de-escalation—to maintain a balanced approach to defend Taiwan, deepen security ties with the United States, while engaging in some limited cooperation with China.

KMT's intraparty differences over the 1992 consensus and relations with China	The 1992 consensus should focus only on "one China," leaving out respective interpretations; supporting a peace agreement to pave the way for eventual unification (Hung Hsiu-chu)	The 1992 consensus is "one China, respective interpretations"; with the KMT's interpretations that one China is the ROC (Ma Ying-jeou, Wu Den-yeh, Eric Chu)	The 1992 consensus is squarely based on conforming with Taiwan's democracy, sovereignty, security, ROC Constitution; explicitly rejecting "one country, two systems" (Johnny Chiang, Hou Yu-ih)
U.S. interests	No	Ambiguous/No	Ambiguous/Yes
PRC interests	Yes	Ambiguous/Yes	No

Table 8.1: KMT's Intraparty Differences over 1992 Consensus and Interests of the US and PRC

Beijing Should Accept the ROC's Continued Existence

The KMT need not eschew or discard their China roots, for that's the party's history, culture, and identity. Denying it would only make the KMT look disingenuous and hypocritical. Taiwan's voters will be the ones to ultimately judge and decide whether they can endorse the KMT's platform. However, there should be a red line drawn: the KMT must not permit any more respective interpretations to the notion of "one China" to appease Beijing. That approach has only backfired by strengthening the PRC's monopolizing power in both the cross-strait and international arenas regarding the Taiwan Strait impasse. The KMT needs to make it crystal clear to Beijing that it will have to accept the reality of the ROC's continued existence to ameliorate cross-strait tensions and mistrust. The ROC and its sovereign jurisdictions may mean different things to different groups and constituents within Taiwan, but Taiwan's public preferences have shown that the ROC is a widely supported institutional arrangement and most compatible with securing the cross-strait status-quo. Polls in Taiwan have consistently found a great majority of respondents rejecting defining one China as merely the PRC and unification under Beijing's one country two

[108] Ibid.

systems model. Yet, when asked about one China, respective interpretations, with the ROC being that China, respondents have reacted with more positive attitudes. Roughly 60 percent supported that between 2005 and 2019.[109] Even in the wake of Xi's January 2019 speech, still roughly 46 percent of respondents expressed their support for OCRI, with the ROC being the "one China."[110] Hou Yu-ih asserted that the ROC and Taiwan are "inseparable," underscoring that the existence of the ROC should be recognized by the international community. More specifically, Hou told reporters that Taiwanese society should have a consensus that the ROC and Taiwan cannot be separated from each other, just like "glass and water.". When a glass is broken, the water in the glass would spill over.[111] As noted, Hou affirmed he would accept a version of the "1992 consensus" that conformed to the ROC Constitution, not the interpretation of the consensus as "one country, two systems." He also strongly opposed the DPP's "stigmatization" of the consensus.[112]

The 2024 presidential election in Taiwan pitted KMT's Hou against former Taipei mayor Ko Wen-je of the Taiwan People's Party, and the DPP's William Lai (who is now the DPP's chairman and Taiwan's vice president). Lai had claimed to be a "pragmatic worker for Taiwan independence," though he later clarified his position and stressed that the DPP, under his watch, would follow Tsai's cross-strait status-quo platform. All three candidates rallied behind the ROC, in line with Taiwan's general public sentiments. Nonetheless, the KMT has remained the only party that still sticks with the "1992 consensus," in order to maintain some level of amicable relations with Beijing while assuring the Taiwanese voters, Washington, and the international community of the party's resolve and resilience in deterring and defending the island democracy against the PRC aggressions. If the Xi government truly endeavors to pursue a peaceful approach towards Taiwan and wants to convince the people there to back the "1992 consensus," then it must revise its obdurate position on one China and the one country two systems. Facing up to the reality of the continued existence of the ROC seems to be the most pragmatic way to foster goodwill and ameliorate cross-strait animosities. The ROC seems to be the most viable institutional arrangement to bridge the China-Taiwan divide while keeping some attributes of the one-China concept, however ambiguously conceptualized. Without showing greater understanding and empathy toward Taiwan people's desires for a democratic way of life, freedom, and participation in

109 Wang and Cheng, "Threat Perception."

110 The Taiwan National Security Studies Survey, October 27–31, 2020.

111 "ELECTION 2024/Possible presidential candidate likens ROC and Taiwan to 'glass and water,'" *Focus Taiwan News* (April 28, 2023), accessible: https://focustaiwan.tw/politics/202304280022.

112 "ELECTION 2024/KMT's Hou Backs '1992 consensus that Conforms with ROC Constitution," *Focus Taiwan News* (July 4, 2023), https://focustaiwan.tw/cross-strait/202307040017.

global activities, the PRC may find their distance across the Taiwan Strait continue to widen and further escalation of tensions to the detriment of all involved. Xi must not let his nationalist ambition blind a clear and sensible path forward for greater peace and stability across the Strait.

Dr. **Dean P. Chen** is Professor of Political Science at Ramapo College of New Jersey. He holds his Ph.D. in Political Science from the University of California at Santa Barbara. He is the author of *U.S.-China-Taiwan in the Age of Trump and Biden: Towards a Nationalist Strategy* (New York: Routledge, 2022), *U.S.-China Rivalry and Taiwan's Mainland Policy: Security, Nationalism, and the 1992 Consensus* (New York: Palgrave Macmillan, 2017), and *U.S.-Taiwan Strait Policy: The Origins of Strategic Ambiguity* (Lynne Rienner, 2012). His articles have appeared in *Asian Survey, Asian Security, Asian Politics & Policy, Pacific Focus, International Relations of the Asia-Pacific*, and *American Journal of Chinese Studies*. Commentaries have appeared in *The National Interest, Global Taiwan Brief, Taiwan Insight*, and *China-US Focus*. Between 2014–16, Chen was coordinator of the Conference Group on Taiwan Studies of the American Political Science Association. He was a MOFA-ROC Taiwan Fellow in 2014 and a Fulbright U.S. Scholar in 2017–18. Currently, Chen serves on the board of directors of the American Association for Chinese Studies.

Bibliography

Bolton, John. *The Room Where It Happened: A White House Memoir* (New York: Simon & Schuster, 2020).

Bush, Richard. *Difficult Choices: Taiwan's Quest for Security and the Good Life* (Washington DC: Brookings Institution Press, 2021).

Chen, Chien-Kai. "Comparing Jiang Zemin's Impatience with Hu Jintao's Patience Regarding the Taiwan Issue," *Journal of Contemporary China* 21, no. 78 (2012), pp. 955–972.

Chen, Dean P. "The Strategic Implications of Ma Ying-jeou's 'One ROC, Two Areas' Policy on Cross-Strait Relations," *American Journal of Chinese Studies* 20, no. 1 (2013), pp. 23–41.

———. "Constructing Peaceful Development: The Changing Interpretations of One China and Beijing's Taiwan Strait Policy," *Asian Security* 10, no. 1 (2014), pp. 22–46.

———."Security, Domestic Divisions, and the KMT's Post-2008 'One China' Policy: A Neoclassical Realist Analysis," *International Relations of the Asia-Pacific* 15, no. 2 (2015), pp. 319–365.

———. *U.S.-China Rivalry and Taiwan's Mainland Policy: Security, Nationalism, and the 1992 Consensus* (New York: Palgrave Macmillan, 2017).

Chen Qimao. "The Taiwan Straits Situation since Ma Came to Office and Conditions for Cross-Straits Political Negotiations," *Journal of Contemporary China* 20, no. 68 (2011), pp. 153–160.

Clark, Cal, Alexander Tan, and Karl Ho. "Was 2016 a Realigning Election in Taiwan?" *Asian Survey* 60, no. 6 (2020), pp. 1006–1028.

deLisle, Jacques. "United States-Taiwan Relations: Tsai's Presidency and Washington's Policy," *The China Review* 18, no. 3 (2018), pp. 13–60.

Hass, Ryan, Bonnie Glaser, and Richard Bush, *U.S.-Taiwan Relations: Will China's Challenge Lead to a Crisis?* (Washington DC: Brookings Institution Press, 2023).

Hickey, Dennis. *Foreign Policy Making in Taiwan* (New York: Routledge, 2007).

Ho Szu-yin, "Cross-Strait Relations," in Kharis Templeman, Yun-han Chu, and Larry Diamond, eds., *Dynamics of Democracy in Taiwan* (Boulder, CO: Lynne Rienner Publishers, 2020), pp. 339–360.

Huang Nian, *Liangan Da Jiagou: Da Wuding Xia De Zhongguo [The Cross-Strait Framework: A One-China Roof]* (Taipei, Tianxia Wenhua Publishers, 2013).

Kan, Shirley. "China/Taiwan: Evolution of the 'One China' Policy—Key Statements from Washington, Beijing, and Taiwan," *Congressional Research Service Report for Congress* (June 24, 2011), p. 75

Lampton, David, ed. *The Making of Chinese Foreign and Security Policy in the Era of Reform* (Stanford University Press, 2001).

Lee, Wei-chin, ed. *Protests, Pandemic, and Security Predicaments: Hong Kong, Taiwan, China, and the US in the 2020s* (New York: Palgrave Macmillan, 2023).

Lin, Syaru Shirley. *Taiwan's China Dilemma: Contested Identities and Multiple Interests in Taiwan's Cross-Strait Economic Policy* (Stanford, CA: Stanford University Press, 2016).

Medeiros, Evan. ed. *Cold Rivals: The New Era of US-China Strategic Competition* (Washington DC: Georgetown University Press, 2023).

Miller, Chris. *Chip War: The Fight for the World's Most Critical Technology* (Scribner, 2022).

Rigger, Shelley. *Why Taiwan Matters* (Lanham, MD: Rowman & Littlefield, 2011).

———. "The 2012 Elections," in Kharis Templeman, Yun-han Chu, and Larry Diamond, eds. *Dynamics of Democracy in Taiwan* (Boulder, CO: Lynne Rienner Publishers, 2020), pp. 39–54.

Shirk, Susan. *Overreach: How China Derailed Its Peaceful Rise* (New York: Oxford University Press, 2022).

Su Chi, *Taiwan's Relations with Mainland China: A Tail Wagging Two Dogs* (New York: Routledge, 2008).

Swaine, Michael. "Decision-Making Regarding Taiwan, 1979–2000," in David Lampton, ed., *The Making of Chinese Foreign and Security Policy in the Era of Reform* (Stanford University Press, 2001), pp. 289–336.

Templeman, Kharis, Yun-han Chu, and Larry Diamond, eds. *Dynamics of Democracy in Taiwan* (Boulder, CO: Lynne Rienner Publishers, 2020).

Wang, T.Y., and Su-feng Cheng, "Threat Perception and Taiwan's 2020 Presidential Election," in Wei-chin Lee, ed., *Protests, Pandemic, and Security Predicaments: Hong Kong, Taiwan, China, and the US in the 2020s* (New York: Palgrave Macmillan, 2023), pp. 121–145.

Weldes, Jutta. "Constructing National Interests," *European Journal of International Relations* 2, no. 3 (1996), pp. 275–318.

Wong, Chun Han. *Party of One: The Rise of Xi Jinping and China's Superpower Future* (New York: Avid Reader Press/Simon & Schuster, 2023).

Xin Qiang. "Beyond Power Politics," *Journal of Contemporary China* 19, no. 65 (2010), pp. 525–539.

———. *Mainland China's Taiwan Policy: From Peaceful Development to Selective Engagement* (New York: Routledge, 2022).

Zhao, Suisheng. "Chinese Nationalism and Beijing's Taiwan Policy: A China Threat?" *Issues & Studies* 36, no. 1 (2000), pp. 76–99.

CHAPTER NINE

Beijing's Military Power and East Asian-Pacific Hot Spots

Xiaobing Li

UNIVERSITY OF CENTRAL OKLAHOMA

Abstract: *Xi has continued military modernization and carried on a pro-active defense strategy in the Taiwan Strait and South China Sea. As Asia's largest air force, the PLAAF has over 2,250 combat aircraft, including 1,800 fighters, strategic bombers, tactical bombers, multi-mission tactical and attack aircraft. The Air Force continues to promote the "leap-over" approach for aviation technological improvement. By 2020, the PLAN had 240,000 naval officers and sailors with an overall battle force of 350 surface ships and submarines—the USN had 293 warships at that time. The Chinese Navy also had 15,000 marines and 26,000 naval aviation personnel with 690 aircraft. Its tonnage totaled 1.82 million tons in 2019 as the second largest navy in the world, only after the US Navy. It continued its expansion into the 2020s, commissioning new warships and constructing more naval facilities. The rapid development of the PLA's air, naval, and strategic forces enabled Beijing to reposition China as the Asia-Pacific regional epicenter, despite experiencing unprecedented demands, facing new challenges, and creating new problems.*

Keywords*:* East China Sea; Military strategy; People's Liberation Army (PLA); PLA Air Force; PLA Navy; South China Sea; Strategic force; Taiwan Strait

2012–2022 became one of the most important decades in the modernization of the People's Liberation Army (PLA, China's armed forces, including army, navy, air force, and strategic force). After taking office as PLA's commander in chief in 2012, Xi Jinping carried on an active defense strategy, enhanced the party's control of the military, continued close military relations with Russia, and promoted the "leap-over" approach for PLA technological improvement. In April 2013, Beijing announced in its annual *Defense White Paper* that it is a strategic task of China's modernization drive as well as a strong guarantee for China's development to build a strong national defense and powerful armed forces, which are commensurate with China's international standing and meet the needs of its security and development interests. China's armed forces must meet the new requirement of

China's national development and security strategy.[1] Xi repositioned China as the Asia-Pacific regional epicenter, despite experiencing unprecedented demands.

This chapter provides a brief historical survey of the PLA's modernization and operations during the first two terms of Xi Jinping's tenure from 2012–2022. It focuses on changes, development, and problems in the PLA's evolution of its air, naval, and strategic forces. This work also explains how China used its new military power to challenge U.S. East Asian-Pacific strategy around Taiwan and the disputed islands in the East and South China Seas, and this kind of behavior remains evident today. The chapter connects China's new military power to U.S.-China relations and characterizes the PLA not only by what they have, but also by who they are and what they can do. The goals of China's military modernization and Beijing's approach to warfare are very important for a better understanding of today's PLA.

Xi's War Strategy, Military Technology, and Russia Policy

Chinese military leaders have new security concerns that are different from the Western specialists' argument that China feels safer than ever before. My findings show that some PLA officers believe they live in a dangerous world in the twenty-first century with many uncertainties and potential challenges to China's security.[2] Their concerns are confirmed by Beijing's high command in the *White Paper: China's National Defense*, which made it clear that the country is facing "unprecedented" challenges because "new security threats keep emerging."[3] Their justification and calculation seem reasonable and logical in terms of the on-going globalization.

Chinese leaders today face some familiar international and domestic issues, which prioritized their security concerns, national defense, economic development, and domestic control in the 1950s. Although the international environment dramatically changed after the end of the Cold War, the PRC apparently replaced the former Soviet Union as the primary challenge to the US and the post-Cold War world. Of course, China is nothing like it was in 1950, but the CCP's dominant leadership, continuing insecurity, and Xi Jinping's call for the "fighting spirit" against the United States carry on the party's doctrine and Mao Zedong's legacy as one of the few Communist survivors as well as a "beneficial participant" in the Cold War.

[1] Information Bureau, PRC State Council, 2013.

[2] Among the interviews with the PLA officers by the author are Major Sun Lizhou, Second Department of the PLA General Staff, Beijing; the deputy commander, Jilin Provincial Command, Changchun, Jilin; and Major General Guan Zhichao (retired), at the PLA Political Academy, Nanjing.

[3] Information Bureau, PRC State Council. "The Security Situation," in *White Papers of China's National Defense in 2008*.

On October 23, 2020, Xi Jinping called to expedite the PLA's modernization at the Korean War's 70th anniversary in Beijing. He told the country, "Without a strong army, there can be no strong motherland."[4] He believes in the PLA's active defense by challenging the current East Asian-Pacific security system under the US leadership. During Mao Zedong's era, the PLA adopted the active defense strategy by challenging the Cold War international system, in which two superpowers dominated global affairs. First, the PLA fought the American armed forces in Korea in 1950–1953, and then fought the Soviet Union along their borders in 1969–1971. Since Mao's era, the CCP has successfully controlled the PLA by providing resources and technology, managing personnel, and mobilizing social support for the armed forces. The Party Center channels the military elite interests and individual consciousness, prejudice, and conflict of the rank and file through the existing political institution. Since the state has adapted well to economic and social changes and effectively responded to the rising demands and expectations of the PLA, its political institutions may be able to manage some of the discontent or different opinions of the PLA in the near future.[5] These activities are still within the boundaries of the Party Center's preference and control.

Xi Jinping reaffirms Jiang Zemin's post-Cold War doctrine and continues to employ nationalism as an ideology to unite the country and fight for its superpower status, perhaps resulting in one more source of legitimacy for the CCP as the country's ruling party. Xi promoted his global plan "New Silk Road and Economic Belt" to establish a China-centric global system excluding America. Moreover, Xi Jinping conducted a massive reorganization of the PLA, culminating in a highly centralized chain of command under his new leadership. In the most sweeping institutional reform since 1949, Xi abolished all the general departments and regional commands, and instead established fifteen functional departments and five theater commands under the CMC with himself as the chairman. The new reform included accelerated

[4] Reuters, "On War Anniversary."

[5] For example, Major General Zhu Chenghu, Dean at PLA National Defense University, spoke to a group of foreign journalists in July 2005 that China would attack over one hundred American cities with nuclear weapons if the United States interferes in a war between China and Taiwan. US Congress called for the sacking of the Chinese general. The Chinese government, however, did not reject Zhu's speech and a spokesperson from the Ministry of Foreign Affairs said that Zhu's speech was his own personal opinion. This spokesperson declined to comment on whether or not the speech represented the Chinese government's view. Jonathan D. Pollack pointed out that while China becomes more involved in "sub- and pan-regional security affairs," it is "acquiring military capabilities that it believes will ultimately enable a short-warning, high-intensity attack against Taiwan. These include a growing inventory of short-range ballistic missiles, advanced conventionally powered submarines and other naval platforms, longer-range aircraft, and a host of related capabilities." See Wang, "U.S. Congress Calls for Sacking of Chinese General"; Shambaugh, "The Rise of China." 11; Pollack, "The Transformation of the Asian Security Order." 339.

development of army aviation troops, light mechanized units, digitalized units, and special operations forces. The changes gradually made PLA units small, modular and multi-functional to enhance their capabilities for air-ground integrated operations, long-distance maneuvers, rapid assaults, and special operations.

In 2012–2022, the new transformation of the PLA certainly affects such areas as strategy, doctrine, operational concepts, and combat techniques. For example, an important on-going change in the PLA doctrine moves away from the traditional defense principle of "never open fire first" in war. It dismisses the timing issue and instead justifies the war efforts as defensive in nature even though Chinese troops may have to open fire first. The new strategy and transformations require the PLA to build up a combat force to win local wars in conditions of informationization. It requires the PLA to prepare itself for defensive operations under the most difficult and complex circumstances. The US Department of Defense pointed out in 2009, "the pace and scope of China's military transformation have increased in recent years, fueled by acquisition of advanced foreign weapons, continued high rates of investment in its domestic defense and science and technology industries, and far-reaching organizational and doctrinal reforms of the armed forces."[6] The development of a new cold war between the two countries is ever looming, if the latter continues efforts in creating "one world, two systems." History will repeat itself if a complete break in diplomatic relations between the two countries, or a limited hot war in the 2020s, occurs.

The Chinese military has also made some recent technological developments, including new fighter jets, anti-missile systems, missile defense capability, Shenzhou-8, and a series of space shuttle launches. In line with the strategic requirements of mobile operations and multi-dimensional offense and defense, the PLA has reoriented from theater defense to trans-theater mobility. You Ji points out that the PLA has transformed itself "from a tactical homeland defensive force to one that is capable of strategic offensive missions beyond national borders... as a credible fighting force globally."[7] However, the PLA had only limited indigenous technological capabilities in the 2010s. It remained as a "learner" rather than an "innovator" in many areas of aviation, naval, missile, space, and nuclear technology up until the 2020s. Tai Ming Cheung places China in the "lower parts of the Tier 2 category" as one of the "adapters and modifiers" in the global defense industry because China "demonstrates few capacities for designing and producing relatively advanced conventional weapons system."[8]

[6] U.S. Secretary of Defense, *Annual Report to Congress: Military Power of the People's Republic of China, 2009*.

[7] You, *China's Military Transformation*: 144, 227.

[8] Cheung, "Introduction," in *Forging China's Military Might*: 5.

Beijing continued its close military relations with Moscow. Xi Jinping made eight trips to Moscow between 2012 and 2020 with the purpose of strengthening strategic support for China. By 2014, the two nations announced a new era of military collaboration as part of an enhanced strategic partnership. In a long-term view, the PLA's investment in Soviet technology and advisory assistance between 1950–1960 paid significant dividends during the PLA's modernization in the 1980s–2000s. The partnership between the PRC and Russian Federation air forces continues to grow through collaborative engagement launched in the 2010s. This raises serious questions over the future of American security, and whether the United States has anything to fear from a potential military superpower in Communist China. The latest Chinese purchase included Su-35 fighters, accounting for over $1 billion annually from 2012 to 2017. In May 2015, the Chinese and Russian forces conducted a joint air/naval exercise, code-named *Joint Sea 2015*, in the Mediterranean Sea. In August, a larger scale operation, *Joint Sea II*, was held in international waters, about 250 miles from Japan, and involved 22 warships and 20 aircraft. Vice Admiral Aleksandr Fedotenkov, Deputy Commander of the Russian Navy, was satisfied with the joint training's results, which "showed that Russian and Chinese forces can effectively fulfill tasks in such a difficult region."[9] In the same year, the PLA conducted three large-scale military exercises in the East China Sea. The third live-fire exercise from August 24–28 involved more than 100 naval vessels, dozens of aircraft, and information warfare units. Chinese warships fired nearly 100 various missiles.[10]

PLA's Way of Air War

In 2014, Xi visited PLAAF HQ and instructed air force generals "to improve air force structure, build up new combat capacity, and make a rapid transition to a balanced air power for both defense and offense."[11] He regards the PLAAF highly not only because he served in the Air Force for six years, but also because he believes in the Air Force's dominant role in future warfare.[12] The face of battle shifted the PLAAF from tactical support for the army and navy to a leading strategic role in winning the next war. *China's Defense White Paper 2018* indicated the PLAAF's

[9] Vice Admiral Fedotenkov's praise was quoted in Gady, "Russian and China Kick off Naval Exercise."

[10] Rajagopalan, "China Conducts Air, Sea Drills in East China Sea." 1–2.

[11] Xi Jinping's speech at the PLAAF headquarters on April 14, 2014, www.chinanews.com/gn/2019/04-14/8808584.shtml [Accessed May 23, 2022].

[12] Xi served as Political Commissar of the Fujian First Air Defense Division (reserve), PLA Air Force, from 1996–2002, while he was the lieutenant governor and governor of Fujian province.

mission and tasks transitioned from territorial air defense to "offensive and defensive operations."[13] The Chinese Air Force's war preparation is designed for offense as building an offensive air force is faster and cheaper than building a defensive one, in terms of combat effectiveness, for a large country. Moreover, an offensive force has greater deterrence power that compensates for vulnerabilities in China's overall national defense. Ye Zhan states that PLAAF offensive doctrine includes long-range pre-emptive operations in the oceanic direction for air control, air strike, and air defense.[14] It should play a key role in joint amphibious landings, coastal blockade, joint firepower strike, island defense, airborne, and nuclear counterstrike campaigns. It will also serve as a comprehensive strategic force capable of strategic early warning, air and missile defense, information countermeasures, long-range airpower projection, and comprehensive support.[15]

Former PLAAF commander Xu Qiliang claimed that the Chinese Air Force established a defense/offense balance through its reorganization up to 2020. General Xu became Air Force Commander in 2007, Vice Chairman of the CMC in 2012, and a member of the CCP Politburo in 2013. He was the first air force general in PLA history to achieve top Chinese military leadership. From the 2010s–2020s, Xu Qiliang emphasized China's aerospace power and air force digitalization. As China's top leader next to Xi Jinping, General Xu continued his effort to build a strong air force as he administrated the PLA's daily operations, managed China's defense budget, and completed military reorganization from 2016–2020. The PLAAF reorganized its divisions into brigades commanded by the air force bases in the PLA's five theater commands (TCs).[16] Each TC air force (TCAF) has seven to ten fighter brigades; each brigade has three to six fighter groups, totaling 30–50 aircraft. Each flight group (wing or battalion) has one type of six fixed-wing aircraft, including J (*Jian*)-class fighters, JH (*Jianhong*)-class fighter-bombers, H (*Hong*)-class bombers, Q-class ground attack aircraft, Y (*Yun*)-class transport, and JZ (*Jianzi*)-class reconnaissance aircraft.[17] Each flight group has two to three flight squadrons, and each squadron has three to five aircraft.

As Asia's largest air force, the PLAAF has over 2,250 combat aircraft, including 1,800 fighters, strategic bombers, tactical bombers, multi-mission tactical and attack aircraft. Among the PLAAF's 1,100 fourth-generation fighters are the J-10C, J-11B, and J-16 (comparable to the US F-16/F-18), armed with the latest air-to-air missiles

[13] China's *Defense White Paper* quoted in Office of the US Secretary of Defense, *Annual Report to Congress: Military and Security Developments involving the People's Republic of China, 2021*, 55.

[14] Ye, *Lun xinxi zhan* [*On Informatized Operations*]: 238.

[15] Information Bureau, PRC State Council, *China's Military Strategy*, May 2015.

[16] Mulvaney, *PLA Aerospace Power:* 17–18.

[17] U.S. Secretary of Defense, *Annual Report to Congress: Military and Security Developments involving the People's Republic of China, 2021*, 56.

(AAMs). During the 2019 military parade, the Chinese Air Force demonstrated its fifth-generation J-20 fighters. Thereafter, it received more than 150 J-20s, which have bolstered Chinese air-to-air capabilities for the J-11A and J-11B with high maneuverability, stealth characteristics, and an internal weapons bay.

As a J-10 fighter pilot himself for 20 years, Air Force commander Chang Dingqiu in 2017 deployed enough strike fighters and bombers to the frontline bases to mount a credible first strike. These bases are used to serve as the takeoff point for offensive operations against the enemy's airplanes and air defense sites. It was a shift from traditional PLAAF deployment as Kenneth Allen and others described it in a "front light, rear heavy" formation.[18] Lawrence "Sid" Trevethan points out, the Chinese also reorganized other types of units into a brigade structure, including unmanned aerial vehicles (UAV), flight testing and training, airborne forces, and transport fleets.[19]

Currently, the PLAAF has more than 450 bombers, including the H-6N as its first nuclear-capable, air-to-air refuellable bomber and as the airborne leg of China's nuclear triad. As of 2020, the PLAAF has operationally fielded the H-6N bombers, providing China's nuclear platform with an air component. In recent years, the PLAAF has also fielded greater numbers of the H-6K, a modernized H-6 bomber that integrates standoff weapons, features the PLAAF's long-range precision strike capabilities, and can target ranges in the Second Island Chain from home airfields on the mainland and increase PLA anti-access/area-denial (A2/AD) capabilities.[20] The Chinese Air Force has more than 250 JH-7A fighter-bombers in service. Meanwhile, China is developing a new generation of H-20 bombers with a long range of at least 8,500 km and a 10-ton payload for both conventional and nuclear bombs. The Chinese Air Force also has 400 transport planes and 150 special mission aircraft.

The Chinese Air Force's missile defense is composed of domestically produced CSA-9 (HQ-9) and HQ (*Hongqi*)-9b battalions. The PLAAF is developing its indigenous CH-AB-X-02, or HQ-19, with ballistic missile defense (BMD) capability. In 2019, China publicly debuted its new Y-9G and Y-9DZ communications jamming/electronic countermeasures aircraft (known as the GX-11). The Chinese aviation industry continues to advance with deliveries of more than forty domestic Y-20A and Y-20B large transport aircraft and completion of the world's largest seaplane, the AG-600. In November 2018, the PLAAF displayed its largest suite ever of UAV aircraft. China has armed and capable reconnaissance UAVs like the *Yunying*, CH (*Caihong*)-4 and CH-5, and *Yilong* (or *Wing Loong*) series of aircraft. 2020 was the PLA Airborne

[18] Allen, Krumel, and Pollack, *China's Air Force Enters the 21st Century*.

[19] Trevethan, *"Brigadization" of the PLA Air Force*: 2, 7.

[20] U.S. Secretary of Defense, *Annual Report to Congress: Military and Security Developments involving the People's Republic of China, 2021*, 56.

Force's 70th anniversary. Its Airborne Corps has six airborne brigades equipped with combat vehicles for more mobility and better ability to engage armored forces in the attack.[21] The Air Force is expanding in all respects except fixed wing transport, which is stable. Moreover, *Shenzhou* 14 launched in the summer of 2022 sent three more astronauts to space. The *Cheng'e* moon landings and the *Tiangong* space station have been successful experiments. The *Beidou* space system is capable of military intelligence gathering and real-time communication. The recent attack on a satellite proves Chinese precision missile strike on defenseless satellites in space and indicates Chinese strategic thinking of a space offense as the next IT war. They become a key component of the PLAAF's area denial to reduce and undermine US military superiority and space dominance.

The PLAAF continues to promote the "leap-over" approach for aviation technological improvement. In line with the strategic requirements of mobile operations and multi-dimensional offense and defense, the PLAAF has reoriented from theater defense to trans-theater mobility. Lu Xiaoping argues, the introduction of the new J-10 fighter jet in 2006 marked a "milestone in the development of both China's aviation industry and the PLAAF weaponry and equipment."[22] China's Military-Civil Fusion (MCF) policy secured adequate financial resources and provided the PLAAF a rapidly rising budget for air power exploration. Civil-military integration cultivated intellectual expertise and promoted aviation science and technology industries. The Chinese Air Force recently made technological developments that included new fighter jets, anti-missile systems, missile defense capability, and a series of space shuttle launches.

In November 2016, the PLAAF conducted another large-scale air exercise in the ADIZ, involving H-6K heavy bombers, Su-30 fighters, and air tankers. The drill included reconnaissance and early warning, attacks on air and sea surface targets, and in-flight refueling to test the PLAAF fighting capacity on the high seas. The PLAAF used three Y-20 large transit airplanes to transport Chinese troops and airlift heavy equipment to Russia for the *Kavkaz 2020* joint military exercise. Pilot Chen Liu flew the J-10C and J-16 before becoming a J-20 pilot in 2018 for the Western TCAF. His wing employs informatized simulation training to shorten air combat power generation cycles. The Chinese transitioned from their traditional combat focus on high-altitude dogfighting for territorial defense. Chen Liu and other pilots were trained to "fight and win" through beyond-the-horizon air engagement, ground strikes, and air assaults against maritime targets. Because of their excellent realistic combat training record, fifteen J-20 fighters from his wing participated in Beijing's military parade on July 1, 2021, celebrating the CCP's 100th birthday.[23]

[21] Cheng, "Assessing Threats to US Vital Interests: China."

[22] Lu, *The PLA Air Force*: 114.

[23] Xinhuashe [Xinhua News Agency], "Youth Diary from the Blue Sky: J-20 Pilot Chen Liu."

Maritime Interests and New Naval Power

The analysis explored the PLAN's continuing re-organization, modernization, professionalization, and digitalization, which started in the late 20th century and define the PLAN's characteristics in the 21st century. After Deng Xiaoping's retirement, Jiang Zemin continued military reform in favor of the Navy as the commander in chief of the PLA from 1990–2002. As he shifted the Party's political goals, Jiang faced new challenges such as Taiwan and disputed islands in the East and South China Seas. Jiang Zemin supported Admiral Liu Huaqing's perception of China's sea power, maritime interests, and oceanic sovereignty. Admiral Liu Huaqing became the CMC's vice chairman in 1990, and a Politburo Standing Committee member in 1992. The PLAN received the lion's share of Jiang's new defense budget as he concurred with Admiral Liu's focus on China's naval development. Jiang Zemin told PLA leaders, "We must prioritize the naval construction."[24] The PLA moved away from traditional ground war preparation, and focused on new naval warfare. He added more than twenty surface warships to the naval force with upgraded missile firepower and control systems and six submarines, including three nuclear ballistic missile submarines.[25] The newly designed destroyers had electronic combat capabilities with *HQ-9* missiles (comparable to US *Patriot* missiles), known as the "Chinese Shield."[26] All the new warships and submarines were blue water capable.[27] In the 1990s, the PLAN sent out second-generation destroyers to visit four countries in the Americas.

In the later 2000s, when China had the second largest economy in the world, the country became more dependent on overseas trade. Hu Jintao, Jiang's successor from 2002–2012, deliberately maintained successful naval reforms. Yet from their inception, the PLAN's continuously adaptive reforms made its modernization dependent upon economic success and possibly forever trailing behind Western armed forces. From 2002–2012, Hu Jintao nurtured the PLAN's relationship by supporting a growing military professionalism with an emphasis on educational credentials and a merit-based system of officer promotion. According to Hu and the new high command, the Navy needed a "leap-over" transition from electronic means to digital capabilities. In 2010, China became the largest shipbuilder in the world after its total building tonnage exceeded the long-time leader South Korea. Chinese news agency *Xinhua News* reported, "China built ships with a total deadweight capacity of 65.5 million tons, accounting for 43 percent of the deadweight

24 Chen, Yuan and Si, "Ride the Spring Wind and Waves: 300.

25 Liu, *Liu Huaqing huiyilu* [*Memoir of Liu Huaqing*]: 477.

26 Gao, *The PLA Navy:* 107.

27 Li, *Haishang changcheng:* 55.

capacity of ships built in the world."[28] The PLAN was ready to improve its logistical support system for long-time maritime missions by providing a better fleet train. The *China's National Defense White Paper in 2010* indicated the accelerated construction of "large support vessels."[29] By 2010, the PLAN totaled 300,000 personnel and more than 600 warships, including an aircraft carrier and nuclear submarines. The Chinese navy has an air arm of 430 warplanes and 35,000 personnel, and commands China's 12,000-strong Marine Corps. You Ji examines the PLAN's transformation in the 2000s–2010s when it was "extending its operations from coastal defense to far-seas power projection."[30] Cole believes that the Chinese have "the idea that a great country should have a great Navy." He links Chinese naval efforts to "the nation's economic development" and to "dependence on overseas trade," which have been principally overlooked by other works in the field. He concludes that Chinese maritime strategy attempts to "achieve near-term national security objective and long-term regional maritime dominance."[31]

In 2008, PLAN Commander Wu Shengli ordered the South Sea Fleet to prepare for participation in international anti-piracy operations off the coast of Somalia to protect Chinese commercial shipping. From December 2008 to February 2011, the PLAN sent ten group formations to the Gulf of Aden and African coast against the pirates, including twenty-five warships, eighteen airplanes and helicopters, totaling 8,400 sailors, marines, and naval special force. They escorted 4,411 Chinese and international commercial ships and rescued fifty-one cargo ships. The special force troops launched twenty-two rescue operations on thirty-three commercial ships, and successfully rescued Chinese and foreign sailors without any casualties. It was the first time the Chinese Navy conducted joint operations to defend national strategic interests in the far seas. It was also the first time for the PLAN to continue its trans-oceanic military missions for such a long period. On November 30, 2011, the spokesman for China's Defense Ministry announced, "China will continue to dispatch naval convoy formations to the waters of the Gulf of Aden and Somalia for escort work and to further carry out international convoy cooperation."[32] On February 23–24, 2012, the PLAN hosted the first International Symposium on Counter-Piracy and Escort Operations at the PLA Naval Command College in Nanjing. More than five hundred naval officers attended the international symposium, including eighty-four naval representatives from international organizations such as the European Union, NATO, and Baltic and International Maritime Conference. More

[28] Wang, "China Rises to Top in Ranks of Ship Makers."

[29] Information Bureau, PRC State Council, *China's National Defense in 2010*.

[30] You, *China's Military Transformation*, 181.

[31] Cole, *The Great Wall at Sea:* xix, 187, 190.

[32] Chinese Defense Ministry's spokesman's announcement quoted in Gao, *The PLA Navy*, 148.

than twenty foreign navies sent their representatives to the symposium, including the United States, United Kingdom, France, Germany, and Russia.

Xi Jinping inherited PLA's traditional naval doctrines, drew on its Cold War strategic concepts, but modified China's maritime policy. Among the factors influential in China's maritime strategy are national security concerns, international relations, economic resources, and political and social conditions. The shift in approach to war from a land conflict to naval warfare reflects current security concerns, evolving strategic thoughts, and emphasis on naval combat readiness.

In August 2013, CMC chairman Xi Jinping visited the aircraft carrier *Liaoning*, commenting that China should build an even stronger naval force.[33] In November, China began construction of its second aircraft carrier. After Wu Shengli retired, Shen Jinlong became the PLAN Commander from 2017–2021. Admiral Shen made it clear that the PLAN became more prominent after the turn of the century due to a change in China's economic growth, international status, new security concerns, and global strategic priorities. China is developing a blue water navy. On April 26, 2017, the PLAN launched its new aircraft carrier *Shandong*, *Type-002*, at the Dalian shipyard. As a modified version of the *Liaoning* (Russian *Kuznetsov*) design, it uses a ski-jump takeoff method for its J-15 fighters. Later that year, Admiral Jiang Weilie, Commander of PLAN South Sea Fleet, had an interview after his fleet's sixteen-day exercise in the Western Pacific and through the first chain of islands. The PLAN admirals said that the purpose of the exercise was to test long distance operations, anti-missile capabilities, and anti-submarine attacks as well as coordination among battleships and fighter jets. They treated the exercise as a real war.[34]

To match China's economic superpower status, the Chinese Navy acquired more ships, improved its technology, and conducted frequent naval exercises. By 2020, the PLAN had 240,000 naval officers and sailors with an overall battle force of 350 surface ships and submarines—the USN had 293 warships at that time. The Chinese Navy also had 15,000 marines and 26,000 naval aviation personnel with 690 aircraft. Its tonnage totaled 1.82 million tons in 2019 as the second largest navy in the world, only after the US Navy. It continued its expansion into the 2020s, commissioning new warships and constructing more naval facilities. Moreover, for the PLA Navy's next class of aircraft carriers and as a future naval fighter for export, China developed the smaller J-31 fighter. Naval aviation is developing new carrier born AEW (air-born early warning) aircraft. As the second largest navy in the world in terms of tonnage, the Chinese Navy has a strength of 240,000 personnel, including 15,000 marines, with an overall battle force of 350 surface

[33] Huang and Ng, "Xi Jinping Sends Signal." 1–3.

[34] General Jiang Weilie, quoted interview with a reporter on April 9, 2013, PRC Defense Ministry's website, www.mod.gov.cn [Accessed December 10, 2021].

ships and submarines. The Navy Air Force has 26,000 naval aviation personnel with 690 aircraft.

The PLA Navy expanded its amphibious assault capabilities by building more landing ships, including amphibious transport docks.[35] Among its most publicized developments is a growing Chinese carrier fleet. The Chinese Navy has also expanded its ballistic missile submarine fleet, including *Type 094 Jin*-class SSBNs and long-range *JL-2 SLBM*.[36] Currently, many American and Japanese naval strategists predict that there will be a naval clash, sooner or later, between their navies or air forces and the PLAN or PLAAF, both of which have become more and more aggressive after acquiring Russian military technology.[37]

Strategic Force and Space War

Today, China's strategic force, the PLA Rocket Forces (PLARF, reorganized from SAC in 2015), totaling 100,000 troops, controls 320 nuclear warheads. The PLA has the largest land-based missile arsenal in the world. It includes 85–100 active inter-continental ballistic missiles (ICBM), mobile nuclear delivery systems with a range of more than 13,000 kilometers and can reach most locations within the continental United States (CSS-4). PLARF also has 200–300 medium-range ballistic missiles (MRBM), 300–400 ground-launched cruise missiles, and 1,200 armed short-range ballistic missiles (SRBM). Finkelstein warns, "For these and many other reasons, we can never discount or ignore this situation. It casts a large shadow over the entire region… It always possesses high potential for major destruction and disruption."[38] What has not been clear is China's relative benign nuclear doctrine. Unfortunately, no official Chinese documents confirm its doctrine; much about it was inferred from the very beginning. Mao pledged that China and its people were not afraid of nuclear weapons; and neither was China afraid to fight a nuclear war to defend itself after nuclear weapons became available. China's nuclear weapons remained for self-defense purposes. In 1964, China adopted a no-first-use (NFU) principle, namely, it would not use nuclear weapons first under any circumstances.[39] China

[35] U.S. Defense Intelligence Agency, *China Military Power: Modernizing a Force to Fight and Win:* 70.

[36] Cheng, "Assessing Threats to US Vital Interests: China."

[37] The author's research paper presented at the conference, "Large-scale Amphibious Warfare in Chinese Military Strategy," organized by China Maritime Studies Institute, US Naval War College, May 4–6, 2021.

[38] Finkelstein, "Three Key Issues Affecting Security," 113.

[39] *The White Papers of China's National Defense in 1998* said, "From the first day it possessed nuclear weapons, China has solemnly declared its determination not to be the first to use such weapons at any time and in any circumstances, and later undertook unconditionally not to use or

also supported the "nuclear disarmament, the 'Fissile Material Cut-off Treaty' (FMCT), security assurance to non-nuclear-weapon states, and prevention of an arms race in outer space."[40] As Shambaugh points out, however, "China has consistently taken the 'high ground' on global nuclear disarmament but has itself been unwilling to enter into negotiations to reduce its own stockpiles until the other declared nuclear powers reduce their inventories to China's level first."[41] Alastair I. Johnston indicates some changes in China's nuclear doctrine from minimum deterrence toward limited deterrence (*youxian weishe*).[42]

Since the 2000s, China has focused on the development of cyber warfare (or informationization warfare) as a major military task. According to Hu Jintao, the PLA should make a "leap-over" transition from a conventional army to an army equipped with digital facilities. General Zhang Zhen, vice chairman of the CMC, anchored in the "leap-over" idea and believed that the next war will take place where China centers its technology.[43] Xi Jinping's high command gave its priority to the new technological development in the armed forces, "to strengthen the capabilities for ... conducting strategic counter-strikes" since cyberspace is offense-dominant.[44] In 2015, China established the PLA Strategic Support Force (SSF) as a cyber force to develop reconnaissance, cyberattacks, electronic warfare, network attack, space warfare, and cyber-defense capabilities. Chinese generals of cyber warfare believe the PLA can respond with a precise counter-attack after the first round of a cyberattack. Thus, the PLA is building up both an effective cyber offense and a strong cyber defense. To reach its goal, General Xiong Guangkai argued that the PLA had to reform virtually all aspects of its gigantic institution in order to prepare for the "new era of information warfare."[45] The PLA considers cyber warfare to be a strategic priority in the twenty-first century, just like nuclear war in the twentieth century. According to the Chinese definition, cyber warfare has broader significance to national defense and international politics beyond the military.

threaten to use nuclear weapons against non-nuclear-weapons states or nuclear-weapon-free zones." In Information Bureau, PRC State Council, *White Papers of the Chinese Government* (Beijing: Foreign Languages Press, 2000), 2: 412.

40 Information Bureau, PRC State Council, *White Paper of China's National Defense in 2004*, 4: 703.

41 Shambaugh, *Modernizing China's Military*: 102.

42 Johnston, "Prospects for Chinese Nuclear Force Modernization."

43 General Zhang Zhen spoke to the participants of the "Joint Warfare Seminar" at the National Defense University in 1997, in *Lun lianhe zhanyi* [*On Joint Warfare*], ed. Yu Shusheng (Beijing: National Defense University Press, 1998), 2. Zhang was the Vice Chairman of the CMC.

44 Information Bureau, PRC State Council, *White Papers of China's National Defense in 2004*: 645.

45 Xiong, "On Revolution in Military Affairs." 182–83.

Chinese leaders remain concerned about international competition and possible conflict in space; the world's major powers have recently mimicked one another in initiating strategic space forces and expedited special weapons research and development. Expanding the battlefield to space could greatly change the international military balance of power. PLAAF is rapidly catching up to Western air forces and has achieved air-space integration according to Commander Chang Dingqiu.[46] As the youngest four-star general of the PLA, Chang believes the best way for the PLAAF to be successful in the next air offense is to integrate air and space operations. In response to the changing ways of air war, PLAAF commanders sought strategic and tactical applications of military force, via platforms operating or passing through air and space, as a key instrument for Chinese security statecraft. Wang Xingwang explains the Chinese view that, without an operational space force, the PLA would not qualify as a major military power. The PLAAF's space program is the core in an informatized war machine and key to the air force's leap-forward aviation strategy.[47] In 2015, the CMC created the PLA's Strategic Support Force (SSF) as a theater level command to centralize the PLA's strategic space, cyber, electronic, and psychological warfare missions and capabilities. At the CCP's 18th Congressional Third Plenum, Xi told party leaders that building a fully-fledged combat space army is part of creating a "new type" of combat force.[48] He made a "three-step" plan for a strong space power in April 2021.

Chinese leaders see a space war less costly in human casualties when compared to a naval or ground war. Additionally, space warfare is also more cost-effective as a *Dongfeng* space missile, costing $200,000, can destroy a low-earth-orbit military satellite worth more than $200 million. Nevertheless, war planners at the PLA's National Defense University project China's space actions as retaliative and preventive when a Chinese satellite is attacked, an imminent attack is signaled, a PLA amphibious landing campaign is interrupted, or a large direct bombardment against China occurs. With a similar doctrine for nuclear warfare, the PLAAF must possess reliable space capabilities for retaliation (or second-strike capabilities) and destruction against a powerful enemy. Moreover, the PLA planners continue designing a "limited space war," rather than an all-out star war, by identifying vulnerable but critical points in enemy space systems. They also argue that China's increased space power can also serve as a means of war deterrence since all powers' space assets are vulnerable.

[46] Xu, "Accelerating Change in Capability-generation Model.". Xu was Commander of the Chinese Air Force from 2007–2012.

[47] Wang, "Developing Space Weapons Is the Key." 83.

[48] Xi's speech quoted in You, *China's Military Transformation*, 154.

Tension in the Taiwan Strait

As his signature project, Xi Jinping's "One-Belt and One-Road" endeavors to connect China with Africa, Asia, Europe, and Latin America by exploring energy sources, constructing modern transportation, and building new channels for trade, finance, and communication. On October 24, 2017, the Belt and Road Initiative was added to the CCP's Constitution at the Nineteenth Party Congress in Beijing. Mao Zedong and Xi Jinping's strategies on active defense diverge as the latter shifted from engaging land wars to preparing for naval warfare. The core of Mao's active defense strategy was to defend China outside its territory in neighboring countries like Korea and Vietnam. Xi has adopted the active defense strategy by projecting the next war into the Taiwan Strait, East China Sea, and South China Sea. From Mao's regime in the 1950s–1970s to Xi's government in the 2010s–2020s, Beijing employed its diplomatic efforts and concentrated military resources to deal with Taiwan. To stop a possible PLA attack on Taiwan, the United States sent its armed forces to the strait in 1954–1955, 1958, and 1995–1996.

Taiwan has emerged as the most dangerous flashpoint in the growing US-China rivalry. Chinese attacks on Taiwan, to protect Beijing's so called "core interests," are part of China's strategy. Taiwan plays an important strategic and political role in the security and stability of the South China Sea sub-region. During Mao's era, Chinese leaders blamed their failure in Taiwan's liberation on the technological gap between the PLAN and USN. After Mao died in 1976, his successor Deng Xiaoping tried to bide time and hide strength while focusing on Chinese naval, air, and strategic forces' modernization from 1978 to 1990.[49] The PLAN developed and manufactured new combat warships, submarines, and large support vessels for oceangoing operations. By the 1980s, they were equipped with new-type guided missile destroyers, fighter-bombers, antisubmarine helicopters, and other high-performance equipment and weapons. The missile carrying warships increased from 20 to 200 by the end of the 1980s. The submarine force grew and increased from 35 to 100 conventional submarines.

With his new military power, Jiang Zemin challenged the Cold War status quo of the Taiwan Strait. In 1995, ROC president Lee Teng-hui (Li Denghui)'s visit to Cornell University in the U.S. tested Jiang's new political agenda and military power. Beijing decided to use force in isolating Taiwan, oppose U.S. government permission for Lee's trip, and stop the further distortion of Sino-American relations. The Second Artillery Corps (SAC) conducted its first round of missile launches from July 21–28 in an area 36 miles north of Taiwan. On July 21, it launched two short-range ballistic *Dongfeng-15* (*M-9*) missiles about 70 nautical miles from Taiwan's coast. On July 22,

[49] Shambaugh, *Modernizing China's Military*, 16–17.

the SAC fired two *DF-15* missiles and hit an area within 40 miles north of Taiwan. Two more missiles were fired on July 24 and hit the same area.[50] Simultaneously, the PLA concentrated large naval and landing forces and launched one military exercise after another, including a joint amphibious landing exercise in the Taiwan Strait.[51] From August 15–25, the East Sea Fleet deployed 59 warships and naval vessels for a large-scale naval attack and amphibious landing exercise. The PLAAF launched 192 sorties and scrambled its fighters and bombers during the naval attack exercise. From October 31 to November 23, the PLA launched another joint amphibious landing campaign on Dongshan Island off the Fujian coast, including 63 warships, landing crafts, and support vessels; and 50 fighters, bombers, and other planes to the joint campaign.[52] By the late fall, Beijing's military aggression caused the most serious international crisis since Beijing and Taipei engaged in military conflict over the islands of Jinmen and Mazu in 1958. It became the Third Taiwan Strait Crisis of 1995–1996.

To deal with a possible PLA invasion of the island, in December 1995, the Clinton administration sent the aircraft carrier *Nimitz* to pass through the Taiwan Strait in response to PLA activities. Between January and February 1996, the PLA concentrated 100,000 troops along the coast across the strait from Taiwan and launched another large-scale landing exercise to send a stronger signal to both Taipei and Washington. Through the winter of 1995–1996, tensions remained heightened in the strait.[53] In early 1996, Taiwan prepared for its first presidential election since 1949 and Lee Teng-hui ran on the GMD ticket.

To discourage the Taiwanese from voting for Lee, Jiang Zemin conducted a new set of missile tests, accompanied by live fire and naval exercises. He used the military to threaten Taiwanese voters. On March 8, 1996, the PLA fired more missiles, three *DF-15* surface-to-surface missiles, just 20 miles off Kaohsiung and about 29 miles off Keelung.[54] On the same day, the United States announced the deployment of the *Independence* carrier battle group to international waters near Taiwan. On March 11, the U.S. deployed the *Nimitz* carrier battle group to the Taiwan area. This was the largest U.S. naval movement in the Asia-Pacific region since the Vietnam War. In response to US naval deployments, China announced more live-fire exercises near Penghu, an ROC-held island group near Taiwan. From March 18–25, the PLA deployed 300 airplanes, guided missile destroyers, and submarines in a joint exercise at Pingtan Island with 150,000 troops, about 70 nautical miles from the

50 Zhang, *Lun lianhe zhanyi* [*On Joint Warfare*], 608.

51 Chen, "The Taiwan Strait Crisis." 131–34.

52 Zhang, *Lun lianhe zhanyi* [*On Joint Warfare*], 610.

53 Perry and Carter, *Preventive Defense:* 92–93.

54 Tyler, *A Great Wall: Six Presidents and China*: 33, 195.

Taiwanese-held islands. The exercise included amphibious landing, paratroopers, and mountain assaults. Meanwhile, several nuclear submarines left their base at Qingdao. Without identifying the Chinese nuclear submarines' locations, the U.S. positioned the *Nimitz* 350 miles away from the strait.[55] Fortunately, the Third Taiwan Strait Crisis did not evolve into a war between China and the United States when Lee Teng-hui was elected as Taiwan's President on March 23, 1996.

Taiwan is located at a critical strategic point on the South China Sea's northern edge and faces the direction where potential invaders must pass, and the defender must hold. Consequently, the chain of islands running north to south along the coast of East Asia, has become not only a forward post line or early warning line, but the northern front line for the safety and security of the South China Sea. Taiwan is a strategic fulcrum to defend or invade the South China Sea region. When the Imperial Japanese Army attacked Southeast Asia in World War II, the invading army used Taiwan as the base for its offensive campaigns. Taiwan guaranteed Japan's military success and strategic control of the South China Sea region, including the Philippines, Vietnam, Hong Kong, Thailand, Malaya, Burma, Timor, East Indies, Borneo, Singapore, and India.[56] Since these countries control both sides of the Strait of Malacca, it becomes critical for any naval powers to provide or prevent a concentration of naval forces in the Pacific or Indian Ocean.

As the most northerly island of the region, Taiwan protects the gateway to the South China Sea. Its loss means the opening of the SCS in the north, allowing the Russian Pacific Fleet, Chinese North Sea Fleets (NSF), and its East Sea Fleet (ESF) to enter the South China Sea, and even the Indian Ocean, prior to the U.S. Seventh Fleet. The safety of America's west coast depends on a U.S. defense perimeter along an island chain in the Western Pacific, and Taiwan is part of it. Its loss means the breaching of the Pacific defense and creating a direct threat to the security of America's west. After WWII, Taiwan also protected Japan's western flank and its sea transportation line, which its economy depended on for international trade through the Cold War. If Taiwan falls into the hands of an adversary, Japan will lose its maritime safety zone and face threats to its national security line in the south. The loss of Taiwan to a hostile force would isolate Australia and New Zealand from Asia and even America.[57]

Although Taiwan is geopolitically disfavored for breaking away from China since the Chinese Civil War (1946–1949), it still holds a geo-positional edge in

[55] William Perry's public statement on March 11, 1996, about the large U.S. naval maneuver near the Taiwan Strait, *American Forces Press Service*, March 11; the U.S. Department of Defense, *News Briefings*, March 12, 14, and 16, 1996.

[56] Li, *The History of Taiwan*:107–108.

[57] Yu, "The Meaning of Taiwan." 9–10.

contending with and containing China, and its potential power influence cannot be underestimated by any means. ROC President Tsai Ing-wen supported Barack Obama's East Asia policy, which highlighted the new Trans-Pacific Partnership (TPP) removing trade barriers between the United States, Taiwan, and several other Pacific Rim countries, and continued the sale of military equipment to Taiwan.[58] In early December 2016, Tsai Ing-wen had an unprecedented telephone call with President-elect Donald Trump. It was the first time that an ROC President had spoken with a US President since January 1979.[59] Tsai tried to depart from the "Southward Policy" under both Lee Teng-hui and Chen Shui-bian governments by focusing on the Pacific Island countries. President Tsai Ing-wen emphasized a "New Southward Policy" with a focus on India and Southeast Asia. In her second term from 2020–2024, Tsai Ing-wen faced new challenges with uncertainty and unstable factors in East Asia. Destabilizing factors in the region first came from the COVID-19 pandemic in 2020 and from China's "zero COVID policy" that produced uncertainties and in-stability. Xi Jinping clarified that China has emerged as a superpower, and that it was to be treated as a global power.

Since the 2000s, China has begun to claim its maritime interests and oceanic sovereignty in both the South and East China Seas. However, with Taiwan in the middle, China finds it difficult to project its sea power over the South China Sea and challenge the U.S. dominance in the region. Taiwan's safety and security fit into U.S. Asian-Pacific policy to deal with China and contain Beijing's aggressive behavior since it is a key link in the "First Island Chain" against China. Taiwan has become the testing ground for US determination to contain the "China threat" in the South China Sea region. A failed defense of Taiwan would undermine the sub-regional countries' trust and confidence in the US commitments and responsibilities. In the late 2010s, the U.S. shifted its policy toward Taiwan from an "ambiguous strategy" to a "clear strategy" by clarifying its commitment to the island's defense.[60]

The PLA has significantly escalated its military activities directed at Taiwan, including air patrols in the Taiwan Strait, joint exercises to simulate landing campaign, and anti-ship missile exercises aimed largely at American intervention against possible PLA attacks on Taiwan. In June 2021, the PLA conducted an amphibious landing exercise in waters near Taiwan amid renewed tensions between Beijing and Washington. According to CCTV, "the 72nd Group Army explored the tactics of emergency loading, long-distance transport, beach assaults under complicated sea situations, and the troops' amphibious combat."[61] The PLA Navy

[58] Harris, "Vietnam Arms Embargo."

[59] Heavy, "Taiwan's Tsai: No Major Policy Shifts."

[60] Chen, *US-China Rivalry and Taiwan's Mainland Policy:* 183.

[61] Catapano, "China Conducts Assault Landing Drills."

also expanded its amphibious assault capabilities by building more landing ships, including amphibious transport docks.[62] Among its most publicized development is a growing Chinese carrier fleet with several conventional takeoff/barrier landing carriers.

In August 2022, the PLA launched its largest military exercise ever by sending 140 fighters and bombers, deploying 10 destroyers, and firing 12 missiles around Taiwan, after two US congressional delegations visited the ROC.[63] The Western nations were shocked and wondered how the US would respond if Chinese armed forces conducted an amphibious invasion of Taiwan. After consolidating his perpetual power at the CCP's 20th National Congress in October, Xi Jinping emphasized that the CCP "will never promise not to use force" to liberate Taiwan and unify the country.[64] He ensured his party that China's strategy had shifted from defensive to a defensive offense by removing a traditional principle of "never open fire first" in war and now justifying China's future attacks as preventive or retaliatory.

Disputed Islands in the South and East China Seas

The disputed islands in the East China Sea are also possible sources for international discontent and present increasing tension between China and the United States, Japan, and other surrounding countries. China's maritime strategy is influenced by national security concerns, international relations, economic resources, and political and social conditions. Perhaps the most important factor, and the most crucial in the new century, is China's worldview as primarily related to global and regional threats of conflict.

The Belt and Road Initiative (BRI) brought massive trade, transportation, and energy programs, by both sea and land routes, from Chinese coasts to other continents along the ancient Silk Road. As Xi Jinping made his strategic shift, he took the challenge and made new aggressive initiatives in the East and South China Seas. In November 2013, Beijing began using "China's East Sea" (*Zhongguo Donghai*) to define the area and announced the establishment of an Air Defense Identification Zone (ADIZ), which included the disputed Diaoyu/Senkaku Islands.[65] ADIZ requires all international aircraft to file a flight plan and submit radio frequency or transponder information to Chinese authorities before entering the zone. Thereafter, the PLAAF regularly patrolled the zones to strengthen the effective control over the

[62] U.S. Defense Intelligence Agency, *China Military Power:* 70.

[63] Tsao, "Hong Kong Crackdown Sparks."

[64] Wei, "Full Text of Xi Jinping's Speech."

[65] You, *China's Military Transformation*, 10, 72, 77–78.

zone. Shen Jinke, spokesman for the PRC Defense Ministry, said that the PLAAF's routine patrols set out to verify the identities of foreign aircrafts and administer official warnings, and that it should not impact commercial air traffic. He stated that the PLAAF patrols "are purely defensive and consistent with international norms," and that the PLAAF would also conduct routine air drills in the zone for dealing with any emergency situations.[66]

In 2016, the territorial conflict escalated to military confrontation involving naval vessels, coast guard gunboats, and fighters in the East China Sea's disputed areas, promoting more worries from the international community. The East China Sea has become one of the most worrisome flash points in Asia, an important source of insecurity in the Western Pacific, and possibly a point of contention between US against PLA forces in East Asia. In November, the PLAAF conducted another large-scale air exercise in the ADIZ, involving H-6K heavy bombers, Su-30 fighters, and air tankers. The drill included early warning, reconnaissance, attacks on air and sea surface targets, and in-flight refueling to test the PLAAF fighting capacity on the high seas. The Japanese Air Force surpassed a previous, Cold War annual record by scrambling 1,168 fighter jets in 2017 in response to PLAAF aircraft encroachment into Japanese airspace and provoked 851 incidents. Thereafter, China replaced Russia as the major threat to Japanese airspace since the Cold War.

The PLAN developed and manufactured new combat warships, submarines, and large support vessels for oceangoing operations. By the 1980s, they were equipped with new-type guided missile destroyers, fighter-bombers, antisubmarine helicopters, and other high-performance equipment and weapons. The missile carrying warships increased from 20 to 200 by the end of the 1980s. The submarine force increased from 35 to 100 conventional submarines. Meanwhile, the Chinese Navy developed nuclear attack submarines (SSN) and nuclear-powered ballistic missile submarines (SSBN).[67]

In March 1988, the PLAN defeated the Vietnamese Navy and seized several islands in the Battle of the Spratly Islands in the South China Sea. In September 1988, the PLAN's successful underwater launch of a ballistic missile by a nuclear submarine showed that they could provide underwater strategic deterrence and limited nuclear counterattacks. The PLAAF began testing *JH-7* "Flying Leopard" (the *FBC-1* is the export version) in 1988, while adopting the Russian-made *Su-27* fighters.[68] Thus, by the 1990s, the PLA's overall technological level became competitive with other global militaries.

66 *PLA Daily*, "China's Establishment of the Air Defense."

67 Liu, *Liu Huaqing huiyilu* [*Memoir of Liu Huaqing*], 398.

68 Liu, *Liu Huaqing huiyilu* [*Memoir of Liu Huaqing*], 403.

In 2015, the PLAAF began patrolling the South China Sea, including the disputed Paracel and Spratly Islands. The PLA's outposts in the South China Sea extend the Air Force's possible operating areas. Deployments of Chinese warplanes from Spratly Island outposts can extend range and loiter time over the South China Sea and even reach the Indian Ocean. The PLAAF's medium-range H-6K bombers carry up to six precision-guided CJ-20 air-launched cruise missiles (ALCMs) each, giving it the ability to engage US armed forces as far away as Guam and Okinawa. The Southern TCAF was the first to receive the H-6J maritime strike bombers. All the PLAAF's twenty-four Su-35s are assigned to the Southern TCAF. Therefore, confrontation between Chinese and American armed forces in the South China Sea has aroused serious concerns in the international community about security and stability in the Indo-Pacific region. The USAF continues flying military aircrafts through the ADIZ without informing China, defying China's declaration that the region falls into a Chinese airspace defense zone. Public debates and strategic research in America focus on what these events may mean to the United States, and how to best deal with the PLA in case of crisis or even a war in the Pacific. In December 2019, Beijing commissioned its newly manufactured aircraft carrier, *Shandong*, into service at Hainan Island's Yulin Naval Base in the Southern TC; additionally, the PLA successfully established its military base in Djibouti, Africa, to sustain PLAAF regional and global air operations.

In the 2020s, Xi Jinping's Cold War II may include a "strategic triangulation" of China-US-Europe relations, in which Beijing can look for new bargaining chips with Washington. In the coming new cold war, China will deter the US from a full-scale hot war with its nuclear arsenal as well as newly developed cyber and space powers. In case of war with the US, China has prepared a new battleground in Africa as America's next quagmire; though the Biden administration faces the pandemic, climate catastrophes, and racial tensions at home. The survival lessons learned by the CCP helped to re-define the party's strategy and changed its perceptions of the world in numerous ways. Its leaders will act according to their own consistent logic in the political agenda, with their diplomatic experience within the context of Chinese society and the new international environment.

While factors of insecurity and instability remain, China is surrounded by an unfavorable security environment, a constant since the founding of the PRC. Due to all the above challenges, the PLA has an arduous task to safeguard China's national unification, territorial integrity, and development interests. The Chinese armed forces will continue to fulfill its mission by carrying on its tradition and culture while evolving through adaptation and improvement for mechanization and digitalization. Through its foreign war experience, the PLA confronted four key issues: planning, learning, making changes, and political control. Military planning or war strategy has been the most prominent and foremost of PLA operations. The

PLA's planning has received the most attention and become an important part of its culture. Political doctrine garners more attention in all military papers, from Mao Zedong to Xi Jinping, than any other military-related topic.

The Chinese military's new mission is to strengthen its combat readiness and effectiveness and make innovative efforts to protect the national security. According to Chinese experts, the ocean means a great deal to China as it is the international communication waterway and holds strategic resources for the world's sustainable development. China has its own strategic interests from the oceans. Many estimate that at some point, China's major threat will come from its surrounding waters. The second point concerns international competition and possible conflict in space. The world's major countries have recently followed one another in initiating strategic space forces, and expedited special weapons research and development. Expanding the battlefield to space could greatly change the international military balance of power, and create serious challenges for China's national security. The third threat arises from cyberspace, the symbol of the information age and has become an emerging strategic area that threatens a nation's security and development. It impacts the older, conventional forms of battle by emersion, affects, and decisive factors. Other major countries have followed suit and established their own cyber forces, to reinforce their cyber war capability, and compete vigorously for cyberspace development rights, dominant position, and control rights.

2023–2049 is the most important time-period for China's rejuvenation as well as when the PLA will reach three milestones for its modernization. Within 26 years, the PLA will integrate its mechanization, informatization, and intelligentization by 2027; complete the modernization of national defense by 2035; and fully transform the PLA into a "world-class force" by 2049. Due to all the above challenges, the PLA has an arduous task to safeguard China's national unification, territorial integrity, and development interests. The Chinese armed forces will continue to fulfill its mission while evolving through adaptation and improvement for informatization and intelligentization. Through its operational experience in the Taiwan Strait, Vietnam, and the South China Sea, the PLA confronts four key issues: planning, learning, changing, and political control. War planning and aerospace strategy have been the most prominent and foremost of PLA's operations.

Dr. **Xiaobing Li** is professor of history and Don Betz Endowed Chair in International Studies at the University of Central Oklahoma. He is currently the editor of *Chinese Historical Reviews*. He has authored, edited, and co-edited books, including *Sino-American Relations: A New Cold War* (Amsterdam University Press, 2022); *The Dragon in the Jungle: The Chinese Army in the Vietnam War* (Oxford U Press, 2020); *Attack at Chosin: The Chinese Second Offensive in Korea* (U of Oklahoma Press, 2020);

A Century of Student Movements in China: The Mountain Movers, 1919–2019, first co-editor (2020); *Building Ho's Army: Chinese Military Assistance to North Vietnam* (U Press of Kentucky, 2019); *China's War in Korea: Strategic Culture and Geopolitics* (Palgrave Macmillan, 2019); *The History of Taiwan* (Santa Barbara, CA: ABC-CLIO, 2019); *East Asia and the West: An Entangled History* (2019), *Corruption and Anti-corruption in Modern China* (2019), *Power vs. Law: Cities, Courts, and the Communist Party* (2018), *The Cold War in East Asia* (2018), *Urbanization and the Party Survival* (2017), *Modern China: Understanding Modern Nations* (2016), *Ethnic China: Identity, Assimilation, and Resistance* (2015), *China's Battle for Korea* (2014) *Oil: A Cultural and Geographic Encyclopedia of Black Gold* (2014), *Evolution of Power: China's Struggle, Survival, and Success* (2013), *Modern Chinese Legal Reforms* (2013), *China at War* (2012), *Civil Liberties in China* (2011), *Voices from the Vietnam War* (2010), *A History of the Modern Chinese Army* (2007), *Voices from the Korean War* (2004), and *Taiwan in the 21st Century* (2003).

Bibliography

Allen, Kenneth, Glenn Krumel, and Jonathan Pollack. *China's Air Force Enters the 21st Century*. Santa Monica, CA: RAND, 1995.

Catapano, Kevin. "China Conducts Assault Landing Drills as Invasion Attempt Looks Inevitable." *The Western Journal*, June 10, 2021. http://westernjournal.com/china-conducts-assault-landing-drills-invasion-attempt-looks-inevitable/ [Accessed August 25, 2021].

Chen, Dean P. *US-China Rivalry and Taiwan's Mainland Policy: Security, Nationalism and the 1992 Consensus*. London: Palgrave Macmillan, 2017.

Chen, Qimao. "The Taiwan Strait Crisis: Causes, Scenarios, and Solutions." In *Across the Taiwan Strait: Mainland China, Taiwan, and the 1995–1996 Crisis*, ed. Suisheng Zhao. London: Routledge, 1999.

Chen Wanjun, Yuan Huazhi, and Si Yanwen. "Ride the Spring Wind and Waves: Historical Records of President Jiang Zemin's Efforts in the Modernization of the People's Navy." In *Guojia lingxiu yu haijun jiangling* [*Chinese Leaders and the Navy*], eds. Wu Dianqing, Yuan Yong'an, and Zhao Xiaoping. Beijing: Ocean Wave Publishing, 2000.

Cheng, Dean. "Assessing Threats to US Vital Interests: China." 2021. www.heritage.org/2021-index-us-military-strength/assessing-threats-us-vital-interests/china [Accessed August 25, 2021].

Cheung, Tai Ming. *Forging China's Military Might; A New Framework for Assessing Innovation*. Johns Hopkins University Press, 2014.

Cole, Bernard D. *The Great Wall at Sea: China's Navy in the Twenty-first Century*, 2nd ed. Annapolis, MD: Naval Institute Press, 2010.

Finkelstein, David M. "Three Key Issues Affecting Security in the Asia-Pacific Region." In *Asia-Pacific Security: New Issues and New Ideas*, ed. International Military Committee, China Association for Military Science. Beijing: Military Science Press, 2014.

Gady, Franz-Stefan. "Russian and China Kick off Naval Exercise in Sea of Japan." *The Diplomat*, August 24, 2015. http://thediplomat.com/2015/08/Russian-and-china-kick-off-naval-exercise-in-sea-of-japan [Accessed February 22, 2023].

Gao Xiaoxing. *The PLA Navy*. Beijing: China Intercontinental Press, 2012.

Guan Zhichao. Interview by the author at the PLA Political Academy, Nanjing, 2008.

Harris, Gardiner. "Vietnam Arms Embargo to Be Fully Lifted, Obama Says in Hanoi." *New York Times*, May 23, 2016. http://www.nytimes.com/2016/05/24/world/asia/vietnam-us-arms-embargo-obama.html?_r=0 [Accessed August 28, 2022].

Heavy, Susan. "Taiwan's Tsai: No Major Policy Shifts, despite Trump Call," *Reuters*, December 6, 2016. https://www.reuters.com/article/us-usa-trump-china-tsai-idUSKBN13V1T7 [Accessed October 2, 2022].

Huang, C. and Teddy Ng. "Xi Jinping Sends Signal to Neighbors with High-profile Tour of Liaoning Aircraft Carrier." *South Chinese Morning Post*, August 31, 2013.

Information Bureau, PRC State Council. *White Papers of China's National Defense*, 1998. Beijing: Foreign Languages Press.

Information Bureau, PRC State Council. *White Paper of China's National Defense*, 2004. Beijing: Foreign Languages Press.

Information Bureau, PRC State Council. *White Papers of China's National Defense*. 2008. http://English.people.com.cn/90001/90776/90785/6578688.html [Accessed February 20, 2023].

Information Bureau, PRC State Council. *White Papers of China's National Defense*, 2010. http://www.gov.cn/english/official/2011-03/31/content_1835499.htm [Accessed January 12, 2023].

Information Bureau, PRC State Council. *White Papers of China's National Defense*, 2013. http://www.chinadaily.com.cn/language_tips/news/2013-04/17/content_16414985.htm [Accessed November 4, 2020].

Information Bureau, PRC State Council. *White Papers of China's National Defense*, 2015. http://www.chinadaily.com.cn/china/2015-05/26/content_20820628.htm [Accessed April 12, 2022].

Jiang Weilie. Interview by a reporter on April 9. PRC Defense Ministry, 2013. www.mod.gov.cn [Accessed December 10, 2021].

Johnston, Alastair I. "Prospects for Chinese Nuclear Force Modernization: Limited Deterrence versus Multilateral Arms Control." In *China's Military in Transition*, eds. David Shambaugh and Richard H. Yang. New York: Oxford University Press, 1997.

Li Qiong. *Haishang changcheng: zhongguo renmin jiefangjun haijun 60 nian* [*The Great Wall at Sea: 60 Years of the PLA Navy*]. Jilin: Jilin Publishing Group, 2011.

Li, Xiaobing. *The History of Taiwan*. Santa Barbara, CA: ABC-CLIO, 2019.

Li, Xiaobing. "Large-scale Amphibious Warfare in Chinese Military Strategy." A conference paper presented at the China Maritime Studies Institute, US Naval War College, May 4–6, 2021.

Liu Huaqing. *Liu Huaqing huiyilu* [*Memoir of Liu Huaqing*]. Beijing: PLA Press, 2004.

Lu Xiaoping. *The PLA Air Force*. Beijing: China Intercontinental Press, 2012.

Mulvaney, Brendan S. *PLA Aerospace Power: A Primer on Trends in China's Military Air, Space, and Missile Forces*, 2nd ed. Montgomery, AL: China Aerospace Studies Institute, USAF, 2020.

Perry, William and Ashton Carter. *Preventive Defense: A New Security for America*. Washington, DC: Brookings Institute, 1999.

PLA Daily. "China's Establishment of the Air Defense Identification Zone (ADIZ) in the East China Sea, January 22, 2014." http://eng.chinamil.com.cn/view/2014-01 [Accessed September 10, 2022].

Pollack, Jonathan D. "The Transformation of the Asian Security Order: Assessing China's Impact." In *Power Shift: China and Asia's New Dynamics*, ed. Shambaurgh. Berkeley: University of California Press. 2005.

Rajagopalan, M. "China Conducts Air, Sea Drills in East China Sea." *Reuters*, August 27, 2015. http://www.retuers.com/articles/us-china-defense-idUSKCN0QW1EX20150827 [Accessed September 14, 2021].

Reuters. "On War Anniversary, Xi Says China's Interests Won't be Undermined." *South China Morning Post*, October 23, 2020. www.news.yahoo.com/xi-says-china-not-let-030107278.html [Accessed October 27, 2020].

Shambaugh, David. *Modernizing China's Military: Progress, Problems, and Prospects*. Berkeley: University of California Press, 2002.

Shambaugh, David. *Power Shift; China and Asia's New Dynamics*. Berkeley: University of California Press, 2005.

Sun Lizhou. Interview by the author at the Peking University, Beijing, 2005.

Trevethan, Lawrence "Sid". *"Brigadization" of the PLA Air Force*. Montgomery, AL: China Aerospace Studies Institute, USAF, 2020.

Tsao, Nadia. "Hong Kong Crackdown Sparks 'Fundamental Change' in US Taiwan Policy: Trump Adviser," *Radio Free Asia*, November 13, 2020. www.rfa.org/english/news/china/crackdown-11132020095826.html [Accessed January 10, 2023].

Tyler, Patric. *A Great Wall: Six Presidents and China.* New York: Public Affairs, 1999.

U.S. Defense Intelligence Agency. *China Military Power: Modernizing a Force to Fight and Win*. Washington, DC: U.S. Government Printing Office, 2019.

U.S. Secretary of Defense. *Annual Report to Congress: Military Power of the People's Republic of China.* 2009. http://www.defenselink.mil/pubs/pdfs/China_Military_Report_09.pdf [Accessed August 2, 2022].

U.S. Secretary of Defense. *Annual Report to Congress: Military and Security Developments involving the People's Republic of China*, 2021. http://www.defense.gov/News/Releases/Release/Article/2831819/dod-release-2021-report-on-military-and-security-developments-involving-the-pe/ [Accessed May 29, 2022].

Wang Guangqun. "China Rises to Top in Ranks of Ship Makers." Xinhua News Agency, May 9, 2011. http://news.xinhuanet.com/english2010/china/2011-05/09/c_13865547.htm [Accessed November 5, 2022].

Wang Xingwang. "Developing Space Weapons Is the Key to the PLA's Leap Strategy of Weapons Equipment." *Guofang daxue xuebao* [*Journal of the PLA National Defense University*]. No. 10, 2002.

Wang Zheng. "U.S. Congress Calls for Sacking of Chinese General." *The Epoch Times*, 2005. http://www.theepochtimes.com/news/5-7-25/30545.html [Accessed June 10, 2019].

Xi Jinping. Speech at the PLAAF headquarters on April 14, 2014. www.chinanews.com/gn/2019/04-14/8808584.shtml [Accessed May 23, 2022].

Xinhuashe [Xinhua News Agency]. "Youth Diary from the Blue Sky: J-20 Pilot Chen Liu." *Zhongguo kongjun wang* [*Chinese Air Force website*], May 23, 2022. www.81.cn/kj/2022-05-23/content_10156891.htm [Accessed June 1, 2022].

Xiong Guangkai. "On Revolution in Military Affairs." In *Guoji zhanlue yu xinjunshi biange* [*International Strategy and Revolution in Military Affairs*], ed. Xiong. Beijing: Tsinghua University Press, 2003.

Xu Qiliang. "Accelerating Change in Capability-generation Model." *Kongjun bao* [*Air Force Daily*], February 27, 2012.

Ye Zhan. *Lun xinxi zhan* [*On Informatized Operations*]. Beijing: Military Science Press, 2007

You Ji. *China's Military Transformation*. Cambridge, UK: Polity, 2016.

Yu, Miles. "The Meaning of Taiwan." *Taipei Times*, January 10, 2022. www.taipeitimes.com/News/editorials/archives/2022/01/10/2003771062 [Accessed December 13, 2022].

Yu Shusheng, ed. *Lun lianhe zhanyi* [*On Joint Warfare*]. Beijing: National Defense University Press, 1998.

CHAPTER TEN

Towards a More Joint Strategy: Assessing Chinese Military Reforms and Militia Reconstruction

Lei Duan

Sam Houston State University

Abstract: *Since Xi Jinping came to power in 2012, China's armed forces have undergone unprecedented reforms in their scale and scope of organizational and strategic changes. With the goal of modernizing and strengthening the Chinese military, Xi has adopted the most comprehensive reforms with a focus on efficiency, technological innovation, and joint operations. China has also strengthened its militia organization and training works. The maritime militia has been integrated closely with the regular navy and has played an increasing role in supporting China's strategies. This chapter explores these reforms, particularly the collaboration between the People's Liberation Army and the maritime militia, illustrating the government's strategy of combining military and paramilitary forces to realize China's ambitions.*

Keywords: Xi Jinping; Military reform; Joint operation; Militia reconstruction

Introduction

In early November 2014, the Military Political Work Conference convened in Gutian, a small county situated in the northeastern region of Fujian province. In front of 420 generals and senior military officials, the Chairman of the Central Military Commission, Xi Jinping articulated a pivotal discourse on the military-political work. Emphasizing the unwavering dominion of the Chinese Communist Party (CCP) over the military apparatus, he reaffirmed a historic sentiment, "The Party commands the Gun." This proclamation resonated with Mao Zedong's fundamental principles aimed at bolstering the ideological and political underpinnings of the nation's armed forces.[1] While Xi presented a generally favorable evaluation of the contemporary advancements in the military sphere, he candidly highlighted

1 "New Gutian Meeting: Another Milestone."

many challenges within the military. These encompassed the problems in "ideals and beliefs, principle of party spirit, revolutionary spirit, and organizational discipline."[2] In advocating for a resolution, Xi underscored the significance of political endeavors within army development. He contended, "[W]e must profoundly recognize the important role of political work in the army building and pass on to the following generations all the great traditions which were forged in blood by our ancestors."[3]

The choice of Gutian as the location for the conference was steeped in historical resonance. The town epitomizes the CCP's foundational principles. The 1929 Gutian Congress, convened at the same locale, was crucial in establishing the principle of party control over the military, a doctrine that has since been central to the CCP's ideological framework.[4] Xi Jinping aimed to connect with this historical legacy and reinforce the Party's longstanding commitment to military supremacy. Xi's admonition to his military was by no means impulsive nor arbitrary. The CCP history resolution passed at the Sixth Plenary Session of the 19th Central Committee admitted that "[F]or a period of time, the party's leadership over the military was obviously lacking. If this problem had not been completely solved, it would not only have diminished the military's combat capacity but also undermined the key political principle that the party commands the gun."[5]

Since his ascendancy to the role of General Secretary of the CCP and chairman of the Central Military Commission in 2012, Xi Jinping has been the promoter of a transformative era in China's military history. Under his leadership, the period of his first ten years has been marked by an unprecedented drive to reform the People's Liberation Army (PLA), aligning it with military powerhouses in capability and sophistication. This transformation has entailed ambitious and comprehensive reforms, ranging from organizational restructuring to embracing modern military technology and executing innovative joint military operations. At the core of these reforms is a revival of the military principles that have been foundational to the CCP, with a particular emphasis on loyalty within the ranks. This focus is deeply rooted in the historical significance of the town of Gutian, the site of the seminal 1929 Gutian Congress, where Mao Zedong emphasized the necessity of a politically loyal and ideologically aligned military for CCP's survival. Xi Jinping's rigorous Anti-Corruption Campaign, which has led to investigations of high-ranking officers including Xu Caihou and Guo Boxiong, reflected his determination. In this meeting,

2 "All-Army Political Work Conference Held in Gutian."
3 "Xi stresses CPC's Absolute Leadership Over Army."
4 Ven Hans, "New States of War," 343.
5 "Full Text: Resolution of the CPC Central Committee."

Xi "called for serious reflection on the discipline and law violations" by Xu Caihou.[6] By reinforcing loyalty as a fundamental value, Xi aimed to ensure an advancement of military modernization, minimizing internal discord. The pursuit of the "Chinese Dream," a concept developed and championed by Xi, underscores the role of a robust and competent military in realizing national rejuvenation. This plan has materialized in the form of enhanced integration across various military branches. Strategic initiatives to foster cooperation between the Army, Navy, Air Force, the crucial Rocket Force, and even the militia forces are invaluable in this respect aiming to elevate combat and strategic effectiveness.

China's commitment to its military reform is evident despite economic challenges. A consistent increase in defense spending over recent years is a testament to this dedication, providing the financial support for the expansive military agenda. In the 2023 fiscal year, China's defense budget experienced a significant increase, indicative of its growing focus on military enhancement. The budget, set at $224.79 billion, marked a 7.2 percent increase from the previous year, signaling an escalated commitment to military expansion.[7] A major consequence of this increased investment is the remarkable growth of China's naval power, now recognized as the largest fleet globally in terms of size.[8]

This expansion of military capabilities is paralleled by an increase in China's territorial assertiveness, notably beyond its immediate borders. This is particularly evident in its approaches to some contentious areas such as the South China Sea and the East China Sea. Within this context, the transformation of China's maritime militia, often referred to as the "Fishing Militia," has drawn significant attention.[9] Various analyses highlight the dual nature of this militia, functioning in both civilian and military capacities. As an integral component of China's armed forces, the maritime militia has effectively integrated with the regular navy. This strategic alignment is a clear indicator of China's shift towards a combined defensive-offensive maritime strategy. The maritime militia has served as a key auxiliary force, through which China is asserting its influence in regional power dynamics.

This chapter examines the depths of China's military reforms by posing several critical questions that aim to uncover the complexities of these transformations. The first question seeks to understand the historical motivations driving Xi Jinping's focus on military reform. This section will discuss how the historical context has shaped Xi's perspectives and policies regarding military reform initiatives. The second question discusses the progression of these reforms, asking for a detailed

6 "Xi Urges Serious Reflection On Xu Caihou's Case."

7 Jash, "China's 2023 Defense Spending: Figures, Intentions and Concerns."

8 "PLA Advances in Arms, Ability over Past Decade"; Office of the Secretary of Defense, 44.

9 Johnson and De Luce, "Fishing Disputes Could Spark a South China Sea Crisis."

account of how they have evolved over time. This section includes identifying the specific features and strategies that characterize these reforms, providing a clear picture of the changes during Xi's first ten years. The third aspect of this chapter is the examination of the synergy between China's militia force and its regular military. This section explores how these two components of China's military apparatus worked together to achieve the nation's military agenda. The chapter proposes that a critical element of China's strategy lies in the harmonized integration of its regular and paramilitary forces, asserting that this synergy is central to furthering China's military ambitions. Drawing from a diverse range of historical and contemporary sources, this chapter aims to provide a detailed and multifaceted understanding of China's military reform under Xi Jinping, and examines its role in defining both the present and future course of China's military development.

Military Reform: Historical Background and Driving Factors

From the late nineteenth to the early twentieth centuries, China underwent a significant military transformation, primarily driven by a quest for "wealth and power." This period, riddled with internal strife and external invasions, compelled Chinese reformists and advocates of self-strengthening to adopt foreign military technology, training programs, and Western organizational models. These initiatives aimed to enhance China's defensive capabilities in an increasing industrial world.[10] The Republican period (1912–1945) witnessed an unprecedented ascendancy of military influence over Chinese socio-political spheres. This period was characterized by predatory warlord dominance and relentless confrontations with external forces. During this time, the Nationalist government had been trying to modernize and impose central control over its military. However, the reform trajectories during the twilight of the Qing dynasty and the subsequent Republican period faced significant challenges. These included inadequate administrative expertise, and political fragmentation, geographical divisions, and frequent armed conflicts. Throughout the first half of the twentieth century, China's political landscape was further fragmented by regional power blocs, which frequently hindered the central authority's statecraft endeavors. Despite Chiang Kai-shek's attempts at political centralization and military reform, his authoritarian governance was continually undermined by the intricate interplay of regional geopolitics and the burgeoning Communist movement. This historical precedent underscored for

[10] Horowitz, "Beyond the Marble Boat." 153– 174; Rowe, *China's Last Empire:* 201– 230.

the later Communist leaders the critical importance of political centralization in promoting any reform initiatives.[11]

The formation of the Chinese Communist force, initially known as the Red Army, in 1927 was a critical moment in China's military history, emerging amidst intense power struggles, factionalism, and conflicts among various military factions. During the late 1920s, Mao Zedong and Zhu De spearheaded the organization and training of a formidable Communist military. Initially lacking in resources, these forces ingeniously employed guerrilla tactics, relying on swift, hit-and-run operations to compensate for their material shortcomings. Despite enduring significant setbacks, notably during the encirclement and suppression campaigns, the Communist forces resiliently survived the arduous Long March.[12] They subsequently flourished during World War II, expanding their strength through mass mobilization efforts behind enemy lines. By WWII's end, the Communist military had grown exponentially, boasting about 2 million militia members and over 900,000 regular troops. This amazing expansion paved the way for their ascendancy during the Civil War from 1946 to 1949. In 1947, the Communist forces were reorganized into the People's Liberation Army, primarily operating as a guerrilla army reliant on the support of Chinese peasants. By the time of the People's Republic of China's establishment on October 1, 1949, the PLA had increased to around 5.5 million personnel, predominantly light infantry.[13] This expansion signified the military's central role in the Chinese Communist system, with its allegiance exclusively to the CCP. The unique bond between the CCP and the military was further institutionalized in 1954 with the creation of the Central Military Commission (CMC), chaired by Mao Zedong until his death in 1976. As the supreme military command and control authority, the CMC aligned the PLA with the State Council in terms of bureaucratic status.[14]

The CCP has consistently regarded the military as an indispensable instrument for sustaining its rule, safeguarding the CCP's interests, and propagating its ideology. This perspective has profoundly shaped the trajectory of China's military development and its role within the broader political framework. Over the next four decades, the PLA underwent a complex transformation, mirroring shifts in doctrinal paradigms, institutional structures, equipment modernization, and its role in society. In an increasingly bipolar world, the early PRC government sought guidance from the Soviet Union, a tendency that intensified following the Korean War. Influenced by Soviet military practices, the PLA restructured its organizational

[11] See Mitter, *A Bitter Revolution*.

[12] See Li, *A History of the Modern Chinese Army*: 13– 78.

[13] Blasko, "Always Faithful: The PLA from 1949 to 1989," 249.

[14] For the role of the PLA in the PLA's government structure, see Godwin, *The Chinese Communist Armed Forces*.

framework and strategic approaches. At the core of the PLA's operational structure were the three general departments: the General Staff Department, overseeing military operations; the General Logistics Department, handling logistical support; and the General Armament Department, responsible for weapons and equipment management.[15]

Another notable restructuring occurred in 1956, when the central government organized the nation into thirteen military regions, each covering several provinces. This reorganization was designed to support the command hierarchies and enhance the oversight of the military's extensive national presence. The evolution of these military regions over time illustrated the PLA's adaptability to changing strategic requirements and administrative reforms. The variations in the number and boundaries of these regions underscored the dynamic nature of China's military and administrative strategies.[16] From the mid-twentieth century to its later decades, broader objectives of military expansion and increased fiscal investment in the military budget were subsumed into the CCP's strategic calculus. This indicated a symbiotic relationship between the military's evolution and the Party's political goals, reflecting a nuanced understanding of the PLA's role not only as a defense force but also as a key player in the broader political landscape of China.

Mao Zedong's strategic vision, shaped by China's economic challenges and the protracted-war doctrine, suggested that the PLA could only achieve modernization by building a strong civilian industrial base. During the turbulent Cultural Revolution (1966–1976), the PLA was thrust into a role of ideological leadership for the Chinese people. Amidst growing societal unrest, the military structure became more robust. This era saw the PLA's ranks swell to over seven million, a significant increase. To quell the escalating unrest during the violent phase, military leaders were appointed to key positions in government and state-owned economic entities. However, numerous academic analyses argue that, amidst these tumultuous changes, the PLA's pursuit of modernization and professionalization encountered significant setbacks.[17]

As the 1970s concluded, the military's dominant position within China's government structure began to wane. This shift became particularly evident following Deng Xiaoping's rise to power after the Cultural Revolution. Deng introduced the Four Modernizations, aimed at restoring China's economy. However, the modernization of national defense was not prioritized in terms of investment and construction. This strategic shift was rooted in the belief that a strong military

[15] Jencks, essay, in *From Muskets to Missiles:* 301.

[16] Shambaugh, *Modernizing China's Military:* 108–173. For a detailed analysis during this period, see Nelsen, *The Chinese Military System.*

[17] Li, *A History of the Modern Chinese Army*, 204–240.

foundation required a prosperous economy and stable nation. Deng and other leading officials recognized that rapid military transformation demanded substantial resources, necessitating a shift in focus towards economic development. In pursuit of this goal, Deng initiated a significant reform of the military structure. This reform included reducing the number of army personnel and placing greater emphasis on specialized training. As the 20th century approached its end, China's military financing was constrained. Yet the PLA discovered an innovative approach to ensure its growth trajectory: engaging in commercial ventures. A network of PLA-affiliated businesses emerged, integrating into the broader landscape of profit-driven commercial activities.[18]

Since the early 1990s, the Chinese political and military leadership, particularly under Jiang Zemin and Hu Jintao, has begun acknowledging the necessity for a comprehensive transformation of the PLA. This realization was driven by a combination of external and internal factors. The evolution of modern warfare, particularly evident in the late 20th and early 21st centuries, had transcended traditional land battles to encompass joint operations across land, sea, air, cyber, and space domains. The Gulf War in the early 1990s had served as a stark example of the effectiveness of joint operations and high-tech weaponry, showcasing the potential of a technologically advanced force to swiftly incapacitate a conventional army.[19] These insights were keenly observed by China's leaders, aspiring to establish a global power. The nature of China's strategic challenges, ranging from the Taiwan Strait issues to territorial disputes with neighboring countries like India, Vietnam, and the Philippines, necessitated a military capable of operating fluidly across various spheres. This required a strategy that not only incorporated traditional warfare but also embraced new dimensions such as information warfare, extending into maritime and aerospace arenas. However, the need for reform was not purely driven by external pressures. Internally, the PLA faced systemic issues. Power within the military was heavily centralized in the general departments and Military Regions (MRs), leading to bureaucratic inefficiencies. The MRs were not adequately equipped to handle the demands of modern warfare. The compartmentalized structure of the PLA, with the Army, Navy, and Air Force often operating in isolation, hampered the effectiveness of joint operations. This lack of integration, compounded by insufficient oversight, raised concerns about unchecked power and widespread corruption in the military.[20] Recognizing these challenges, Hu Jintao addressed in 2006 these shortcomings in the PLA's structure. He emphasized the importance of establishing a joint operation command system to address the

[18] Johnston, *Cultural Realism*: 184.

[19] Algora Blog.

[20] Wuthnow and Saunders, *Chinese Military Reform*: 23–36.

realities of contemporary warfare. Additionally, he called for a reformed training approach to ensure that the PLA could operate effectively as a unified entity across all warfare domains.[21]

Under the leadership of Jiang Zemin and Hu Jintao, China's military strategy and structure underwent some changes, reflecting a commitment to modernizing the PLA and adapting to the changing geopolitical environment. These reforms were both structural and personnel-focused, aimed at reshaping the PLA's strategic vision and operational capabilities. A key aspect of this transformation was the downsizing of the PLA, which signified a transition from a large, conventional army to a smaller, technologically advanced force. This shift spoke to the global military trends where the emphasis on the quality of equipment and training took precedence over sheer numbers. It represented a strategic move towards building a more centralized and capable military force. Another significant reform was the diversification of the leadership within the CMC, the PLA's highest decision-making body. For the first time, commanders from the Navy, Air Force, and the Second Artillery Corps (later reorganized as the Rocket Force) were included in the CMC. This move marked a historic development in the PLA's history, signaling China's expanding focus on maritime, aerial, and strategic military capabilities. It also broke the long-standing tradition of the CMC being dominated by army generals, indicating a move towards a more integrated defense strategy. Both Jiang and Hu also recognized the increasing importance of information in modern warfare. The focus on "informatization" led to the creation of specialized divisions within the military, dedicated to leveraging technology for intelligence, operations, and strategy. The establishment of the Informatization Division was a clear indication of China's intent to evolve from a traditional military force to a modern, information-centric army. This shift was aligned with global military trends, where dominance in information technology often equates to superiority on the battlefield.[22]

The reforms initiated under Jiang and Hu were relatively modest in comparison to the extensive and transformative changes later implemented by Xi Jinping. Xi's approach to military reform was driven by various political and strategic factors, and reflected a profound sense of urgency regarding China's geopolitical standing. Xi Jinping perceived an urgent need to overhaul the military in response to the rapidly evolving international security landscape. This landscape was characterized by new forms of warfare and potential threats, which often blurred the traditional lines of conflict. A key objective for Xi was to ensure the Chinese military's ability to develop and deploy combat capabilities in an informationalized environment.

[21] "Hu Jintao Speaks at the Whole Army Training Meeting" 胡锦涛在全军军事训练会议上发表重要讲话, available at, http://zqb.cyol.com/content/2006-06/28/content_1430531.htm.

[22] Cliff, *China's Military Power:* 50–54.

This sense of necessity was further solidified by volatile global and regional situations. China faced multiple security and strategic challenges, including perceived threats from the U.S. rebalancing strategy in the Asia-Pacific, which Beijing saw as a response to China's rise in Asia. Beyond the U.S. factor, the tensions near China posed significant concerns for China. For example. tensions in the Korean Peninsula and territorial disputes over the Senkaku Islands, Taiwan, and the South China Sea added to the complex geopolitical situation. These issues underscored the need for a military that was not only strong but also effective, coordinated, and modernized.

Another factor driving Xi Jinping's push for military reform was the inadequacy of the PLA's joint operation structure. Historically, the PLA had been an army-centric force, a legacy of its origins and strategic focus on land-based threats.[23] However, the nature of modern warfare had evolved, with the maritime, aerospace, cyber, and electromagnetic domains gaining extreme significance. Without robust joint operations capabilities, the PLA risked being disadvantaged in potential conflicts. The existing PLA structure, characterized by decentralized command structure and lack of interoperability among the branches and regions, was not compatible for modern warfare. The lessons from global military trends had demonstrated the importance of joint operations, particularly how technology and information could lead to swift and decisive victories. The PLA's structure, with its overemphasis on ground forces and insufficient integration was increasingly outmoded in the contemporary strategic context. Xi Jinping recognized that joint operational capabilities were essential for a modern and effective military.

Increasing Central Coordination: Military Reform Initiatives under Xi Jinping

"We must endeavor to comprehensively transform the people's armed forces into a world-class military by the mid-21st century." This visionary proclamation was made by Xi Jinping during the landmark 19th Party Congress in 2017.[24] In his address, he meticulously charted distinct milestones for the PLA's modernization journey. He set an ambitious goal: finalize the modernization phase by 2035, and by 2049—the 100th anniversary of the People's Republic of China—elevate the PLA to the stature of a "world-class military." This timeline wasn't just symbolic; it was deeply intertwined with China's national narrative of rejuvenation and global rise. Since assuming leadership of the CCP in October 2012, Xi Jinping swiftly set into motion a series of sweeping and transformative reforms within the PLA. His

[23] Li, *A History of the Modern Chinese Army*, 1–13.

[24] "Full Text of Xi Jinping's Report at 19th CPC National Congress," *Xinhua News*, 3 November 2017, available at, http://www.xinhuanet.com/english/special/2017-11/03/c_136725942.htm.

vision was clear: a military machine that was not only numerically formidable but also technologically advanced, coordinated, and strategically efficient. To achieve this, considerable initiatives were directed towards research and development, as well as the integration of cutting-edge technologies into the PLA's operational framework.

In November 2013, during the 18th Central Committee of the CCP, Xi Jinping marked a new era in China's military strategy and organization by announcing the start of comprehensive national defense and military reform. Recognizing the need for a dedicated and specialized oversight body, a small yet influential leading group was established on March 15th, 2014, with Xi Jinping himself as its leader.[25] This group was charged with the complex task of conceptualizing, planning, and implementing the proposed reforms. After two years of meticulous preparation, the "Deepening National Defense and Military Reform" initiative was formally announced in November 2015 by the Central Military Commission's Central Leading Group for Military Reform. During the CMC Reform Work Conference, Xi Jinping outlined several key reform proposals. These included (1) the establishment of a leading organization for the PLA's ground force, enhancing the CMC's role in coordinating the four general departments, (2) reorganizing the PLA's command structure, and (3) creating the CMC Discipline Inspection Commission and the CMC Politics and Law Commission. These latter two bodies were designed to regulate and oversee the interaction between politics and military operations.[26]

On January 1, 2016, the Central Military Commission issued an important document titled "Deepening National Defense and Military Reform." This document was crucial in outlining the CMC's comprehensive responsibilities, which extended across various military and paramilitary entities, including the People's Liberation Army, the People's Armed Police, militia, and reserve forces. The essence of these guidelines was a call for a significant and thorough restructuring of the military apparatus. By delineating these responsibilities and calling for profound changes, the document set the stage for a series of reforms that were intended to modernize and enhance the operational capabilities of China's military forces.[27]

In a significant shift from previous practices, the reform under Xi Jinping led to the replacement of the four traditional general departments of the Chinese military. In their place, fifteen specialized departments, commissions, and offices were established, all under the strategic leadership of the Central Military Commission.

[25] Wuthnow and Saunders, *Chinese Military Reform*: 37–42.

[26] "PLA to Announce Overhaul".

[27] For an overview of the reform, see "Graphics: China's Military Reform in Past 5 Years," 1 August 2020, available at, http://eng.chinamil.com.cn/CMC/Departments/OfficeforReformandOrganizationalStructure/10055567.html.

This restructuring was aimed at creating a more efficient and responsive military command structure. The reform introduced seven functional departments at the core of military operations and support: the General Office, Joint Staff Department, Political Work Department, Equipment Development Department, Training and Management Department, Logistic Support Department, and National Defense Mobilization Department. Each of these departments was tasked with handling specific aspects of military operations, ranging from personnel management to equipment development and logistical support.

Complementing these functional departments were three specialized commissions: the Discipline Inspection Commission, the Politics and Law Affairs Commission, and the Science and Technology Commission. These commissions were responsible for maintaining discipline, overseeing legal affairs, and fostering scientific and technological advancements within the military, respectively. Additionally, the reform blueprint established five critical operational offices: the Strategic Planning Office, Reform and Organization Office, International Military Cooperation Office, Audit Bureau, and Organ Affairs General Management Bureau. These offices were instrumental in strategic planning, implementing reforms, managing international military cooperation, overseeing financial audits, and handling the general management of organizational affairs. The overarching aim of this comprehensive restructuring was to support the military establishment, enhancing command control and adopting a meticulous, specialized approach to its diverse functions. This reorganization was a crucial step in realizing Xi Jinping's vision of transforming the PLA into a world-class military, capable of addressing modern security challenges effectively and efficiently.[28] (Figure 10.1)

On February 1, 2016, China initiated a major strategic realignment, replacing its legacy system of seven military regions with five newly established Theater Commands: Northern, Southern, Western, Eastern, and Central. This reorganization was more than a redrawing of territorial lines; it represented a profound shift towards integrated military strategies and joint operations command structures. Each Theater Command was designed to function as a unified entity, capable of conducting joint operations across different branches of the military. This approach was a clear departure from the previous system, where operations were often segmented by military branches and regions. The leadership within these Theater Commands was carefully structured to reflect this new integrative focus. Commanders with strong backgrounds in ground operations were appointed to

[28] Wuthnow and Saunders, *Chinese Military Reform*: 42–49.

lead, underscoring the continued importance of ground forces and territorial expertise in military strategy.[29]

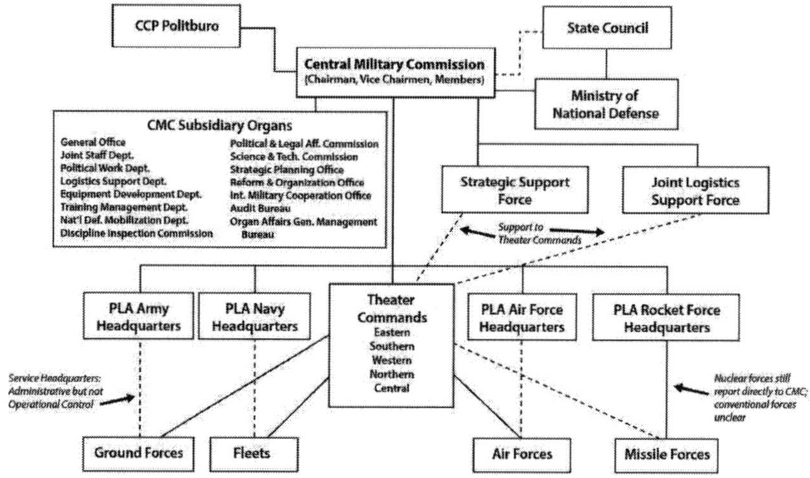

Figure 10.1: New PLA Structure
Source: Joel Wuthnow and Phillip C. Saunders, *Chinese Military Reform in the Age of Xi Jinping: Drivers, Challenges, and Implications* (Washington. D.C.: National Defense University Press, 2017), 27.

In a move that further emphasized the integrated nature of these reforms, military commanders were selected from different military branches. This diverse command structure ensured that the strategic perspectives of the navy and air force were incorporated into each Theater Command. Such policy was crucial for fostering an effective and rapid approach to military operations, enhancing the ability of each theater to respond effectively to various security challenges. The transition to Theatre Commands was aimed at improving joint operations capabilities, increasing the PLA's readiness and combat effectiveness, and aligning the military's structure with the demands of modern warfare. This reorganization was a key component of Xi Jinping's broader military reform agenda, reflecting his vision of transforming the PLA into a more integrated force.

The transition to the theater command system represents a strategic evolution in China's military organization, allowing for more efficient coordination and

[29] Ziyu Zhang, China's Military Structure: What are the Theatre Commands and Service Branches, "15 August 2021, available at, https://www.scmp.com/news/china/military/article/3144921/chinas-military-structure-what-are-theatre-commands-and-service.

integration of forces across different services. This structure facilitates simplified command and control, particularly during wartime situations. In this setup, the command and control of forces within a specific theater can be rapidly established as needed. In times of conflict or emergency, the relevant theater command can be swiftly activated, enabling more effective and coordinated military responses. This shift underscores China's commitment to modernizing its military structure, aligning it with contemporary warfare concepts that prioritize joint operations and the ability to project power across various domains. The theater command system enhances operational flexibility and strengthens the PLA's capacity to address regional and global security challenges.

Aligned with centralizing the command structure, the PLA transitioned its service headquarters into a centralized entity, the "Army Leading Organ." This creation underscores the significance China attributes to its ground forces, establishing a centralized and dedicated office to oversee and coordinate the operations and development of the PLA's ground components. Its establishment aimed to work with the broader military reform agenda, emphasizing the importance of joint operations and integrated warfare capabilities.[30] Another critical step in the PLA's transformation was the decision to reduce its personnel by approximately 300,000 soldiers by the end of 2017. This reduction mainly affected non-combat roles, including those specializing in cultural and academic works. The primary objective behind downsizing the PLA was to enhance operational efficiency. By eliminating redundant positions and optimizing the chain of command, the PLA aimed to become a more flexible force, better equipped to meet the demands of modern warfare. This downsizing allows for a reallocation of resources towards research, development, and the acquisition of advanced weaponry and technologies, including unmanned systems, cyber capabilities, and artificial intelligence.[31]

The Militia Reconstruction

Under Xi Jinping's leadership, the concept of military-civil fusion has become an important part of China's national strategy. This approach is particularly evident in the utilization and modernization of the militia forces, which was not only a reserve military force, but also seen as an important player in the national defense system. These forces are not only vital for maintaining local stability against internal disturbances but also serve as a critical auxiliary force, seamlessly integrating with the PLA during conflicts and emergencies. The historical significance of militia

30 Lowsen, "Predictions on the Chinese Military's New Army Leading Organ."

31 "System Overload? The 2015 PLA Force Reduction."

forces in China dates back to periods long before the Communist Party's rise to power. During the decline of the Qing dynasty, local militias played a crucial role in maintaining social order. The militia forces, tasked with a range of responsibilities from protecting communities against rebels and bandits to upholding law and order, were crucial in safeguarding society when the state presence was limited in local society. Their importance was particularly pronounced during major upheavals like the Taiping Rebellion, where they actively participated in suppressing the insurrection and preserving imperial stability.[32]

During the Chinese Communist Revolution, the CCP particularly emphasized the role of the militia forces. Recognizing the critical importance of grassroots support, the CCP leveraged the tradition of mass mobilization. These militias, largely composed of peasants, became the front-line defenders of communist revolution, playing diverse roles from protecting villages, implementing land reforms, providing logistic support, repelling external threats, to consolidating communist-controlled areas.[33] From the early 1950s to the late 1970s, the role of the maritime militia was significant, especially in the context of national defense and territorial assertion. Early PRC leaders, recognizing the strategic importance of the seas, deemed the establishment of an organized maritime militia crucial for countering Nationalist incursions into the PRC's coastal waters. This initiative was part of a broader strategy to integrate local resources into national defense, aligning with Mao Zedong's "People's War" doctrine. The Bureau of Aquatic Products played a key role in this endeavor, initiating the collectivization of local fisheries. This facilitated the organization of maritime militias under the guidance of People's Liberation Army Navy (PLAN) officers. A notable instance of this integration was the appointment of Admiral Yuan Yelie, a vice commander of the PLAN, as Vice Minister of the Bureau of Aquatic Products in 1960.

The PLAN further institutionalized this initiative by establishing militia schools in its three fleets based in Qingdao, Shanghai, and Guangzhou. These schools were instrumental in training fishermen in military tactics and operations, thereby enhancing their effectiveness as a maritime militia. This synergy between civilian maritime activities and military objectives was a distinctive feature of the Chinese approach to naval warfare during this period.[34] The effectiveness of the maritime militia was most prominently demonstrated in two significant naval confrontations. First, in the Battle of the Paracel Islands against South Vietnam, the maritime militia played a central role. The presence of Chinese fishing vessels around the Paracels,

[32] See Kuhn, *Rebellion and Its Enemies.*

[33] Scholarships on the CCP's mobilization of the militia forces include Chen, *Making Revolution;* Wou, *Mobilizing the Masses: Building Revolution in Henan.*

[34] Muller, *China as a Maritime Power*: 168.

backed by the PLAN, effectively slowed down the South Vietnamese forces. During the swarming operations at the Senkaku/Diaoyu Islands in the East China Sea in 1978, the maritime militia again proved its strategic value. By employing a large number of fishing vessels in these operations, the militia demonstrated its capacity to assert Chinese territorial claims and influence regional maritime dynamics.

Thus, Xi Jinping's emphasis on revitalizing and modernizing the militia reflects a continuation and recognition of its historical and ongoing importance in China's defense and political framework. Xi's focus represents an acknowledgment of the militia's longstanding role and its strategic importance in the future of China's defense strategy. The continued support of militia has been a strategic move towards enhancing China's comprehensive national defense capabilities. The maritime militia stands as a formidable yet often overlooked component. In recent years, its importance has received scholarly attention mostly from scholars outside China.[35] Many American observes believed that the People's Armed Forces Maritime Militia (PAFMM) serves as an inevitable element in China's military establishment, particularly in the areas of maritime sovereignty disputes. Recognized as the world's largest maritime militia, its role extends far beyond that of conventional fishermen or mariners.[36] It was established as a specialized unit, meticulously developed and maintained by the local military jurisdictions of the PLA. It comprises a diverse array of vessels and crew members, each trained and equipped for specific maritime operations. This strategic composition of the PAFMM has led to its characterization as the "little blue men," reflecting its perceived covert operations and integral role in supporting Beijing's ambitious maritime strategy. This characterization underscores the militia's significance as a tool of statecraft in China's broader geopolitical objectives, particularly in contested maritime territories.[37]

According to many American reports, the maritime militia plays a supplemental role in Beijing's strategy in the South China Sea, operating within a complex and strategic framework. This strategy is multi-layered, aiming to assert China's disputed claims, when possible, strategically delaying addressing issues that are untenable, and exerting calibrated pressure on adversaries—all while avoiding actions that could escalate to full-blown military conflict. This approach, often referred to as "gray zone" operations, is designed to impact the maritime status quo without provoking open hostilities with its neighbors. This delicate balance can be seen as a nuanced power game, balancing assertiveness with restraint, and is critical in understanding the militia's role as China's Third Sea Force, complementing

[35] See Hongzhou Zhang and Sam Bateman, "Fishing Militia, the Securitization of Fishery and the South China Sea Dispute," *Contemporary Southeast Asia*, Vol. 39, No. 2 (2017), 288–314.

[36] Erickson, "Shinning a Spotlight."

[37] Erickson, "Understanding China's Third Sea Force."

the Navy and Coast Guard. While international attention often focuses on the more visible elements of China's maritime power, the maritime militia operates frequently under the radar, playing a crucial role in various significant incidents. Their involvement in frontline confrontations, especially in the South China Sea, highlights the complex nature of China's maritime strategy and Beijing's determination to achieve its maritime objectives through a mix of visible and covert operations.[38]

Under Xi Jinping's leadership, a significant emphasis has been placed on modernizing China's militia forces, making them compatible with current security challenges and equipped with technological advancements. This modernization encompasses a comprehensive upgrade in training, equipment, and capabilities, aimed at boosting combat readiness and incorporating modern technologies into militia operations. The government advocates for a deeper integration and coordination between the militia and the PLA. This strategy involves enhancing communication channels, sharing vital information, and conducting joint training exercises to bolster the effectiveness and cooperation of both forces. The overarching goal is to forge a unified and efficient defense system capable of responding adeptly to a variety of security situations. The reconstruction of China's militia has been characterized by a focus on modernization, integration, and a heightened role in local defense and stability. These initiatives aim to forge a militia force that is not only more capable but also highly responsive, effectively complementing the PLA and contributing to the broader national defense strategy.[39]

A significant aspect of this transformation under Xi's leadership is the development and strategic deployment of the maritime militia. This paramilitary force, comprising civilian vessels and personnel, operates in synergy with the PLAN and other maritime law enforcement bodies. Embracing the concept of "People's War at Sea," Xi has underscored the importance of integrating civilian maritime forces into the nation's defense and security framework. This approach plays a significant role in China's stance on maritime disputes, leveraging non-military actors to advance national interests and counter perceived adversaries. Efforts to enhance the capabilities of the maritime militia under Xi's regime have been notable. Training programs have been introduced to improve the maritime skills of militia personnel, and investments have been made to equip them with modern technologies and communication systems, thereby boosting their operational effectiveness and coordination with the PLAN and other maritime forces.

Furthermore, the maritime militia has been actively involved in information warfare and psychological operations within the maritime domain. These activities

[38] Luo and Panter, "China's Maritime Militia."

[39] Grossman and Ma, "A Short History of China's Fishing."

range from disseminating propaganda and conducting influence operations to shaping public perception in support of China's narratives and goals, particularly in contested maritime areas. The role of the maritime militia exemplifies Xi Jinping's strategic vision of leveraging a diverse range of assets to strengthen China's national defense and assert its maritime claims. The expanded role and assertiveness of China's maritime militia in the South China Sea under Xi Jinping's leadership have indeed been a source of increasing concern and tension with neighboring countries and other regional stakeholders. The maritime militia's heightened activity in these contested waters plays a significant part in China's strategy to safeguard its maritime interests, reinforce its sovereignty claims, and influence the regional maritime order.

This increased utilization of the maritime militia in the South China Sea has been a key factor in exacerbating existing maritime disputes. The presence and operations of these civilian vessels, often in sensitive or disputed areas, have raised alarms about the potential for misunderstandings, miscalculations, or direct incidents at sea. These concerns stem from the ambiguity surrounding the militia's operations and their dual-use nature, blurring the lines between civilian and military activities. The strategic employment of the maritime militia by China under Xi Jinping thus not only highlights its role as a critical instrument in Beijing's broader maritime strategy but also underscores the complexities and challenges in managing maritime relations and ensuring stability in a region marked by overlapping territorial claims and strategic rivalries.

Thus, China's vision of civil-military fusion is particularly relevant to the militia. This concept seeks to create synergies between the civilian and military sectors, utilizing technological innovations and expertise from both areas to mutual advantage. In the context of militia reform, this means tapping into civilian resources, skills, and technological advancements to increase the militia's operational capabilities. Such integration is key to reinforcing the militia's role in national defense and ensuring it remains an effective component of China's overall security strategy.

Assessment and Conclusion

Under Xi Jinping, China's military has seen a dramatic transformation, diverging sharply from the modest approaches of his predecessors, Hu Jintao and Jiang Zemin. Earlier reforms were incremental and moderate, but Xi's changes were comprehensive and radical, marking a significant shift in the military's structure and strategy. This involved a major reform of the organizational framework. The four traditional general departments, long-standing pillars of the military, were abandoned. The Central Military Commission introduced a multi-department system comprising various functional departments, commissions, and offices. This new structure was designed to be more efficient and responsive to contemporary demands of warfare and defense, reflecting a profound change in China's military orientation under Xi's leadership.

The military reform has placed a significant emphasis on joint operations, transforming the traditional structure of the armed forces. This shift moves away from the previous dominance of ground forces, promoting a more balanced and integrated military approach. This focused on jointness aligned with global military trends, ensuring that the PLA remains effective in the evolving landscape of modern warfare. A key strategic decision in these reforms is the reduction of troop numbers, reflecting an understanding of the changing nature of warfare. As discussed above, resources are being reallocated to bolster the capabilities of the air force, rocket force, and navy, which are crucial for modern power projection, deterrence, and defense. Moreover, the transition from numerous military regions to fewer, more focused theater commands marks a departure towards a combat-ready military posture. Each Theatre Command is designed to address specific strategic challenges, allowing for more efficient and high-intensity joint military operations. This structural realignment enhances the PLA's ability to respond quickly and effectively to various threats, embodying an active defense strategy. This restructuring has significantly enhanced the role of the CMC, with Xi as its chairman, as the central hub of military command and control. The reforms centralized authority that was previously distributed across the four general departments, leading to more efficient decision-making, clearer command structures, and improved coordination between different military departments. This centralization served a strategic purpose beyond mere consolidation of power. It also reinforced the CMC chairman responsibility system, where the chairman holds ultimate authority over the military. Increasing the power and scope of the CMC, and consequently Xi Jinping, has not only solidified his status as China's political leader but also as the foremost military authority. These changes underscore Xi's commitment to creating a modern and centralized Chinese military, in line with his broader vision for the nation's defense capabilities.

Xi Jinping's military reforms in China have notably embraced the concept of civil-military fusion, a strategic approach that integrates civilian resources, expertise, and technology into military development. This initiative aims to harness civilian sector advancements to foster innovation within the PLA. A key element of this strategy is the enhanced role of the maritime militia, a crucial part of China's defense framework. The maritime militia has been further integrated into the national defense strategy, functioning as a well-coordinated force that enhances China's naval capabilities and serves as a versatile instrument in advancing its maritime interests. Particularly notable is its involvement in gray zone operations in the South China Sea, highlighting its critical role in China's strategic and defense planning.[40]

In conclusion, through these reforms, Xi has not only addressed existing challenges within the PLA but has also transformed the military into a more efficient, technologically sophisticated entity. This repositioning aligns the military more closely with China's global ambitions, ensuring it remains a potent force in the international arena. The focus on civil-military fusion thus marks a significant shift in China's approach to military development and strategic operations. Xi Jinping's military reforms in China, while groundbreaking, face significant challenges. A key concern is the PLA's lack of recent combat experience. Over four decades of peace have contributed to China's economic growth but have left the PLA without real-world combat exposure. This gap raises questions about the army's readiness and adaptability in actual conflict situations, as training, no matter how advanced, cannot fully replicate the complexities of live combat. Another issue is the impact of Xi's sweeping anti-corruption campaign within the military. While it has successfully identified and penalized corrupt officers, setting a strong precedent, the extent of corruption's entrenchment and the effectiveness of the purges in completely eradicating it remain uncertain. Moreover, the intensity of the anti-corruption drive might inadvertently inhibit initiative and innovation among senior military officers, who may fear the risks of being perceived as overstepping boundaries.

Additionally, a central focus of Xi's reforms is fostering joint operations across the PLA's various branches. Transitioning from a service-centric model to a truly integrated joint operation framework presents its own set of challenges. Each military branch has its distinct culture, operational doctrine, and priorities, and merging these into a cohesive whole requires not only structural changes but also a significant shift in mindset and operational culture. The PLA's future effectiveness will largely depend on how successfully it can implement and operationalize this aspect of Xi's military reform agenda.[41]

Dr. **Lei Duan** is an assistant professor of East Asian history at Sam Houston State University. His research centers on the interplay between social violence and state power in modern China. He is currently finishing work on his first monograph, *Arming and Disarming: The Culture and Politics of Guns in Modern China*. His research has been supported by distinguished research fellowships from the

[40] For example, the Beihai City in Guangxi Province developed a maritime militia during the 2010s. See "In Joint Operations, The Militia Must Not be Absent," People's Daily Online, 25 January 2016, available at, http://military.people.com.cn/n1/2016/0125/c1011-28081634.html.

[41] Wuthnow and Saunders, *Chinese Military Reform in the Age of Xi Jinping*, 42–48.

Harry Frank Guggenheim Foundation, the American Historical Association, the Association for Asian Studies, and various libraries and archives. He has published multiple articles, reviews, and book chapters. He was a postdoctoral fellow at the Lieberthal-Rogel Center for Chinese Studies at the University of Michigan from 2017 to 2019. He received his Ph.D. in history from Syracuse University.

Bibliography

"All-Army Political Work Conference Held in Gutian; Xi Jinping Attends Meeting, Delivers Important Speech." November 1, 2014. http://www.xinhuanet.com//politics/2014-11/01/c_1113074055_3.htm.

Algora Blog. "How the Gulf War Sparked China's Military Revolution." Algora Blog, February 4, 2021. https://www.algora.com/Algora_blog/2021/02/03/how-the-gulf-war-sparked-chinas-military-revolution.

Blasko, Dennis J. "Always Faithful: The PLA from 1949 to 1989." In *A Military History of China.* edited by David A. Graff and Robin Higham. Lexington, The University Press of Kentucky, 2012.

Chen, Yung-fa. *Making Revolution: The Communist Movement in Eastern and Central China, 1937–1945*. Berkeley: University of California Press, 2021.

"China Military." China Military. Accessed September 10, 2023. http://eng.chinamil.com.cn/CMC/Departments/OfficeforReformandOrganizationalStructure/10055567.html.

"China's Modernizing Military." Council on Foreign Relations. Accessed September 10, 2023. https://www.cfr.org/backgrounder/chinas-modernizing-military.

Cliff, Roger. *China's Military Power: Assessing Current and Future Capabilities.* New York: Cambridge University Press, 2015.

Erickson, Andrew S. "Shining a Spotlight: Revealing China's Maritime Militia to Deter its Use," The National Interest, 25 November 2018, https://www.andrewerickson.com/2018/12/the-complete-china-maritime-militia-bookshelf-latest-greatest-4/.

Erickson, Andrew S. "Understanding China's Third Sea Force: The Maritime Militia." Fairbank Center for Chinese Studies, July 7, 2022. https://fairbank.fas.harvard.edu/research/blog/understanding-chinas-third-sea-force-the-maritime-militia/.

"Full Text of Xi Jinping's Report at 19th CPC National Congress." Xinhua. Accessed September 10, 2023. http://www.xinhuanet.com/english/special/2017-11/03/c_136725942.htm.

"Full Text: Resolution of the CPC Central Committee on the Major Achievements and Historical Experience of the Party over the Past Century." November 16, 2021. https://english.www.gov.cn/policies/latestreleases/202111/16/content_WS6193a935c6d0df57f98e50b0.html.

Godwin, Paul H.B. *The Chinese Communist Armed Forces.* Maxwell Air Force Base, AL: Air University Press, Center for Aerospace Doctrine, Research, and Education, 1988.

Grossman, Derek and Logan Ma, "A Short History of China's Fishing Militia and What it May Tell Us," 6 April 2020, https://www.rand.org/pubs/commentary/2020/04/a-short-history-of-chinas-fishing-militia-and-what.html.

Horowitz, Richard S. "Beyond the Marble Boat: The Transformation of the Chinese Military, 1850–1911." In *A Military History of China*, edited by David A. Graff and Robin Higham. Lexington, The University Press of Kentucky, 2012.

"Hu Jintao Speaks at the Military Training Meeting."http://zqb.cyol.com/content/2006-06/28/content_1430531.htm.

"In Joint Operations, The Militia Must Not be Absent," *People's Daily Online*, 25 January 2016. http://military.people.com.cn/n1/2016/0125/c1011-28081634.html.

Jash, Amrita. "China's 2023 Defense Spending: Figures, Intentions and Concerns." *China Brief.* April 14, 2023. https://jamestown.org/program/chinas-2023-defense-spending-figures-intentions-and-concerns/#:~:text=In%20March%2C%20at%20the%20opening,from%20last%20year%20(State%20Council.

Jencks, Harlan W. *From Muskets to Missiles: Politics and Professionalism in the Chinese Army, 1945–1981*, 301. Boulder, CO: Westview Press, 1982.

Johnson, Keith and Dan De Luce. "Fishing Disputes Could Spark a South China Sea Crisis." *Foreign Policy.* April 7, 2016. http://foreignpolicy.com/2016/04/07/fishing-disputes-could-spark-a-south-china-sea-crisis/.

Johnston, Alastair I. *Cultural Realism: Strategic Culture and Grand Strategy in Chinese History.* Princeton: Princeton University Press, 1998.

Kuhn, Philip A. *Rebellion and Its Enemies in Late Imperial China.* Cambridge, Mass: Harvard University Press, 1970.

Li, Xiaobing. Essay. In *A History of the Modern Chinese Army*, 13–78. Lexington, KY: University Press of Kentucky, 2009.

Luo, Shuxian and Jonathan G. Panter, "China's Maritime Militia and Fishing Fleets, A Primer for Operational Staffs and Tactical Leaders," *Military Review,* January-February 2021, https://www.armyupress.army.mil/Journals/Military-Review/English-Edition-Archives/January-February-2021/Panter-Maritime-Militia/.

Lowsen, Ben. "Predictions on the Chinese Military's New Army Leading Organ," *The Diplomats*, 29 March 2016, https://thediplomat.com/2016/03/the-chinese-plas-new-army/.

Mitter, Rana. *A Bitter Revolution: China's Struggle with the Modern World.* Oxford: Oxford University Press, 2010.

Muller, David G. *China as a Maritime Power.* New York: Routledge, 2018.

Nelsen, Harvey W. *The Chinese Military System: An Organizational Study of the People's Liberation Army* Boulder, Colo.: Westview Press, 1977.

"New Gutian Meeting: Another Milestone." *Xinhua News*, February 11, 2015. http://www.xinhuanet.com/mil/2015-02/11/c_127483366.html.

Office of the Secretary of Defense, *Military and Security Developments Involving the People's Republic of China, 2020.*

"PLA Advances in Arms, Ability over Past Decade," *China Daily*. August 16, 2022. https://www.chinadaily.com.cn/a/202208/16/WS62fadodba310fd2b29e724e0.html.

"PLA to Announce Overhaul: Five 'Strategic Zones' Will Replace Regional Commands, Most Army HQ to Be Scrapped." South China Morning Post, December 20, 2015. https://www.scmp.com/news/china/diplomacy-defence/article/1893468/peoples-liberation-army-be-split-five-combat-regions.

Rowe, William T. Essay. In *China's Last Empire: The Great Qing*, 201–30. Cambridge, MA: Belknap Press of Harvard University Press, 2012.

Schillinger, Nicolas. *The Body and Military Masculinity in Late Qing and Early Republican China: The Art of Governing Soldiers*. Lanham: Md., 2016.

Shambaugh, David. *Modernizing China's Military: Progress, Problems, and Prospects.* Berkeley: University of California Press, 2002.

"System Overload? The 2015 PLA Force Reduction, Military-Locality Relations, and the Potent." National Defense University Press, February 5, 2019. https://ndupress.ndu.edu/Media/News/News-Article-View/Article/1748788/system-overload-the-2015-pla-force-reduction-military-locality-relations-and-th/.

Ven Hans, Van de. “New States of War: Communist and Nationalist Warfare and State Building (1928–1934).” Essay. In *Warfare in Chinese History*, edited by Van de Ven Hans. Leiden: Brill, 2000.

Wou, Odoric Y. K. *Mobilizing the Masses: Building Revolution in Henan*. Stanford, CA: Stanford University Press, 1994.

Wuthnow, Joel, and Phillip C. Saunders. *Chinese Military Reform in the Age of Xi Jinping: Drivers, Challenges, and Implications*. Washington. D.C.: National Defense University Press, 2017.

“Xi Stresses CPC’s Absolute Leadership over Army,” November 2, 2014. https://english.www.gov.cn/news/202307/21/content_WS64ba72bbc6d0868f4e8de04d.html.

“Xi Urges Serious Reflection on Xu Caihou’s Case,” *China Daily*, November 1 2014, https://usa.chinadaily.com.cn/china/2014-11/01/content_18840748.html.

CHAPTER ELEVEN

From Trade War to New Cold War: Popular Nationalism and the Global Times on Weibo under Xi Jinping

Lin Mao

GEORGIA SOUTHERN UNIVERSITY

Abstract: *The United States and the People's Republic of China have been waging what the Chinese social media called the most "epic trade war in human history" since early 2018. This ongoing trade war has attracted unprecedented attention from all types of Chinese media. While Xi Jinping's government tries to maintain a tight control of public opinion, it cannot always shape the narrative of the trade war based on official policies. This chapter examines how popular nationalism has evolved over time and shaped China's response to the trade war, focusing on the influential Global Times and how it used the social media platform, Weibo, to frame the trade war. During the early months of the trade war, China's response was largely defensive. Chinese public opinion claimed China as an innocent victim of the trade war, initiated by a reckless Trump administration. Many, especially those on social media, were also optimistic, believing that the trade war would be over once the U.S. government came to its senses. After Washington imposed sanctions on Huawei, a popular Chinese high-tech company, the public opinion shifted to an offensive mode. Many now argued that America was not looking for fair trade policies but trying to block China's rise as a global power. Furthermore, Chinese popular nationalists started to argue that China's model of development was superior to America's liberal democracy. Other issues on Xi Jinping's policy toward Taiwan, Hong Kong, Tibet, Xinjiang, and the South China Sea from 2018–2022 further confounded the bilateral relationship and led to the rise of popular nationalism.*

Keywords: New cold war; Popular nationalism; *The Global Times*; Weibo

"America has fired the first shot of a trade war!" On March 22, 2018, the *Global Times* (hereafter the *GT*) broke the news on its Weibo account that the US President Donald Trump signed a memorandum to impose tariffs on $60 billion of Chinese goods.[1] Between then and January 15, 2020, when Beijing and Washington signed the Phase

[1] "Trump Officially Signed the China Tariff Memo," March 20, 2018, https://weibo.com/1974576991/G8Cs93pdK

One Trade Agreement, the *GT* generated 2,238 posts on its Weibo platform related to the trade war and US-China relations.[2] Indeed, the *GT* and its controversial chief editor, Hu Xijin, have played a leading role in framing the US-China trade war and shaping the Chinese public's perceptions of US-China relations. In Chapter Two, Guolin Yi pointed out that Xi Jinping has tightly restricted public media, and the *GT*, being affiliated with CCP's main mouthpiece *The People's Daily*, has grown to become one of the most influential media outlets in China covering international affairs. Hu Xijin's writings, often nationalistic and provocative, have led to numerous public battles against his critics and made himself one of the top opinion influencers in China. Almost a household name now, Hu's personal Weibo account has 24.82 million followers, while the Weibo account of *GT* has 31.02 million followers.[3]

Since early 2018, the trade war between the United States and the People's Republic of China (PRC), the world's two largest economies, has not only destabilized the global economy, but also expanded beyond the economic realm to raise questions about national security and international order. Inside China, the trade war has attracted unprecedented attention from all types of Chinese media. Immediately after Trump's March 22 memorandum, Chinese social media were swarmed with discussions about the most "epic trade war in human history."[4] Nationalism has played a primary role in framing the Chinese media coverage of the trade war. As scholars have argued, "public discussions of the trade war in China…were driven by a number of factors that had little to do with economics and more with questions of nationalism and sense of self."[5]

This chapter systematically examines the 2,238 Weibo posts by the *GT* and discusses its efforts to frame the trade war and control the narrative of Chinese nationalism. It argues that the *GT* cannot be simply dismissed as a state-controlled propaganda outlet promoting popular nationalism bordering on xenophobia. Rather, an in-depth analysis of its Weibo posts shows that while the *GT* often follows the official policies laid out by the Chinese Communist Party (CCP), its status as commercial media allows Hu Xijin and his team to believe that they can genuinely represent grassroots concerns of the Chinese public. The editorial stance of the *GT*, therefore, can help us better understand the shifting landscape of Chinese nationalism and how it affects the Chinese public's perceptions of China's role in the world and US-China relations.

[2] This number is based on the Weibo posts accessible to the author during research. It does not include the posts that may have been deleted since their publication.

[3] https://weibo.com/huxijin and https://weibo.com/u/1974576991

[4] The term was first coined by Mei Yuxin, a researcher associated with the Chinese Ministry of Commerce, and quicky went viral. https://finance.ifeng.com/a/20180404/16058513_0.shtml

[5] Ha and Willnat, eds. *The U.S.-China Trade War*, p. x.

This chapter first discusses the history of *GT* in the context of the rising Chinese nationalism. It then discusses the two stages of *GT*'s Weibo coverage of the trade war, separated by the Canadian authorities' arrest of Meng Wanzhou, the Chief Financial Officer of Huawei and daughter of the company's founder, in December 2018. During the first stage, the Weibo coverage mainly focused on narrowly defined trade issues. After Meng's arrest, however, the coverage shifted beyond Sino-American trade issues, with a special focus on a possible new cold war between the two nations.

The *Global Times* and China's "Left Turn" since the 1990s

Founded in 1993 as a subsidiary of the *People's Daily*, the most authoritative mouthpiece of the CCP, the *GT* was designed as a "tabloid" newspaper covering international news and affairs. Initially published as a weekly newspaper, the *GT* became a daily in 2006 and launched its English version in 2009. In 2010, the *GT* opened its account on Sina Weibo, a leading social media platform in China. By the time the US-China trade war broke out, the *GT* had already become a media conglomerate that owned numerous companies spanning across the Chinese media landscape. With a daily circulation of more than 2 million copies, the *GT* has a professional team of more than 500 journalists stationed in 150 plus countries and has been consistently ranked as a top media brand in China.[6]

The rapid growth of the Internet in China since the 1990s has made the *GT* even more influential. As of March 2020, China boasted 904 million netizens and its Internet coverage had reached 64.5 percent. About 897 million Chinese netizens used mobile devices to gain access to the Internet, with 99.3 percent of them using mobile phones. About 731 million or 80.9 percent of China's Internet users got their news online.[7] For Chinese netizens, Weibo, a microblogging application that combines features of Facebook and Twitter, has become a leading source for news and information. Although Weibo is the second largest social media after WeChat measured by the number of users, it is primarily a public platform while WeChat is more private. The bloggers can discuss issues with netizens they do not know in real life and build mass followings. Weibo therefore becomes an ideas platform for the Chinese public to discuss issues such as the US-China trade war. While multiple Chinese companies provide Weibo services, Sina Weibo, which was launched by Sina Corporation in 2009, is the best known one in China. In fact, the term Weibo

6 "About the Global Times," https://hd.globaltimes.cn/article/44O8GBcr4ld

7 Chinese Internet Network Information Center, "The 45th China Statistical Report on Internet Development," April 2020. https://www.cnnic.net.cn/n4/2022/0401/c88-1088.html

is almost used exclusively to refer to Sino Weibo. The latest Sina report shows that as of the end of 2021 its Weibo had 573 million monthly active users and 249 million daily active users.[8] The importance of Weibo was further highlighted when in April 2019, China's National Library declared that it would archive Weibo posts "for research and policymaking purposes."[9]

The *GT* has taken full advantage of China's new digital age. Its Weibo account has been ranked as one of the top three influential Weibo accounts managed by official media for years. For example, the *GT*'s Weibo posts were retweeted 12.7 million times in 2017, next only to the *People's Daily*.[10] Its posts also spread across China's social media platforms. In 2018, the *GT* on Toutiao, a popular news application, was the most read account with more than 7 billion visits.[11] Financially, the *GT* has been turning a profit since 2015. In 2020, it reported a total revenue of 176 million CNY with a net profit of 24.5 million CNY, which tripled from the 8 million CNY net profit of 2015.[12] The combined media and financial successes have made the *GT* one of the most powerful opinion influencers in China when it comes to international news and affairs.

If the new age of social media provided a platform for the *GT* to become influential, then the rise of Chinese nationalism since the 1990s became the key to *GT*'s success. A commonly accepted definition of Chinese nationalism, however, has so far eluded scholars. Some argue that nationalism has become important in China only since the 1990s when the CCP started to use nationalism to boost the party's legitimacy. Some argue that nationalism in China can be traced back to the 1890s, when the Middle Kingdom suffered at the hands of Western and Japanese imperialists. Neither do scholars agree if it is proper to apply the concept of nationalism to China. Some argue that nationalism is a historical and social construct based on the European historical experience, thus it cannot be applied to China. But others argue that China's long history has produced enough common cultural traits to make China a nation, if not a modern state.[13] Despite the diverse understandings, scholars

[8] "Weibo 2021: Environmental, Social, and Governance Report," http://ir.weibo.com/static-files/44f43977-536d-4d2e-8b4d-0a3fb20a33c2

[9] Wang Mengzhen, "China's National Library to Archive 200 billion Sina Weibo Posts," May 19, 2019. https://news.cgtn.com/news/3d3d674d79677a4e34457a6333566d54/index.html

[10] "2017 Annual Report of Media Convergency," http://media.people.com.cn/n1/2018/0402/c14677-29901624.html

[11] "2018 Annual Report of Media Convergence," http://media.people.com.cn/n1/2019/0327/c120837-30996998.html

[12] "2020 Annual Report," http://static.sse.com.cn/disclosure/listedinfo/announcement/c/new/2021-04-16/603000_20210416_4.pdf

[13] See Duara, *Rescuing History from the Nation*; Zhao, *A Nation-State by Construction*; Gries, *China's New Nationalism*

agree on two features about Chinese nationalism. First, the so-called narrative of victimhood is central to the Chinese people's understanding of nationalism. This narrative consistently portrays China as a victim invaded, bullied, and exploited by foreign powers since the early 19th century until the founding of the PRC. With the rise of China since the 1990s, many believe that it is time for China to reclaim its position in the world as a respected power.[14] Second, Chinese nationalism has various manifestations, which often come into conflict with each other. The CCP does not have a monopoly on the meaning of nationalism. Rather, different breeds of nationalism often emerge "largely independent of official propaganda."[15] As this paper shows, the *GT* primarily used a hybrid type of nationalism, which combines state nationalism and popular nationalism, to frame the US-China trade war.

The rise of Chinese nationalism has brought about a "left turn" in Chinese politics since the 1990s. Two concurrent trends contributed to the rise of a grass-roots pan-leftism. On the one hand, China's rapid economic growth widened the gap between the rich and the poor and produced new social problems such as unemployment and pollution. As Jude Blanchette observed, marginalized groups—workers, peasants, disillusioned intellectuals, and others—gradually came together to forge a pan-leftist movement. Those groups were held together by the belief that "the Communist Party was abandoning socialism and embracing economic growth at all costs...to the benefit of an elite few and at the expense of the majority."[16] They urged the CCP to revive certain policies during the Maoist era, when the Chinese society was supposed to be more egalitarian.

On the other hand, many pan-leftists believed that a rising China was encountering growing hostilities from the West, especially from the United States. They complained that the Western media either misunderstood China or intentionally demonized China. A series of events since the 1990s, including the Taiwanese President Lee Teng-hui's 1995 visit to America, the 1999 NATO bombing of the Chinese embassy in Belgrade, the 2001 mid-air collision between an American spy plane and a Chinese jet, the clash with Japan over the Diaoyudao/Senkaku islands in the early 2000s, the 2008 Tibetan riot, and the 2008 human rights controversy over China's hosting of the Olympic Games, all convinced the pan-leftists that America and its allies were trying to bully China and maintain the US hegemony. The Internet provided a platform for them to express their grievances. For example, several Chinese college students spontaneously established the Anti-CNN website in 2008 and made waves criticizing the Western media.[17] Indeed, the online expression of

[14] Wang, *Never Forget National Humiliation.*

[15] Zhao, *A Nation-State by Construction*, p. 11.

[16] Blanchette, *China's New Red Guards*, p. 66.

[17] The website was later renamed the April Media.

Chinese nationalism became so prominent that scholars started to treat popular nationalism in China's cyberspace as a serious subject.[18]

Popular nationalism, however, is a double-edged sword for Chinese policy makers. It can be garnered to support the CCP, but it can also damage the credibility and legitimacy of the regime if the leadership appears too soft on certain issues. The Chinese government has been walking a tightrope between maintaining cordial relations with other nations and defending China's interests more aggressively. When the anti-Japanese sentiments appeared to grow out of control over the Diaoyudao/Senkaku Islands in 2006, for example, the government used censorship to silence online discussions.[19]

The thorny problem of popular nationalism created a grey area in which the *GT* thrived. The *GT* seems to be caught in a dilemma. It is both a state-run and a market-driven newspaper. In an interview, Hu Xijin admitted that the *GT* has two bosses: the government and the market. "In the long run, the two are equally important." Hu said: "If we lose the support of ordinary people and lose our influence, the government won't care about us anymore. Without ordinary people, our paper will die."[20] In practice, the *GT* often allowed the market to be the main driving force. "From the day it was launched, the *Global Times* tentatively broke away from the journalistic tradition seen as normal in the Chinese media landscape, which avoids touching upon conflict and confrontation." So declared the *GT*'s editorial team in 2009.[21] To market itself, the *GT* frequently used nationalistic rhetoric to frame its publications. "Most mainstream publications were so propaganda-heavy, so filled with party lingo and news of top leaders' endless meetings," the *Guardian* observed: "that the arrival of the plain-talking, eye-catching *Global Times* must have felt like an episode of *Sex and the City* beamed into the middle of a long sermon."[22] "[I]ts position is to make money—nationalism is *Global Times'* positioning in the market," the *Foreign Policy* agreed: "It's like any Rupert Murdoch publications; It's Fox News, essentially."[23]

[18] Wu, *Chinese Cyber Nationalism*; Jiang, *Cyber-Nationalism in China*; Schneider, *China's Digital Nationalism*.

[19] Wu, *Chinese Cyber Nationalism*, pp. 73–87.

[20] Zheping Huang, "Global Times Editor Hu Xijin on US-China Relations," August 9, 2016, *Quartz*, https://qz.com/741931/qza-with-hu-xijin-editor-in-chief-of-global-times

[21] "About Us," https://www.globaltimes.cn/about-us/index.html

[22] Han Zhang, "China's Troll King: How a Tabloid Editor Became the Voice of Chinese Nationalism," December 14, 2021, *The Guardian*, https://www.theguardian.com/news/2021/dec/14/china-troll-king-hu-xijin-tabloid-editor-became-voice-chinese-nationalism

[23] Christina Larson, "China's Fox News," October 31, 2011, *Foreign Policy*, https://foreignpolicy.com/2011/10/31/chinas-fox-news/

The *GT* took fully advantage of its ambiguous position. Hu Xijin admitted that the *GT* enjoyed a special relationship with government officials. In an interview Hu said that as a Communist party member who was appointed by the party to be the chief editor, he had access to insider information. The government officials "need to lay down and carry out policies, so they are more cautious. They can't speak willfully, but I can." Hu explained: "Some of my words are in line with their thinking, but it won't necessarily become state policy."[24] Hu seemed to imply that the *GT* used some of its provocative pieces as test balloons. But sometimes this strategy backfired. For example, in 2016, the *GT* was reprimanded by the government for discussing sensitive topics such as using force to take Taiwan and the June Fourth Incident of 1989.[25] In other cases, however, the *GT* was able to get away with running afoul of party lines. When the 2008 Olympic torch relay was disrupted by pro-Tibet protesters in Paris, Hu decided to report what happened. While the *GT* report conflicted with the official Chinese report which described the relay as a success, Hu recalled that he did not get into any trouble with the Chinese officials even as the *GT* piece angered the French ambassador.[26] Thus, the *GT* and the Chinese propaganda authority appeared to have a mutually beneficial relationship. The government gave the *GT* enough leeway to report, as long as the latter did not venture too far, and the *GT* thrived commercially. In return, the *GT* could frankly discuss issues that the government was unwilling to discuss openly. And if the *GT* crossed the government's bottom line, the latter could always rein in the nationalistic sentiments with plausible deniability.

Yet Hu genuinely regards himself as a professional journalist with a mission, which is to shape public opinion in a constructive way to make China stronger. In 2013, Hu made headlines again when he published *A Complicated China*, a collection of *GT*'s editorials. He used the book to systematically explain the *GT*'s editorial philosophy. The book, together with a series of interviews Hu did afterward, provided an opportunity for Hu to lay bare his understanding of nationalism.

Hu believed that China should promote patriotism, a "healthy" kind of nationalism, although he frequently used the terms "nationalism" and "patriotism" interchangeably. This belief was largely produced by the heated debates between the pan-leftists and liberals. In 2014, Mao Yushi, a prominent liberal economist, suddenly came under attack from pan-left groups and most of the official media. Mao had already become a public enemy of the pan-left groups because of his sharp

[24] Huang, "Global Times Editor Hu Xijin on US-China Relations."

[25] "Internet Regulator Asked the *Global Times* to Rectify Its Sensitive Polls," May 13, 2016, *BBC News*, https://www.bbc.com/zhongwen/simp/china/2016/05/160513_china_global_times_internet_regulator.

[26] "A Conservation with Hu Xijin," June 24, 2011, *Southern People Weekly*, http://news.sina.com.cn/c/sd/2011-06-24/154322700397_2.shtml

criticism of Mao Zedong and leftist policies. This time, Mao drew fire from his critics when he discussed a new buzzword "patriotic traitor" on his Weibo account.[27] Mao defined the "patriotic traitors" as those who pursued their own interests and defended the ruling elite at the expense of the public while doing so in the name of patriotism. Some of his more radical followers even argued that it was righteous to be a "traitor" in an "autocracy." The *GT* sharply criticized Mao, arguing that the term was a vicious attack against patriotism, not the traitors.[28] "We promote a healthy patriotism," Hu argued: "China is still relatively weak. If you don't love and protect it, it will be ruined. This kind of nationalist sentiment is perfectly normal. The *Global Times* will promote patriotism."[29]

The term "patriotic traitor," however, quick went viral and became a frequently used word in online trolling. A frustrated Hu complained that "nowadays criticizing our nation is becoming a new vogue."[30] To him, the polarization of Chinese public opinion was dangerous. "People either say that China is the best, or they say China is the worst." Hu explained: "the polarization of public opinion is very obvious."[31] Hu's solution was the "complicated China" perspective. He recognized that China faced many problems, but he insisted that China's achievements in the past decades should not be dismissed. "China's development is extremely unbalanced." Hu argued: "We have some highly developed regions but also some very backward regions. China is both a powerful country in the world and a backward one."[32] He thus urged the media to adopt a more balanced perspective. "Don't be a leftist or a rightest," Hu declared: "Be a pragmatist."[33]

For many, Hu's "complicated China" was not a new theory at all. Rather, it echoed the official party lines and sounded like a different expression of "socialism with Chinese characteristics." Some argued that Hu's approach was just an excuse to defend the government and fend off future reforms. To Hu, however, his critics missed the point. Hu believed that the criticism leveled against the government was based upon a flawed assumption. People who criticized China relied too heavily on Western ideas and theories. "All the popular social sciences and social theories

[27] Mao's Weibo account was shut down in 2017. His original Weibo post is no longer available, but its screenshot can still be found online. http://biweeklyarchive.hrichina.org/repost/22305.html

[28] "'Patriotic Traitor' Targets Patriotism, Not Traitor," October 22, 2014. *GT*, https://opinion.huanqiu.com/article/9CaKrnJFIvi

[29] "A Conservation with Hu Xijin."

[30] "Interview with Hu Xijin," March 2, 2015. http://theory.people.com.cn/n/2015/0302/c168825-26621292.html

[31] *Guanchazhe*, "Interview with Hu Xijin," August 20, 2013, *Guanchazhe*, https://www.guancha.cn/Media/2013_08_20_166959.shtml?web

[32] Ibid.

[33] "A Conservation with Hu Xijin."

were invented by the West, and they described and summarized the collective behavior and mentality of the West." Hu argued: "When you apply those theories to China, they don't fit."[34] The chief editor paid particular attention to America. "In the age of globalization, it is inevitable that China has been influenced by the West. And China's opening to a large extent is opening to America."[35] China can learn a lot from America, but China cannot import American ideas and institutes wholesomely. "China needs to think independently and decide what to do and what not to do."[36]

The "complicated China" thesis not only reflected the pan-leftist suspicion of the West and particularly of the United States, but also the general political atmosphere in Xi Jinping's China. Since becoming China's leader in 2012, Xi has initiated a series of reforms aimed at strengthening the power of the CCP and promoting more assertive foreign policies. While his anti-corruption campaign was widely popular, Xi also launched ambitious programs such as the Belt and Road Initiative and Made in China 2025. To mobilize public support, Xi touted the term "Chinese Dream" to achieve the "great rejuvenation of the Chinese nation." In foreign policy, the Xi administration shifted away from the policy of "keeping a low profile" that had been followed since the time of Deng Xiaoping and turned to more assertive policies such as a tougher stance in the South China Sea. Xi Jinping particularly emphasized ideological struggles, built a "Great Firewall," and tightened censorship. Popular nationalism quickly dominated public opinion, with movies like *Bravo! My Nation* getting applauded and netizens chanting the Wolf Warrior Diplomacy. Despite his frequent pledge to continue "reform and opening up," Xi's China has been perceived in the West as reversing that policy.[37]

Hu Xijin, however, was determined to tell China's story from his own perspective, even if that required using nationalistic rhetoric. "We can no longer avoid discussing sensitive topics," Hu explained regarding the *GT*'s coverage of international news: "We can only face them directly."[38] He dismissed the criticism that the *GT*'s nationalistic pieces could damage China's image abroad. "If the outside world wants to criticize us, let them do it."[39] Hu's idea of a healthy patriotism and the *GT*'s decision to tell China's story, as the rest of the paper shows, played a crucial role in framing the US-China trade war.

[34] *Guanchazhe*, "Interview with Hu Xijin."

[35] Ibid.

[36] Ibid.

[37] Economy, *The Third Revolution*.

[38] Hu Xijin, "China Telling the Truth," https://book.douban.com/reading/13772756/

[39] Huang, "Global Times Editor Hu Xijin on US-China Relations."

Framing the Trade War: China as a Defender of Free Trade, March–December 2018

Trade tensions had been building up between America and China long before Donald Trump and Xi Jinping became the leaders of their respective countries. Trump, however, was the first presidential candidate who made trade with China a primary issue in his campaign. He frequently singled China out as a villain ripping off America on trade for years and must be dealt with. Some analysists even argued that "[i]f Chinese import growth had been 50 percent slower than it was…[t]hat would have been enough (for Hilary Clinton) to defeat Donald Trump."[40] Thus, a trade war was not entirely unexpected in China, but it still shocked the Chinese public when it happened. On March 22, 2018, the Trump administration released the report of its investigation of China under Section 301 of the Trade Act of 1974, which accused China of practicing a wide range of unfair trade activities.[41] Trump then signed the memorandum and demanded China reduce the trade deficit by $100 billion.[42]

Hu Xijin and his *GT* were ready to punch back. "Trump savagely attacked China with tariffs," the *GT*'s Weibo account declared: "Washington mistook us as cowards. The only way to stop a war is to fight a war." The post then argued that China should hit back with tariffs on American soybeans, which would hurt farmers who voted for Trump. "China needs to knock off Trump's front teeth and let him face his voters toothless."[43]While this kind of tough talk fit with the *GT*'s writing style, its Weibo posts did not always use radical nationalistic tones. Instead, the Weibo posts zigzagged between nationalistic and moderate tones.

Between March 22 and the December 1 meeting between Trump and Xi during the G20 Summit in Argentina, the *GT* produced 754 posts on its Weibo account related to the trade war and the general US-China relations. Those posts were roughly divided into three categories. The first category consisted of news and statements from various agencies of the Chinese government. A total of 362, or 48 percent of the total 754 posts, fell under this category. The *GT* was clearly doing its job as a government affiliated media by keeping the netizens informed about the progress of the trade war and China's reactions. The second category consisted of editorials and commentaries for which the *GT* had been known. Hu Xijin took

[40] Davis and Wei, *Superpower Showdown*, p. 134.

[41] Office of the United States Trade Representative, "President Trump Announces Strong Actions to Address China's Unfair Trade," March 22, 2018. https://ustr.gov/about-us/policy-offices/press-office/press-releases/2018/march/president-trump-announces-strong

[42] *GT* Weibo Post (hereafter GTWP), untitled, March 22, 2018, https://weibo.com/1974576991/G8ChAwq18

[43] GTWP, untitled, March 22, 2018, https://weibo.com/1974576991/G8xtj9bMK

pride in those pieces, which he considered as the crown jewels of his newspaper.[44] A total of 310, or 41 percent of the total 754 posts, belonged to the second category. The last category included reproduced contents from foreign media, and a total of 82 pieces were posted.

The primary goal of those posts was not to report news matter-of-factly, but to frame the trade war into a narrative of an innocent and defensive China fighting against the American bully to preserve the global system of free trade. At first glance, the *GT* appeared to be neutral when it simply transmitted news and statements from the Chinese government. However, the Chinese government itself tried to frame the trade war in a similar way, albeit with a much more moderate tone since the statements were often written in rigid diplomatic rhetoric. The *GT* then piled on with its own evaluative editorials and commentaries. The reproduced contents from foreign media were also highly selective, as the *GT* only chose contents either critical of America or sympathetic toward China. The readers had no way to know if the Weibo posts quoted the foreign media out of context.

One way to defend China was to place the blame for the trade war squarely at the Trump administration's feet. The Chinese government did not deny that trade problems between the two countries existed, but Beijing refused to admit that China practiced unfair trade. Further, it was wrong for the Trump administration to use tariffs to address the trade disputes. The first government statement that appeared on the *GT*'s Weibo came from the Ministry of Commerce, followed by a similar statement from the Chinese embassy in America. While the former protested that America "ignored China's efforts to protect intellectual properties and the rules of the WTO" and pursued "unilateral actions and trade protectionism,"[45] the latter urged Washington to "pause on the brink of the precipice and make prudent decisions so as not to put bilateral trade relations in jeopardy."[46] The two statements were formulaic and followed the standard Chinese diplomatic rhetoric. The *GT*, however, quickly followed with more colorful language. "The unbalanced US-China trade has many complicated reasons, and it is a natural product of the international division of labor," one editorial argued. "One American administration cannot hope to change the situation with a magical scalpel. Washington wants to reduce the trade deficit by $100 billion. This is wishful thinking, the craziest plan in the world." The editorial ended with a scoff: "History will laugh at today's American administration for using outworn tariff tools to solve the problems in

[44] Wu Yuanchun, "Hu Xijin: How Do We Produce the Editorials," July 8, 2011, *GT*, https://china.huanqiu.com/article/9CaKrnJrASc

[45] GTWP, untitled, March 22, 2018, https://weibo.com/1974576991/G8Fodaavr

[46] GTWP, untitled, March 22, 2018, https://weibo.com/1974576991/G8EWrhI9C

the largest bilateral trade relationship of the world."[47] The *GT* also offered data-driven analysis trying to show that the Trump administration set up a strawman argument. Quoiting a report released by the Deutsche Bank, a *GT* editorial argued that America's calculation of the trade deficit was seriously flawed. The value of the goods produced by American companies in China was not included in Washington's calculation, while goods produced by Japanese and South Korean companies in China but exported to America were attributed to China. "The trade deficit is $30 billion," the editorial concluded, "and it is a far cry from the $360 billion Washington claimed."[48]

The Weibo posts rebutted the Trump administration's charges of China's theft of intellectual property and forced technology transfers, the key findings of the Section 301 investigation. "This is a big lie," one editorial put it bluntly. Washington was "trying to create an impression that China's modernization was achieved through theft." The editorial admitted that China did fail to protect intellectual property during the early years of China's economic reforms, but "now China has already established laws to protect intellectual property."[49] The post insisted that there were no forced technology transfers. US companies often did not provide their cutting-edge technologies and only offered less advanced technologies that China could find from somewhere else. Moreover, the editorial argued that technology transfer was a fair price for US companies to pay to gain access to the Chinese market. "By offering such technologies, these companies receive generous paybacks." The editorial then concluded that "[t]his is how a market economy works and there is no room for the Trump administration to forcefully change the rules."[50]

In line with Hu Xijin's idea of promoting a healthy patriotism, the *GT* sharply refuted liberal voices that blamed the trade war on China. Those voices argued that China's unfair trade practices and assertive foreign policies triggered the trade war. They also wanted a more cautious response, given America's overall economic strength and the trade war's negative impact on the economy. "Some people think no matter what China does, it's still China's fault," one editorial fumed. "We cannot expect that their voices will entirely disappear, but they do not represent public

[47] GTWP, "The More America Pushes, The More China Will Push Back," March 27, 2018. https://weibo.com/1974576991/G9qChpDPc

[48] GTWP, untitled, "US Companies in China Were Not Included," April 3, 2018. https://weibo.com/1974576991/GamCyd9IH

[49] GTWP, "Washington Suffers from IP-Theft Paranoia," March 31, 2018 https://weibo.com/1974576991/G9UZEFwx1

[50] Ibid.

opinion."[51] Hu Xijin also blamed the liberal voices for undermining China's effort to forge a unified response to the trade war.[52]

The *GT* went beyond defending China and argued that Trump was bluffing and blackmailing China for trade concessions. "This is Trump's trade war, not a trade war that America wanted," said one editorial. "Trump's real goal is to scare China into making concessions."[53] On April 5, Trump said that he was considering a new round of tariffs on an additional $100 billion of Chinese imports. The *GT* immediately called Trump a "tariff maniac." "President Trump is throwing a temper tantrum against China and the world," one editorial mocked the additional tariffs, "and this has become America's way of treating the rest of the world."[54] China, however, would not be intimidated. Making concessions to America would be a policy of appeasement and further whet Trump's appetite. "The problem is that Trump may want a lot more from China," one editorial argued. "In fact, Trump wants to get all he wants to get support for his 'America First' strategy and make sure that economically China will never surpass America."[55] China, therefore, was being pushed into a corner. "This is our Battle of Stalingrad," another editorial made clear that China could not cave in, "and let's fight an epic trade war of self-defense."[56]

The *GT* was particularly angry that the trade war targeted the "Made in China 2025" plan, which aimed at turning China into a leading manufacturing power in ten high-tech areas. "The White House has admitted," one Weibo post announced, "that the trade war's real target is Made in China 2025. Fair trade? What a flimsy excuse!" Angry netizens quickly flooded the commentary section. "Do we need the world's permission to make an economic plan? None of your business!" fumed one netizen. "America wants Chinese people to be cheap labor for them forever. What a despicable idea!" cursed another.[57] When the Chinese government started to criticize America's targeting of "Made in China 2025," the *GT* followed with a call to arms. "America wants to attack 'Made in China 2025' and some American elites arrogantly want to beat China back into the last century," one editorial declared. "Let's hit them

[51] GTWP, "People Who Dampen China's Counterstrikes Pretending to Be Rational," March 25, 2018, https://weibo.com/1974576991/G92gktTF4

[52] GTWP, untitled, March 25, 2018, https://weibo.com/1974576991/G92S5lVOn

[53] GTWP, "Trump Will Be Defeated," March 22, 2018, https://weibo.com/1974576991/G8FK9gHfP

[54] GTWP, "Trump Intimidates China, What a Joke," April 5, 2018, https://weibo.com/1974576991/GaNQ87Y4n

[55] GTWP, "US-China Trade Conflict, Not That Simple," March 23, 2018, https://weibo.com/1974576991/G8K3VtV7l

[56] GTWP, "China Will Fight to The End," March 25, 2018, https://weibo.com/1974576991/G98pvn3Gs

[57] GTWP, untitled, March 29, 2018, https://weibo.com/1974576991/G9CG8vHwM

hard."[58]The editorial then suggested that China impose tariffs on American cars and agricultural products, which presumably would hurt Trump's political base. "China needs to fight America the same way we fought them during the Korean War," Hu Xijin added. "We need to firmly smash Washington's arrogance."[59] "China is not America's colony," another editorial claimed. "No one can block China's development."[60]

While using terms like "the Battle of Stalingrad," "the Korean War," and "colony" to stoke nationalistic sentiments, the *GT* was confident that China would prevail in the trade war. A typical argument was that the US economy relied more heavily on the Chinese market than the other way around. One editorial argued that China could easily import soybeans from Brazil and Russia while America would have a hard time finding alternative suppliers of consumer goods.[61] "China will soon surpass America as the world's largest consumer market," another editorial observed. "China has been the largest market for cars in the past nine years, the largest market for smart phones, and the largest market for clothes, e-commerce, tourism, and agricultural products."[62]Therefore, America would have no choice but continue to rely on the Chinese market.

In addition, the *GT* believed that the Chinese people were more unified behind the government and could endure more pressures, compared with a domestically divided America. "Chinese people know that we are forced to fight against an unjust war," one editorial reassured its readers. "The advantages of our system will help Chinese people and companies negatively affected by the trade war."[63] When China reported that its GDP grew by 6.8 percent during the first quarter of 2018, the *GT* touted the number as an indicator of a healthy economy. "The trade war is just a small problem," one editorial boasted. "China's strong development is the best rebuttal of outside challenges."[64] The Weibo posts rarely discussed the trade war's negative impact on the Chinese economy. When this topic came up, the posts usually gave it a fleeting mention, always with a reassuring message. By contrast, the *GT* frequently reported how American soybean farmers, hog farmers, cherry farmers and other businesses suffered from the trade war.[65]

[58] GTWP, "If We Fight the Trade War, Hit America Hard," April 4, 2018, https://weibo.com/1974576991/GavEV41Mp

[59] GTWP, untitled, April 7, 2018, https://weibo.com/1974576991/Gb1Y3skq2

[60] GTWP, "Trump Distorted Trade," April 10, 2018, https://weibo.com/1974576991/GbqtUm9ci

[61] GTWP, "Easy to Boycott US Soybeans," March 22, 2018, https://weibo.com/1974576991/G8wzM6DoE

[62] GTWP, "Market Size Shows American Advantages Not Real," March 26, 2018, https://weibo.com/1974576991/G9ieIAq7a

[63] GTWP, "China Is Firm And Calm," March 24, 2018, https://weibo.com/1974576991/G8ROftMob

[64] GTWP, "China's Economy in Great Shape," April 18, 2018, https://weibo.com/1974576991/GcDLLkZyS

[65] GTWP, "US GDP Up by 4.1%," July 30, 2018, https://weibo.com/1974576991/GsqUenPlm

The *GT* also examined the trade war in the global context, presenting China as a defender of the free trade system and the World Trade Organization (WTO). Indeed, the WTO was mentioned 154 times in the 754 Weibo posts under study here. Four days after the trade war started, the *GT* reposted a sharp critique from the Chinese government that America's sanction against China, based on the 301 Section investigation, a domestic law, went against the rules of WTO. The government spokesperson urged other WTO members to work together against American unilateralism.[66] Another post from the Ministry of Commerce argued that China had fulfilled its obligations under the WTO rules by lowering its average tariff from 15.3 percent to 9.8 percent. Thus, it was America that violated WTO rules by taking unilateral actions against China.[67] On June 28, the *GT* summarized on Weibo a white paper titled "China and the World Trade Organization," published by the State Council.[68] China emerged as a defender of free trade and WTO rules. In July, the *GT* further criticized America's attempt to change the rules of the WTO.[69]

While the Chinese position on WTO was repeated throughout the Weibo posts, the *GT* devoted 251 or 33 percent out of the total 754 posts to issues not directly linked to the trade war. The 251 posts covered a wide range of issues. Some posts aimed at exposing the "American hegemony" and sounding the alarm about the threats Washington posted to world peace. One editorial, for example, accused America and its allies of bypassing the United Nations and attacking Syria.[70] Another editorial warned that America should not toy with US-Russian relations. "American failed to appreciate the real possibility that US-Russian relations would deteriorate," the post pointed out. "America is the number one superpower of the world, but now it has become the biggest threat to world stability."[71] The *GT* also blamed America for sabotaging China-Latin American relations[72] and asked America to bury the Monroe Doctrine once and for all.[73]

China tried to drive a wedge between America and its allies. In May 2018, the Chinese Premier Li Keqiang visited Japan, and the Japanese Prime Minister Shinzo

66 GTWP, untitled, March 26, 2018, https://weibo.com/1974576991/G9hs1i47Y

67 GTWP, untitled, March 29, 2018, https://weibo.com/1974576991/G9C3hn9l2

68 GTWP, untitled, June 28, 2018, https://weibo.com/1974576991/Gnsg2EBEo

69 GTWP, "America: Don't Even Think About Challenging WTO," July 17, 2018, https://weibo.com/1974576991/Gqt8ucAIN

70 GTWP, "Shameful for US, UK, and France to Attack Syria," April 15, 2018, https://weibo.com/1974576991/GckgbyFX7

71 GTWP, "Washington Should Not Recklessly Toy with Russia," August 9, 2018, https://weibo.com/1974576991/GtY61r82r

72 GTWP, "US Driving a Wedge between China and Latin America," October 20, 2018. https://weibo.com/1974576991/GEV8oE9B9

73 GTWP, "US Should Bury Monroe Doctrine," December 3, 2018, https://weibo.com/1974576991/H5EBEzBNi

Abe visited China in October. The *GT* closely followed the visits on Weibo and posted no less than 19 editorials and commentaries. "Japan's best interest is to maintain relative neutrality between America and China, rather than ganging up with one against the other," said Hu Xijin.[74] Another editorial put it more bluntly. "As the second and third biggest economies of the world, China and Japan should work together, without being influenced by America."[75] China also tried to woo America's European allies. When Li Keqiang visited Germany in July, the *GT* posted an editorial that argued "China had no intention to harm the interests of the European Union."[76] A few days later, the *GT* celebrated the joint communique of China and Germany. Tapping into the tariff war between America and its European allies, Hu Xijin insisted that "no one is talking about China and the EU joining forces against America. But China and Germany need to work together since Trump is bullying everyone."[77]

Besides American allies, the *GT* paid special attention to North Korean to remind Trump that he needed China on this issue. Its Weibo account produced 29 editorials and commentaries on the Chinese-North Korean-American entanglement and used the North Korea issue as leverage in the trade war. On May 3, an editorial warned that America should not try to marginalize China on the North Korea issue. "China is a huge mountain beside the Korean Peninsula, not a haystack," said the post. "The North Korea issue will never be solved without China."[78] When Trump and the North Korean leader Kim Jong-un were planning their first summit meeting, Hu Xijin argued that "China is indispensable to a peaceful solution of the North Korean problem because only China can persuade North Korea that it can trust America. Without China, the Trump-Kim summit will not succeed."[79]

The *GT* did not forget that America, too, had leverages. Its Weibo devoted 130 posts, or 51 percent of the total 251 non-trade related posts, to other US-China bilateral issues. These posts included 44 pieces on Taiwan, 28 on alleged Chinee espionage and travel restriction, 26 on the South China Sea, 10 on Xinjiang, 9 on military relations, 5 on human rights, 5 on "One Belt One Road," 3 on Hong Kong, 2 on Tibet, and 1 piece on fentanyl. Most of those posts and editorials involved tit-for-tat refutations against American accusations in those areas. The *GT* was not particularly alarmed by those conflicts. In an early editorial, it had already warned that "America may use

[74] GTWP, untitled, September 2, 2018, https://weibo.com/1974576991/GxxWzdEic

[75] GTWP, "China-Japan Relations Should Avoid External Influences," September 12, 2018, https://weibo.com/1974576991/Gz8T9mwoj

[76] GTWP, "China-EU Relations Should Be Positive," July 6, 2018, https://weibo.com/1974576991/GoExo3eeQ

[77] GTWP, untitled, July 10, 2018, https://weibo.com/1974576991/Gpl3a3smS

[78] GTWP, "China Is a Mountain, Not a Haystack," May 3, 2018, https://weibo.com/1974576991/GeVXVpgzN

[79] GTWP, untitled, May 23, 2018, https://weibo.com/1974576991/GioE1ipMJ

Taiwan, South China Sea or other issues to wage the trade war, but China is strong enough to hold its lines."[80] Those posts were also not very nationalistic. After all, protesting the US navy sailing through the South China Sea or warning America not to intervene with China's domestic affairs appeared to be routine. And the Weibo readers had got used to them. One editorial, for example, calmly declared that China was confident about handling the Taiwan situation on its own terms.[81]

While the *GT* presented a confident China prepared to fight to the end, the trade war showed no signs of ending. On the contrary, it continued to escalate. On April 16, the US Commerce Department announced a seven-year ban on the Chinese telecommunication company ZTE.[82] On May 3 and 4, the US trade delegation which included Treasury Secretary Seven Mnuchin, Commerce Secretary Wilbur Ross, and the U.S. trade representative Robert Lighthizer held a new round of negotiations in Beijing. The American team presented eight demands which included cutting the bilateral trade deficit by $200 billion, stopping state support for "Made in China 2025," canceling financial support of state-owned enterprises, protecting press freedom, and other harsh demands. The Chinese side was so shocked by this "surrender or die" approach that it leaked the eight demands to the media.[83] Both Chinese and American media concluded that those demands were unrealistic and dimmed the prospect of an early trade deal.[84]

Surprisingly, the *GT* posted an editorial that presented the negotiation in a positive way. For readers who know how to read between the lines, the editorial hinted that a trade settlement was not within sight. "The Chinese side repeatedly told the Americans that China would not sacrifice its core interest for a trade deal," the editorial reported. "Of course, America and China cannot solve all their problems just by one talk." The editorial then said that Washington had softened its stance. "They came to us to talk, and all the heavyweights on trade came to us," the editorial argued. "This is very different from the beginning of the trade war when Washington arrogantly threatened China with tariff." The editorial concluded that "China's counterstrikes are working" and the deadlock was going to be broken soon.[85]

[80] GTWP, "China Will Fight to The End."

[81] GTWP, "Beijing Decides How to Play Chess," April 8, 2018, https://weibo.com/1974576991/GbfSmdxB2

[82] US Department of Commerce, "ZTE Denial Order," April 16, 2018, https://www.commerce.gov/files/zte-denial-order

[83] Davis and Wei, *Superpower Showdown*, pp. 220–221.

[84] Keith Bradsher, "U.S.-China Trade Talks End with Strong Demands, but Few Signs of a Deal," May 4, 2018, *The New York Times*. Sina News, "No Country Will Accept the US Eight Demands," May 6, 2018, https://news.sina.com.cn/o/2018-05-06/doc-ihacuuvu0524334.shtml

[85] GTWP, "Trade Conflict Tilting Toward Negotiation," May 6, 2018, https://weibo.com/1974576991/Gf6WXb1eX

In fact, the overall tone of the *GT*'s Weibo posts moderated after the early May negotiation. While still insisting that China must be prepared to fight, most of the posts started to plead for a negotiated settlement. In middle May, the Vice Premier Liu He, whom Xi Jinping trusted and put in charge of the trade negotiation, led a delegation to Washington for another round of talks. On May 19, the two sides rolled out a joint statement that promised to cut tariffs and stop the trade war.[86] The *GT* hailed the agreement as a win-win for both nations, although it refuted the perception that China had surrendered to American demands.[87] The agreement, however, did not hold and the trade war resumed in June. While accusing America of negotiating in bad faith, the overall tone of the *GT* continued to be moderate, urging the two sides to settle. After a couple of new rounds of negotiation through September, Hu Xijin expressed his frustration on Weibo. "China obviously underestimated the Trump administration's toughness, and the White House underestimated China's resistance," Hu mused. "What is to be done? Let the confrontation continue? Escalate the trade war into a comprehensive new cold war? And then trigger a hot war with a military incident? This is unthinkable! We are talking about two nuclear powers!" Hu then launched a tirade playing down China's strengths. "China will not surpass America even by the end of this century." Hu concluded. "America and China should work together instead of fighting against each other." The change of tone was so obvious that one netizen teased in the commentary area: "Are you preparing to surrender?"[88]

Hu's concern of a new cold war was the main reason why the *GT* toned down its nationalistic rhetoric. The Weibo posts reflected the Chinese government's uncertainty about the real intention of Washington. Did America try to get a good trade deal? Or did America try to launch a new cold war aimed at containing China? The mixed signals made it hard for China to reach a clear-cut conclusion. On the one hand, the Trump administration lifted the ban on ZTE in July and said multiple times that America did not want to contain China. On the other hand, the trade war continued to escalate. One thing was clear though. It was not in China's interest to initiate a new cold war. Thus, despite its nationalistic tone, the *GT* carefully limited its discussion of a new cold war. Among the 754 posts under study here, only 26 posts discussed whether the trade war could escalate into something bigger. The term "Cold War" was used 29 times, but it was used to mean a "new cold war" only 5 times. The term "decoupling" only appeared 2 times. The *GT* did not provide a firm conclusion, but in a late November editorial, it argued that America and

[86] GTWP, "US-China Joint Statement," May 19, 2018, https://weibo.com/1974576991/Ght7PnRPo

[87] GTWP, "Trade War Stopped, Win-Win for the Two Nations," May 19, 2018, https://weibo.com/1974576991/GhtVjtGnZ

[88] GTWP, untitled, October 12, 2018, https://weibo.com/1974576991/GDzjUfXon

China must seek "the greatest common divisor." The complicated bilateral relations and the two nations' economic interdependence made it unfeasible to launch a new cold war. "The so-called 'decoupling' is only a utopian idea cooked up by a minority," declared the editorial.[89] As the trade war continued into 2019, however, the issue of a new cold war quickly emerged as the front-runner problem.

Toward a New Cold War?

The meeting between Trump and Xi during the G20 Summit in Argentina raised the hope that Beijing and Washington were heading toward a settlement. An editorial published before the Trump-Xi meeting downplayed the new cold war thesis and urged the G20 nations to work together. "Based on the signals from Washington, the trade war certainly involves geopolitical considerations, but Washington apparently focuses primarily on economic gains." The editorial then argued that the American and Chinese economies "are highly complementary to each other" and the G20 should work together to defend "global trade based on multilateralism."[90] The two leaders agreed to put the trade war on hold for 90 days. Trump agreed to keep the tariffs on $200 billion Chinese imports at the 10 percent rate, instead of raising it to 25 percent. Xi agreed that China would start to purchase a substantial amount of product from China. A White House statement said that the two leaders "have agreed to immediately begin negotiations on structural changes with respect to forced technology transfer, intellectual property protection, non-tariff barriers, cyber intrusions and cyber theft, services and agriculture."[91]

The *GT* followed the truce with an editorial that welcomed the agreement as a win-win result. "After more than a half year's trade war, the two sides have come to understand each other's determinization, core interests, and bottom lines," the editorial analyzed. "Both sides have realized that it is in their interest to end the trade war." The editorial noticed that Trump appeared to have dropped the "Made in China 2025" issue. "America does not have the capacity to really damage China's core interests," the editorial said confidently. "The trade war may escalate again (after 90 days), but it sure will not lead to decoupling like what happened

[89] GTWP, "Difficult Mission Seeking US-China Greatest Common Divisor," November 28, 2018, https://weibo.com/1974576991/H4SGtjlN2

[90] GTWP, "G20 Please Support Multilateralism," November 30, 2018, https://weibo.com/1974576991/H5bplbA7v

[91] "Statement from the Press Secretary Regarding the President's Working Dinner with China," December 1, 2018, https://trumpwhitehouse.archives.gov/briefings-statements/statement-press-secretary-regarding-presidents-working-dinner-china/

under the Cold War."[92] A few days later, Hu Xijin told the audience of the 2019 *GT* annual meeting that China must avoid a new cold war. In this revealing speech, Hu worried that extreme nationalistic sentiment might give a boost to the extreme leftists, which would backfire and hurt China's reforms. "That's why the *Global Times* has adjusted its overall tone in the past few months," Hu said frankly, "and we have emphasized that it is one of China's core interests that a new cold war will not happen between America and China."[93]

The arrest of Meng Wanzhou on December 1 in Canada, however, quickly dampened the optimism generated by the Trump-Xi meeting. Meng was arrested on behalf of the United States. Washington alleged that Meng, as one of Huawei's top executives, played a leading role in Huawei's business operations in Iran, which violated American sanctions. Washington thus wanted Meng arrested and extradited. Meng's arrest caused a nationalist outrage in China. "To many Chinese, the U.S.-directed action was equivalent to Beijing ordering the arrest of Ivanka Trump."[94] Public opinion in China immediately sensed a conspiracy behind Meng's arrest. "As the chief editor of a Chinese media," Hu Xijin denounced the arrest on Weibo, "I want to tell America that while you cannot beat Huawei in the market, do not use despicable means and play dirty."[95] When Trump himself hinted that he might weigh in if it could help settle the trade war, the President's words only confirmed China's worst suspicion that America was willing to break all the international norms. One *GT* editorial argued that "Washington and Canada, without doubt, are abusing their legal system.... Washington should not use its domestic laws to wage diplomatic offensives and weaponize its long-arm jurisdiction."[96] The editorial compared Huawei with ZTE and wondered aloud why instead of fining or sanctioning Huawei, like what happened to ZTE, Washington decided to arrest Meng instead.

The answer was obvious to many Chinese. Unlike ZTE, Huawei had long been regarded as a vanguard in China's high-tech industries. The company invested heavily in research and became the world's largest supplier of telecommunications network equipment and second-largest maker of smartphones. While foreign companies filed lawsuits against Huawei on alleged intellectual property infringement, Huawei was generally regarded in China as the hope of China's indigenous innovations, especially since the company, arguably, was privately owned. Its founder,

[92] GTWP, "US-China 90-Day Truce," December 3, 2018, https://weibo.com/1974576991/H5EtxlxBg

[93] GTWP, "Hu's Speech," December 7, 2018, https://weibo.com/1974576991/H6fM8Fxk3

[94] Davis and Wei, *Superpower Showdown*, p. 307.

[95] GTWP, untitled, December 5, 2018, https://weibo.com/1974576991/H5We7ggOf

[96] GTWP, "US Canada Should Not Open the Pandora Box," December 11, 2018, https://weibo.com/1974576991/H6ReUxowy

Ren Zhengfei, a former military officer who became one of China's most successful entrepreneurs, was almost regarded as a folklore hero. "Forget about making a trade deal with the Americans," one angry netizen posted, "because they don't just want to cost China an arm and a leg. They want China's head. Let's fight. What do we have to lose?"[97]

Naturally, Huawei became a frequently discussed topic on the *GT*'s Weibo account. Between Meng's arrest and the Phase One trade agreement, the *GT* produced 1,484 Weibo posts related to the trade war and U.S.-China relations, which had a similar overall structure to those published before. The posts included 607 pieces (41 percent) coming from the Chinese government, 670 editorials and commentaries (45 percent), and 207 pieces (14 percent) of reproduced content from foreign media. Out of the 1,484 posts, 269 posts (18 percent) were specifically devoted to Huawei, not to mention hundreds more that touched upon the Huawei controversy.

Although overshadowed by the Huawei incident, U.S.-China trade negotiations struggled forward. In a December 29 editorial, the *GT* reported that Trump and Xi just talked over the phone and confirmed that the two countries were following up with the Trump-Xi agreement reached during the Argentina G20 Summit. "This is good news," the editorial cheered. "This is a New Year gift from the two leaders to the whole world." But the editorial also expressed its concerns. "Does America primarily want to contain China as a strategic competitor, or does America primarily want to get a fair-trade deal with China? Does America send out mixed signals because of the lack of internal coordination, or is that a kind of strategy? Frankly, China is confused. So are American allies."[98]

When the U.S.-China vice-ministerial level consultation in Beijing was extended for another day, the *GT* took the extension as a sign that the two sides were moving toward a deal. An editorial argued that two factors contributed to the thaw of relations. On the one hand, the trade war's negative impact on the American economy forced Trump to seek a deal. On the other hand, China initiated certain reforms to address the structural issues raised by the American side. "Some of the structural changes align with China's own needs and China can respond positively, such as lowering tariffs and protecting intellectual property," the editorial tried to present Chinese concessions in a positive way: "Of course, the Americans know that some issues regarding China's basic institutes and ideology are off limits."[99] When Liu He

[97] GTWP, untitled, December 6, 2018, https://weibo.com/1974576991/H61C7p5sV

[98] GTWP, "Xi-Trump Phone Call Releases Positive Signals," December 29, 2018, https://weibo.com/1974576991/H9B3YvwfI

[99] GTWP, "US-China Trade Negotiation Moving Forward," January 10, 2019, https://weibo.com/1974576991/HbhWuvOCW

led a delegation to Washington in January 2019, the *GT* increased its optimism. One editorial reported that Liu He's visit had achieved "substantial progress." There were still thorny problems to be solved. "But those problems are minor compared with the benefits of an agreement," the editorial argued. "The trend toward the end of the trade war is now becoming irresistible."[100]

The early battle cry of an epic trade war was now replaced with more moderate rhetoric. The concern about a new cold war played a major role in bringing about this change of tone. Settling the trade war obviously would help in scaling down the tensions between America and China. At the same time, the *GT* responded to the looming new cold war by trying to control the narrative of Chinese nationalism. On the one hand, Hu Xijin and his team had to fight against what they considered as extreme nationalists, meaning those who wanted to fight America at all costs. On the other hand, they had to insist that China would not make too many concessions to appease Washington. This was not just a strategy to calm down the nationalist sentiment. It also reflected Hu Xijin's idea of a "complicated China" and the belief that China should pursue its own development model without being excessively influenced by the West.

On December 23, 2018, Hu Xijin dismissed a "rumor" that the Chinese government ordered to ban Christmas in China. While extreme nationalists supported such a ban, Hu urged people to be more tolerant and open. "It's perfectly normal to see Christmas decorations around China," said Hu.[101] On Christmas Day, however, Hu celebrated the 125th anniversary of Mao Zedong's birthday. "More and more netizens are calling today *mao dan* (birthday of Mao) instead of *sheng dan* (Christmas)," Hu said. "Mao Zedong is a great man. And let's hope China will continue to develop without repeating his mistakes."[102] After appealing to both the liberals and the leftists, Hu expressed his biggest concern in an editorial. "Washington's designation of China as a strategic competitor is shaping its overall policy," the editorial warned. "More and more American elites have accepted that the US-China rivalry is now inevitable." The editorial acknowledged that with the rise of China, Sino-American relations were bound to change. China could no longer keep a low-profile, because "China's rise could no longer be suppressed or hidden." But Washington was not ready to launch an all-out Cold War against China yet. The editorial argued that China still had time to prevent the worst scenario from happening. "As long as we keep our door open, America cannot shut it from its side completely." The editorial then urged China to be calm and rational. "Under no circumstance should

100 GTWP, "Negotiation on Track Based on Trump-Xi Agreement," February 1, 2019, https://weibo.com/1974576991/HeLjAqH5v

101 GTWP, untitled, December 23, 2018, https://weibo.com/1974576991/H8BQOexBD

102 GTWP, untitled, December 25, 2018, https://weibo.com/1974576991/H8Z2kfmjo

we proactively escalate conflicts with America," the editorial cautioned. "The two nations have no desire to fight a hot war. But China can defend its core interests, including preventing an independent Taiwan."[103] On December 30, Hu Xijin penned a post celebrating the 40th anniversary of the normalization of U.S.-China relations. "In the past four decades, America has played a positive role in China's reform and opening up," Hu said candidly. "We know that frictions are growing between America and China, but both nations need to prevent those frictions from getting out of control." Hu then urged public opinion to remain calm and rational. "As long as we say NO firmly to the new cold war, the new cold war will not be ignited. When some Americans are talking about a new cold war, we should not act so impulsively as to turn the new cold war into a reality."[104]

Can China avoid a new cold war unilaterally? Hu seemed to think that China could. While opposing a new cold war appealed to the liberals, Hu's argument was also built to satisfy the leftists: the new cold war already failed before it was launched due to China's strengths. In an April editorial, the *GT* argued exactly that. "Washington has been smearing China's 'One Belt One Road,' but has been ignored by the developing nations," the editorial teased. "Italy now officially joined the "One Belt One Road' initiative." "America's effort to suppress Huawei has also failed to achieve the desired result," the editorial piled on, "and it is doubtful that its military pressures against China regarding Taiwan and the South China Sea will work." The editorial concluded that "America's containment failed because Washington misjudged China's strengths, strategic goals, and its own ability to mobilize domestic forces and allies to contain China." With that said, the editorial added that "China has no intention to upend the international order and seek domination."[105]

The *GT*'s effort to wish away a new cold war, however, was undermined by the escalated trade war. The trade negotiation fell apart again at the beginning of May. On May 5, Trump announced that he would increase the tariffs on the $200 billion Chinese imports from 10 percent to 25 percent. The Chinese government urged the American side to continue the negotiation, and Liu He was heading to America for another round of negotiation.[106] The Chinese government did not reveal the details of the ten rounds of trade negotiation the two countries had done so far, but its statements clearly indicated that Washington was pressuring Beijing on issues that the latter could not compromise on. The *GT* likened Liu He's trip to Washington

[103] GTWP, untitled, "The Biggest Question Mark from 2018," December 25, 2018, https://weibo.com/1974576991/H8Z5KDsBp

[104] GTWP, untitled, December 30, 2018, https://weibo.com/1974576991/H9JnCpwmV. Emphasis original.

[105] GTWP, "Containing China Failed as a Delusion," April 4, 2019, https://weibo.com/1974576991/Ho3rRwsgU

[106] GTWP, untitled, May 6, 2019, https://weibo.com/1974576991/HsWs2AVKw

to the "Hongmen Banquet," a well-known historical story in China. Liu Bang, the founder of the Han Dynasty, was once invited to a banquet by his chief rival Xiang Yu at a place called Hongmen. Xiang Yu planned to kill Liu Bang at the banquet, but Liu was saved by one of his lieutenants who broke into the banquet hall carrying his sword. "We Chinese know all about the Hongmen Banquet," Hu Xijin said defiantly, "and this time our delegates bring their swords with them too." The analogy had another implied meaning. After all, Liu Bang ultimately defeated Xiang Yu and established one of the greatest Chinese dynasties. And China could ultimately prevail in the trade war. But for now, Hu was worried about the domino effect. Echoing the official propaganda lines, Hu argued that China must fight against "the American strategy of maximum pressures," because "if we cave in, America will follow up on issues of Taiwan, the South China Sea, nuclear arms limitation, and the 5G technology."[107]

Indeed, it appeared that Washington was stepping up its pressures on Beijing from all directions. On April 29, Kiron Skinner, the US State Department's director of policy planning, declared that the U.S.-China competition was "the first time that we will have a great-power competitor that is not Caucasian."[108] Skinner since then has been criticized for promoting a new version of Samuel Huntington's "clash of civilizations" thesis while bordering on racism. The *GT* responded on May 5 with an editorial that accused America of using the "false thesis of clash of civilizations" to "mobilize the entire West against China." The editorial accused the Secretary of State Mike Pompeo of turning the State Department into another CIA that had fabricated lies about China.[109] On May 6, the *GT* reported that two American destroyers sailed near China-controlled islands in the South China Sea and argued that China must respond to each American intrusion with "increasing sternness."[110] On the same day, the Chinese government strongly refuted the US Assistant Secretary of Defense Randall Schriver's claim that China had detained 3 million Muslims in concentration camps in Xinjiang.[111] On May 8, Meng Wanzhou appeared in a new round of extradition hearings in Canada, and the *GT* emphasized again that Meng had been wrongfully arrested.[112] Meanwhile, the Chinese government strongly accused the US House for passing the Taiwan Assurance Act, which designated

107 GTWP, untitled, May 9, 2019, https://weibo.com/1974576991/Htr29b1Lp

108 Paul Musgrave, "The Slip That Reveals the Real Trump Doctrine," May 2, 2019, *Foreign Policy*, https://foreignpolicy.com/2019/05/02/the-slip-that-revealed-the-real-trump-doctrine/

109 GTWP, "US State Department Using Clash of Civilization to Trick the West," May 5, 2019, https://weibo.com/1974576991/HsUcYcV4f

110 GTWP, "US Provocations in South China Sea Are Pathetic," May 6, 2019, https://weibo.com/1974576991/Ht41M1uWU

111 GTWP, untitled, May 6, 2019, https://weibo.com/1974576991/HsYVkf9Nl

112 GTWP, untitled, May 8, 2019, https://weibo.com/1974576991/HtmmifXho

Taiwan as an important part of America's Indo-Pacific strategy and urged more sales of defense weapons to Taipei.[113]

The *GT* responded to the series of events with more nationalistic posts. On May 4, China's Youth Day, Hu Xijin celebrated the anniversary of the 1919 May 4th Movement and promoted his healthy patriotism. "China needs to build democracy and respect science, but we must do so in the context of patriotism," Hu said. "It is important to promote patriotism when China and America have frictions about the model of developments."[114] In a separate post, Hu encouraged China's younger generation in "the mission of the rejuvenation of the Chinese nation." "It is highly likely that the U.S.-China relations will never go back to the pre-trade war time," Hu pleaded. "But today's Chinese youths must be firm and confident. They must make sure that China's rejuvenation will not be hijacked by America and the West."[115] On May 8, Hu Xijin published a post in memory of the three Chinese journalists killed in the 1999 NATO bombing of the Chinese embassy in Belgrade.[116] In a May 9 editorial, the *GT* declared that China would fight the escalated trade war head-on. "We don't want a trade war, but Washington has forced us to fight one. Bring it on then."[117]

For Hu Xijin, while ending the trade war could help with preventing a new cold war, fighting the trade war fiercely could help too. Echoing his early concern about a domino effect, Hu argued that "clearly the timing is yet right to end the trade war.... We must fight until Washington agrees to respect us."[118] On May 15, Trump signed an executive order that laid the groundwork to ban Huawei from doing business in America.[119] The US Department of Commerce immediately added Huawei to the so-called "Entity List."[120] American companies were prohibited from selling semiconductors and other items critical to Huawei's operation to the Chinese company. The next day, the *GT* posted an open letter from the CEO of HiSilicon, a Huawei subsidiary focusing on research, to the company's employees. Written in a solemn tone, the letter pledged that Huawei develop its own chips and technologies at all

113 GTWP, untitled, May 8, 2019, https://weibo.com/1974576991/HtfyaeAYu

114 GTWP, untitled, May 4, 2019, https://weibo.com/1974576991/HsDIqlLZd

115 GTWP, untitled, May 4, 2019, https://weibo.com/1974576991/HsZ8h746v

116 GTWP, untitled, May 8, 2019, https://weibo.com/1974576991/HteZQFyMt

117 GTWP, "China Does Not Want a Trade War, But We Can Fight One," May 9, 2019, https://weibo.com/1974576991/HtwjghCAo

118 GTWP, untitled, May 13, 2019, https://weibo.com/1974576991/HuoLocq6Z

119 "Executive Order on Securing the Information and Communications Technology and Services Supply Chain," May 15, 2019, https://trumpwhitehouse.archives.gov/presidential-actions/executive-order-securing-information-communications-technology-services-supply-chain/

120 "Department of Commerce Announces the Addition of Huawei Technologies Co. Ltd. To the Entity List," May 15, 2019, https://web.archive.org/web/20200305133531/https:/www.commerce.gov/news/press-releases/2019/05/department-commerce-announces-addition-huawei-technologies-co-ltd

costs.[121] On Weibo, Hu Xijin likened Huawei's plight to the Shangganling Campaign, or the Battle of Triangle Hill, one of the toughest battles during the Korean War. The trade war "is going to be a prolonged struggle…but let's remember Shangganling…. Let's not sing an elegy, but a high-spirited marching song."[122]

But the concern about a new cold war only grew bigger. As if to further escalate the tensions between Beijing and Washington, pro-democracy protests engulfed Hong Kong in June. The Chinese government immediately suspected America's involvement and warned Washington not to intervene in China's domestic affairs.[123] In a June 12 editorial, the *GT* charged that the protestors were being used by foreign hostile forces to destroy Hong Kong.[124] Like Huawei, Hong Kong quickly became the new trending topic on Weibo. Between June and January 2020, the *GT* produced 193 editorials and commentaries on Hong Kong, 13 percent of the total 1,484 posts under study here. Altogether, the *GT* devoted 534 posts, or 36 percent out of the total 1,484 posts to issues not directly linked to the trade war, a 3 percent increase compared with the first stage of the *GT*'s coverage. But the percentage of posts related to China's core interests such as Hong Kong, Taiwan, Xinjiang, Tibet, and the South China Sea increased to 43 percent, compared with the 38 percent from the first stage. If we include posts on Huawei into the category, then the percentage of posts not directly linked to the trade war jumps to 50 percent, and the percentage of posts on China's core interests jumps to 61 percent. The changes in numbers reflected China's growing concern that the trade war was heading toward a larger new cold war.

In June, the Trump-Xi meeting in Japan raised the hope of a trade deal again, but not for too long. Xi Jinping told Trump that China and America should work together as partners and avoid confrontations, and he was clearly worried about a new cold war.[125] Trump claimed that the meeting went extremely well, and he even suggested that he might ease some restrictions on Huawei. A Chinese spokesperson welcomed Trump's decision "if he will really do that."[126] In August, however, Trump announced 10 percent tariffs on the remaining $300 billion of Chinese imports after another round of negotiation. China retaliated with tariffs on $75 billion of American imports. The *GT* complained that America's inconsistency and arbitrary moves now became the biggest barrier to a trade settlement. "Washington complained that China did not fulfill its promise to buy more agricultural products, but its own Commerce Department admitted that China has been buying," the editorial mused.

121 GTWP, untitled, May 16, 2019, https://weibo.com/1974576991/HuA1vq8mA

122 GTWP, untitled, May 17, 2019, https://weibo.com/1974576991/HuJJioBe7

123 GTWP, untitled, June 11, 2919, https://weibo.com/1974576991/HyqkviR3Q

124 GTWP, "HK Riots Make Friends Sorrow Enemies Happy," June 12, 2019, https://weibo.com/1974576991/HyGzUDXcT

125 GTWP, untitled, June 29, 2019, https://weibo.com/1974576991/HAZ5pyyho

126 GTWP, untitled, June 29, 2019, https://weibo.com/1974576991/HB9LYy5ir

"White House's greed is too much for this planet to bear."[127] On August 24, Trump announced an additional 5 percent tariff on all Chinese imports, after he ordered American companies to leave China on Twitter.[128] The *GT* responded by claiming that "the trade war now has become a war of attrition" and urged China to be firm and patient.[129] On August 27, the US company Costco opened a store in Shanghai. It attracted so many customers that the store was forced to close after a couple of hours. The *GT* put out an editorial teasing Trump's Twitter order. "Costco did not leave China as ordered but went to Shanghai instead," the editorial gleefully reported. "American companies voted with their feet and proved decoupling is a delusion."[130]

The Trump administration, however, continued to increase pressures on China. While the turmoil continued in Hong Kong, the US State Department approved $8 billion in arms sales to Taiwan, the biggest since the normalization of Sino-American relations.[131] When the US Senate passed the Taiwan Allies International Protection and Enhancement Imitative Act in late October, the *GT* warned Taiwan that "America will not save you."[132] Xinjiang became another front of the Beijing-Washington rivalry. While the Western media had been accusing Beijing of oppressing the Uyghurs for years, the criticism intensified in 2019. On March 21, a *GT* editorial accused the Western media of smearing China's Xinjiang policy. The West ignored Xinjiang's economic development and criticized China while rejecting Muslim refugees.[133] On August 15, the Chinese government published a white paper on Xinjiang, which argued that the training centers in Xinjiang were necessary to fight against terrorism and promote economic growth.[134] In December, the Chinese government strongly protested when the US Congress passed the UIGHUR Act. "The US congress members are high on something," Hu Xijin teased. "They are producing anti-China legislations faster than elementary school students writing essays."[135]

The mounting pressures, however, clearly made Hu frustrated. "The beacons are being lit everywhere on China's 'Great Wall'—Hong Kong, Xinjiang, and the

[127] GTWP, "US Breach of Promise," August 5, 2019, https://weibo.com/1974576991/IoNquxKod

[128] GTWP, untitled, August 25, 2019, https://weibo.com/1974576991/I3UivtuVn

[129] GTWP, "China Has Enough Tools to Counterstrike," August 25, 2019, https://weibo.com/1974576991/I3FTl5brT

[130] GTWP, "Costco Taught America a Lesson," August 27, 2019, https://weibo.com/1974576991/I4htcF70G

[131] GTWP, "Purchasing F16V Will Only Create More Risks for Taiwan," August 21, 2019, https://weibo.com/1974576991/I3nasD5SW

[132] GTWP, "US Will Not Dominate Taiwan," October 30, 2019, https://weibo.com/1974576991/IeoOZdynk

[133] GTWP, "West Criticism Against Xijiang Went Nowhere," March 21, 2019, https://weibo.com/1974576991/Hm3QsraVo

[134] GTWP, untitled, August 15, 2019, https://weibo.com/1974576991/I2sJBjmny

[135] GTWP, untitled, December 4, 2019, https://weibo.com/1974576991/IjfSgojGo

trade war," Hu said in a post. "What challenges do we have to face? What on earth does the enemy want from the central plain?" While the term "central plain" is a Sinocentric word that regarded China as the center of the world, in this revealing post Hu replaced the Chinese character *di* (敌) for enemy with another character *di* (狄) for barbarians. "A rising great power naturally feels isolated," Hu told his readers. "Don't expect the rest of the world to understand us. We need to be calm and confident."[136] But China's priority was still to avoid a new cold war. "We should never act the way the radical American elites want us to act," an editorial argued. "We must avoid the Thucydides Trap. This will be China's, and America's contribution to the 21st Century."[137]

A silver lining of hope finally appeared. In October, the Chinese delegation headed by Liu He visited Washington for the 13th round of trade negotiation. On October 11, Trump announced that the two nations were close to an agreement and decided to postpone tariffs that were scheduled to take effect on October 15.[138] The *GT* welcomed the breakthrough but cautioned that this was still a fluctuating situation. It urged the two sides to focus on the big picture and not be distracted by other issues.[139]On October 15, the Chinese Ministry of Foreign Affairs confirmed that the two sides had reached an agreement.[140] To the *GT*, a trade agreement meant that a new cold war could at least be postponed. On October 24, one editorial noticed that the US Vice President Mike Pence delivered a harsh speech against China. "The Vice President repeated all the usual attacks against China including Xinjiang, Taiwan, Hong Kong, and other issues," the editorial observed. "But at the end of his speech he said that America would not seek decoupling. He left an Easter egg."[141] On December 13, Beijing and Washington announced that they had reached an agreement on the text of the trade deal. China agreed to purchase more agricultural products and services from America, tighten intellectual property protection, and open further its financial market to American companies. America agreed to gradually reduce its tariffs on Chinese goods.[142]

On January 15, 2020, America and China signed the Phase One trade deal in Washington. The *GT* put out a series of editorials to reflect on the long trade war. One editorial argued that China should not underestimate the strengths of America.

136 GTWP, untitled, November 28, 2019, https://weibo.com/1974576991/IilUUf7lw

137 GTWP, "China Will Have the Last Laugh When the New Cold War Comes to Naught," December 5, 2019, https://weibo.com/1974576991/Ijut6cymw

138 GTWP, untitled, October 11, 2019, https://weibo.com/1974576991/Ib8e1q2Vs

139 GTWP, "US-China Talk Yield Positive Results," October 11, 2019, https://weibo.com/1974576991/Ib8e1q2Vs

140 GTWP, untitled, October 15, 2019, https://weibo.com/1974576991/IbCCN2uSN

141 GTWP, "Pence Said No Decoupling," October 24, 2019, https://weibo.com/1974576991/Id6I1iKBV

142 GTWP, untitled, December 13, 2019, https://weibo.com/1974576991/IkDh4u1Zm

The editorial indirectly refuted the nationalistic sentiment that chanted China's rise and argued that given the asymmetrical relations between America and China, "we have to be on the defensive."[143] But being on the defensive did not mean that China could not fight back when pressured. The *GT* argued that the trade war had made the Chinese people more mature and confident. China fought fiercely and proved that it could defend its core interests. The strength of China's political and economic institutes was the main reason why the nation could stand up to America. The *GT* argued that China should continue to pursue its own model of development.[144] The *GT* further argued that the Phase One trade agreement did not mean that China made too many concessions. China agreed to buy more products and services from America, but those were not forced sales. On the contrary, China would make purchase plans based on China's own needs. Structural changes such as intellectual property protection and opening more economic sectors to foreign investment served China's own need to deepen its reforms. In other words, China did not capitulate.[145]

Looking forward, the *GT* argued that China would need to fight smartly. Instead of fighting against America on all fronts, China should focus on the core issues and ignore the noise. "America is going to badmouth China anyway," one editorial argued. "China does not need to talk back every time. But when it comes to our core interests, we need to fight back firmly." At the same time, China should work with other nations to resist America's unilateral actions.[146] But still, China should not fight a new cold war against America. "How to handle relations with America is going to be the most difficult issue for China's foreign policy," one editorial argued. "China must stay rational and never fight a new cold war. We need to both fight America and talk with it without a showdown."[147]

Conclusion

Washington and Beijing had conduced 13 rounds of major negotiations and more small-scale talks before they reached a truce in early 2020. The U.S.-China trade war indeed was an epic one. The *GT*'s coverage of the trade war provided a window through which we can better understand China's perceptions of the trade disputes and its overall relations with America. While the *GT* frequently framed the trade

143 GTWP, "Understanding America," January 7, 2020, https://weibo.com/1974576991/IouUU2vbu

144 GTWP, "Trade War Made China More Confident," January 8, 2020, https://weibo.com/1974576991/IoFwsssxB

145 GTWP, "How to Understand More Imports from America," January 16, 2020, https://weibo.com/1974576991/IpSpXelRN

146 GTWP, "US-China Relations in 2020," January 2, 2020, https://weibo.com/1974576991/InKz7pAL2

147 GTWP, "China in the 2020s," January 9, 2020, https://weibo.com/1974576991/IoO27A21H

war from a nationalistic angle, it did not consistently promote popular nationalism, contrary to many contemporary observations. Instead, the *GT* had to battle against what it considered to be extreme positions both from the Left and the Right. It opposed making more concessions that would infringe on China's basic political and economic institutes, but it also opposed the extreme nationalistic sentiments that would provoke America needlessly. This vacillation largely reflected the evolving positions of the Chinese government. During the early months of the trade war, China was determined to fend off American demands. When the trade war threatened to evolve into a new cold war, China concluded that reaching a trade deal would prevent such an outcome.

The *GT* thus struggled to control the narrative of nationalism. At the core of this narrative was the pride China took in its achievements. This national pride was deeply connected to China's past, as China finally started to rise again from the "Century of Humiliation." Yet China felt that it was being frequently misunderstood by the West. While the *GT* fought a tit-for-tat verbal war against America, it concluded that China should stop caring too much about how America perceived China. On the other hand, the *GT* argued that China should continue to focus on its own model of development, which made it harder for America to persuade China to initiate structural changes.

Despite the Phase One trade deal, however, the fear that the U.S.-China trade war would evolve into a new cold war has continued to cloud the *GT*'s analysis of the bilateral relations. From early 2020 to the end of 2022 when the draft of this article was finalized, Beijing and Washington appeared to move closer to an all-out confrontation. The breakout of the COVID-19 pandemic further complicated the already tense relationship. Thanks to the pandemic, China not only failed to reach the goal of purchasing $200 billion of US exports by the end of 2021, which was stipulated in the Phase One deal, but the politicized origins of the pandemic further reduced the remaining good faith between the two nations. The election of Joseph Biden as the new American president in late 2020 only produced an attitude from the *GT* editorial board that could be best described as cautiously optimistic. For example, participants of the 2021 *GT* annual meeting agreed that while the Biden administration was likely to abandon the Trump administration's head-on collision against China, the new administration would nonetheless continue to contain China through softer means. Yet a softened American approach also meant that there would be more maneuvering to prevent a new cold war. The participants thus recommended rebuilding US-China cooperation through initiatives such as joint efforts to fight the pandemic.[148]

[148] GTWP, untitled, December 4, 2020, https://weibo.com/1974576991/Jx2ozid48

Indeed, between 2020 and 2022, the *GT*'s Weibo posts paid even less attention to trade issues per se and focused almost exclusively on issues related to the pandemic, Taiwan, the South China Sea, the semiconductor industry, the Ukrainian-Russian War, and other sensitive strategic and political problems. During the 2023 *GT* annual meeting held in December 2022, the participants concluded that the US-China decoupling had become a reality. Yet they still believed that it would be difficult for America to launch a new cold war unilaterally considering the economic integration of China into the world.[149] In short, new developments since the early 2020 have further deepened the fear about a new U.S.-China cold war, but those developments deserve another article.

The *GT*, of course, was not the only voice in China. But with the rise of pan-leftism in China, it has become more influential. Hu Xijin once said that the *GT* frequently conducted market surveys and had loyal readers from all social groups.[150] Thus the *GT* to a certain extent did reflect China's public opinion. Moreover, it sometimes also had an impact on public officials. As Susan L. Shirk once observed, the GT frequently "mobilize(s) public opinion on foreign policy and then feed(s) it back into the foreign policymaking process."[151]

In sum, the *GT*'s coverage played an important role in the Chinese public's perceptions of the trade war and relations with America. While the *GT* argued against a new cold war, it still presented a hostile America bent on containing China. This image has damaged the overall positive attitude most Chinese had toward America. Perhaps this will be the major problem for future Sino-American relations.

Dr. **Mao Lin** is an associate professor of history at Georgia Southern University. His research focuses on American foreign relations, the Cold War, modern China, and especially US-China relations. Lin's articles have appeared in a number of academic journals, covering a wide range of topics related to US-China relations. He has received several scholarships, including the 2022 Wilson Center China Fellowship, the 2020 Fulbright-Hays Seminars Abroad in Taiwan, the 2011 National Endowment for the Humanities, and the 2009 Marshall-Baruch Fellowship from the George C. Marshall Foundation. Currently he is working on a book project with the working title "U.S.-China Relations and the Diplomacy of Modernization, 1966–1979."

149 GTWP, "Experts on Decoupling," December 16, 2022, https://weibo.com/1974576991/MjZIbcAYO

150 "A Conservation with Hu Xijin," June 24, 2011.

151 Shirk, ed., *Changing Media, Changing China*, pp. 227–228.

Bibliography

Blanchette, Jude. *China's New Red Guards: The Return of Radicalism and The Rebirth of Mao Zedong.* Oxford: Oxford University Press, 2019.

Davis, Bob and Lingling Wei, *Superpower Showdown: How the Battle Between Trump and Xi Threatens a New Cold War*. New York: HarperCollins Publishers, 2020.

Duara, Prasenjit. *Rescuing History from the Nation: Questioning Narratives of Modern China.* Chicago: University of Chicago Press, 1995.

Economy, Elizabeth C. *The Third Revolution: Xi Jinping and the New Chinese State.* Oxford: Oxford University Press, 2018.

Gries, Peter Hays. *China's New Nationalism: Pride, Politics, and Diplomacy.* Berkley: University of California Press, 2004.

Ha, Louisa and Lars Willnat, eds. *The U.S.-China Trade War: Global News Framing and Public Opinion in the Digital Age.* East Lansing: Michigan State University Press, 2022.

Hu, Xijin. *A Complicated China.* Beijing: People's Daily Publisher, 2013.

Jiang, Ying. *Cyber-Nationalism in China: Challenging Western Media Portrayals of Internet Censorship in China.* Adelaide: University of Adelaide Press, 2012.

Schneider, Florian. *China's Digital Nationalism.* Oxford: Oxford University Press, 2018.

Shirk, Susan L. ed., *Changing Media, Changing China.* Oxford: Oxford University Press, 2011.

Wang, Zheng. *Never Forget National Humiliation: Historical Memory in Chinese Politics and Foreign Relations.* New York: Columbia University Press, 2012.

Wu, Xu. *Chinese Cyber Nationalism: Evolution, Characteristics, and Implications.* Lanham: Lexington Books, 2007.

Zhao, Suisheng. *A Nation-State by Construction: Dynamics of Modern Chinese Nationalism.* Stanford: Stanford University Press, 2004.

CONCLUSION

Xi's China: Continuing Evolution in a New Direction

Xiaobing Li and Qiang Fang

UNIVERSITY OF CENTRAL OKLAHOMA AND UNIVERSITY OF MINNESOTA DULUTH

The chapter authors have provided a historical assessment of Xi Jinping's policy and China's experience between 2012 and 2022. Their findings are different from the standard image in the West concerning the CCP's political reforms, PRC economic growth, and social changes in China during the past decade as reactive, full of self-doubt, confusion, anxiety, and returning to the "old way" in the revolutionary period of the 1950s–1970s. China at present has little in common with the Cold War China. The country has transformed because Xi Jinping's priorities and ruling methodologies changed tremendously through the decade and indicated many differences from his bland predecessors Jiang Zemin and Hu Jintao. However, the Chinese Communists have strong links to their revolutionary past, and any understanding of Chinese political culture, perspectives on leadership, and military transition may have to begin with a study of the CCP's history. Meanwhile, the Chinese political system had also evolved in terms of leadership, organization, and world view in the past decade. The society appears to be flexible and able to adapt to economic and political changes and to respond to rising demands and expectations of the Party in the 2020s.

Moreover, Xi and his advisors believe they live in a dangerous world in the 21st century with many uncertainties and potential challenges to China's security.[1] Their concerns are confirmed by Beijing's high command in the *White Paper: China's National Defense*, which made it clear that the country is facing "unprecedented" challenges because "new security threats keep emerging."[2] Their justification and calculation seem reasonable and logical in terms of the on-going globalization. Xi has made it clear that China is a superpower, and that it wants to be treated

[1] Among the interviews with the PLA officers by the author are Major Sun Lizhou, Second Department of the PLA General Staff, Beijing; the deputy commander, Jilin Provincial Command, Changchun, Jilin; and Major General Guan Zhichao (retired), at the PLA Political Academy, Nanjing.

[2] Information Bureau, PRC State Council. "The Security Situation."

as a global power. He proclaims to the Chinese people that "we must achieve the great revival of the Chinese nation, and we must ensure there is unity between a prosperous country and a strong military."[3]

Therefore, the new generation of CCP leaders in Xi's administration has faced disharmonious factors and unstable elements in China as well as in the world like the global pandemic and U.S.-China trade war. These problems and limitations made adaptation and flexibility necessary and were an important component for the Party's survival during the hard times. Henry Kissinger points out that "Each of the five generations of leaders since the founding of the People's Republic of China has represented a particular aspect of the Chinese experience. Xi's is that of the children of those Chinese who traversed the purgatory of the Cultural Revolution. He found his own life disrupted, since he was sent to the countryside for seven years."[4] Power struggles over Xi Jinping's leadership after his second term characterized the political culture of the CCP in the 21st century. As a result, the tremendous growth and development of Chinese society has been all but hidden behind this apparent circular motion of political affairs.

Party Control: Continuity and Selective Adaptation

Factional politics, which has been particularly noticeable during the current power transition, resulted in new struggles, scandals, and even more crises for Xi Jinping's third term. After the CCP's 18th National Congress in November 2012, the growing diversity of political elites provided more challenges and opportunities, as well as more difficulties and hopes for the future. It appeared that the new leadership would work to maintain economic growth at home while seeking a growing role on the global political stage. Power-sharing among competing political camps has not entailed a more dynamic and institutionalized decision-making process and yet developed better policies.

Xi Jinping carries on the CCP doctrines and principles, calling for "continuing struggle" against the perceived threats from the West and the U.S. It seems to Xi that the early communists established the CCP for just one purpose which was national salvation. He advises Chinese Communists: "Never forget the original intent and stick firmly to the mission."[5] During the pandemic, Xi called in 2021 for the party and Chinese people to study the CCP history and stick to the direction set up by the CCP. He considers Mao Zedong as a great leader who mobilized the Chinese to

[3] Xi Jinping's words quoted in Hannah Beech, "How China Sees the World," *Time*, June 17, 2013, 28.
[4] Henry Kissinger, "Xi Jinping" 64.
[5] Xi Jinping, *Lun Zhongguo*: 159.

join the revolution and seized the country through armed rebellion. Some chapter authors compare Xi's "fighting spirit" with Mao's legacy of the "continuing revolution" in the 1950s–1970s. During Mao's era, the Party Center adopted an active anti-containment strategy by challenging the Cold War international system, in which the superpowers dominated global affairs. Beijing sent 3 million Chinese troops to the Korean War in 1950–1953, 410,000 troops to the Vietnam War in 1965–1973, and 220,000 troops to invade Vietnam in 1979. Mao Zedong promoted China's international status in the world and the PRC became one of the few Communist survivors as well as a "beneficial participant" in the Cold War. Patrick F. Shan states in his chapter, "Xi is so passionate about 1921 and 1949 that he applies them to yardstick his lofty 'Two Centennials' to turn China into a moderately prosperous country in 2021 and to make China a middlingly developed nation in 2049."[6] Shan also emphasizes Xi's way of controlling the military. "Xi makes it clear that it is a convention for the Chinese soldiers to be loyal to the party, defend the party, and fight for the party."[7]

With a negative attitude toward Western influence in 2012–2022, Xi Jinping continued to criticize some ideas of the West like multi-partisan politics, freedom of speech and press, and individual rights. However, the Party Center has made some changes in imported governing methods, such as spokesmen system, complaint and reports, direct government hotlines, and officials' email contacts. It has also been willing to increase the power of the National People's Congress (NPC), and able to work with local governments and non-government organizations. Xi Jinping has attempted to fit those ideas into whatever he felt was needed, making the best use of imported methods, and letting all things serve their purpose when convenient while meeting certain social and political demands. This selective adaptation for the Xi administration seems to have worked in the past ten years. During the 20th Party's National Congress, held in 2022, Xi Jinping solidified his dominant authority over the highest ranks of the CCP. The 20th Party Congress once again enshrined Xi Jinping Thought on Socialism with Chinese Characteristics for a New Era and highlighted the importance of Party discipline and loyalty to the Party's leadership. The "two safeguards" were added to the new party constitution, calling for greater unity within the Party and emphasizing the importance of "staying true to the original aspiration and founding mission" of the Party.

Xi promoted his global plan "New Silk Road and Economic Belt" to establish a China-centric global system excluding America. His plan was to connect Africa, Asia, Europe, and Latin America while China is repositioning itself by creating a new

[6] Patrick F. Shan, "What Did the CCP Learn from the Past? An Analysis of Xi Jinping's Dexterous Utilization of History," in chapter one, 24.

[7] Shan, "What Did the CCP Learn from the Past?" 25.

center of gravity in the Asia-Pacific region. On October 24, 2017, the Belt and Road Initiative was added to the Party's Constitution at the CCP 19th National Congress. The most direct approach to visualize China's commitment to the 21st Century Maritime Silk Road is via its investment in participating countries. According to Ting Jiang, between 2013 to 2023, worldwide Chinese investments and construction reached a cumulative record of $1,016 billion with 1,524 projects in Asia, Africa, Arabia and the Middle East, South America, Europe, and Oceania. Almost half of it ($402 billion) is marked for Belt and Road projects. Her analysis shows that the majority of the investments ($316 billion) goes directly to the 521 Maritime Silk oad projects across various industrial sectors.[8] In January 2016, China and Djibouti signed an MOU to lease the Port of Djibouti for a length of 10 years. In July 2017, the People's Liberation Army (PLA) established its military base in Djibouti, whose task is to conduct anti-piracy operations off the coast of Djibouti and around the Horn of Africa, as well as safeguard China's security interests in Africa, the Middle East, and the Indian Ocean.

Party State: Centralization and New Military Power

Three generations of Chinese leadership after Mao Zedong pursued the establishment of collective leadership, the decentralization of authority, and a balanced power structure between the party and the state. However, since Xi Jinping's ascent to power in 2012, he has significantly deviated from this trajectory by restructuring the roles of the party and the state, and exercising control over historical narratives and linguistic constructs to bolster his legitimacy. Xiaojia Hou in her chapter points out, at the 19th Party's National Congress, Xi Jinping filled the top positions of the Politburo Standing Committee (PSC) with mostly his supporters.[9] In the 20th Party Congress, all the members of PSC and Politburo were considered Xi's adherents.[10] Not only did Xi secure his third term as the party leader, he also avoided naming a successor. In ten years, Xi Jinping has dramatically centralized authority under his personal leadership.

Moreover, this increased concentration of power in the hands of Xi Jinping aligned with the simultaneous reinforcement of Party leaders' positions at all levels of the party state. The increased flexibility given to local Party leaders in recruitment and evaluation procedures tended to reinforce the clientelist aspects of the

[8] Ting Jiang, "Belt and Road by the Sea—21st Century Maritime Silk Road," chapter eleven, 10, 17.

[9] Economy calculates four of the seven members of the PSC and 15 out of 18 Politburo members were allies of Xi. Economy, *The Third Revolution*: 18.

[10] Wu, "Killing the Different Dreams."

party-state cadre management system. A recent survey conducted among Chinese officials revealed that recognition from superiors was considered the most crucial criterion for promotion, surpassing competence or achievements. By granting local Party leaders greater authority and discretion over recruitment and promotion decisions, the subjectivity of the Party secretary becomes increasingly central.

To keep the CCP in power, a continuing coalition between the PLA and the CCP seems necessary for Beijing. At the National People's Congress in 2013, Xi Jinping's vision for a "strong military" became government policy for the PLA's development in 2013–2022. To achieve a modern military in a new time, it is important to build on the PLA's long and rich traditions and to preserve them in innovative ways. The PLA needs to follow the fundamental principle and system of absolute Party leadership over the armed forces. In other words, the PLA should support the Xi administration by showing their loyalty to the Party Center. The rank and file should accept party authority, as well as value social harmony, sharing ideas, and living with them as social norms. The high command should contribute to various forms of rationale in order to promote social harmony. In this socio-economic climate, the concept of harmony is becoming increasingly valuable and pertinent to Chinese society as well as that of the rest of the world.

The PLA still belongs to the Party, since the latter controls the resources and personnel management for military budgets and professional careers under the current leadership. The Party Center can channel the military elite interests and individual consciousness, prejudice, and conflict of the rank and file through the existing strong political institution. Since the state has adapted well to economic and social changes and has effectively responded to rising demands and expectations of the PLA, its political institutions may be able to manage some of the discontent or differing opinions of the PLA in the near future.[11] These activities are still within the boundaries of the Party Center's preference and control. In the meantime, the PLA should also provide new military capabilities for this policy since there are serious

[11] For example, Major General Zhu Chenghu, Dean at PLA National Defense University, spoke to a group of foreign journalists that China would attack over one hundred American cities with nuclear weapons if the United States interferes in a war between China and Taiwan. U.S. Congress called for the sacking of the Chinese general. The Chinese government, however, did not reject Zhu's speech and a spokesperson from the Ministry of Foreign Affairs said that Zhu's speech was his own personal opinion. This spokesperson declined to comment on whether or not the speech represented the Chinese government's view. Jonathan D. Pollack pointed out that while China becomes more involved in "sub- and pan-regional security affairs," it is "acquiring military capabilities that it believes will ultimately enable a short-warning, high-intensity attack against Taiwan. These include a growing inventory of short-range ballistic missiles, advanced conventionally powered submarines and other naval platforms, longer-range aircraft, and a host of related capabilities." See Wang, "U.S. Congress Calls"; Shambaugh, "The Rise of China and Asia's New Dynamics," 11; Pollack, "The Transformation of the Asian Security Order," in Shambaugh ed., ibid., 339.

disharmonious factors and unstable elements in China, as well as in the rest of the world. As we know, in the past two decades, disparity in wealth, unsettled social political infrastructure, and international conflicts have resulted in a new set of uncertainties and challenges for China's sustained development.

"We must endeavor to comprehensively transform the people's armed forces into a world-class military by the mid-21st century." This visionary proclamation was made by Xi Jinping during the landmark 19th Party Congress in 2017.[12] In his address, he meticulously charted out distinct milestones for the PLA's modernization journey. He set an ambitious goal: finalize the modernization phase by 2035, and by 2049—the 100th anniversary of the People's Republic of China—elevate the PLA to the stature of a "world-class military." This timeline wasn't just symbolic; it was deeply intertwined with China's national narrative of rejuvenation and global ascendancy. Lei Duan states in his chapter, since assuming leadership of the Chinese Communist Party in October 2012, Xi Jinping has swiftly set into motion a series of sweeping and transformative reforms aimed at the PLA.[13] His vision was clear: a military machine that was not only numerically formidable but also technologically advanced, agile, and strategically efficient. Xi's vision for the military was both radical and swift, marking a tectonic shift in its structural and strategic orientation. As such, significant resources and attention were funneled into research, development, and the integration of cutting-edge technologies within the PLA's operational matrix.

Lei Duan continues the discussion on the PLA's modernization and operations from 2012–2022. The author focuses on changes, development, and problems in the PLA's evolution of its air, naval, and strategic forces. The chapter also explains how China used its new military power to challenge U.S. East Asian-Pacific strategy around Taiwan and the disputed islands in the East and South China Seas, and this kind of behavior remains evident today. Lei connects China's new military power to U.S.-China relations and characterizes the PLA not only by what they have, but also by who they are and what they can do. Due to all the above challenges, the PLA has an arduous task to safeguard China's national unification, territorial integrity, and development interests. The Chinese armed forces will continue to fulfill its mission by carrying on its tradition and culture while evolving through adaptation and improvement for mechanization and digitalization. Through its foreign war experience, the PLA confronted four key issues: planning, learning, making changes, and political control. Military planning or war strategy has been the most prominent

[12] "Full Text of Xi Jinping's Report at 19th CPC National Congress," Xinhua News, accessed September 10, 2023, http://www.xinhuanet.com/english/special/2017-11/03/c_136725942.htm.

[13] Lei Duan, "Toward a More Joint Strategy: Assessing Chinese Military Reforms and Militia," chapter seven, 3.

and foremost of PLA operations. The PLA's planning received the most attention in the chapters and became an important part of its culture. Political doctrine garners more attention in military papers, from Mao Zedong to Xi Jinping, than any other military-related topic. Mao and Xi's strategies on active defense diverge as the latter shifted from engaging land wars in neighboring countries like Korea and Vietnam to preparing for naval warfare in the East China Sea and South China Sea.

After consolidating power at home, Xi adopted an increasingly more assertive and bellicose domestic and foreign policy. He has gradually abandoned Deng Xiaoping's low-profile foreign policy and Hu Jintao's peaceful rise policy, and followed a proactive and belligerent foreign policy, such as wolf-warrior diplomacy, which is partly reflected in his uncompromising policy toward Xinjiang, Tibet, Hong Kong, Taiwan, the U.S. and other sensitive issues.[14] As Dean P. Chen indicates in his chapter, "As ties between Washington and Beijing become more competitive and adversarial over a range of divergent issues, including trade, military, espionage, human rights, governance, and high technologies that are pivotal in determining the global distributions of power of the 21st century, the world also pays greater attention to the security and freedom of Taiwan."[15] Xi Jinping warned his government and military, the Taiwan issue "cannot be passed down from generation to generation," implying a sense of urgency on China's longstanding reunification goal.[16]

Diplomacy, Society, and Social Media

Beset by diplomatic woes and mishaps elsewhere, especially in East Asia and the Indo-Pacific, the Xi administration has become all the more keenly aware of the growing significance of Central Asia, with the region featuring prominently in the formulation and execution of its foreign policy. Arguably, Central Asia is a bright spot in China's increasingly challenging geopolitical landscape. It is no coincidence that Kazakhstan, the largest Central Asian country, was the site of both Xi Jinping's announcement of China's One Belt One Road Initiative (BRI) in September 2013 and the destination of his first state visit abroad nine years later after reemerging from his COVID-19 isolation. During the same trip, Xi also visited Uzbekistan, where he

[14] Guo, "Repackaging Confucius", 13, 34; Glaser et al., "The Changing Ecology" ; Ding, et al., *Chinese Politics and Foreign Policy*; Huang, "'Wolf Warrior' and China's Digital Public Diplomacy," 37–40.

[15] Dean P. Chen, "Xi Jinping and the Derailment of the KMT-CCP '1992 Consensus'," chapter eight, 1.

[16] "Xi says 'China Must Be, Will Be Reunified' As Key Anniversary Marked," *Xinhua News* (January 2, 2019), http://www.xinhuanet.com/english/2019-01/02/c_137714898.htm.

was received with considerable fanfare and effusive praise for his statesmanship.[17] Chapter author Yi Sun examines the contour of the Chinese economic and cultural policies toward Central Asia during the past three decades, particularly during the Xi administration, as part of Beijing's broader geopolitical strategies. She points out, China's strategic pivot to Central Asia was prompted by two main factors: natural resources, including oil and gas; and security concerns over the stability of Xinjiang, "where ethnic conflicts between the Uighurs and the Han Chinese had continued for decades, and where government oppression and mistreatment of the Muslims had intensified the latter's resistance."[18] Although China's foreign policy toward Central Asia has some achievements in terms of massive investment, loans, and labor for the construction and updating of transportation and communication infrastructure in that region, the Chinese "soft power" through the use of Confucius Institutes and generous scholarships for Central Asian students were not as successful as expected.

Shuhua Fan continues to discuss China's soft power in her chapter and explains the rise and fall of Confucius Institutes in the world in general and in the United States in particular. She argues, after Xi Jinping took over in 2012, a relatively open and favorable international environment for China to continue its cultural diplomacy like Confucius Institutes changed significantly. According to her research, the change was partially caused by domestic changes in China. Xi's hardline policy caused concerns among American leaders and led to increasing conflicts with the United States. Fan argues, "U.S. leaders have realized more clearly than before that China's domestic and foreign policy, including using Confucius Institutes to carry out its cultural diplomacy, has threatened American national security and national interests."[19] They had noticed that China under Xi has been fast moving toward a different direction, unlike what they had expected. China became the second largest world economy in 2010,[20] but has not conducted political reforms to import Western democracy and other values while becoming more authoritarian at home and more belligerent in foreign policy. The U.S. leaders believed that what China has exported via CIs and other "charm offensives" has served only China's national interests and conflicted with and threatened American values and ideas such as democracy, freedom of speech, freedom of religion, and human rights.

[17] Bradsher, "In the 'Great Game.'"

[18] Yi Sun, "Necessitated by Geopolitics: China's Economic and Cultural Initiatives in Central Asia," chapter nine, 4.

[19] Shuhua Fan, "Confucius Institutes in the Xi Jinping Era: From Peak to Demise in the United States," chapter six, 13.

[20] Barboza, "China Overtakes Japan."

At the turn of the century, the digital revolution had a strong and positive impact in the public arena and civil society in China. As the Chinese people become better informed and connected, however, both the result of the internet communication and change in social democratization are still uncertain. In China, there was a "golden age of critical journalism" before Xi's era. Part of the reason, according to Yi Guolin, was the commercialization of newspapers, radio stations, and TV companies in the 1990s–2010s, which had to find ways to support themselves financially after they lost some government subsidiaries.[21] The news market demanded more autonomy and freedom in terms of readers' rating and advertisers' interests. And the private sector began to invest and become involved in the news industry. The government adopted more flexible policies toward the media with an emphasis on rights guaranteed by the constitution.

Between 2012 and 2022, however, the Xi administration tightened its control of the mass media, commercial outlets, and the internet. The first means of control is through government regulations. The government rules and regulations have become more and more repetitive, expansive, and elaborate in restrictions. According to Yi, in 2013, Beijing announced the "Seven Speak-Nots" which included seven topics that were not allowed to be discussed by the media or in public places. They were universal values, press freedom, civil society, human rights, historical mistakes of the CCP, crony capitalism, and legal independence. The party and government controlled the mass media and used the press and internet as a means to articulate and build support for their policies. The second means of state control of media is government ownership, certification, and licensing process. The control of the mass media reached new heights in 2019, when the Party Center required all journalists to take tests before getting their license renewed. The decade was characterized by the decline of critical journalism and the expansion of party propaganda. As Xi Jinping became the most powerful leader since Mao, the Chinese media has been used to promote his personality cult. The third method of media control is government censorship of sensitive stories and reports. Each reporter must know the line between what is permitted and what is forbidden. They are expected to practice self-censorship, since their jobs are on the line. Yi's analysis indicates that government censorship also plays an important role in controlling the internet. For example, in 2014, the CCA (China Cyberspace Administration) issued the "Account Ten Rules," "WeChat Ten Rules," and "Regulatory Talks Ten Rules." As their names suggest, they targeted internet news providers and regulated what was allowed to appear online. Although these regulations are not law, they did set the rules and played an important role in controlling China's cyberspace. Government

[21] Guolin Yi, "From "Seven Speak-Nots" to "Media Surnamed Party": Media in China from 2012 to 2022," chapter 2.

surveillance and internet policing have increased in response to the internet's growing popularity and its use as a medium for activism throughout China.

When the new age of social media arrived in China in the 1990s–2000s, the Chinese nationalism rose with a new and popular platform. Mao Lin provides a detailed survey of Weibo of the *Global Times*, and states that the magazine and its Weibo platform played an important role in framing the U.S.-China trade war and shaping the Chinese public perceptions of U.S.-China relations. Weibo, a leading social media platform in China and a microblogging application that combines features of Facebook and Twitter, has become a leading source for news and information. Although Weibo is the second largest social media site after WeChat measured by the number of users, it is primarily a public platform while WeChat is more private. The bloggers can discuss issues with netizens they do not know in real life and build mass followings. Weibo therefore becomes an ideas platform for the Chinese public to discuss issues such as the U.S.-China relationship online. According to Lin, as of March 2020, Chinese netizens increased to 904 million, and China's internet coverage had reached more than 64 percent. About 897 million Chinese netizens used mobile devices to gain access to the internet, with 99 percent of them using mobile phones. About 731 million or 81 percent of China's internet users got their news online.

However, the chapter author concludes that the *Global Times* as commercial media was controlled by the Chinese government, and it became one of the most influential media outlets in China covering international affairs. Its Weibo account has more than 31 million followers. The chapter author followed the Weibo account from March 22, 2018, to January 15, 2020, when Beijing and Washington engaged in tariff disputes over Chinese goods imported to the U.S. He examines thousands and thousands of *Global Times* generated posts and looks into its editor's intention and behavior, which made its Weibo influential over U.S.-China trade issues. Its Weibo generated thousands of posts to expand the tariff issues beyond the economic realm and raised questions about national security and international order. Therefore, in China, the trade war has attracted unprecedented attention from all types of Chinese media. Chinese social media was swarmed with discussions of the most "epic trade war in human history."[22] Nationalism has played a primary role in framing the Chinese media coverage of the trade war. As some Western scholars have argued, "public discussions of the trade war in China...were driven by a number of factors that had little to do with economics and more with questions of nationalism and sense of self."[23]

[22] The term was first coined by Mei Yuxin, a researcher associated with the Chinese Ministry of Commerce, and quicky went viral. https://finance.ifeng.com/a/20180404/16058513_0.shtml

[23] Ha and Wilnat, eds. *The U.S.-China Trade War*: x.

Following the 20th CCP National Party Congress in October 2022 and the 14th National People's Congress in March 2023, Xi Jinping successfully secured and consolidated an unprecedented third term in office as the CCP general secretary, president of the PRC, and chairman of the Central Military Affairs Commission (CMC). He must face and solve his own problems, consisting of, but not limited to, economic recession, pandemic, corruption, power abuse, law infringement, human rights violation, and urban mismanagement. These factors all delay China's growth and impede improvement of the Sino-U.S. relationship. The possibility of a tragic repetition in the development of a new cold war between the United States and China is ever looming, if the latter continues efforts in creating "one world, two systems." In Beijing's bi-polar world, one system is the existing American-centric global community; the other is a China-centered international system. History will repeat itself if a complete break in diplomatic relations between the two countries, or a limited hot war in the 2020s occurs. With no single enemy to unite against, and with the PRC emerging as a major economic power, the relationship between the U.S. and China arrives at a historical crossroads. Miles M. Yu, China's policy advisor to Secretary Michael Pompeo, emphasized that President Donald Trump made a fundamental change in U.S. policy toward China by terminating "common ground" policy principles and stopping playing the "China card." China presents a major threat to the United States, which should fight back against China as its potential enemy whenever it can.[24]

The outbreak of Covid-19 in late 2019 and Russia's aggression against Ukraine further compound the already tense relations between China and the United States. The Sino-US relations were at their nadir. President Joe Biden continued Trump's hardline policy, and described China as the "strategic competitor" of the U.S. Capitalizing on China's tough stance and a flurry of bellicose policies toward its neighbors, the Biden administration has gradually cemented military alliances with Japan, South Korea, the Philippines, and Australia. Even India, a founding member of the Non-Alignment Movement in the Cold War, has leaned toward the United States in light of its military cooperation and economic ambition to outshine China as the new world factory.

After the U.S. and its allies in Europe and Asia demonstrated a strong resolve in standing up to China during the pandemic and Ukraine war, Xi Jinping seems to have sensed the adverse consequences of his assertive policies. Despite the embarrassing balloon incident in early 2023, Xi has recently tried to take a more conciliatory move toward the West by removing the Wolf-Warrior spokesman and sending a moderate diplomat to be China's ambassador in the United States. Furthermore, Xi has repeatedly assured Western countries that China will not provide arms to

[24] Yu, "Special Interview of China Policy Advisor."

Russia, albeit it continues to provide Russia with diplomatic support, conduct joint naval drills, and to flow billions of dollars to buy Russian oil and wheat. In return, the Biden administration responded by dispatching several top officials to China in the summer of 2023. Biden also publicly reiterated that it was not in the best interest of the U.S. to contain China.[25] However, the persistent ideological distrust, big-power competition, China's growing assertiveness to take Taiwan by force and its threats to its neighbors and American dominance and interest will not be eased any time soon. The U.S. government ramps up economic and technological sanctions and bans certain investments in China and slowly forms military alliances around China. With most congressmen holding an animosity or distrust toward China, there is little sign of possible improvement of the U.S.-China relationship in the coming years. No matter which party wins the 2024 American presidential election, the ongoing tensions between the two superpowers will not diminish.

For China, so long as Xi Jinping and other Chinese leaders insist on putting all their shoulders to the wheel on a Communist ideology and cling to power and reject Western values such as the rule of law, democracy, human rights, and a market economy, the West led by the U.S. will never see China as "one of us" and accordingly the outlook that the CCP will cultivate a long-term and amicable relationship with the U.S. and its major neighbors is inconceivable any time soon.

Bibliography

Barboza, David. "China Overtakes Japan to Become No. 2 Global Economic Power," *New York Times*, Aug. 15, 2010. http://www.nytimes.com/2010/08/16/business/global/16yuan.html, accessed June 26, 2011.

Beech, Hannah. "How China Sees the World." *Time*, June 17, 2013.

Bradsher, Keith. "In the 'Great Game' of Central Asia, China's Leader Seeks the Advantage," *New York Times*, September 16, 2022. https://www.nytimes.com/2022/09/16/world/asia/china-xi-central-asia.html [Accessed February 22, 2023].

Economy, Elizabeth. *The Third Revolution: Xi Jinping and the New Chinese State.* Cambridge: Oxford University Press, 2018.

Guan Zhichao. Interview by the author at the PLA Political Academy, Nanjing, 2008.

Ha, Louisa and Lars Wilnat, eds. *The U.S.-China Trade War: Global News Framing and Public Opinion in the Digital Age.* East Lansing: Michigan State University Press, 2022.

Information Bureau, PRC State Council. *White Papers of China's National Defense*, 2008. http://English.people.com.cn/90001/90776/90785/6578688.html [Accessed February 20, 2023].

Kissinger, Henry. "Xi Jinping: Helmsman of an Evolving Superpower." *Time*, April 29, 2013.

[25] Nicholas, "Biden Insists He's Not Trying."

Nicholas, Peter. "Biden Insists He's Not Trying to 'Contain' China as He Courts Beijing's Rivals" in NBC News, September 10, 2023. https://www.nbcnews.com/politics/joe-biden/biden-insists-s-not-trying-contain-china-courts-beijings-rivals-rcna104273; Accessed September 13, 2023.

Pollack, Jonathan D. "The Transformation of the Asian Security Order; Assessing China's Impact." In *Power Shift: China and Asia's New Dynamics*, ed. Shambaurgh. Berkeley: University of California Press, 2005.

Shambaugh, David. *Power Shift; China and Asia's New Dynamics*. Berkeley: University of California Press, 2005.

Sun Lizhou. Interview by the author at the Peking University, Beijing, 2005.

Wang Zheng. "U.S. Congress Calls for Sacking of Chinese General." *The Epoch Times*, 2005. http://www.theepochtimes.com/news/5-7-25/30545.html [Accessed June 10, 2019].

Wu Guoguang. "Killing the Different Dreams, Keeping the Same Regime: Xi Jinping's ten-year struggle to remake CCP elite politics." *China Leadership Monitor,* September 1, 2022. https://www.prcleader.org/wu-september-2022 [Accessed May 14, 2023].

Xi Jinping. *Lun Zhongguo gongchandang lishi* [*On the History of the Chinese Communist Party*]. Beijing: CCP Central Archival and Manuscript Press, 2021.

Xi Jinping. *Report at 19th CPC National Congress*. 2017. http://www.xinhuanet.com/english/special/2017-11/03/c_136725942.htm [Accessed September 10, 2023].

Yu, Miles M. "Special Interview of China Policy Advisor to Secretary Pompeo," *Radio Free Asia*, November 12, 2020. www.rfa.org/mandarin/yataibaodao/junshiwaijiao/nt-11122020220695.html [Accessed June 2, 2021].

Index

FSC
www.fsc.org
MIX
Papier | Fördert
gute Waldnutzung
FSC® C083411

Kolibri 360 GmbH
Ferdinand-Jühlke-Straße 7
99095 Erfurt, Deutschland
produktsicherheit@kolibri360.de